# Acknowledgments

It takes an All-Star team of talented, creative individuals to produce a publication as challenging as the *STATS Baseball Scoreboard.* The following people made valuable contributions to the team effort.

John Dewan, STATS President and CEO, has charted STATS' course as the company has conquered new and unexplored frontiers. No challenge is too great. STATS Chief Operating Officer Marty Gilbert coordinates and oversees the many tasks of our ever-growing company. They are assisted by Heather Schwarze, who always seems to have whatever is needed right at her fingertips.

As Vice President of Publications, Don Zminda oversaw every step of this book's production from start to finish. Don not only sifted the gems out of a virtually endless list of essay ideas, but he also penned a good number of the pieces you'll find on the following pages.

Other purveyors of prodigious prose are Publications Staff members Jim Callis, Ethan D. Cooperson, Kevin Fullam, Jim Henzler, Tony Nistler, and the guy who does my laundry, Mat Olkin. STATS' John Sasman both conceived and composed several essays, and Steve Moyer and Pat Quinn contributed valuable ideas. For the second straight year, loyal reader Steve Schulmann penned an essay, while Joseph Weindel provided the idea for another. Special thanks to Bill James for contributing his writing and insights.

As always, Chuck Miller went above and beyond the call of duty to pull the book together and whip it into shape. Kevin Fullam relieved Chuck when he got winded, and Ethan D. Cooperson checked the stats. Chad Huebner, Thom Henninger and the entire Publications department worked together to edit out every last dangling participle. We think.

Legendary programmer Stefan Kretschmann was responsible for translating our requests into computerese, and he extracted much of the data that appears in this book. He was ably assisted by programmers Steve Moyer, Brent Osland, David Pinto, Allan Spear, Jeff Schinski and Kevin Thomas.

Of course, STATS owes a considerable debt of gratitude to its managers: Art Ashley, Mike Canter and Sue Dewan (Systems); Doug Abel (Vice President of Operations); Steve Byrd (Vice President of Marketing); Jim Capuano (Vice President of Sales) and Bob Meyerhoff (Vice President of Finance and Administration). Stephanie Seburn (Human Resources) and Susan Zamechek (Administration) assist Bob Meyerhoff.

Finally, we thank STATS' dedicated staff: Kristen Beauregard, Andrew Bernstein, Grant "Willie" Blair, Dave Carlson, Jeff Chernow, Brian Cousins, Steve Drago, Marc Elman, Drew Faust, Dan Ford, Ron Freer (whose handiwork appears on the cover), Angela Gabe, Mike Hammer, Mark Hong, Sherlinda Johnson, Antoinette Kelly, Jason Kinsey, Tracy Lickton, Walter Lis, Betty Moy, Jim Musso, Jim Osborne, Oscar Palacios, Dean Peterson, Corey Roberts, Carol Savier, Taasha Schroeder, Matt Senter, Leena Sheth, Lori Smith, Mike Wenz and Peter Woelflein.

—Mat Olkin

I dedicate this book to Donat C. Quinn,
a quiet man living a life of patience, kindness, fairness,
and healthy living. What an excellent role model!
Thank you Dad, for giving me gifts I never can repay.
—Patrick Quinn

# Table of Contents

## II. GENERAL BASEBALL QUESTIONS 77

## III. QUESTIONS ON OFFENSE 107

## IV. QUESTIONS ON PITCHING                         141

# Foreword
### by Roland Hemond
### Arizona Diamondbacks
### Senior Vice President of Baseball Operations

The growth of baseball continues in so many aspects. The game's expansion on a global scale in the last decade or so has been astounding.

The blossoming of the game's statistical records has also skyrocketed and STATS, Inc. has been one of the powers of the analytical information. We in the game have availed ourselves of the numerous publications published by STATS, Inc. I doubt that any major league or minor league office fails to get STATS, Inc. books.

The legendary baseball writer, Leonard Koppett, always has been a baseball statistical genius. His in-depth analysis of the true value of a player's contribution to a club or a team's performance surpassing the apparent statistics was highly educational for not only the average fan but also the astute baseball person in a club's front office. In other words, when Leonard originally outlined his detailed analyses, he was ahead of his time. It was a great asset for baseball operators to study Koppett's teachings. He described the game as a thinking person's game; he was so right.

Managers of the past and present have displayed intellect that led to their success. Earl Weaver was a forerunner of keeping statistics of hitters vs. pitchers on index cards and Earl is now a member of baseball's Hall of Fame. The managers of today have access to much more data thanks to works provided by STATS, Inc. and others in baseball.

Managers and front office people cannot and should not base all their decisions on statistical information. It is an important tool, but there are also parts of a player's game; physical strengths and weaknesses, makeup and other intangibles that come into focus and are included in reports from each organization's scouts.

I have found that all of STATS, Inc. baseball publications are spellbinding. It is impossible to open any of the covers without simply being drawn to continue devouring the information, and the curiosity to check one more item is overwhelming. Time passes before, reluctantly, one has to march on to other pressing assignments.

*STATS Baseball Scoreboard* is another example of this captivating hold. There is an old cliché, "No one knows everything about baseball and we can always learn more." Well, STATS, Inc. proves this, without a doubt. Fans and people in baseball, including players, are indebted for the knowledge that can be gained by scrutinizing what STATS, Inc. publishes.

STATS, Inc. will undoubtedly continue to be a force in the preaching of baseball worldwide, thus assuring a prosperity in the decades ahead. All of STATS, Inc. publications belong in the National Baseball Hall of Fame Library in Cooperstown, where baseball history is preserved in book form.

# Introduction

In the beginning, Cartwright created the *run*.

The first box score appeared in a newspaper on October 22, 1845, only one month after Alexander Cartwright had laid down baseball's first set of rules. That box score did not credit anyone with a hold, and it did not reflect any blown save opportunities. If any home runs were hit during the game in question, the box score failed to account for them. In fact, there wasn't even any mention of stolen bases or the identities of the winning and losing pitchers. For each player, the box score simply listed two categories: runs and outs.

Welcome to the 1998 *STATS Baseball Scoreboard.* We've come a long way, baby.

Since that first attempt to summarize the results of a baseball game on the printed page, the development of baseball statistics has been continually evolving. One of the pillars of what's now known as the "Triple Crown," the "run batted in," was introduced by a newspaper in Buffalo, N.Y. in 1879. The National League adpoted it as an official stat in 1891 but dropped it by the end of year after official scorers all but ignored the new-fangled stat. It was another 29 years before the major leagues began counting RBI again.

The earned run average was born in 1912, the year after Cy Young retired. The save debuted in 1969, six years before Dennis Eckersley did, and on-base percentage was born in 1985, when Rod Carew was in the final season of his career. Since then, the computer revolution has enabled us to view the game in breathtaking detail. For example, we can now find out not only how many runs a player drives in, but how many baserunners he *doesn't* drive in.

The data and essays on the following pages represent the state of the art in baseball information and analysis. STATS' vast database sheds light on discussions as old as the game itself. Find out which players really are the best bunters in the game. Take a look at the list of players who drive in the highest percentage of baserunners, or the second basemen who turn the double-play pivot most effectively.

Our unique analytical tools also allow us to shed light on many of today's issues. For instance, would Paul Molitor have approached Pete Rose's career hit record if he'd been able to avoid the injuries that plagued his early career? Which team got the better end of the Kenny Lofton/David Justice deal? And how will Darryl Kile perform with the Colorado Rockies? We'll do more than just give you our opinions—we'll also back them up.

At present, much of the statistical information in this book is impossible to get anywhere else. Beyond the data, you'll find lively, informative essays from STATS' expert analysts. And John Grimwade's distinctive illustrations bring the numbers to life.

Once again, we invite you to write to us with comments and suggestions for future editions of the *Scoreboard.* For the second straight year, reader Steve Schulmann has penned an essay for us; you'll find it on page 167. Steve is just one of the many readers whose input has helped the *Scoreboard* to continue to evolve and improve.

The *Scoreboard* represents the best that we have to offer, and we feel that this year's edition is the best yet. Turn the page and take a peek into baseball's future.

—Mat Olkin

# I.  TEAM QUESTIONS

## Anaheim Angels: Is Salmon the Best Non-All-Star?

You'd think a guy who worked for Disney would get more attention than this, but Tim Salmon might be the best-kept secret in baseball. In his five full major league seasons, Salmon has topped the 30-home run mark four times; the only year he missed was 1994, the strike year, when he had 23 homers in only 100 games. Over the last three seasons, Salmon has batted .303, slugged .536 and averaged 30 doubles, 32 homers, 110 RBI, 99 runs scored and 93 walks per season. He's also a fine defensive player who led American League right fielders last year with 15 assists. About the only thing he can't do is steal bases (25 for 54 in his career).

That's an impressive resumé, but Salmon has yet to be selected for an American League All-Star team. That got us wondering who were the best active position players never to be selected for an All-Star team. Here's what we came up with:

### The "Non-All-Star" All-Stars

| Pos | Player | AB | H | HR | RBI | R | BB | BA | OBP | SLG |
|-----|--------|-----|------|-----|-----|------|------|------|------|------|
| C | Chris Hoiles | 2553 | 669 | 136 | 393 | 379 | 397 | .262 | .367 | .467 |
| 1B | Eric Karros | 3371 | 891 | 154 | 535 | 441 | 276 | .264 | .319 | .455 |
| 2B | Jeff Kent | 2705 | 728 | 107 | 439 | 386 | 188 | .269 | .324 | .455 |
| 3B | John Valentin | 2576 | 763 | 83 | 378 | 411 | 313 | .296 | .375 | .479 |
| SS | Omar Vizquel | 4046 | 1072 | 27 | 333 | 536 | 368 | .265 | .326 | .335 |
| OF | Tim Salmon | 2667 | 782 | 153 | 503 | 464 | 426 | .293 | .392 | .527 |
| OF | Bernie Williams | 3179 | 927 | 100 | 469 | 537 | 421 | .292 | .374 | .464 |
| OF | Tony Phillips | 6975 | 1865 | 141 | 749 | 1190 | 1201 | .267 | .375 | .387 |

(active players; minimum 2,500 career PA)

Not a bad team at all. Others we considered included J.T. Snow, Mike Lansing, Delino DeShields, Todd Zeile and Walt Weiss.

So is Salmon the best non-All-Star? His numbers in the key categories— on-base percentage, slugging, homers per time at bat—are clearly better than anyone's on the list. So Salmon's the pick, but we were more than a little surprised to discover that his ex-teammate, Tony Phillips, has never made an All-Star team. The versatile Phillips has ranked as one of the best of the best leadoff hitters in baseball for a number of years while compiling more than 1,800 major league hits. Considering his age (39 this year) and the fact that a drug arrest ended Phillips' association with the Angels last year, he may *never* make an All-Star team.

— Don Zminda

## Baltimore Orioles: What Happens When a Division Winner Changes Managers?

1997 was just another successful campaign in the managerial career of Davey Johnson. He piloted the Baltimore Orioles to an American League-best 98-64 record, and led the club to victory over the Seattle Mariners in the Division Series before falling to the Cleveland Indians in the ALCS. It was Johnson's sixth trip to the postseason in his 12 years as a manager.

During the offseason, however, Johnson resigned his post—perhaps to avoid the indignity of being fired by Orioles owner Peter Angelos. If Angelos had beaten Johnson to the punch, it wouldn't have been the first time that Johnson had been canned after bringing home a division crown. In fact, the last manager to be fired after winning a division title was Johnson, who was replaced by Ray Knight as manager of the Cincinnati Reds following the 1995 season. Since the advent of division play in 1969, only nine division-winning clubs have changed managers over the offseason:

### Division-Winning Teams Which Changed Managers

| Team | Yr | Manager | W-L | Yr | New Manager | W-L (Place) |
|------|-----|---------|------|-----|-------------|-------------|
| Min | '69 | Billy Martin | 97-65 | '70 | Bill Rigney | 98-64 (1) |
| Pit | '71 | Danny Murtaugh | 97-65 | '72 | Bill Virdon | 96-59 (1) |
| Oak | '73 | Dick Williams | 94-68 | '74 | Alvin Dark | 90-72 (1) |
| Oak | '75 | Alvin Dark | 98-64 | '76 | Chuck Tanner | 87-74 (2) |
| Yanks | '80 | Dick Howser | 103-59 | '81 | Gene Michael/ Bob Lemon | 59-48 (1/5) |
| Cal | '82 | Gene Mauch | 93-69 | '83 | John McNamara | 70-92 (5) |
| Tor | '85 | Bobby Cox | 99-62 | '86 | Jimy Williams | 86-76 (4) |
| Tex | '94 | *Kevin Kennedy | 52-62 | '95 | Johnny Oates | 74-70 (3) |
| Cin | '95 | Davey Johnson | 85-59 | '96 | Ray Knight | 81-81 (3) |

*The Rangers had the best record in the AL West when play was stopped on August 12, 1994.

It's significant to note that not all of these men were *fired.* After winning the 1971 World Series, Pittsburgh manager Danny Murtaugh stepped down due to a heart condition, although he later returned and won two more division titles. Oakland's Dick Williams went out on top as well; his affliction was the A's incurable owner, Charlie O. Finley. Gene Mauch resigned in 1982 after his California Angels blew a two-games-to-none lead in the (then five-game) ALCS. Like Murtaugh, Mauch later returned, but he was driven back into retirement after his Angels blew a similar three-games-to-one lead in the 1986 ALCS. Toronto's Bobby Cox stepped down to take a job as the Braves' GM after he won the AL East in 1985. George Steinbrenner insisted that Dick Howser had chosen to "resign" after the 1980 season, but at the press conference, Howser's cool silence in the face of Steinbrenner's announcement suggested a different story.

That leaves only four managers who were explicitly fired. The Twins showed uncommon prescience by giving Billy Martin the boot while he was still on top. With Bill Rigney at the helm, they captured their second straight division title—something Martin accomplished only once in his managerial career. While Finley didn't get to fire Williams, he did ax his replacement, Alvin Dark, after the A's were swept in the 1975 ALCS. In '94, there was no postseason, and the Rangers' division-best 52-62 record was more of a quirk of fate—and an unrewarded one at that—than anything else. There was little backlash when manager Kevin Kennedy was dismissed that winter. The replacement of Johnson with Knight in Cincinnati was one of the weirder escapades in recent years. The move was prearranged by Reds owner Marge Schott, and Knight spent the entire season on the bench as a coach while Johnson piloted the team to a division title.

Overall, the departed managers' replacements didn't fare as well as their predecessors had, but that's hardly surprising, since most division-winning teams fail to defend their title, regardless of any managerial change. Three of the nine teams successfully defended their crown, while six of the nine declined in the won-lost column. To see if this pattern was unusual, we created a "control" group as a basis for comparison. For each of the division-winning teams above, we selected the team from the same season with the most similar won-lost record. Through this process, we obtained a list of nine teams that had similar records to the nine teams above but hadn't made any managerial changes over the two-year span. Did stability result in more wins on the field?

| Group | Year 1 W-L | Pct | Year 2 W-L | Pct | +/− |
|---|---|---|---|---|---|
| New Managers | 820-570 | .590 | 737-638 | .536 | −.054 |
| Control | 818-573 | .588 | 741-636 | .538 | −.050 |

From what we can tell, the managerial turnover didn't seem to have much of an effect on the division winners—as a group, they declined almost exactly as much as the control group did. Despite this, Baltimore fans may rightfully fret over losing Johnson. He may be a special case, but the facts are undeniable: the last two teams he's left—the Mets and the Reds—suffered sudden collapses soon after he departed.

—Mat Olkin

## Boston Red Sox: Was Garciaparra the Best Rookie Shortstop Ever?

The Red Sox created quite a stir in spring training when they announced that they would shift John Valentin, their starter at shortstop for the previous four seasons, to second base. The move was made to accommodate rookie shortstop Nomar Garciaparra, a top prospect regarded as an outstanding fielder and a very good hitter.

Garciaparra had hit 16 homers in half a season in Triple-A in 1996, and finished that year by hitting .241 with four more homers for Boston in September. The Red Sox believed he would help them offensively in '97, but they certainly didn't expect this: a .306 average, .342 on-base percentage and .534 slugging percentage; American League bests with 209 hits and 11 triples; plus 44 doubles, 30 homers and 22 steals.

A terrific season, to be sure, one that earned Garciaparra the AL Rookie of the Year award. In fact, it was the best ever for a rookie shortstop in the modern era of baseball in terms of runs created. The runs created formula, devised by Bill James to boil down all of a player's offensive contributions into one number, shows that Garciaparra created 117 runs in 1997. By comparison, the three other rookies who were regular shortstops last year—Detroit's Deivi Cruz, Cincinnati's Pokey Reese and Pittsburgh's Kevin Polcovich—combined to create 95 runs.

Here's the list of the most runs created by a shortstop who hadn't exceeded 130 career at-bats (the modern rookie standard) entering a season, since 1901; we considered a player to be a shortstop if he played short at least as much as he played any other position.

### Most Runs Created, Rookie Shortstops—1901-97

| Shortstop | Year | RC |
|---|---|---|
| Nomar Garciaparra, Bos | 1997 | 117 |
| Joe Sewell, Cle | 1921 | 110 |
| Dick Howser, A's | 1961 | 102 |
| Tom Tresh, Yanks | 1962 | 102 |
| Johnny Pesky, RSox | 1942 | 97 |
| Freddy Parent, RSox | 1901 | 93 |
| Harvey Kuenn, Det | 1953 | 92 |
| Stan Rojek, Pit | 1948 | 88 |
| Donie Bush, Det | 1909 | 85 |
| Vern Stephens, Browns | 1942 | 85 |
| Cal Ripken, Bal | 1982 | 85 |

(maximum 130 previous at-bats)

Besides Garciaparra, three of the five other shortstops who debuted after the Rookie of the Year award was introduced in 1947 came away with that honor: Tom Tresh, Harvey Kuenn and Cal Ripken. Dick Howser finished one vote behind Red Sox righthander Don Schwall, who won 15 games, while Stan Rojek didn't receive a vote. Rojek, you may have noticed, is the only National League player among the 11 on the list.

Most of the star rookie shortstops went on to have long, productive careers. Joe Sewell was elected to the Hall of Fame, and Ripken will join him five years after he retires. The 10 shortstops besides Garciaparra averaged 12 seasons in the majors, and the seven who debuted after the creation of the All-Star Game in 1933 averaged five appearances in the midsummer classic.

Garciaparra's season also stacks up against the best for any shortstop, rookie or otherwise, in the modern era. His 117 runs created are tied for 29th among shortstops in the modern era, and are tied for 10th since 1957. Seattle's Alex Rodriguez created 147 runs in 1996, the best total this century:

**Most Runs Created, Shortstops—1957-97**

| Shortstop | Year | RC |
|---|---|---|
| Alex Rodriguez, Sea | 1996 | 147 |
| Robin Yount, Mil | 1982 | 136 |
| Alan Trammell, Det | 1987 | 129 |
| Cal Ripken, Bal | 1991 | 125 |
| Ernie Banks, Cubs | 1958 | 123 |
| Ernie Banks, Cubs | 1959 | 121 |
| Ernie Banks, Cubs | 1957 | 120 |
| Travis Fryman, Det | 1993 | 120 |
| Rico Petrocelli, Bos | 1969 | 118 |
| Cal Ripken, Bal | 1983 | 117 |
| John Valentin, Bos | 1995 | 117 |
| Nomar Garciaparra, Bos | 1997 | 117 |

Notice that Garciaparra as a rookie matched Valentin's best season ever. Add in Garciaparra's defensive superiority and it's clear that the Red Sox made the right decision, even if it didn't sit well with Valentin.

—Jim Callis

A more complete listing for this category can be found on page 212.

## Chicago White Sox: Is The Big Hurt Unique?

It's right there, on page 314 of our *1998 Major League Handbook*. At the top of the on-base percentage chart for active career batting leaders is one Frank Edward Thomas at .452. And next to that, atop the slugging percentage leaders, is Frank Thomas at .600. Which got us to wondering: Is he the first player to lead his era in both categories—the two most important offensive statistics for individual players?

First, we had to define the eras. We divided baseball into six periods, each ending with a significant event: 1876-1900, 1901-1919 (the deadball era), 1920-1945 (the lively ball), 1946-60 (the end of World War II and expansion), 1961-76 (free agency) and 1977 to date. Here are the leaders in on-base and slugging percentage for each:

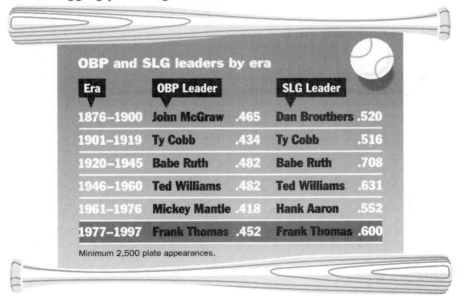

**OBP and SLG leaders by era**

| Era | OBP Leader | | SLG Leader | |
|-----|------------|------|------------|------|
| 1876–1900 | John McGraw | .465 | Dan Brouthers | .520 |
| 1901–1919 | Ty Cobb | .434 | Ty Cobb | .516 |
| 1920–1945 | Babe Ruth | .482 | Babe Ruth | .708 |
| 1946–1960 | Ted Williams | .482 | Ted Williams | .631 |
| 1961–1976 | Mickey Mantle | .418 | Hank Aaron | .552 |
| 1977–1997 | Frank Thomas | .452 | Frank Thomas | .600 |

Minimum 2,500 plate appearances.

Well, we've come up with yet another way to compare Frank Thomas to Ted Williams, and we've thrown in Ty Cobb and Babe Ruth for good measure. While Thomas' dual leadership isn't unique, The Big Hurt is certainly in exalted company. Barring a complete catastrophe, it's hard to imagine that Thomas won't join those three as first-ballot Hall of Famers.

—Jim Callis

A more complete listing for this category can be found on page 213.

### Cleveland Indians: Who Got the Best of Last Spring's Blockbuster Trade?

Without a doubt, last season's biggest and most-talked-about transaction was the blockbuster trade that sent Atlanta's Dave Justice and Marquis Grissom to Cleveland for Kenny Lofton and Alan Embree. Immediately after the deal was struck, our office e-mail system was flooded from all sides with commentary concerning the trade—mirroring the debate that was raging throughout the baseball world. A sizable percentage of "experts" declared the Indians' braintrust got the better of the Braves in the swap; after all, so the reasoning went, Cleveland received two All-Stars (Justice & Grissom) in exchange for only one (Lofton) and a throwaway reliever (Embree). In addition, the Indians had already decided that they weren't going to be able to re-sign Lofton, who would become a free agent after the '97 season. . . so why should they see another star walk without receiving any compensation in return (a la Albert Belle)?

The other side of the argument, however, was also powerful:

1) Replacing Lofton with Grissom in center field would definitely cost the Indians a substantial amount of offensive production.

2) In view of Justice's age (31) and injury history, expecting him to step in and perform at an All-Star level was quite optimistic, at the very least.

3) The Indians weren't being totally honest when they said they made the deal for financial reasons. They acquired two sizable contracts along with Justice and Grissom (around $7-8 million annually for the two players), who together wouldn't be making much less than what they believed Lofton himself would have commanded on the open market.

4) Cleveland's acquisition of Grissom and Justice would take away playing time from younger talents such as Brian Giles.

#### Statistical Comparison: Braves/Indians Trade—1997

| Player, Team | Avg | OBP | Slg | Runs | HR | RBI | RC/27 Outs |
|---|---|---|---|---|---|---|---|
| Lofton, Atl | .333 | .409 | .428 | 90 | 5 | 48 | 6.36 |
| Grissom, Cle | .262 | .317 | .396 | 74 | 12 | 66 | 4.34 |
| Justice, Cle | .329 | .418 | .596 | 84 | 33 | 101 | 8.91 |

Point 1 was definitely true; Lofton didn't quite live up to expectations in Atlanta—but he had a much better year than Grissom did. Grissom got off to a sluggish start and was exiled to the No. 9 spot in the Indians' lineup by the end of year; he posted an OBP of only .317, and scored just 74 runs despite spending part of the year as the leadoff hitter for a powerful Cleveland offense.

Of course, point 2 turned out to be completely wrong, as Justice posted the best offensive numbers of his career, hitting .329 while slugging .596. Call me a stubborn cynic, but I still feel that Justice can't possibly keep up his current level of production over the next few seasons. Not only is he entering a stage in his career where decline is almost unavoidable, but it was revealed during the summer that he's been playing with a partially torn knee tendon for the last several years. If *that's* not the definition of risk, what is?

As for point 3, well. . . how often have you seen a team trade a player in the last year of a contract specifically because it felt it couldn't retain him—and then sign the *same* player after the season for far *less* than what it originally had offered him? Not often. But that's exactly what happened with Lofton, who returned to Cleveland at the end of the '97 season for about $4 million per season—about half of what he was asking for last spring.

The Brian Giles issue—point 4—turned out to be a moot issue, since the Indians were able to find Giles playing time at the DH and left-field (after Justice could no longer man the position) slots. In his first taste of extended action, Giles played as well as could be expected, hitting .268 and slamming 17 homers in 377 at-bats.

Though he wasn't mentioned much at the time of the trade, reliever Alan Embree delivered a surprisingly strong performance last year—by far the best season of his young career. The 27-year-old appeared in 66 games for the Braves last year, posting a 2.54 ERA and racking up nearly a strikeout per inning. Now that Lofton will be suiting up for the Tribe again in '98, Embree is the only commodity the Braves have retained from the deal. Rather than invest in Lofton, Atlanta has decided to move young phenom Andruw Jones from right field to center next season, sliding fellow prospect Michael Tucker in at right. The money the team has saved from Grissom's and Justice's long-term contracts were used to both cement its starting rotation (both Tom Glavine and Greg Maddux inked contract extensions in 1997) and to lure Andres Galarraga from Colorado over the winter.

What has Cleveland retained from the deal? In December, it shipped off Grissom to Milwaukee in a three-way trade and came away with Ben McDonald, Ron Villone and Steve Karsay. McDonald and Karsay are starting pitchers who have had arm troubles throughout the last several years, while Villone is a mediocre reliever who's been shipped around a number of teams in his short career. If the Indians hadn't been able to bring back Lofton—and were planning to start Grissom in center field next season—then Justice would have had to maintain his stellar offensive production in order to save the deal; now, it stands that they picked up Justice and the trio of hurlers in exchange for Embree and a one-year "rent" of Lofton. A *much* better transaction.

What's hard to figure, though, is exactly *why* the Braves let Lofton go. They invested twice as much money in signing Galarraga when they could have moved Ryan Klesko from left field to first—and filled Klesko's slot with either Jones or Tucker. It doesn't exactly make sense, but who are we to argue with the Braves' front office?

—Kevin Fullam

## Detroit Tigers: Can They Continue to Improve?

Life is good if you're a Tigers fan. After going 53-109 in 1996, Detroit jumped to 79-83 last season. The Tigers cut 1.82 runs off their ERA. Justin Thompson looks like a future Cy Young Award winner. Todd Jones is a legitimate closer. Tony Clark looks like Cecil Fielder, minus about 50 pounds. Brian Hunter is the club's biggest basestealing threat since Ron LeFlore. Bobby Higginson isn't quite Al Kaline, but he's Detroit's best outfielder since Kirk Gibson. The farm system is revitalized, with outfielder Juan Encarnacion the first of many impact players on the way. A new state-of-the-art stadium is scheduled to be completed for the 1999 season.

Yes, life is good. And with the Tigers moving from the American League East to the comparatively weaker AL Central, they could contend for a division title if they can improve by just half as much as they did in 1997.

How likely is it that Detroit will continue to move forward in 1998? Let's take a look at the teams that have posted a .150 gain in winning percentage since the expansion era began in 1961. Fifteen teams, including the 1997 Tigers, make the cut:

### Biggest Improvements—1961-97

| Team | Year 1 | Year 1 Pct | —Year 2— Pct | —Year 2— Change | —Year 3— Pct | —Year 3— Change |
|---|---|---|---|---|---|---|
| Orioles | 1988 | .335 | .537 | +.202 | .472 | −.065 |
| Phillies | 1961 | .305 | .503 | +.198 | .537 | +.034 |
| Giants | 1992 | .444 | .636 | +.192 | .478 | −.158 |
| Braves | 1990 | .401 | .580 | +.179 | .605 | +.025 |
| Athletics | 1979 | .333 | .512 | +.179 | .587 | +.075 |
| Cubs | 1966 | .364 | .540 | +.176 | .519 | −.021 |
| Rangers | 1973 | .352 | .522 | +.170 | .488 | −.034 |
| Phillies | 1992 | .432 | .599 | +.167 | .470 | −.129 |
| Mets | 1968 | .451 | .617 | +.166 | .512 | −.105 |
| Tigers | 1996 | .327 | .488 | +.161 | — | — |
| Brewers | 1977 | .414 | .574 | +.160 | .590 | +.016 |
| White Sox | 1976 | .398 | .556 | +.158 | .441 | −.115 |
| Cubs | 1983 | .438 | .596 | +.158 | .478 | −.118 |
| Rangers | 1985 | .385 | .537 | +.152 | .463 | −.074 |
| White Sox | 1989 | .429 | .580 | +.151 | .537 | −.043 |

The 1989 Orioles top the list, going from an 0-21 start the year before to season-long contention. The 1969 Miracle Mets won the World Series, while the 1991 Braves and 1993 Phillies captured National League pennants and the 1984 Cubs took the NL East title.

Of the 14 teams besides the 1997 Tigers, just four improved in the following year. This isn't a big surprise. Bill James pointed out years ago that teams or players who improve or decline significantly one season tend to head in the other direction the next. The average change in winning percentage for the 14 teams was -.051, which would put Detroit in line for a 71-91 year.

As for postseason aspirations, just two of the 14 clubs made the playoffs in the season following their huge improvement. The 1992 Braves won their second straight pennant, and the 1981 Athletics reached the AL Championship Series. The average wait to reach the postseason was eight years, and the Cubs and Phillies haven't been back since 1984 and 1993, respectively.

Life *is* good if you're a Tigers fan. It's just not likely to get any better in 1998.

—Jim Callis

A more complete listing for this category can be found on page 215.

### Kansas City Royals: What Kind of Manager Will Muser Be?

Tony Muser landed his first big-league manager's job when he was handed the reins of the Kansas City Royals at last year's All-Star break, replacing Bob Boone. During his time at the helm of the Kansas City Royals, Boone had established one of the most unique managerial styles in the majors, so it was hardly surprising that Muser's approach turned out to be quite different. Let's take a look at what Muser accomplished over the second half to see what we might expect from his Royals in the near future.

Last year, the most obvious difference between Boone and Muser was Boone's heavy reliance on veterans compared to Muser's willingness to cast his lot with younger players. Under Boone, less than one-sixth of the team's at-bats were devoted to players with a seasonal age of 25 or younger. After Muser took over, the young hitters' percentage of the team's at-bats more than doubled:

| Manager | AB, Age 25 & Younger | Tot Team AB | %AB, Age 25 & Younger |
|---|---|---|---|
| Bob Boone | 462 | 2,808 | 16.5 |
| Tony Muser | 1,006 | 2,791 | 36.0 |

In retrospect, it's easy to understand why Boone was so reluctant to play the kids while Muser was so willing to do so. Going into the season, the Royals had added Chili Davis, Jeff King and Jay Bell to the lineup—moves which were expected to propel Kansas City back into contention. Royals President Mike Herman had even gone on record predicting a 92-win season. Even though the Royals had given Boone a contract extension over the winter, Boone knew that significant improvement was expected. The club's short-term goals did not seem to include building for the future.

All of that had changed by the time Boone was dismissed at the All-Star break. By then, the Royals were a half-game out of the American League Central cellar, 10 games under .500, nine games out of first place, and even further out of contention in the AL wild-card race. Muser took over when the club's focus had shifted from the present to the future, and he used the opportunity to look at the club's younger talent. He took extended looks at several youngsters who hadn't played much in the first half, and expanded the roles of some who had.

Two of the most significant changes involved outfielder Johnny Damon and catcher Mike Sweeney, a pair of well-regarded prospects who hadn't quite lived up to expectations to that point. Damon, a natural center fielder whose only shortcoming afield was a weak throwing arm, had been moved to right field by Boone so that Tom Goodwin could play center. Boone had also dropped Damon to the bottom third of the lineup, despite the fact that Damon is seen as the team's future leadoff hitter.

Three weeks after Muser took over, Goodwin was traded to the Rangers. This cleared the way for Muser to return Damon to center, which he did immediately. At first, he batted Damon low in the order, while giving him occasional starts in the No. 2 spot. As the weeks passed, he gave Damon more and more time in the two-hole, and began to bat him leadoff as well. By the end of the year, Damon was batting first or second exclusively. Although Damon's batting average fell as he readjusted to hitting at the top of the lineup, he improved his plate discipline and put his speed to good use on the bases. He still promises to be a better leadoff man and center fielder than Goodwin ever was.

Muser also reversed the roles of catchers Mike Sweeney and Mike Macfarlane, giving Sweeney the bulk of the playing time after Macfarlane had handled most of the chores over the first half. Although Sweeney's power fell off somewhat in the second half, he proved that he could hold up under everyday play while contributing with both the bat and the glove. Sweeney is expected to develop into one of the better young catchers in the league, and may take another step forward this year.

Muser also gave considerable playing time to rookies Jed Hansen, who took over as the regular second baseman in August after Jose Offerman was injured, and Yamil Benitez, who played regularly in left and right field in the second half. Both Hansen and Benitez showed enough to figure in the club's future, though Benitez was lost in the expansion draft. Others who got long looks included first baseman Larry Sutton, utilityman Shane Halter and outfielder Rod Myers, who each played quite a bit during the season's final month.

Young pitchers Glendon Rusch and Jim Pittsley struggled, but Muser remained patient with them, resisting the urge to drop them from the starting rotation. Rusch showed significant improvement over the last two months and may contribute more this season.

The other major change Muser instituted was to do away with Boone's NL-style offense. Boone's Royals always had attempted more stolen bases than any other club in the league, and they made liberal use of the sacrifice and the hit-and-run as well. Boone's lineup selection illustrated his preference for speed over power, as he often played players with little pop at "power" positions (Jose Offerman at first base, Joe Randa at third and Johnny Damon in right field are but a few examples).

With the trade of Goodwin for power-hitting Dean Palmer, Muser moved Damon back to center and made slugger Benitez a regular, adding power at two spots at once. Later in the year, Bip Roberts was unloaded, enabling Muser to get both Benitez and Jermaine Dye into the lineup at the same time.

Overall, the club declined by 3½ games in the second half, but it was clear that Muser's first half-season was a success. He devoted his attention to uncovering and developing players who could grow into significant contributors, and he showed admirable patience as some of the youngsters suffered through the inevitable rough stretches. He also showed flexibility in his offensive strategy, tailoring it to utilize the talent on hand. The Royals may not zoom back into contention overnight, but under Muser, they look like they're finally back on the right track.

—Mat Olkin

## Minnesota Twins: What Might Have Been for Molitor?

Without a doubt, Paul Molitor is headed for Cooperstown. His legacy includes a .308 career batting average, 3,178 hits and one World Series championship, and he's still adding to it. His totals across the board are striking. So are the number of incomplete seasons.

In 1980, Molitor was leading the American League in batting when he pulled a ribcage muscle, which cost him more than three weeks. The following year, he tore ligaments in his left ankle and was placed on the 60-day disabled list. He remained healthy throughout 1982 and 1983, then missed all but 13 games in 1984 when he needed reconstructive surgery on his right elbow. Hamstring strains led to three stints on the disabled list in 1986 and 1987, and he headed back to the DL twice in 1990 with a broken right thumb and a fractured knuckle on his left index finger.

The injury bug that kept biting Molitor is quite uncommon. We did a study of the 37 players, including Molitor, who have played in 2,500 major league games. We compared their games played to the games played by their teams in those years. All games missed because of military service were counted. We didn't include any season before a player's first 100-game year, or his last season (unless the player was active), because those are often partial years. As it turned out, only four longtime players missed a higher percentage of their teams' game than Molitor:

### Highest Percentage Of Team Games Missed

| Player | Years | G | Team G | Pct Missed |
|---|---|---|---|---|
| Willie McCovey | 1960-79 | 2,488 | 3,223 | 22.8 |
| Tony Perez | 1965-85 | 2,688 | 3,338 | 19.5 |
| Rabbit Maranville | 1913-34 | 2,621 | 3,211 | 18.4 |
| Bill Buckner | 1971-89 | 2,466 | 3,012 | 18.1 |
| Paul Molitor | 1978-97 | 2,557 | 3,119 | 18.0 |
| **Totals** | | **99,166** | **112,745** | **12.0** |

(minimum 2,500 G)

What could Molitor have accomplished had he stayed injury-free? For the sake of discussion, we prorated his statistics as if he had played in 155 games in each of the seasons in which he lost time to injury. For strike-shortened 1981, we prorated his stats as if he had played in 105 games. And for 1984, when he played in just 13 games, we prorated his 1983-85 numbers to 155 games to get a more accurate sample. This healthy Molitor would have missed just 6.3 percent of his team's games, making him the fifth-most durable longtime player.

Here are the results:

### Real vs. Healthy Molitor

|         | G     | AB     | H     | 2B   | 3B   | HR   | R     | RBI   | SB   | Avg  |
|---------|-------|--------|-------|------|------|------|-------|-------|------|------|
| Real    | 2,557 | 10,333 | 3,178 | 576  | 109  | 230  | 1,707 | 1,238 | 495  | .308 |
| Rank    | 31st  | 13th   | 12th  | 12th | —    | —    | 21st  | 89th  | 34th | 99th |
| Healthy | 2,923 | 11,816 | 3,610 | 660  | 123  | 263  | 1,960 | 1,383 | 578  | .306 |
| Rank    | 10th  | 4th    | 5th   | 6th  | 93rd | —    | 6th   | 52nd  | 20th | —    |

Molitor would have 3,610 career hits, just 87 behind all-time leader Pete Rose at the same stage of their careers. How much of a chance would he have to surpass Rose's total of 4,256? Bill James developed a formula, the Favorite Toy, to answer just such a question. We'll spare you the math and just tell you that Molitor would have a 27 percent chance of becoming the new Hit King. His chances would have been greatly enhanced had he agreed to manage the Blue Jays, which meant he could have kept penciling his name into the lineup as Rose did in his last years with the Reds.

Molitor also would have a 26 percent chance of passing Ty Cobb's record of 2,245 runs scored and the same chance of breaking Tris Speaker's mark of 792 doubles. One further note that doesn't show up on the chart: Molitor would have scored 150 runs in 1987, becoming the first player to reach that plateau since Ted Williams in 1949.

Because he has stayed healthy for the last seven seasons and has gotten better with age, Molitor actually has been able to fashion a long career. Only 30 hitters have played in more major league games. But if he had been able to avoid injuries, some of the game's most coveted records might have been his.

—Jim Callis

A more complete listing for this category appears on page 216.

### New York Yankees: Who's the Leading Winner From Each Nation?

Imagine, if you will, that you're George Costanza, beleaguered member of the Yankees' front office. You've been called on the carpet by your boss, The Boss. George Steinbrenner wants you to justify the Hideki Irabu signing. Of course, it was Steinbrenner who arranged the deal to send $3 million and top prospects Ruben Rivera and Rafael Medina to the Padres for the rights to Irabu. It was Steinbrenner who reportedly nixed a spring-training trade of Rivera for Philadelphia's Curt Schilling. And it was Steinbrenner who gave Irabu a four-year contract worth a guaranteed $12.8 million. But none of this matters. He wants *you* to explain.

Billed as the Japanese Nolan Ryan, Irabu wasn't even the Japanese Ken Ryan. Irabu went 5-4, 7.09 in 13 appearances and wasn't a factor in New York's failed drive to repeat as World Series champions. And Steinbrenner is even more displeased after San Diego used Medina as one of two key prospects in a trade for Marlins ace Kevin Brown. He already has fired Irabu's interpreter, and you get the feeling that you might be next.

So now it's up to you to explain what good, if any, came from the Irabu signing. You come up with the fact that Yankees attendance was up an average of more than 10,000 fans for each of Irabu's four home starts, but surprisingly Steinbrenner is impressed. Desperately seeking some way to manufacture some addtional positive spins for Irabu, you ask yourself, "Where does Irabu stand on the list of winningest Japanese pitchers ever in the major leagues?"

Good question. In fact, we were wondering who the all-time leading winner was from each nation. Major league pitchers have been born in 36 different countries, though three (Austria, the Panama Canal Zone and Finland) haven't produced any who won a game.

The illustration on the following page lists the winningest pitcher by country for those nations that can claim at least one 100-game winner in the major leagues. Cy Young, of course, takes top billing overall, while Bert Blyleven is our top "foreigner" with 287 victories for The Netherlands:

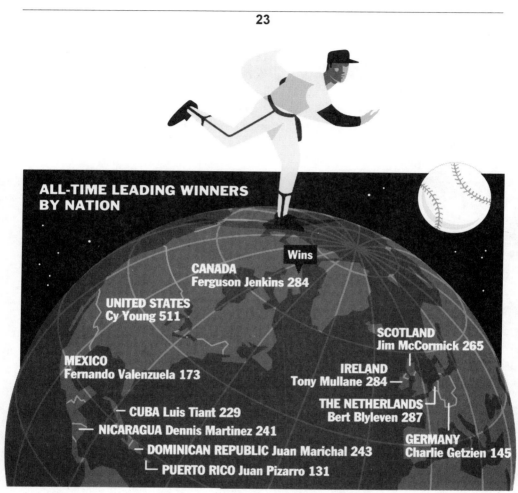

## ALL-TIME LEADING WINNERS BY NATION

Wins

CANADA
Ferguson Jenkins 284

UNITED STATES
Cy Young 511

SCOTLAND
Jim McCormick 265

MEXICO
Fernando Valenzuela 173

IRELAND
Tony Mullane 284 —

THE NETHERLANDS
Bert Blyleven 287

— CUBA Luis Tiant 229

GERMANY
Charlie Getzien 145

— NICARAGUA Dennis Martinez 241

— DOMINICAN REPUBLIC Juan Marichal 243

└ PUERTO RICO Juan Pizarro 131

Minimum 100 wins for a nation.

Now let's take a look at the rest of our list—the leading winners from nations who can't boast a 100-game winner:

### Winningest Pitchers By Nation—Nations With No 100-Game Winner

| Nation | Pitcher | W |
| --- | --- | --- |
| Wales | Ted Lewis | 94 |
| Poland | Moe Drabowsky | 88 |
| England | Danny Cox | 74 |
| Venezuela | Wilson Alvarez | 71 |
| Switzerland | Otto Hess | 70 |
| Panama | Juan Berenguer | 67 |
| Virgin Islands | Al McBean | 67 |

| Nation | Pitcher | W |
|---|---|---|
| France | Charlie Lea | 62 |
| West Germany | Craig Lefferts | 58 |
| Japan | Hideo Nomo | 43 |
| Sweden | Eric Erickson | 34 |
| Italy | Marino Pieretti | 30 |
| South Korea | Chan Ho Park | 19 |
| Russia | Rube Schauer | 10 |
| Australia | Mark Hutton | 9 |
| Aruba | Calvin Maduro | 3 |
| Norway | Jimmy Wiggs | 3 |
| Spain | Bryan Oelkers | 3 |
| Afghanistan | Jeff Bronkey | 2 |
| Austria-Hungary | Joe Hovlik | 2 |
| South Vietnam | Danny Graves | 2 |
| Bahamas | Wenty Ford | 1 |

Hideo Nomo of the Dodgers is the Japanese kingpin with 43 victories. Other pitchers who lead their nations and were active in 1997 include Nicaragua's Dennis Martinez, Mexico's Fernando Valenzuela, Venezuela's Wilson Alvarez, South Korea's Chan Ho Park, Australia's Mark Hutton, Aruba's Calvin Maduro and South Vietnam's Danny Graves.

Now back to George. You point out that Irabu is tied for second place on the Japanese list with Masanori Murakami. But with Hideki's meager total of five lifetime victories, you'd better think of something else quick.

—Jim Callis

## Oakland Athletics: How Small Was Aaron's Win Total?

Oakland righthander Aaron Small chased a baseball record down to the second-to-last week of the 1997 season. His pursuit received little attention, probably because the mark is far from coveted.

Small topped the Athletics in wins last year with the paltry total of nine. The fewest victories ever for a team leader in a non-strike season is seven, a distinction shared by Scott Bailes, Tom Candiotti and Phil Niekro of the 1987 Indians and Omar Olivares of the 1996 Tigers. Small did his best to equal the record, not winning a single game for nearly two months after beating the Indians on July 25 for his seventh victory. But on September 20, Izzy Molina homered in the bottom of the 15th to give Small a 4-3 victory over the Mariners, and he beat Seattle again on the final day of the season.

Small became the 34th pitcher in the modern era to lead a team with fewer than 10 victories, not counting the strike seasons of 1981 and 1994. He was the 13th in the last two decades:

### Fewest Wins By A Team Leader—1978-97

| Year | Team | Leader | W |
|------|------|--------|---|
| 1987 | Indians | Scott Bailes, Tom Candiotti, Phil Niekro | 7 |
| 1996 | Tigers | Omar Olivares | 7 |
| 1988 | Orioles | Jeff Ballard, Dave Schmidt | 8 |
| 1995 | Cardinals | Rich DeLucia | 8 |
| 1996 | Athletics | John Wasdin | 8 |
| 1979 | Blue Jays | Tom Underwood | 9 |
| 1985 | Giants | Scott Garrelts | 9 |
| 1985 | Indians | Bert Blyleven, Neal Heaton | 9 |
| 1986 | Cubs | Scott Sanderson, Lee Smith | 9 |
| 1988 | Braves | Rick Mahler | 9 |
| 1996 | Phillies | Curt Schilling | 9 |
| 1997 | Athletics | Aaron Small | 9 |
| 1997 | Rockies | Roger Bailey, Darren Holmes | 9 |

(1981 and 1994 strike seasons not included)

Most of these teams shared two things in common: they were bad teams with bad pitching staffs. Eight of the 13 had their league's worst record, and eight had their league's worst ERA. Oakland did both in 1997, with a 65-97 mark and a 5.48 ERA. The average winning percentage for the 13 teams was .395, which translates into a 64-98 record, and the average ERA was 4.82.

Team leaders with fewer than 10 wins are becoming more common. The average for the first eight decades of this century was three teams per decade with single-digit win leaders, with the most being four in the 1940s. The 1980s and 1990s have had six each, even with the strike seasons discounted. There are more teams than ever, leading to greater extremes in their quality and thus more bad teams. Teams also are using more pitchers than ever, thus spreading the wins around more than in the past.

While Small couldn't win more than seven games, he did help the Athletics achieve another dubious distinction. With John Wasdin leading the way for the A's with eight wins in 1996, Oakland became the first team since the 1927-28 Phillies to have consecutive win leaders fall shy of double digits (strike seasons excluded).

—Jim Callis

A more complete listing for this category can be found on page 217.

## Seattle Mariners: Will Griffey Shatter the Home-Run Record?

**H**ere's a quick baseball intelligence quiz: Player A is 28 years of age. He's coming off a season in which he just hit 34 home runs, raising his career total to 253. Player B is also 28 years old. But he hit *56* homers the previous season, raising his lifetime total all the way up to 294. Based on this information, which of these sluggers do you think will finish with more lifetime homers?

Well, since this *is* the Seattle Mariners' team essay, you probably already know that Player B is Ken Griffey Jr. Likewise, based on the title of the essay, it doesn't take a genius to figure out that Player A is Hank Aaron. As for the question that we posed, well, the Einstein of Sabermetrics, Bill James, has generated a formula which can help answer that.

The Favorite Toy is one of those fun kind of stats developed by James, like Brock2 or MLEs, in which we're able to pull out the crystal ball and try to peer into the future. The Toy attempts to answer big questions such as whether a player will reach 3,000 hits or 500 home runs. It bases those answers on three criteria: how far the player is from a particular goal, how fast he's getting there, and how much time he has to arrive. That time remaining is itself based on seasonal age. For our purposes, the seasonal age for active players was their age on July 1, 1997.

In the case of Griffey and his homers, the Toy recognizes that

| | AGE | CHANCE | HOME RUNS |
|---|---|---|---|
| Mark McGwire | 33 | 94% | 387 |
| Barry Bonds | 32 | 91% | 374 |
| Ken Griffey Jr. | 27 | 88% | 294 |
| Juan Gonzalez | 27 | 78% | 256 |
| Albert Belle | 30 | 56% | 272 |
| Frank Thomas | 29 | 53% | 257 |
| Sammy Sosa | 28 | 41% | 207 |
| Rafael Palmeiro | 32 | 36% | 271 |
| Jay Buhner | 32 | 35% | 253 |
| Jose Canseco | 32 | 35% | 351 |

he's virtually a lock to reach a milestone which will almost guarantee immortality—500 homers. But he isn't the only active player with a better than one-in-three chance.

Of the 15 men with 500 lifetime homers, 14 are in the Hall of Fame. The 15th, Eddie Murray, has just retired. But for Griffey, 500 homers may be aiming too low; he's on target for even loftier heights. Recall the numbers we presented in the opening paragraph, and it's apparent that Griffey is *ahead* of the pace of the all-time career leader in home runs.

Griffey turned 28 last November, after completing the '97 season with 294 lifetime homers. Only two other players in baseball history, Jimmie Foxx (302) and Eddie Mathews (299), had hit more homers through their age-27 season. But what separates Griffey from Foxx, Mathews and others is the *rate* at which he's moving. Junior has averaged 52.5 homers the past two seasons. By comparison, Foxx (40.0) and Mathews (38.5) were moving at a slower pace. As a result, no other player has ever entered his age-28 season with a higher established chance at reaching the magic number of 756 homers:

### Best Chances For 756 Home Runs—Through Age 27

| Player | HR | %Chance |
| --- | --- | --- |
| Ken Griffey Jr. | 294 | 27 |
| Jimmie Foxx | 302 | 17 |
| Ralph Kiner | 215 | 17 |
| Harmon Killebrew | 223 | 15 |
| Eddie Mathews | 299 | 13 |
| Juan Gonzalez | 256 | 13 |
| Babe Ruth | 197 | 12 |
| Frank Thomas | 182 | 12 |
| Roger Maris | 191 | 8 |
| Rocky Colavito | 209 | 6 |

Interestingly, Aaron had established just a five percent chance at reaching 756 homers by the time he turned 28. But the keys for Aaron were that he was just warming up, and that he seemed to go on forever. Over his next 12 seasons, he *averaged* 38.3 home runs per year, while blasting 40 or more on six occasions, the last occurring at age 39. Whether Griffey can remain that productive as he ages will obviously be the determining factor in his quest for the record.

And remember, having a 27 percent chance at succeeding means he also has a 73 percent chance at *not* breaking the mark. Furthermore, the percentages can demonstrate great fluidity from year to year. For instance, after a 1965 season in which he slugged 52 homers, Willie Mays had established a 41 percent chance at breaking Babe Ruth's career record of 714 home runs. Three years later, Mays' chances were non-existent. Aaron's chances, on the other hand, moved from just four percent in 1965, to 17 in '66, and then to 26, 18, 33 and 44 percent in successive years. By 1971, after hitting 47 homers to reach 639 at age 37, the Toy would give Aaron a 93 percent chance at breaking Ruth's record. It also pegged Hammerin' Hank to finish with 748, not far from his actual final total of 755.

Similarly, should Griffey drop to 35 homers in 1998, his established chance at breaking Aaron's record would drop to 23 percent. But if he repeats another 50-homer campaign, his prospects improve all the way to 38 percent. Though Griffey still has a ways to go before the discussion of Aaron's record gets really serious, it's obvious he's on the right track.

—Jim Henzler

A more complete listing for this category can be found on page 218.

### Tampa Bay Devil Rays: How Many Expansion Franchises Have Had a Milestone Player?

Wade Boggs covets 3,000 hits, and he signed with his hometown team, the expansion Tampa Bay Devil Rays, to continue his pursuit of that goal. He finished 1997 needing 200 hits, and Bill James' Favorite Toy gives him a 49-percent chance of achieving it.

Since the expansion era began with the creation of the Los Angeles Angels and the new Washington Senators in 1961, how many players have reached one of baseball's most treasured milestones (300 wins, 500 homers or 3,000 hits) with an expansion franchise? Let's take a look:

**Milestones Achieved With Expansion Franchises**

| Year | Team | Season | Player | Milestone |
|------|------|--------|--------|-----------|
| 1967 | Astros | 6th | Eddie Mathews | 500 HR |
| 1982 | Mariners | 6th | Gaylord Perry | 300 W |
| 1984 | Angels | 24th | Reggie Jackson | 500 HR |
| 1985 | Angels | 25th | Rod Carew | 3,000 H |
| 1986 | Angels | 26th | Don Sutton | 300 W |
| 1990 | Rangers | 30th | Nolan Ryan | 300 W |
| 1992 | Brewers | 24th | Robin Yount | 3,000 H |
| 1992 | Royals | 24th | George Brett | 3,000 H |

If Boggs reaches 3,000 hits with the Devil Rays, he almost assuredly will do so before their sixth season, thus making them the expansion team to have a milestone player the soonest. The first two were the fastest, with Eddie Mathews hitting his 500th homer in the Astros' sixth year (1967) and Gaylord Perry winning his 300th game in the Mariners' sixth (1982).

Only six of the 12 expansion franchises have had milestone players, and only the Angels have had more than one. Anaheim (then California) had one for three years running, with Reggie Jackson belting his 500th homer in 1984, Rod Carew stroking his 3,000th hit in 1985 and Don Sutton earning his 300th victory in 1986. The Padres could beat the Devil Rays in the race to become the seventh expansion team to have a milestone player, as Tony Gwynn needs just 220 hits to reach 3,000.

—Jim Callis

**Texas Rangers: Will Pudge Burn Out?**

Ivan Rodriguez, the Rangers' All-Star catcher, continues to put up some amazing numbers. Last year, at 25, he batted a career-high .313 and hit 20 home runs, another career best. He also won a Gold Glove, something he's done in each of his six full major league seasons. Rodriguez did all this while catching 143 games, a heavy workload for any receiver but especially for one who plays half his games in the wilting Texas heat.

An obvious question about Rodriguez is whether his workload will shorten his career or reduce his productivity. Through the age of 25, Rodgriguez has caught 853 games, one of the highest figures in history for a player his age. In fact, only one receiver—Johnny Bench—caught more. How did other catchers who were used heavily at such a young age fare during the rest of their careers? Here's the top 10 in games caught through age 25 (seasonal age as of July 1), and their before-and-after offensive figures:

**Most Games Caught Through Age 25**

| | By Age 25 | | | | | After Age 25 | | | | |
|---|---|---|---|---|---|---|---|---|---|---|
| Player | G | BA | OBP | SLG | HR | G | BA | OBP | SLG | HR |
| Johnny Bench | 870 | .268 | .336 | .479 | 179 | 872 | .267 | .346 | .474 | 210 |
| **Ivan Rodriguez** | **853** | **.290** | **.330** | **.439** | **88** | — | — | — | — | — |
| Ted Simmons | 798 | .298 | .353 | .441 | 77 | 973 | .277 | .345 | .435 | 171 |
| Ray Schalk | 776 | .245 | .327 | .303 | 4 | 951 | .261 | .351 | .326 | 7 |
| Butch Wynegar | 735 | .255 | .342 | .343 | 36 | 512 | .253 | .358 | .353 | 29 |
| Tim McCarver | 683 | .282 | .334 | .410 | 51 | 704 | .264 | .339 | .372 | 46 |
| Frankie Hayes | 629 | .278 | .355 | .447 | 73 | 682 | .242 | .333 | .357 | 46 |
| Bill Freehan | 625 | .262 | .337 | .401 | 69 | 956 | .262 | .341 | .419 | 131 |
| Al Lopez | 620 | .284 | .340 | .372 | 17 | 1298 | .250 | .320 | .319 | 34 |
| Darrell Porter | 607 | .238 | .338 | .390 | 70 | 899 | .253 | .364 | .421 | 118 |
| Steve O'Neill | 607 | .233 | .289 | .287 | 2 | 923 | .282 | .384 | .369 | 11 |

There are three Hall of Famers on this list in Bench, Ray Schalk and Al Lopez (though Lopez made it primarily because of his skills as a manager). Ted Simmons is considered a strong Hall of Fame candidate in some circles, and Tim McCarver, Bill Freehan, Darrell Porter, Frankie Hayes and Steve O'Neill were all considered among the best catchers of their day.

Rodriguez' offensive numbers through age 25 are among the best in the group, and he also has to rank near the top defensively as well. His offensive numbers through age 25 are probably most similar to Ted Simmons.

A more detailed comparison:

| | AB | R | H | 2B | 3B | HR | RBI | BB | SO | AVG | OBP | SLG |
|---|---|---|---|---|---|---|---|---|---|---|---|---|
| Simmons | 3204 | 371 | 956 | 177 | 24 | 77 | 495 | 275 | 263 | .298 | .353 | .441 |
| Rodriguez | 3264 | 445 | 948 | 192 | 15 | 88 | 417 | 181 | 419 | .290 | .330 | .439 |

A pretty good match. Simmons, who was nowhere near the defensive player that Rodriguez is, caught only 973 more games after the age of 25, but he played on as a first baseman, DH and pinch hitter until he was 38, finishing with a .285 career average and 2,472 hits. If Rodriguez lasts that long, everybody will be happy, but Simmons' longevity was undoubtedly aided by the fact that he was switched to other positions. Even then, he faded out fairly early; he had only one good season, 1983, after the age of 30, and he was strictly a bench player the last few years of his career.

Rodriguez also bears some similarities to Bill Freehan, the Tigers' catcher of the 1960s and a five-time Gold Glove winner. In 1967, at the age of 25, Freehan had 20 homers, 74 RBI and an on-base plus slugging of .839; Pudge's figures last year were 20-77-.844. Freehan had several more good years after 1967, but his career started winding down at age 30, and he was finished at age 34 after playing in 71 games for the '76 Tigers.

There are also some similarities between Rodriguez and Tim McCarver, who had 14 homers, 69 RBI and an .826 OPS at age 25 for the 1967 St. Louis Cardinals. McCarver, who was less of a home-run threat than Pudge and not nearly as good defensively, had his last good year with the bat at age 29 for the '71 Phillies. Like Simmons, McCarver lasted until he was 38, but that was mostly as Steve Carlton's personal receiver; he never had more than 169 at-bats in a season during the last seven years of his career.

Finally, there is Johnny Bench, the only receiver to catch more games than Rodriguez to this point of his career. Bench had some great years after the age of 25, with three more 100-RBI seasons. But Bench's last 100-ribbie season came at age 29, and he had only one 400-at-bat season after that.

If these players' experience is any guide, Rodriguez figures to have three or four more strong seasons at most before he starts to fade. He's such a good defensive catcher that he could probably hit .240 and still hold onto his job, so a long career is still a possibility if he can stay healthy. Given his heavy workload, that's anything but guaranteed. It's weird to think that the clock is already ticking for a player who's only 26 years old. But that's been the history of heavily-used catchers.

— Don Zminda

## Toronto Blue Jays: Do Young Power Hitters Pan Out?

Rookie Jose Cruz Jr. won over the confidence of the Toronto brass and the hearts of Blue Jays fans with one explosive swing of the bat. On August 1, in his very first game in a Jays uniform after coming over in a deadline-beating trade with the Mariners, Cruz launched a game-winning, two-run homer in the top of the sixth to help lift Toronto to a 7-5 victory over Detroit. He proceeded to go deep eight more times during the month and finished his rookie year with 26 dingers, prompting more than just a few people to second-guess Seattle's thinking in letting him go.

After all, here's a kid who was practically born with a bat in his hands. Baseball genes? Cruz Jr. must have DNA strands shaped like Louisville Sluggers! His father (Jose Sr.) was a two-time All-Star for the Houston Astros, while two of his uncles (Hector and Tommy) also logged time in the major leagues. Was there ever *really* a question of how Jose Cruz Jr. would pay the bills when he grew up? Of course "grown up" is a relative term when it comes to athletes, and Cruz Jr. is no exception. When the 1997 season opened, Cruz was fine-tuning his stroke at Triple-A Tacoma at the ripe old age of 22. On May 31—just six weeks after his 23rd birthday—he was taking his cuts in the Kingdome. By the end of '97, he had become just the 18th rookie with an Opening Day age of 22 or younger to hit at least 26 home runs in that season:

### Rookies With 26+ HR and Opening Day Age of 22 or Younger

| Player, Year | Age | HR | Career HR |
|---|---|---|---|
| Frank Robinson, 1956 | 20 | 38 | 586 |
| Hal Trosky, 1934 | 21 | 35 | 228 |
| *Jose Canseco, 1986 | 21 | 33 | 351 |
| Earl Williams, 1971 | 22 | 33 | 138 |
| Jim Ray Hart, 1964 | 22 | 31 | 170 |
| Ted Williams, 1939 | 20 | 31 | 521 |
| *Pete Incaviglia, 1986 | 22 | 30 | 206 |
| Reggie Jackson, 1968 | 21 | 29 | 563 |
| Willie Horton, 1965 | 22 | 29 | 325 |
| Dick Allen, 1964 | 22 | 29 | 351 |
| Joe DiMaggio, 1936 | 21 | 29 | 361 |
| *Cal Ripken, 1982 | 21 | 28 | 370 |
| Eddie Murray, 1977 | 21 | 27 | 504 |
| George Scott, 1966 | 22 | 27 | 271 |
| **\*Jose Cruz Jr, 1997** | **22** | **26** | **26** |

| Player, Year | Age | HR | Career HR |
|---|---|---|---|
| *Darryl Strawberry, 1983 | 21 | 26 | 308 |
| Bobby Murcer, 1969 | 22 | 26 | 252 |
| Ken Keltner, 1938 | 21 | 26 | 163 |
| (*active player) | | | |

Cruz' rookie effort pales in comparison to the ones turned in by the likes of Frank Robinson, Hal Trosky and Jose Canseco, but it nevertheless puts him in some distinct company. And we should point out that the Toronto left fielder hit his 26 homers in just 395 at-bats—he's a strong candidate for the 30+ mark in 1998.

But what about his long-term prognosis? We'd say his future is quite bright if our "young sluggers" list is any indication. Twelve of the 17 players other than Cruz who made the cut went on to log at least 250 career homers, and 10 players topped the 300 mark. The Hall of Fame is well represented, as is the 500-homer club. In fact, only three players fell short of the 200 plateau, and Jim Ray Hart almost certainly would have made it had it not been for a shoulder injury that turned him into a part-timer after just five full seasons. Only Ken Keltner, who was a whiz in the field but suffered mysterious power outages throughout his career, and Earl Williams, who never was comfortable with his original position of catcher, had a tough time maintaining their pace in the power department for reasons other than injury.

If he also inherited his father's durability genes—Cruz Sr. played 2,353 major league games over 19 seasons—then the sky could be the limit for the young Cruz, who won't celebrate his 24th birthday until April 19. He's a great bet to top his father's home-run mark of 165, and the two have a strong chance of being remembered as one of the greatest father/son duos of all time. Injuries aside, the one thing that could derail Cruz is his lack of plate discipline. He struck out 117 times and worked just 41 free passes last season with Seattle and Toronto, showing his inexperience with breaking pitches and changeups. But selectivity and anticipation come with time, and that's something Cruz has a ton of. His father certainly set a good example, walking nearly as many times (898) as he struck out (1,031) during his career.

Will Cruz Jr. add his name to the list of young power hitters who continued to shower the seats for years and years? According to our calculations, it would be an aberration if he didn't—genes or no genes.

—Tony Nistler

## Arizona Diamondbacks: Will Bank One Ballpark Be a Hitters' Paradise?

When the Rockies joined the National League in 1993, most people seemed fairly sure that their home park, Mile High Stadium, would help the Colorado hitters. The Triple-A American Association's Denver team had been playing there for years, during which time the park had acquired a reputation as a pitcher's worst nightmare. Even with that foreknowledge, however, most people were shocked when Andres Galarraga, Dante Bichette and Charlie Hayes were transformed into fantasy league All-Stars overnight. Despite what was commonly known about the park, most people had failed to anticipate the tremendous magnitude of the park's effects.

We shouldn't allow ourselves to be caught off-guard a second time. This season, the Arizona Diamondbacks will unveil their retractable-roof dome, Bank One Ballpark (or "BOB"). With all that's known about the dimensions of the park and the climate of Phoenix, we can make an educated guess about how BOB will affect the hitters.

Studies of park effects reveal that the two biggest measurable factors in determining a park's effect on offense are its *dimensions* and *elevation*. The dimensions determine not only the difficulty of hitting a home run, but also the amount of territory the outfielders must defend. At higher elevations, batted balls carry further and pitched balls break less sharply. Although other factors (like prevailing wind patterns, the hitting background and the size of foul territory) come into play, the dimensions and elevation will outweigh all the other factors in most cases.

We'll consider BOB's dimensions first. Interestingly, all of the current NL parks have very similar dimensions (with the exceptions of Coors Field and Wrigley Field, which are actually larger than average. Coors measures 347-415-350 and Wrigley measures 355-400-353). When Coors and Wrigley are overlooked, all of the left-field lines measure between 325 and 338 feet, the center-field measurements fall between 395 and 410, and the right-field lines range from 325 to 345. The average NL field measures 334-403-334; BOB's measurements are almost exactly average at 328-402-335. It's fairly safe to say that BOB's dimensions alone shouldn't tip the scale in favor of either the hitters or the pitchers.

While NL ballparks are largely similar in dimension, their elevations differ quite substantially. Coors Field (5,282 feet) is more than five times as high as any other ballpark in the league; Pro Player Stadium, Shea Stadium, Qualcomm Stadium and Veterans Stadium are within 50 feet of sea level, and the rest are somewhere in between.

Furthermore, the parks' elevations correlate very well with their influences on runs and home runs. The eight parks with the lowest elevations are all within 270 feet of sea level. Those parks' average run and home-run indexes (from 1996 through 1997 for San Diego and 1995 through 1997 for all other parks) in our *Major League Handbook* park indexes are 92 and 91, respectively. In other words, most of the league's pitchers' parks fall within this group, and of the eight, the average park depresses scoring by eight percent.

Coors Field is so far off the charts that it must be left in its own category. The five remaining parks fall between 535 and 1,010 feet; when they are studied, it's obvious that they favor the hitters as a group. The five are Busch Stadium, Wrigley Field, Three Rivers Stadium, Cinergy Field and Turner Field. Their average run index is 101 and their average home-run

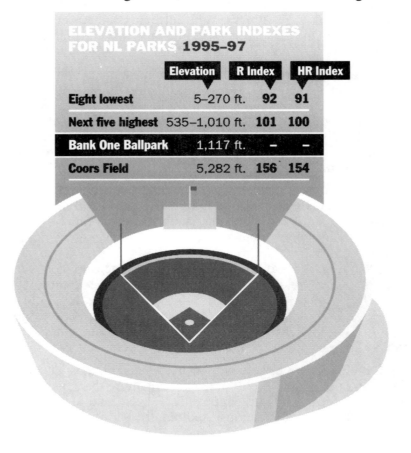

**ELEVATION AND PARK INDEXES FOR NL PARKS 1995–97**

|  | Elevation | R Index | HR Index |
|---|---|---|---|
| **Eight lowest** | 5–270 ft. | 92 | 91 |
| **Next five highest** | 535–1,010 ft. | 101 | 100 |
| **Bank One Ballpark** | 1,117 ft. | – | – |
| **Coors Field** | 5,282 ft. | 156 | 154 |

index is 100. Of the five, the only parks that come out as pitchers' parks are Busch Stadium and Turner Field. Those two have one thing in common: they haven't been around as long. Busch's new grass surface was installed in 1996, so we've only used its home/road data from the last two years. Turner Field favored pitchers in its first year of existence, although it was built to the same dimensions as the old Launching Pad, and it may ultimately prove to be a hitters' park like its predecessor. We used three seasons' worth of data for the other three parks. If one gives more weight to the three-year data, the run and home-run indexes each rise to 103. Not only will BOB's elevation make it comparable to the parks in this group, but it probably will make BOB the most hitter-friendly venue in the group.

If all this seems a little technical, please bear with us. The bottom line is simple: even if you ignore Coors Field, the NL parks with the higher elevations are more hitter-friendly than the rest of the parks, even though their dimensions are all pretty much the same.

But here's the key to the whole discussion: Phoenix' elevation is 1,117 feet above sea level. This would make BOB the NL park with the highest elevation outside of Coors. This alone would indicate that it ought to be a hitters' park.

We wanted to estimate the magnitude of the impact that the elevation can be expected to have on BOB, so we ran a regression analysis on the NL parks' elevations and park indexes. It turns out that a park's elevation correlates very well with its run index, resulting in a correlation coefficient of 0.92. Based on the regression analysis, with an elevation of 1,117 feet, BOB can be expected to have a run factor of 104. This matches the results we obtained above, when we estimated that BOB would likely match or exceed the five hitters' parks' average run index of 103. (And keep one more thing in mind: Coors skews all of the NL park factors. Its run index is so high that there are only four or five other parks in the league with run index above 100. Take away Coors, and a run factor of 103 would zoom up to 107 or 108.)

We will submit one more piece of evidence for your consideration. Although a minor league team has never played at the BOB, the Pacific Coast League's Phoenix Firebirds have been playing in the Phoenix area for years. Since 1992, they've been playing in nearby Scottsdale Stadium. An analysis of the Scottsdale park's characteristics is quite revealing.

Before considering Scottsdale Stadium's park indexes, remember that the Pacific Coast League is a great hitters' league. Several franchises play in hitters' havens, including Albuquerque, Colorado Springs, Las Vegas and

Calgary. There are only two parks in the league that favor the pitcher to any extent. For this reason, a park that might be known as a good hitters' park in another league may come out as a neutral park in the PCL.

In fact, that's exactly how Scottsdale Stadium comes out. Over the last three years, its run index is 99, and its home-run index is 106. It's an average hitters' park for the PCL, so in real-world terms, it's a pretty good place to hit.

But now consider this: its measurements are 360 to left field, 430 to center and 340 to right. So if you take a good hitters' park like Scottsdale Stadium, and move in the fences by 32 feet in left, 28 feet in center and five feet in right, you've got the BOB.

So there you have it. Based on all the available evidence, we're quite confident that BOB will be one of the best hitters' parks in the league. It won't be another Coors Field, of course, but players like Travis Lee, Jay Bell and Matt Williams might easily exceed everyone's expectations. Remember, you heard it here first.

—Mat Olkin

**Atlanta Braves: How Good Is the Glavine/Maddux/Smoltz Trio?**

**B**y their standards, 1997 was not a particularly memorable season for Tom Glavine, Greg Maddux and John Smoltz. Their six-year monopoly on the National League Cy Young Award ended, and for only the second time since Maddux arrived in Atlanta in 1993, the Braves fell short of the World Series. Atlanta's trio of aces combined for 48 wins, impressive to be sure, but also its lowest total in a season not shortened by a strike.

Of course, the standards of Glavine, Maddux and Smoltz are higher than any other starting threesome's. Only one other team (the Dodgers) heads into 1998 with three starters (Ramon Martinez, Hideo Nomo and Ismael Valdes) who have been together for three seasons, each making a minimum of 15 starts each year. In five seasons together, the Braves' big three have combined for 241 wins. Here's how they compare to the best threesomes since 1972:

**Top Starting Threesomes—1972-97**

| Pitchers | Team | Years | W |
|---|---|---|---|
| Gooden (119), Darling (93), Fernandez (78) | Mets | 1984-90 | 290 |
| Glavine (116), Smoltz (100), Avery (72) | Braves | 1990-96 | 288 |
| McGregor (102), Flanagan (95), Martinez (87) | Orioles | 1978-85 | 284 |
| Morris (103), Petry (78), Wilcox (77) | Tigers | 1979-84 | 258 |
| Saberhagen (92), Gubicza (84), Liebrandt (76) | Royals | 1984-89 | 252 |
| **Maddux (89), Glavine (80), Smoltz (72)** | **Braves** | **1993-97** | **241** |
| Seaver (87), Koosman (75), Matlack (75) | Mets | 1972-76 | 237 |
| Flanagan (82), McGregor (75), Palmer (69) | Orioles | 1978-82 | 226 |
| Scott (81), Knepper (75), Ryan (68) | Astros | 1983-88 | 224 |
| Leonard (78), Gura (76), Splittorff (63) | Royals | 1978-82 | 217 |

(minimum 15 GS by each pitcher each year)

Interestingly, Glavine, Maddux and Smoltz aren't even the Braves' best trio of the 1990s. That honor falls to Steve Avery, Glavine and Smoltz, who lasted two years longer and won 47 more games. Glavine, Maddux and Smoltz will move past them this year if they can duplicate their 1998 win total, which also would leave Atlanta's current threesome one victory shy of the top spot.

No. 1 on the list are Dwight Gooden, Ron Darling and Sid Fernandez of the 1984-90 Mets, who helped revitalize a franchise that had finished last five times and next-to-last twice in the seven previous seasons. Not coincidentally, that dismal period began after New York broke up its successful

Tom Seaver-Jon Matlack-Jerry Koosman threesome in 1977 by trading Seaver to the Reds. With Darling, Fernandez and Gooden in their rotation, the Mets never finished worse than second from 1984-90 while winning two NL East titles and the 1986 World Series. Darling was traded and Fernandez was injured in 1991, beginning a streak of six straight losing seasons for New York.

The Mets' periods of success and failure attest to the value of quality starting pitching. The top six groups of starters all brought their teams a World Series championship, and three others led their teams to the Fall Classic. The 10 threesomes combined for 14 pennants and 21 division crowns.

As good as Darling, Fernandez and Gooden were, they rank just 19th on the all-time list. Four-man rotations have gone the way of the reserve clause while the use of relievers continues to rise, making it more difficult for today's starters to win as many games as those of the past. Increased player movement also makes it less likely that a team will keep three starters together for long periods of time. Here's the all-time top 10:

### Top Starting Threesomes—All-Time

| Pitchers | Team | Years | W |
|---|---|---|---|
| Lemon (172), Wynn (163), Garcia (138) | Indians | 1949-57 | 473 |
| Mathewson (215), Wiltse (122), Ames (100) | Giants | 1905-12 | 437 |
| Mathewson (191), McGinnity (151), Taylor (93) | Giants | 1902-08 | 435 |
| Plank (141), Coombs (115), Bender (110) | Athletics | 1906-12 | 366 |
| Rixey (136), Donohue (119), Luque (108) | Reds | 1922-29 | 363 |
| Grove (152), Earnshaw (98), Walberg (94) | Athletics | 1928-33 | 344 |
| Cuellar (125), McNally (111), Palmer (106) | Orioles | 1969-74 | 342 |
| Mathewson (147), McGinnity (112), Wiltse (80) | Giants | 1904-08 | 339 |
| Drysdale (124), Koufax (110), Podres (95) | Dodgers | 1958-65 | 329 |
| Lemon (128), Wynn (112), Feller (85) | Indians | 1949-54 | 325 |

Each of the 10 threesomes features at least one Hall of Famer, while the No. 10 group of Bob Lemon, Early Wynn and Bob Feller includes three Cooperstown inductees. That group wasn't the winningest, though: Lemon and Wynn combined with Mike Garcia to form the most successful and longest-lasting big three ever, winning 473 games for the Indians from 1949-57. Oddly, however, neither of the overlapping Cleveland trios was able to deliver a World Series championship. The Indians won one in 1948, when Garcia had yet to break into the rotation and Wynn was still with the Washington Senators; the Tribe was upset in the 1954 Series after setting an American League record for victories. Cleveland was a perennial contender, but finished ahead of the Yankees only once from 1949-57. For all its success, New York couldn't place a threesome in the top 10. Vic Raschi, Allie Reynolds and Ed Lopat placed 14th by winning 307 games for the 1948-53 Yankees.

Besides the Indians, only one other trio in the top 10 didn't win a World Series, and they were the lone group that never captured a pennant. Pete Donohue, Dolf Luque and Eppa Rixey had 363 victories for the 1922-29 Reds. They came closest to the Fall Classic in 1926, when Cincinnati finished two games behind the Cardinals.

It's quite conceivable that Glavine, Maddux and Smoltz will crack the top 10 before they're through. They're contractually bound to the Braves through the 2000 season, and they'll have 386 combined victories at that point if they keep winning at their current pace. That would leave them about two seasons behind Garcia, Lemon and Wynn. Glavine and Maddux would be 34, with Smoltz 33, so they just might be able to catch them.

—Jim Callis

A more complete listing for this category can be found on page 219.

### Chicago Cubs: Can Rodriguez and Sosa Set the Combined Strikeout Record?

The Cubs traded for Henry Rodriguez on December 12, giving them a matched set of corner outfielders who hit a lot of homers and pile up a lot more strikeouts. In 1997, incumbent Cub Sammy Sosa led the National League with 174 whiffs while Rodriguez ranked third with 149. The year before, Rodriguez topped the Senior Circuit with 160 strikeouts while Sosa placed fourth with 134.

Barring injury, it's almost a given that Rodriguez and Sosa will combine to fan 300 times in 1998. But would that be enough to give them the all-time record for a pair of teammates? Let's go to the vast STATS database:

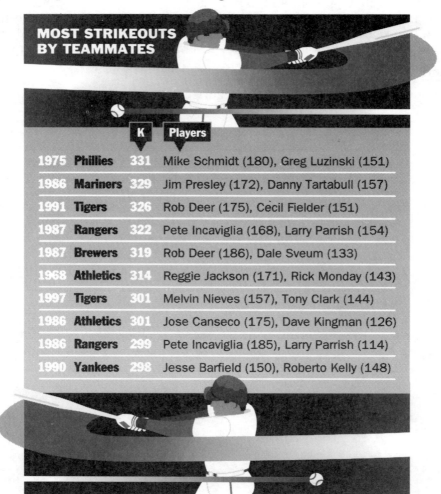

**MOST STRIKEOUTS BY TEAMMATES**

| Year | Team | K | Players |
|------|------|-----|---------|
| 1975 | Phillies | 331 | Mike Schmidt (180), Greg Luzinski (151) |
| 1986 | Mariners | 329 | Jim Presley (172), Danny Tartabull (157) |
| 1991 | Tigers | 326 | Rob Deer (175), Cecil Fielder (151) |
| 1987 | Rangers | 322 | Pete Incaviglia (168), Larry Parrish (154) |
| 1987 | Brewers | 319 | Rob Deer (186), Dale Sveum (133) |
| 1968 | Athletics | 314 | Reggie Jackson (171), Rick Monday (143) |
| 1997 | Tigers | 301 | Melvin Nieves (157), Tony Clark (144) |
| 1986 | Athletics | 301 | Jose Canseco (175), Dave Kingman (126) |
| 1986 | Rangers | 299 | Pete Incaviglia (185), Larry Parrish (114) |
| 1990 | Yankees | 298 | Jesse Barfield (150), Roberto Kelly (148) |

The Cubs hope the addition of Rodriguez will increase their power and help them contend in the National League Central. That could happen, because the first pair of teammates on this list were productive when they made contact. Though Mike Schmidt and Greg Luzinski whiffed a combined 331 times in 1975, Schmidt led the NL in homers and Luzinski topped the league in RBI as the Phillies finished a strong second in the NL East. Four of the nine other teams on the list finished above .500, and the 1986 Rangers and the 1991 Tigers finished second in their divisions.

The record is certainly within the reach of Rodriguez and Sosa. They combined for 323 strikeouts in 1997 and 294 the year before. And if they both were to match their career highs in 1998, they would total 334 whiffs—making them the new champions.

—Jim Callis

A more complete listing for this category can be found on page 220.

## Cincinnati Reds: How Good a Leadoff Man Is Deion?

The answer to the question posed above depends upon what you're looking to get out of your leadoff hitter. If you're after a marketable character who can steal bases, give a colorful postgame quote, and provide a gate attraction for a cash-poor and scandal-marred franchise, then Deion Sanders may be your man. Our definition of a leadoff man's responsibilities is a bit different, however.

As we see it, the leadoff hitter's job is to reach base and, ultimately, score runs. It's quite easy to compare the on-base percentages and runs-scored totals of the various leadoff men, but it has occurred to us that such a limited analysis may be a bit too superficial.

Ponder this riddle for a moment: when is a leadoff man *really* a leadoff man? We're not getting into Zen philosophy here; we're just asking you to consider how often a leadoff hitter *actually* leads off an inning. Obviously, he leads off the first inning of every game, but after that, he's often a leadoff man in name only—he may not lead off an inning for the rest of the game. For example, he may end up as the sixth batter of the second inning, the third batter of the fourth, the fourth batter of the sixth, and the third batter of the ninth. During those final four at-bats, his ability to reach base may have relatively less significance, because even if he reaches base, the inning may end before the run-producers who follow him in the lineup even have a chance to drive him in. If one of his later at-bats comes with two out and a runner on second base, the leadoff man's ability to reach base in that situation becomes far less important than his ability to drive in the run. Therefore, we thought it might be appropriate to focus on leadoff hitters' ability to reach base *in those situations when reaching base is most critical.*

To put it into more concrete terms, we took all the leadoff men who had 300 at-bats in the leadoff spot last year, and looked at how they performed when they led off an inning or batted second in an inning. Our ultimate aim is to see which hitters scored the most runs *per inning* in these situations. Deion's fans may be disappointed to see that he doesn't crack the top 10 in runs per inning:

## Most Runs per Inning by Leadoff Hitters—1997

| Player, Team | Inning Batting 1 or 2 | R | R/Inn. | Avg | OBP |
|---|---|---|---|---|---|
| Craig Biggio, Hou | 439 | 92 | .210 | .288 | .387 |
| Derek Jeter, Yanks | 386 | 76 | .197 | .315 | .373 |
| Tony Phillips, WSox/Ana | 347 | 66 | .190 | .269 | .377 |
| Chuck Knoblauch, Min | 399 | 75 | .188 | .290 | .373 |
| Kenny Lofton, Atl | 321 | 60 | .187 | .330 | .416 |
| Nomar Garciaparra, Bos | 408 | 76 | .186 | .304 | .324 |
| Joey Cora, Sea | 376 | 70 | .186 | .303 | .364 |
| Ray Durham, WSox | 405 | 74 | .183 | .291 | .350 |
| Rickey Henderson, SD/Ana | 319 | 58 | .182 | .235 | .374 |
| Eric Young, Col/LA | 418 | 74 | .177 | .284 | .364 |

(minimum 300 AB as leadoff hitter)

It's no surprise to find that Houston's Craig Biggio led the pack by a wide margin last year. After all, he did score a major league-high 146 runs, the most by a National League hitter in 65 years. Obviously, the key to scoring runs as a leadoff hitter is to get on base. Everyone on the list has an on-base percentage of .350 or better in these situations, except for Boston's Nomar Garciaparra, who made up for it with his uncommon power. Some of these players may have derived a small advantage from having more effective power hitters in the heart of the order to help them score runs, but Biggio and Chuck Knoblauch did just fine without a lot of help from their friends.

Now, let's take a look at the five *worst* leadoff men:

## Fewest Runs per Inning by Leadoff Hitters—1997

| Player, Team | Inning Batting 1 or 2 | R | R/Inn. | Avg | OBP |
|---|---|---|---|---|---|
| Marquis Grissom, Cle | 315 | 45 | .143 | .273 | .333 |
| Deion Sanders, Cin | 313 | 46 | .147 | .283 | .330 |
| Jose Offerman, KC | 256 | 38 | .148 | .300 | .361 |
| Tony Womack, Pit | 389 | 61 | .157 | .261 | .305 |
| Otis Nixon, Tor/LA | 386 | 61 | .158 | .248 | .321 |

Aha! There's Deion—just ahead of Marquis Grissom, who struggled so badly atop the Indians' lineup that he was dropped to the bottom of the order by year's end. Incidentally, Grissom's last-place finish delivers a fatal blow to the argument that the number of runs a leadoff man scores is mostly determined by the bats that follow him in the lineup. It's obvious that Jim Thome, Matt Williams and David Justice aren't to blame for Grissom's failure to score runs last year.

We'll admit that we've been a bit coy; it doesn't surprise us a bit to find Deion coming in next-to-last. You see, despite all his speed, sound and fury, he just doesn't reach base often enough to be an effective leadoff man. In 115 games last year, he scored a total of *53* runs—31 less than the supposedly washed-up Rickey Henderson did in five more games. Batting first or second in an equal number of innings, Craig Biggio would have scored about 43 percent more runs than Deion did.

To our way of thinking, these lists reinforce the notion that players with a low on-base percentage aren't effective leadoff hitters, no matter how many bases they steal. Low-OBP, high-steal players like Sanders, Otis Nixon and Tony Womack all made the bottom five. Meanwhile, sore-legged Kenny Lofton's basestealing efforts were downright miserable, but his unimpaired ability to reach base put him in the top five anyway.

—Mat Olkin

A more complete listing for this category can be found on page 221.

## Colorado Rockies: How Will Kile Pitch at Coors?

Larry Walker's 1997 season amply demonstrates what a true top-flight hitter can do in Coors Field. Now, we're about to find out how well a real No. 1 starter can survive there. During their five-year existence, the Rockies have acquired Bill Swift and Bret Saberhagen, only to see both of them break down. Pedro Astacio was the Dodgers' fourth starter, and he's been arguably the most talented starting pitcher that the Rockies have ever sent to the mound. With the signing of free agent Darryl Kile, the Rockies have netted their first true ace pitcher. Now, the obvious question is: "Can he conquer Coors, or will it conquer him?"

Kile has had the good fortune to spend his entire career in one of the most pitcher-friendly parks in baseball, the Astrodome. Over the last three years, Dodger Stadium is the only NL park that's depressed scoring by a greater margin. By moving to Coors Field, the best hitters' park of all time, Kile is likely to see his numbers greatly affected.

Adjusting his stats for the change in ballparks is a fairly straightforward process. We're well aware of the way that Coors and the Dome affect players' hits, runs, homers, walks and strikeouts. If we assume that the two parks have the same affect on Kile as they do on other players, we can project what Kile's numbers will look like in Coors Field. For example, the Astrodome reduces home runs by about 27 percent, and Coors boosts them by about 66 percent. If we take Kile's home runs allowed at home last year, and add 27 percent for the move away from the Astrodome and add another 66 percent for the move into Coors Field, we can estimate how many home runs he would have allowed at home, had he been pitching in Colorado instead of Houston. We can add that total to his home runs allowed on the road to get an estimate of his total home runs allowed on the season. (Technically, it would be more accurate to adjust his *road* stats as well, since the Astrodome will now replace Coors as one of his road parks. But for simplicity's sake, we'll write off any such effects as *de minimus.*)

Using that methodology, we park-adjusted his 1997 stats, removing him from the Dome and putting him in Coors instead. We've chosen to leave his won-lost record, games started and innings pitched as they were. Compare his actual 1997 season ("Hou") to his park-adjusted line ("Col"):

### Darryl Kile—1997 Adjusted for Coors

|     | W  | L | GS | IP    | H   | HR | BB  | SO  | ERA  |
| --- | -- | - | -- | ----- | --- | -- | --- | --- | ---- |
| Hou | 19 | 7 | 34 | 255.2 | 208 | 19 | 94  | 205 | 2.57 |
| Col | 19 | 7 | 34 | 255.2 | 258 | 33 | 101 | 179 | 3.73 |

Well, that's quite a difference. As dominant as Kile was in 1997, it would have been hard for him to keep his hits-per-inning under 1.0. His homers and walks would have shot up while his strikeouts would have dropped. And the bottom line is that his NL-third-best 2.57 ERA would have risen by well over a full run.

While that approach still gives him a decent stat line, keep in mind that it represents Kile's *best-case scenario.* He pitched more effectively last year than he ever had in his career, and the park-adjusted numbers above represent what he might have done, given that high level of performance. In other words, Kile may have a tough time keeping his ERA under 4.00, unless he approaches the Cy Young-caliber performance he put together last year.

Remember, Kile put up three straight ERAs over 4.00 prior to 1997, and that was in the Astrodome. It seems safe to say that he may backslide a bit this season, even without help from his new park. To create a more realistic scenario, we park-adjusted his numbers as a starting pitcher over the last five years, projecting them into 34 starts. Again, we present what he did in Houston and what he might have done in Colorado:

### Kile as a Starter—1993-97

|     | W  | L  | GS | IP    | H   | HR | BB  | SO  | ERA  |
|-----|----|----|----|-------|-----|----|-----|-----|------|
| Hou | 14 | 11 | 34 | 223.1 | 208 | 16 | 100 | 190 | 3.79 |
| Col | 14 | 11 | 34 | 223.1 | 257 | 27 | 108 | 169 | 5.40 |

Ouch. We can assume that the Rockies will be rather disappointed if Kile's ERA reaches the mid-fives, and they may be underwhelmed by a 14-11 record as well. If he doesn't win as many games as they had expected, they can't blame the park; after all, a pitcher's won-lost record is the one thing that *isn't* seriously affected by the Coors effect. And as a matter of fact, Kile has won more than 12 games only two times during his seven-year career. If Kile crashes to earth in 1998, Coors Field certainly will be a major factor—but it may ot be the entire explanation.

—Mat Olkin

**Florida Marlins: Is the Champs' Fire Sale Unprecedented?**

After spending $89 million on free agents, $79 million on contract extensions for closer Robb Nen and right fielder Gary Sheffield, and $7.5 million on manager Jim Leyland last year, Florida owner Wayne Huizenga proved that you *can* buy a World Series championship. But not necessarily happiness as well.

Huizenga officially put the team up for sale in June, stating that he'd lost $34 million last year, then began slashing Florida's $57 million payroll shortly after the World Series ended. GM David Dombrowski was told to hack the 1998 salaries down to $25 million, and he started by trading left fielder Moises Alou, ace righthander Kevin Brown, first baseman Jeff Conine, lefthander Al Leiter, Nen and center fielder Devon White for minor leaguers. Factor in the loss of fifth starter Tony Saunders to the Diamondbacks in the expansion draft, and seven Marlins out of 16 regulars—defined as the nine position players with the most plate appearances, the five pitchers with the most starts, the reliever with the most save opportunities and the reliever with the most holds—will begin 1998 with new teams.

Had any previous World Series champion ever cast off as many regulars? For the purposes of this essay, we considered only players who started the following season on another major league team. That left out players who were injured, retired, holding out or called to military duty. The 1943 Yankees lost seven players to World War II, but that obviously doesn't compare to Florida's situation.

#### Most Regulars Relinquished—World Series Champions

| Year | Team | No. | Players |
|------|------|-----|---------|
| 1972 | Athletics | 4 | Larry Brown, Dave Duncan, Mike Epstein, Bob Locker |
| 1914 | Braves | 3 | Charlie Deal, Les Mann, Possum Whitted |
| 1918 | Red Sox | 3 | Sam Agnew, Walt Kinney, Dutch Leonard |
| 1948 | Indians | 3 | Wally Judnich, Ed Klieman, Eddie Robinson |
| 1980 | Phillies | 3 | Randy Lerch, Greg Luzinski, Bob Walk |

No other champion decided to part with more than four regulars. You may have expected to see the end of Connie Mack's two Philadelphia Athletics dynasties, but there are a couple of reasons they didn't make the list. First, both the 1914 and 1931 Athletics lost the World Series. Second, Mack didn't sell off all of his stars at once. The 1914 A's do deserve a brief mention for losing three Hall of Famers to other teams (Eddie Collins was sold to the White Sox, while Chief Bender and Eddie Plank defected to the Federal League) and inducing another (Home Run Baker) to hold out for the entire 1915 season.

Let's take a closer look at the five previous champions who relinquished at least three regulars:

**1972 Athletics.** The previous record-holders certainly didn't harm themselves by getting rid of four players, because they won the next two World Series and the next three American League West titles. Infielder Larry Brown was released, but catcher Dave Duncan, first baseman Mike Epstein and reliever Bob Locker all netted players who contributed to the next two championships. Duncan was used in a trade for catcher Ray Fosse with Cleveland, Epstein brought reliever Horacio Pina from Texas and Locker was swapped for Cubs center fielder Bill North.

**1914 Braves.** One of baseball's unlikeliest champions ever lost third baseman Charlie Deal and center fielder Les Mann to the new Federal League. Boston also sold utilityman Possum Whitted to the Phillies. None of these moves critically wounded the Braves, who contended for the next two seasons.

**1918 Red Sox.** The Red Sox haven't won a World Series since Harry Frazee began selling his best players, often to the Yankees, in order to finance his Broadway musicals. The first of those deals sent lefthander Dutch Leonard to New York with two other standouts who had missed the 1918 season because of World War I, left fielder Duffy Lewis and righthander Ernie Shore, for four marginal players and a substantial sum of money. Catcher Sam Agnew was sold to Washington, and lefthander Walt Kinney, a bit player, apparently was released. After winning three of the four previous World Series, Boston wouldn't reach .500 again until 1934.

**1948 Indians.** Like the 1972 Athletics, the 1948 Indians improved their club after winning the World Series. Reliever Ed Klieman and first baseman Eddie Robinson pried All-Star first baseman Mickey Vernon and Hall of Fame starter Early Wynn loose from the Senators. Reserve outfielder Wally Judnich was waived and claimed by the Pirates. Cleveland continued to contend annually, though it only would top the Yankees in 1954, when it won an AL-record 111 games.

**1980 Phillies.** Philadelphia got rid of three regulars in spring training. Starters Randy Lerch and Bob Walk were traded for outfielders Dick Davis (Brewers) and Gary Matthews (Braves), respectively, allowing for the sale of left fielder Greg Luzinski to the White Sox. The Phillies won the first-half title in the National League East in 1981 and reached the World Series two years later.

The team that compares best to the Marlins is the 1918 Red Sox, which doesn't bode well for Florida, even though it has a well-stocked farm system. And the Marlins may not be done breaking up their championship club, as they seem determined to find new teams for reserve outfielders Jim Eisenreich and John Cangelosi. Third baseman Bobby Bonilla and Sheffield could be had, but their huge contracts have scared other teams off. Is it Huizenga whistling "No No Nanette" that we hear?

—Jim Callis

A more complete listing for this category may be found on page 222.

### Houston Astros: Is Bagwell/Biggio the Best Modern Batting Duo?

We note in the runs-created essay (page 111) that Bill James has improved the technique for calculating individual runs-created estimates. The new formula allows us to compute more precisely than ever how many runs each individual hitter is responsible for on any particular team. As a result, conclusions based on the new formula will tend to have greater reliability than those in the past.

One question we were hoping the new runs-created estimates would help answer more definitively was this: which team's batting duo was the most productive for any single season in baseball history? And more importantly for this essay, where do Jeff Bagwell and Craig Biggio, who carried the Houston Astros to the 1997 National League Central title, rank? There are a variety of ways in which we could approach that question. Instead of basing the answer on the raw total of combined runs created, we decided to predicate the results on the *percentage* of team runs that the tandem accounted for.

When we think about the best batting duos through the years, the combos of Ruth-Gehrig, Maris-Mantle and Mays-McCovey immediately leap to mind. But based on our condition, the all-time top tandem played for an eighth-place team that finished 18 games under .500:

#### Top Batting Duos in Percentage of Team's Offense—1901-97

| Year | Team | Runs | Pct | Batters (RC) |
|------|------|------|------|-------------|
| 1965 | Cubs | 635 | 39.5 | Billy Williams (131), Ron Santo (120) |
| 1917 | Tigers | 639 | 39.4 | Ty Cobb (144), Bobby Veach (108) |
| 1937 | Cardinals | 789 | 38.8 | Joe Medwick (163), Johnny Mize (143) |
| 1972 | White Sox | 566 | 38.7 | Dick Allen (123), Carlos May (96) |
| 1948 | Cardinals | 742 | 38.5 | Stan Musial (177), Enos Slaughter (109) |
| 1906 | Browns | 559 | 38.1 | George Stone (127), Charlie Hemphill (86) |
| 1901 | Orphans | 578 | 38.1 | Topsy Hartsel (126), Danny Green (94) |
| 1989 | Giants | 699 | 38.1 | Will Clark (141), Kevin Mitchell (125) |
| 1959 | Braves | 724 | 37.8 | Hank Aaron (143), Eddie Mathews (131) |
| 1963 | Braves | 677 | 37.5 | Hank Aaron (146), Eddie Mathews (108) |

Williams and Santo didn't necessarily come by their ranking cheaply, considering the 1965 Cubs also boasted a fella by the name of Ernie Banks, who created 89 runs himself. Ironically, one of the arguments Hall of Fame voters have used *against* Santo is that, were he inducted, the Cubs team of the late '60s would have featured four Hall of Famers on its roster (including Ferguson Jenkins). For a club with no championships of any kind, that might seem like too many immortals.

However, that logic misses a couple key points. First, Banks wasn't the dominant player in the '60s that he had been in the '50s. Beginning in 1963, it was Banks who finished third every year in runs created behind Santo and Williams. Second, consider the talent level of the Cubs' complementary players in those years. In 1965, for instance, the remainder of the Cub lineup included guys like Don Landrum (46 runs created), Glenn Beckert (46), Doug Clemens (29) and Jimmy Stewart (28). Legends they are not. It's difficult to imagine any team overcoming that level of mediocrity, no matter how good the other core of players may be. And it's one reason Williams and Santo generated the runs-created percentage they did.

The rest of the top-10 tandems features its share of both Hall of Famers and relative unknowns. The Ty Cobbs, Stan Musials and Hank Aarons you might expect. The George Stones, Charlie Hemphills and Topsy Hartsels, maybe not. There are four MVPs represented on the list, but the new runs-created totals would indicate that voters chose the wrong man in 1989. Though Mitchell (.291-47-125) and Clark (.333-23-111) both had wonderful years, Mitchell hit a greater percentage of his home runs with the bases empty. And while Kevin hit .286 with runners in scoring position, Clark hit a whopping .389 in those situations. Add it up, and Clark accounted for more of the Giants' runs.

No tandem of the 1990s, including Bagwell and Biggio, managed to crack the top 10 of all time, though there was a duo that came close last year. Here are the top combos this decade:

### Top Batting Duos in Percentage of Team's Offense—1990s

| Year | Team | Runs | Pct | Batters (RC) |
|------|------|------|-----|--------------|
| **1997** | **Astros** | **777** | **37.2** | **Craig Biggio (147), Jeff Bagwell (142)** |
| 1994 | Giants | 504 | 36.1 | Barry Bonds (104), Matt Williams (78) |
| 1992 | Pirates | 693 | 35.1 | Barry Bonds (130), Andy Van Slyke (113) |
| 1996 | Astros | 753 | 34.9 | Jeff Bagwell (149), Craig Biggio (114) |
| 1992 | Cubs | 593 | 34.7 | Ryne Sandberg (109), Mark Grace (97) |
| 1992 | Padres | 617 | 34.7 | Gary Sheffield (108), Fred McGriff (106) |
| 1994 | Astros | 602 | 34.4 | Jeff Bagwell (114), Craig Biggio (93) |
| 1996 | Marlins | 688 | 34.2 | Gary Sheffield (145), Jeff Conine (90) |
| 1996 | Mets | 746 | 34.0 | Bernard Gilkey (132), Lance Johnson (122) |
| 1993 | Giants | 808 | 32.9 | Barry Bonds (162), Matt Williams (104) |

It's clear from this list that Bagwell and Biggio have meant more to their team than any other duo in recent years. With them, the Astros tied for fifth in the National League with 777 runs in 1997. Without them, they may have finished last. Only one other Astro generated even 74 runs (Bill Spiers).

Perhaps you expected to see some combination of Colorado Rockies on the above chart. While it's true that in 1996 Andres Galarraga (150) and Ellis Burks (146) accounted for more runs (296) than any other pair of teammates this decade, their sum represented just 30.8 percent of Colorado's total of 961 runs. It's the same reason the 1927 duo of Lou Gehrig (182) and Babe Ruth (177) didn't appear on the historical list. Though Gehrig and Ruth created more runs (359) in 1927 than any other duo ever, they accounted for only 36.8 percent of the Yankees' total. An impressive sum, for sure, but not a high enough percentage.

—Jim Henzler

A more complete listing for this category can be found on page 223.

### Los Angeles Dodgers: Did Piazza Deserve the MVP Award?

Ever since Colorado joined the National League in 1993, Rockies hitters have tried to seduce MVP voters with their inflated numbers. Dante Bichette nearly stole the trophy with his second-place finish in 1995, and Ellis Burks finished third in '96. Finally, Larry Walker captured the award last year. He had monster numbers, but was he really more valuable than Mike Piazza?

Before last year, the candidacy of Rockies MVP candidates always had been undermined by their road stats, which exposed them as the mere mortals they really were. Last year, though, Walker compiled road statistics that were equal to his home numbers. This may have legitimized Walker's stats in many voters' minds. It was easy to conclude that Walker's 1997 stats were not simply a Coors illusion. And if his '97 stats are taken at face value, it's impossible to deny Walker the award.

We find such logic fatally flawed, however. It is our contention that Walker was helped by Coors Field in 1997, no matter what he hit on the road. And if the effects of Coors Field and Dodger Stadium are taken into account, the case can be made that Piazza's year was just as productive as Walker's. Furthermore, if consideration is given to the fact that Walker is an outfielder while Piazza is a catcher, it's hard to see why anyone would find Walker to be the more valuable of the two.

Last year, Walker's and Piazza's production on the road was roughly comparable (.346-29-62 for Walker; .368-18-63 for Piazza). The edge would go to Walker, especially in light of the fact that Coors Field was not one of his road parks (while it *was* one of Piazza's).

The real difference in their respective values resulted from their production at their respective home parks. Walker hit well at Coors Field (.384-20-68), but the impact of his contribution there was lessened because it came in an environment where the Rockies and their opponents combined to bat .317 with almost 13 total runs scored per game. By comparison, Piazza's home production (.355-22-61) was much more valuable because it came in the run-starved environment of Dodger Stadium, where the Dodgers and their opponents batted .245 and combined to score less than eight runs per game. Because Piazza played half of his games in a park where each run was much more valuable than in Coors Field, each run he created at home had much more value than each one Walker created at Coors.

One way to put the two of them on equal footing is to park-adjust Piazza's numbers to simulate what he would have hit in Coors Field. We can do that by adjusting his home numbers and adding his road numbers back in (as we noted above, their road numbers were not compiled in exactly the same ballparks, but the effect of this discrepancy is fairly small, and for the sake of simplicity, we'll overlook it here).

To demonstrate how the adjustments are made, let's park-adjust Piazza's home runs. Last year, the Dodgers and their opponents hit 13 percent fewer home runs at Dodger Stadium, while the Rockies hit 27 percent more home runs at Coors Field. Piazza hit 22 home runs at home last year. We give him 13 percent more homers for moving out of Dodger Stadium, and then an additional 27 percent more homers for moving into Coors Field. That would give him a total of 32 home runs in his home games alone. When you factor in his road homers, it adds up to a 50-homer season for Piazza. Here's Piazza's entire park-adjusted stat line, compared to Walker's unadjusted numbers:

| Player | G | AB | R | H | 2B | 3B | HR | RBI | BB | Avg | OBP | Slg |
|---|---|---|---|---|---|---|---|---|---|---|---|---|
| Piazza (@Coors) | 152 | 599 | 137 | 244 | 39 | 1 | 50 | 159 | 70 | .407 | .468 | .726 |
| Walker | 153 | 568 | 143 | 208 | 46 | 4 | 49 | 130 | 78 | .366 | .452 | .720 |

Wow. His total of 244 hits would put him ninth on the all-time single-season list. Furthermore, his 159 RBI would be the highest total in 48 years, and his .726 slugging percentage would place 13th all-time. And we trust you can appreciate the significance of his .407 batting average. These numbers tell us that Piazza's offensive accomplishments were *more* valuable, in their proper context, than Walker's were.

The park adjustments put Piazza safely ahead of Walker, and an additional consideration widens the gap even further. Piazza's position is catcher—where offensive talent is scarce—while Walker's is in the outfield—where hitters are a dime a dozen. If both Piazza and Walker were replaced with scrub-level players, the Dodgers would be hurt far more severely than the Rockies would. The configuration of the Dodgers' and Rockies' rosters illustrates this point very well. The Dodgers don't have a Larry Walker, but they do have a fairly competent right fielder (Raul Mondesi), and if they didn't have Mondesi, they'd still have some fairly productive alternatives, like Billy Ashley. Colorado, on the other hand, has no Mike Piazza, so it's forced to scrape by with Jeff Reed and Kirt Manwaring behind the plate. Even if we were to assume that Piazza and Walker were equally productive with the bat, Piazza's contribution would remain more valuable, because of the two players' respective positions on the field.

Walker's numbers were great, but Piazza put up numbers that were truly historic—and he did it with no help at all from his home park. Piazza's 1997 season was, without a doubt, the greatest offensive season ever put together by a catcher. He became the first catcher in history to get 200 hits (201), breaking the previous record by eight. His .362 batting average was second-best ever, two-tenths of a point behind Bill Dickey's all-time record. Piazza tied for fourth all time with 40 longballs, and his 124 RBI tied for eighth on the all-time list. No catcher has ever come close to matching Piazza's across-the-board domination of the all-time leader boards in one single season.

The clutch-hitting stats favor Piazza, if anyone. Piazza batted .361 with runners in scoring position; Walker hit .364. During September's stretch run, Piazza batted .406 with eight homers and 27 RBI in 24 games. Walker hit .289 in September with nine homers and 21 RBI in 21 games. The Dodgers finished with a better record than the Rockies did.

Some may suggest that Walker's defense rates an edge over Piazza's. We would submit that Piazza's defensive contribution last year was largely underappreciated: he threw out 28 percent of enemy basestealers, which was only slightly below the league average of 33 percent. In addition, the Dodgers' staff ERA was 0.69 runs lower with him behind the plate (which is no fluke—in the previous four seasons, the staff ERA with Piazza has been substantially lower three times: -0.50, -1.59, +0.02 and -1.05). Walker may have been the superior defensive player last year, but Piazza was substantially more valuable with the bat, and there's no way Walker made up the entire difference from his post in right field.

Overall, it seems impossible to defend Walker's MVP selection if the proper adjustments are made for Piazza's and Walker's respective ballparks and defensive positions. And if you still think that Piazza's park-adjusted numbers are unrealistic, consider that in 87 career at-bats at Coors he's batted .471 with 11 homers and 34 RBI.

—Mat Olkin

## Milwaukee Brewers: Have They Been an NL-Style Team All Along?

When Brewers owner Bud Selig announced that his team was moving to the National League, it was said that Milwaukee manager Phil Garner's style would fit in well in the Senior Circuit. Garner earned a reputation as an NL-style manager when he took over the '92 Brewers and moved them into contention with an aggressive running attack. Although Garner's methods have changed over the last five years, the label has stuck. Is it still accurate to characterize his Brewers as an NL-style team?

Below, we've compared the 1997 Brewers to the average '97 AL and NL team. We've focused on the Brewers' reliance on power (home runs per game), their aggressiveness on the basepaths (stolen-base attempts per game and attempted steals of third per game), and their use of strategies like the sacrifice, the squeeze play and the pitchout.

|  | HR/G | SB Att/G | SB Att. of 3B/G | SH/G | Squeeze | Pitchout |
|---|---|---|---|---|---|---|
| AL | 1.09 | 0.98 | 0.12 | 0.24 | 2.2 | 38.6 |
| NL | 0.95 | 1.17 | 0.16 | 0.22 | 6.4 | 53.3 |
| Mil | 0.84 | 0.98 | 0.08 | 0.30 | 7.0 | 55.0 |

(pitchers not included)

As you can see, Garner's '97 club resembled the average AL club in some respects and the average NL club in others, while showing no across-the-board resemblance to either league's average club. Under Garner, the Brewers have shunned power in favor of solid defense and contact hitting, and their below-average home-run power is more suited to the NL.

Contrary to popular belief, however, the Brewers are not the pack of jack-rabbits that they've been said to be. Ever since Garner's '92 club stole a major league-high 256 bases, his reliance on the stolen base has steadily waned. Over the last four years, the Brewers have finished no higher than sixth in the AL in steals in any one season. Last year, they finished eighth in the league with 103 steals, and exactly matched the AL's average rate of steal attempts per game. Furthermore, Garner calls for the steal of third less often than most managers in *either* league.

The Brewers have several skilled bunters, and Garner asks them to sacrifice fairly often. He called an above-average number of sacrifices by AL standards, and his total was above-average by NL standards as well (when the NL's pitchers are removed from the equation, NL teams average *fewer* sacrifices per game than the AL teams do). He does use the squeeze play much more aggressively. The Brewers pulled off seven squeezes last year, four more than any other AL team. His affinity for the squeeze isn't anything out of the ordinary by NL standards, though. His more liberal use of the pitchout will be better-suited for the NL's more aggressive running game.

Although it's safe to say that Garner is far from a typical NL manager, it's hard to predict exactly how he'll handle his club in the NL. If Garner has shown one consistent trait during his managerial tenure, it's *adaptability*. After burning out Bill Wegman and Cal Eldred, he learned to limit his starters' pitch counts, and he now handles his starters as carefully as any manager in the majors. When his club struggled to score runs, he moved players like B.J. Surhoff and Dave Nilsson to less demanding defensive positions to allow them to develop as hitters. And when the reckless basestealing stopped paying off, he stopped relying on it so heavily. Garner may try to employ more of an NL-style attack this year, or he may not, but you can bet he won't be scared to keep trying new approaches until he finds something that works in the Brewers' new circuit.

—Mat Olkin

## Montreal Expos: How Good Could They Be?

It was the same old story in Montreal this offseason. Pedro Martinez' Cy Young Award would have made him just too expensive, so he was traded to the Red Sox. Mike Lansing's career-high 20 homers would have looked too good in arbitration, so he was sent to the Rockies. Henry Rodriguez' 62 longballs over the past two seasons also would have been too costly in arbitration, so he was given to the Cubs for throwaway righthander Miguel Batista. David Segui became a free agent, and the Expos can't ever seem to afford to re-sign a free agent, so he was allowed to join the Mariners.

No, we're not going to beat you over the head with another large-revenue vs. small-revenue argument about the injustices of the national pastime. Hey, we don't even really believe the city of Montreal needs or deserves the Expos.

What we are going to do is give you something to chew on while you watch the Braves roll toward their seventh consecutive National League East title. Namely, if Claude Brochu had the deep pockets of, say, Ted Turner and Time-Warner, and could hold onto players regardless of how high their salaries might spiral, how good could the Expos be? We won't even consider current members of the team.

First, we'll choose a lineup. The eight players we picked combined to hit 200 homers in 1997:

### Best Possible Expos Starting Lineup

| | | |
|---|---|---|
| 2B | Delino DeShields | Cardinals |
| SS | Mike Lansing | Rockies |
| RF | Larry Walker | Rockies |
| LF | Matt Stairs | Athletics |
| CF | Moises Alou | Astros |
| 1B | Andres Galarraga | Braves |
| C | Jeff Reed | Rockies |
| 3B | Doug Strange | Pirates |

Before you start to quibble, Lansing played shortstop throughout his minor league career and when he first came up with Montreal. If we really wanted to cheat, we could have listed Stairs at third base, where he played regularly in Double-A. Among the players who didn't make our starting lineup were Sean Berry, Wil Cordero, Darrin Fletcher, Marquis Grissom, Otis Nixon, Tim Raines, Rodriguez and Segui.

After park adjustments, the eight players in the lineup created an average of 6.69 runs per 27 outs last season. To simplify things, we'll assume that these players would stay in the lineup all year (which benefits us), each of the eight players would get the same amount of plate appearances (which hurts us) and that we'd get no offensive production out of the No. 9 spot (which also hurts us). All this would give us an average of 5.95 runs per game or 964 runs over the course of the season. That's 39 more than the Mariners, the game's highest-scoring team, had in 1997.

On to the pitching staff. We chose five starters and four relievers, who went 98-46 and totaled 80 saves last year:

### Best Possible Expos Pitching Staff

| | | |
|---|---|---|
| SP | Pedro Martinez | Red Sox |
| SP | Randy Johnson | Mariners |
| SP | Jeff Fassero | Mariners |
| SP | Kirk Rueter | Giants |
| SP | Mark Gardner | Giants |
| RP | Butch Henry | Red Sox |
| RP | Dave Veres | Rockies |
| RP | Jeff Shaw | Reds |
| RP | John Wetteland | Rangers |

Others who merited consideration include Kent Bottenfield, Ken Hill, Jeff Juden and Mel Rojas. Not that we need to apologize. After park adjustments once again, our top nine pitchers combined to surrender 3.49 runs—that's runs, not earned runs—per nine innings last season. Over 162 games that translates into 565 runs, 16 fewer than the game's best pitching staff, the Braves, allowed last year.

Using Bill James' Pythagorean Theorem, a team that scored 5.95 runs per game while allowing 3.49 should have a winning percentage of .726. That would mean a record of 118-44, breaking the 1906 Cubs' mark for single-season victories. This assumes that our Expos would stay healthy all year, which is quite an assumption, and that our defense won't hurt us. Still, we feel safe in saying that we believe the 'Spos at least would wrest the NL East crown from the Braves.

Admittedly, this team wouldn't be cheap. The payroll for our top 17 players would be about $65 million. But would you rather pay for success or go to war with what the Expos have to show for those 17 players? Rondell White, a first-round compensation draft pick for Mark Langston (who was acquired for Johnson and others), is a rising star. Carl Pavano, the key player in the Martinez trade, is one of the best pitching prospects in baseball, even if he hasn't pitched in the major leagues. The return on Fassero was Chris Widger, a promising catcher, and Matt Wagner, who might be a decent pitcher if he stays healthy.

Those are the only four players who figure to contribute in the major leagues in 1998. We'd rather spend the money, break the three-million attendance barrier, and watch the Expos win their first World Series. Of course, we don't own the team. That's probably Montreal's loss.

This exercise can be done for any team, but we have a hard time believing other franchises could stack up to the Expos Who Could Have Been. Maybe that's a question for next year's *Scoreboard.* . .

—Jim Callis

# New York Mets: How Weak Was Ordonez?

Mets shortstop Rey Ordonez seems to appear nightly on "SportsCenter" during baseball season, showing off defensive wizardry not seen since Ozzie Smith was in his prime. Though he missed a good chunk of the 1997 season, he won a Gold Glove in just his second year in the big leagues.

But Ordonez is taking the concept of "good field, no hit" to an extreme. He hit .354 in his first month in the majors, but just .228 since then. After missing six weeks of '97 with a broken bone in his left hand, he returned in mid-July and hit an especially feeble .189 the rest of the way. His overall .216 average (second-worst in the National League among players with at least 350 plate appearances) was compounded by his inability to draw a walk or hit for power. Ordonez' .255 on-base percentage ranked last in the NL, and his .256 slugging percentage was the worst in *either* league.

One of the best ways to measure a player's offensive ability is to combine his on-base and slugging percentages. Colorado's Larry Walker led the major leagues with a 1.172 OPS last season, nine other players topped 1.000, and anything over .900 is outstanding. At the other end of the spectrum, Ordonez' .510 OPS (he loses .001 when his raw percentages aren't rounded) not only was the worst in baseball, but 44 points behind Mariano Duncan, the second-worst hitter:

| Worst OPS—1997 | | | |
|---|---|---|---|
| Player (Pos), Team | OBP | SLG | OPS |
| Rey Ordonez (SS), Mets | .255 | .256 | .510 |
| Mariano Duncan (2B), Yanks/Tor | .268 | .286 | .554 |
| Carlos Garcia (2B), Tor | .253 | .309 | .562 |
| Kirt Manwaring (C), Col | .291 | .276 | .567 |
| Pokey Reese (SS), Cin | .284 | .287 | .571 |
| Scott Brosius (3B), Oak | .259 | .317 | .576 |
| Deivi Cruz (SS), Det | .263 | .314 | .577 |
| Gary DiSarcina (SS), Ana | .271 | .326 | .597 |
| Mike Bordick (SS), Bal | .283 | .318 | .601 |
| Ozzie Guillen (SS), WSox | .275 | .337 | .612 |
| (minimum 350 PA) | | | |

Not surprisingly, nine of the 10 men on the list play positions where defense is at a premium and lackluster offense is tolerated. Six are shortstops, including Ordonez, two are second basemen and one is a catcher. The other is third baseman Scott Brosius, who rates quite well in a number of defensive statistics. Manwaring never has been much of a hitter, but it's still stunning to see a Rockie make the list.

Ordonez' offensive season was dreadful, but how dreadful was it? We can determine that by comparing his OPS to his league's (.743), a ratio of .686. Now we'll see how that compares to all players who have had 350 plate appearances in a season since the lively ball was introduced in 1920:

## Worst Relative OPS—1920-97

| Year | Player (Pos), Team | OPS | Lg OPS | Rel OPS |
|------|--------------------|-----|--------|---------|
| 1979 | Mario Mendoza (SS), Sea | .466 | .743 | .627 |
| 1977 | Rob Picciolo (SS), Oak | .475 | .735 | .646 |
| 1933 | Jim Levey (SS), Browns | .477 | .732 | .651 |
| 1937 | Del Young (2B), Phils | .465 | .714 | .652 |
| 1977 | Tom Veryzer (SS), Det | .485 | .735 | .659 |
| 1985 | George Wright (OF), Tex | .483 | .733 | .660 |
| 1936 | Skeeter Newsome (SS), A's | .531 | .784 | .677 |
| 1994 | Matt Walbeck (C), Min | .530 | .779 | .680 |
| **1997** | **Rey Ordonez (SS), Mets** | **.510** | **.743** | **.686** |
| 1989 | John Shelby (OF), LA | .466 | .678 | .688 |

Ordonez' offensive performance was the ninth-worst since 1920. The only NL player ever to swing a weaker stick was Del Young of the 1937 Phillies. Fittingly enough, the man on top of this list is synonymous with offensive ineptitude. George Brett coined the phrase "Mendoza line" in reference to Mario Mendoza's constant struggle to bat .200, and Mendoza's one season as a major league regular was truly historic. His .466 OPS is the worst ever for an American Leaguer since 1920, and his relative OPS is the worst ever for any big leaguer in that period.

Eight of the 10 players on this list played premium defensive positions. Outfielders George Wright and John Shelby never played regularly again after their dismal seasons. Neither did Mendoza, and Jim Levey's career ended after his awful year. The nine players other than Ordonez have combined for just 10 more seasons as major league regulars, and that could become the Cuban shortstop's fate if he can't boost his offensive performance. Considering his Triple-A performance (a .555 OPS in 1995) and his age (25), there's not much reason to expect that he will.

—Jim Callis

A more complete listing for this category can be found on page 224.

## Philadelphia Phillies: Will Their Second-Half Revival Carry Over?

During the first half of the '97 season, the Phillies weren't just bad. . . they were *bad*. At midseason, the Phils had a record of 24-61 and stood 33 games off the pace in the National League East; they trailed fourth-place Montreal by a wider margin (22.5 games) than any other *last*-place team trailed its respective division leader, and were the only team in the majors with a winning percentage below .400 *and* .300. These were tough times, indeed, for the City of Brotherly Love. By the All-Star break, wild rumors were flying amongst the Philly faithful; it was even speculated that the since-departed GM/managerial tandem of Lee Thomas and Jim Fregosi really *had* sacrificed the soul of the team to the devil for their 1993 pennant run. . . or at least it had seemed that way.

But then slowly but surely, things began to change. Ace righthander Curt Schilling—who was initially the only force standing between the team and a catastrophe of the magnitude of the 1962 Mets—was gradually accompanied by a few promising hurlers in the rotation, most notably rookie Garrett Stephenson, who posted a 6-2, 2.57 mark in 10 second-half starts. At the plate, the struggling Philadelphia attack received a boost from midseason acquisitions Midre Cummings and Tony Barron; while the pair were certainly far from "young prospects," the duo helped stabilize a nightmarish outfield situation and delivered some key offensive contributions down the stretch (.295 average in 397 ABs combined). Buoyed by the support, Schilling raised the level of his own game several notches, transforming from a mere rock-solid starter (9-8, 3.59) in the first half of the year to a Cy Young contender (8-3, 2.30, 160 strikeouts) after the break.

### Philadelphia Phillies First/Second Half Comparisons—1997

| | Phillies | | | Opponents | | | | |
| | OBP | SLG | R/G | OBP | SLG | R/G | W-L | Pct |
|---|---|---|---|---|---|---|---|---|
| Pre-ASB | .312 | .372 | 3.60 | .362 | .464 | 5.87 | 24-61 | .282 |
| Post-ASB | .333 | .395 | 4.70 | .319 | .408 | 4.43 | 44-33 | .571 |

The fightin' Phils improved dramatically across the board, improving their scoring output by over 30 percent while decreasing the number of runs allowed by nearly the same margin. The result was a winning percentage that more than *doubled* their first-half mark, a feat never before accomplished since the All-Star break was created in 1933. How historic was the size of Philly's improvement? Here's a list of the 10 biggest "second-half surges" produced in the last 50 years:

### Top 10 Second Half Surges—1948-97

| Year | Team | Before | After | 2nd Half Increase | Overall | Next Year |
|------|------|--------|-------|---------|---------|-----------|
| **1997** | **Philadelphia Phillies** | **.282** | **.571** | **.289** | **.420** | — |
| 1979 | Los Angeles Dodgers | .387 | .623 | .236 | .488 | .564 |
| 1995 | New York Mets | .362 | .587 | .224 | .479 | .438 |
| 1996 | Boston Red Sox | .424 | .636 | .213 | .525 | .481 |
| 1995 | Florida Marlins | .358 | .566 | .208 | .469 | .494 |
| 1986 | Oakland Athletics | .378 | .583 | .206 | .469 | .500 |
| 1973 | Cleveland Indians | .357 | .563 | .205 | .438 | .478 |
| 1984 | New York Yankees | .439 | .638 | .198 | .537 | .602 |
| 1952 | Philadelphia Phillies | .467 | .658 | .192 | .565 | .539 |
| 1949 | Boston Red Sox | .532 | .714 | .182 | .623 | .610 |

Wow. Philadelphia not only headed the list, but *shattered* the competition, posting a whopping 53-point edge over the No. 2 team on the leader board. Notice that the list is obviously biased towards struggling clubs; it's a general rule of thumb that bad teams more often than not tend to improve (and vice versa), and with a club as bad as Philly was last season, there was a *lot* of room for improvement. However, four of the nine other teams on the list took a step backwards during the following season.

How did some of the other more notable teams on the list fare? These two might give Philadelphians some hope:

**1986 Athletics**. Oakland's grim 1986 first-half performance was merely a continuation of the near-uninterrupted string of losing seasons the A's had produced since the collapse of their early-1970s dynasty. But a young manager by the name of Tony La Russa took over the helm in midseason—and things began to dramatically change. La Russa, a master of rebuilding depleted pitching staffs, plucked washed-up hurler Dave Stewart from the Phillies that summer; Stewart would soon become the centerpiece of Oakland's championship-quality rotation, delivering four straight 20-win seasons beginning in 1987. Offensively, La Russa built his lineup around a young slugger named Jose Canseco, who saw his first full season of action in '86; a year later, Mark McGwire was added to the mix, and Oakland would dominate the American League West for the latter part of the decade.

**1979 Dodgers**. After weathering back-to-back World Series losses against the New York Yankees in the 1977-78 seasons, the '79 Dodgers stumbled badly out of the gate. Los Angeles had lost starters Tommy John to the

Yankees and Rick Rhoden to the Bucs over the previous offseason, and when arm injuries sidelined hurlers Bob Welch and Doug Rau, its starting rotation was left in shambles. Stars Steve Garvey, Dusty Baker, and Ron Cey continued to pace a fine Dodger offense, however, and the team began to rebound when the staff, led by rookie Rick Sutcliffe (17-10, 3.46), rounded into form at midseason. Sutcliffe soon lost his effectiveness in L.A., but with the return of Welch and the emergence of dominant screwballer Fernando Valenzuela, Los Angeles stormed to a 92-win season in 1980 before finally capturing the Series in '81.

Although the Phils' second-half improvement was indeed impressive, it'd be difficult to anticipate any championship runs anytime soon for their current squad. Why?

- Outside of third baseman Scott Rolen, the Phillies have virtually no offensive cornerstones to build around. Barron's age (31) and Cummings' inconsistency (.298 career OBP) make them very unlikely to contribute to the team's success in the future. The Phils have major holes in both their infield (second baseman Mickey Morandini and shortstop Kevin Stocker were both traded last winter) and outfield, and compounding the problem is the fact that $10 million of its annual budget is tied up in former stars Gregg Jefferies and Lenny Dykstra. *Then* there's the case of first baseman Rico Brogna, who contributed a .293 on-base percentage last year. . . need we go on?

- Schilling, one of the few pitchers capable of singlehandedly keeping his team above water, was worked awfully hard last season: 254.1 innings, a career high. He's had arm trouble in the past when he's been used extensively, so if manager Terry Francona continues to place heavy workloads on him in the next couple of years, there's a strong chance he could break down again.

While the Phils do have quality young talent in the names of Rolen and collegiate phenom J.D. Drew (should he ever sign), Philadelphia is probably going to need a much more drastic overhaul in order to rebound from its current state of misery—despite its drastic improvement in the second half last season.

—Kevin Fullam

A more complete listing for this category can be found on page 225.

### Pittsburgh Pirates: How Important Is It to Grow Your Own Players?

With the advent of free agency after the 1976 season, the fear was that rich teams would be able to buy pennants. For the most part, that concern proved unfounded. The Yankees *did* win titles in '77 and '78, but George Steinbrenner's millions didn't result in another World Series title until '96. Gene Autry lavished huge sums of money on free agents, but the Angels never have been able to win one for The Cowboy. The only teams besides the Yankees to capture multiple championships in the last 20 years are the Blue Jays, Dodgers and Twins, who developed many of the stars who led them to glory within their own system. In all, 15 different clubs have won the World Series, showing that it's impossible to buy a dynasty.

The argument just won't go away, however. During the bitter negotiations that resulted in the 1994-95 strike, the terms "large-market" and "small-market" got pounded into our brains. Since then, money has seemed to matter. The final four teams in the 1997 playoffs all ranked among the top five payrolls, with only the defending champion Yankees absent.

So we ask the question at the top of this page. To answer it, we focused on each team's 16 regulars: the nine hitters with the most plate appearances, the five pitchers with the most starts, the reliever with the most save opportunities and the reliever with the most holds. We defined a homegrown regular as one who had spent his entire major league career with his present team.

The chart to the right shows the teams with the most homegrown regulars. At first glance, growing your own players looks like a foundation for success. The Pirates were given little chance to contend in the National League Central, but battled down to the final week with a lineup that was almost all Pittsburgh-developed. Atlanta is the consensus best team in baseball, coming off six straight NL East crowns and possessing a homegrown nucleus of Tom Glavine, An-

**MOST HOMEGROWN REGULARS 1997**

| | GROWN | W–L |
|---|---|---|
| Pirates | 12 | 79–83 |
| Braves | 10 | 101–61 |
| Brewers | 10 | 78–83 |
| Dodgers | 10 | 88–74 |
| Twins | 10 | 68–94 |

druw Jones, Chipper Jones, Ryan Klesko, Javy Lopez, John Smoltz and Mark Wohlers. All told, these five teams combined for a .512 winning percentage and an average record of 83-79, certainly better than average.

But before we jump to any conclusions, let's look at the teams with the fewest homegrown regulars. Five had four or fewer:

### Fewest Homegrown Regulars—1997

| Team | Grown | W-L |
|------|-------|-----|
| Padres | 3 | 76-86 |
| Giants | 4 | 90-72 |
| Reds | 4 | 76-86 |
| Rockies | 4 | 83-79 |
| Yankees | 4 | 96-66 |

None of the teams on this list is a big surprise. The Giants and Reds have two of the worst farm systems in baseball, and the Padres were languishing before revitalizing their organization in the last few years. The Rockies are an expansion team, and the Yankees still love free agents. And maybe the Yankees have the right idea. These five teams combined for a .520 winning percentage and an average record of 84-78. They also include two playoff teams and three .500+ clubs, one more in each category than the five teams with the most homegrown players.

This bears further scrutiny. Let's break all the teams down into three nearly equal groups—those who developed at least half of their regulars, those who developed less than a third and those who fell in between:

### Comparing The Philosophies

| Makeup Of Regulars | Teams | W-L | Pct. | Avg W-L | .500 Teams | Playoff Teams |
|--------------------|-------|-----|------|---------|------------|---------------|
| One-Half (8 or more) | 8 | 639-656 | .493 | 80-82 | 3 | 1 |
| In Between (6-7) | 9 | 694-762 | .477 | 77-85 | 2 | 2 |
| One-Third (5 or less) | 11 | 933-848 | .524 | 85-77 | 7 | 5 |

There seems to be no disputing that in 1997, developing your own players didn't necessarily equal success. Five of the eight playoff teams let other organizations produce most of their regulars, including the World Series champion Marlins.

—Jim Callis

A more complete listing for this category can be found on page 226.

## St. Louis Cardinals: Will They Bounce Back After Crashing?

For a team with a history as glorious as that of the Cardinals, the franchise has somehow managed to maintain a tradition it will definitely *not* be bragging about. The Cardinals have captured more World Series championships than any other National League team. That's good. They've totaled more winning seasons since 1920 than any other team in the Senior Circuit. That's good, too. But they've perfected a habit of following their titles with disappointing and downright wretched campaigns. That's bad.

The last four times the Cardinals have won their division, they've failed to break the .500 mark in the ensuing season. It happened once again in 1997, when, a year after coming within a single game of the World Series, they finished with a miserable 73-89 record. The scenario also occurred following World Championships in 1931 and 1964. Judging by the Cardinals' history, we could have predicted last year's meltdown. By the same token, however, perhaps we can now forecast a rebound for St. Louis in 1998:

### Cardinal Titles Followed by Sub-.500 Record

| Title Year | Year1 | Year2 | Year3 |
|------------|--------|--------|--------|
| 1931 | 101-53 | 72-82 | 82-71 |
| 1964 | 93-69 | 80-81 | 83-79 |
| 1982 | 92-70 | 79-83 | 84-78 |
| 1985 | 101-61 | 79-82 | 95-67 |
| 1987 | 95-67 | 76-86 | 86-76 |
| 1996 | 88-74 | 73-89 | —— |

The Cardinals have followed six first-place finishes with losing records the following season. But in each of the first five cases, they've also managed to crack the .500 mark in Year 3. But only once were they able to translate their reborn success into another league or division title.

The "Plexiglass Principle" may have applied to the Cardinals in 1997. That tenet concerns the strong tendency for teams which have improved substantially from one season to the next to then squander those gains in Year 3. In the Cardinals' case, they improved by over 100 percentage points between 1995 and 1996, going from 62-81 to 88-74. So they were ripe for a fall. Even more ominously, they had built their ascent on perhaps the most treacherous of terrains—veteran players. It's tough enough to consolidate those gains under normal conditions. But it's especially risky depending on the likes of 39-year-old third basemen and 42-year-old closers, which the Cardinals discovered while falling from the penthouse to the outhouse.

The Cardinals aren't the only division winner from 1996 that played below .500 in '97. The Padres and Rangers are also in the same boat. Their situations have actually become quite commonplace in recent years. Consider that in the 60 years immediately after the turn of the century, only nine teams went from first place to below .500 in one season. That total increased to 14 teams between 1960 and 1979 alone, and ballooned to 27 teams in the 17 seasons between 1980 and 1996. There are more "winners" than ever before, now that we have six divisions, so that helps explain the explosion of ricocheting teams. And based upon the combined records of such teams in those three eras, it appears the Cardinals may be fortunate to just generate a winning record in '98:

**First-Place Teams Below .500 in Year 2**

| Era | Teams | Year1 | Year2 | Year3 |
|---|---|---|---|---|
| 1900-1959 | 9 | .621 | .448 | .481 |
| 1960-1979 | 14 | .588 | .469 | .530 |
| 1980-1995 | 24 | .588 | .461 | .504 |

We considered the teams with the best *overall* records as the division winners in the strike-shortened season of 1981, and also included those teams that stood in first place at the time of the '94 strike. We didn't include '96 or '97, because those teams haven't completed their three-year cycles. The percentages for the first era (1900-59) are not quite as extreme as they appear. They're affected by one particular club, the Philadelphia A's of 1914, which went from 99-53 (.651) to 43-109 (.283) and 36-117 (.235) in successive seasons. Without them, the combined winning percentages for the other eight teams in their group are .617, .469 and .513, not that far out of character with the percentages of the past 40 years. The .617 winning percentage in Year 1 for that group is higher than the .588 rate since 1960, but that can probably be attributed to the requirements for winning an eight-team league as compared to a four- to seven-team division.

If anything, it appears to be getting *tougher* for teams of this type to rebound in Year 3. The winning percentage in the third season has fallen by roughly 26 percentage points since 1980, which translates to four fewer wins over a 162-game schedule. For a team like St. Louis, which will probably be breaking in a rookie catcher and has only gotten a year older at most positions, it may have to hope a little better than a .500 record is good enough to capture a pedestrian NL Central Division.

—Jim Henzler

A more complete listing for this category can be found on page 227.

### San Diego Padres: Is Gwynn the Best of All Time Relative to His League?

Here's a dilemma for you: How do you find a new way to say that the Beatles were one of the greatest rock bands ever, or how do you find a way to say that Albert Einstein was one of the greatest minds in history, without being cliché? How about this: come up with a new way to expound on the greatness of Elvis, or Babe Ruth, or Sir Lawrence Olivier, or Shakespeare. Just try and say Wayne Gretzky is one of the world's best hockey players, or that Beethoven was one of our greatest composers, without sounding like a broken record. Chances are good that someone else stole your eloquent thunder long ago.

Such is the case with Tony Gwynn, who year-in and year-out reinforces his title as the Beatles, the Elvis, the Shakespeare, the Gretzky, the Olivier of hitting a baseball. If greatness is self-evident, then the numbers hold the truth. In 1997, Gwynn earned his NL record-tying eighth batting title and raised his career average to .340; he reached the .300 mark for the 15th straight season, and joined Ted Williams, Honus Wagner and George Brett as the only men in history to win a hitting crown at age 37 or older; he set career highs in homers (17), RBI (119), doubles (49) and hits (220). He also put the finishing touches on one of the greatest five-year stretches of any hitter in the past 71 years:

| Highest Batting Average, Five-Year Span—1927-97 | |
|---|---|
| Player (Seasons) | Avg |
| Al Simmons (1927-31) | .375 |
| **Tony Gwynn (1993-97)** | **.368** |
| Lefty O'Doul (1928-32) | .365 |
| Rogers Hornsby (1927-31) | .365 |
| Lefty O'Doul (1927-31) | .365 |
| Ted Williams (1953-57) | .362 |
| Bill Terry (1929-33) | .361 |
| Bill Terry (1928-32) | .360 |
| Al Simmons (1928-32) | .360 |
| Chuck Klein (1927-31) | .360 |
| (minimum 2,000 PA) | |

Nearly seven decades have passed since any player has boasted an average of .368 or better over a five-season period. Since the start of the 1993 campaign, Gwynn has not only put his stamp on history but also left his *contemporaries* in the dust. His .368 mark is 31 points better than Mike

Piazza's figure of .337, the second-best average over the past five years among hitters with at least 1,800 plate appearances. That huge chasm between Gwynn and the "next-best" hitters of his generation naturally got us to wondering if he is the top batsman of all time in relation to his league.

Towards that end, we generated an index of the best career batting averages by individuals relative to the overall league average during their careers. We only considered the average of the league in which a hitter played in a given season, and we weighted years, so if Ty Cobb, for example, had 100 at-bats in 1905 and 300 in 1906, his league's average in 1906 carried three times more weight than his league's mark in '05. The only requirement we placed on a given player is that he must have logged at least 5,000 career plate appearances. Using this approach, we wanted to produce a fair comparison between apples and oranges—between hitters from different leagues who played in entirely different eras. As you can see from the following chart, Gwynn fares extremely well:

## HIGHEST CAREER BATTING AVERAGES RELATIVE TO LEAGUE ALL-TIME

| | AVG. | LEAGUE AVG. | INDEX |
|---|---|---|---|
| Ty Cobb (1905–28) | .366 | .265 | 138.4 |
| Joe Jackson (1908–20) | .356 | .260 | 137.1 |
| Pete Browning (1882–94) | .340 | .254 | 133.5 |
| Tony Gwynn (1982–97) | .340 | .256 | 132.4 |
| Ted Williams (1939–60) | .344 | .262 | 131.5 |
| Nap Lajoie (1896–1916) | .338 | .260 | 129.8 |
| Dan Brouthers (1879–1904) | .341 | .264 | 129.5 |
| Rogers Hornsby (1915–37) | .358 | .277 | 129.5 |
| Tris Speaker (1907–28) | .345 | .267 | 128.9 |
| Stan Musial (1941–63) | .331 | .259 | 127.7 |

Minimum 5,000 plate appearances.

Any analysis of hitting that puts the likes of Ty Cobb and Joe Jackson at the head of the class must have at least *some* validity. As for Gwynn, his .340 career average currently ranks 16th on the all-time list, but when you look at that figure compared to what the rest of the National League has hit from 1982 to the present (with years properly weighted), his stock sky-rockets. In fact, using this method he's the *best* hitter for average compared to his respective league of any player whose career falls primarily in the lively-ball era, which began in 1920. Better than Williams. Better than Musial. Better than Hornsby. Better than Ruth. Better than Gehrig. Better than Terry. You get the picture. "But wait a minute," you say. *"Better than Williams?* Better than the guy who wrote the *book* on hitting, literally—a book that Gwynn admitted to reading 'more than a couple of times' in a recent interview with *The Sporting News*?"

Using this approach, the answer is "Yes." Williams may own a higher average, but he built that in a time and in a league when batters across the board were hitting for a higher average. Does this approach punish a hitter like Williams, then? Perhaps, but it wouldn't be an unthinkable leap to assume that Williams' average would go down in a league and a time when everyone else's average was lower. The same holds true for Hornsby, who finishes behind Gwynn despite a career .358 mark.

Does this settle things in the great debate of Gywnn's place in history? Does this definitively answer our initial question about whether he is indeed the greatest hitter for average in history relative to his league? Of course not. That battle will rage on, much like the debates of Sanders vs. Brown, or Gretzky vs. Orr, or Jordan vs. Wilt, or the Beatles vs. the Stones. Our goal is simply to add something meaningful to the discussion. . . while trying to come up with new ways to describe greatness.

—Tony Nistler

A more complete listing for this category can be found on page 228.

## San Francisco Giants: Were the Giants 1997's Biggest Overachievers?

The Los Angeles Dodgers' pursuit of the San Francisco Giants in the National League West race was one of the running stories of the 1997 season. Most agreed that the Dodgers possessed far more talent, and many were puzzled by their inability to catch the Giants. San Francisco's division title ultimately brought the NL Manager of the Year Award to Giants skipper Dusty Baker and intense scrutiny to the ethnically diverse Dodgers clubhouse. Although we can't speculate whether the composition of the Dodgers' roster affected their performance on the field, we can say with certainty that the Giants had no business playing over .500, much less participating in the postseason.

How can we say that with such confidence? Why, it's only common sense. The most basic rule of baseball is that you have to outscore your opponent in order to win the game. Over the course of a full season, the number of games a team will win is a direct function of the number of runs the team scores and allows.

Bill James was able to translate this common-sense rule into a mathematical equation, the *Pythagorean method,* which holds that the ratio of a team's wins to losses will approximate its ratio of runs scored (squared) to runs allowed (squared). The method can be used to estimate—with great accuracy—the number of games that should be won by a team with a given number of runs scored and runs allowed. Last year, three-quarters of the major league teams had win totals that were within five games of their Pythagorean projection.

The Giants were not among the majority. In fact, they exceeded their Pythagorean projection by a greater margin than any other team last year:

### The Luckiest Teams—1997

| Team | W-L | Pct. | Pythag W | Pythag Pct. | +/− |
|------|-----|------|----------|-------------|-----|
| Giants | 90-72 | .556 | 80.1 | .494 | +9.9 |
| Reds | 76-86 | .469 | 68.1 | .421 | +7.9 |
| Phillies | 68-94 | .420 | 62.8 | .387 | +5.2 |
| White Sox | 80-81 | .497 | 75.1 | .467 | +4.9 |
| Brewers | 78-83 | .484 | 73.6 | .457 | +4.4 |

Given the fact that the Giants actually were *outscored* by their opponents by nine runs, they ought to have finished below .500 with an 80-82 record. In other words, they managed to win *10* extra games simply by catching all the breaks in the close games. They played .595 ball in games decided by four runs or less, but won at only a .439 clip in games decided by five runs or more. No other NL contender had a split that was anywhere close. The Dodgers' luck ran the other way: they dominated the blowouts (.686) but were barely over .500 in the rest of their games (.504).

While some would attribute a team's superior record in one-run games to clutch ability, repeated studies have shown that this supposed ability rarely holds up from year to year. We know of no team that's ever been able to consistently win more games than it should have been able to, given the numbers of runs it scored and allowed. For this reason, we tend to regard any major deviation from a Pythagorean projection as a function of luck, rather than clutch ability.

The 1997 Giants were one of the luckiest teams of the expansion era. We can't stress this enough. No other team this decade has exceeded its projection by more than 8.3 games. The Giants outperformed theirs by 9.9 games—a margin almost 20 percent larger than any other team's in the 1990s. During the 1980s, only one team played so far above its ability for a whole season (the 1984 New York Mets).

It's safe to say that the Giants' unique good fortune was almost entirely responsible for putting them in the postseason. If each team in the NL West had performed exactly as it should have, the Giants would have finished third, 12 games behind the division-winning Dodgers and two games behind the Rockies. In fact, if all the teams that ever made the postseason are rated in terms of their predicted winning percentage, the '97 Giants come out as the third-worst postseason team of all time:

### Worst Teams to Make the Postseason—All-Time

| Year | Team | W-L | Pct | Pythag W | Pythag Pct. | +/– |
|------|------|------|------|----------|-------------|------|
| 1987 | Twins | 85-77 | .525 | 79.0 | .487 | +9.9 |
| 1984 | Royals | 84-78 | .519 | 79.5 | .490 | +7.9 |
| 1997 | Giants | 90-72 | .556 | 80.1 | .494 | +5.2 |
| 1995 | Rockies | 77-67 | .535 | 72.1 | .501 | +4.9 |
| 1973 | Mets | 82-79 | .509 | 83.2 | .517 | +4.4 |

As you can see from the Pythagorean winning percentages, only two other clubs have made it into the postseason despite being outscored by their opponents during the regular season. One of them, the '87 Twins, even made it past the Tigers and the Cardinals to claim the World Series championship, although they had to outscore both clubs in order to do so.

—Mat Olkin

# II. GENERAL BASEBALL QUESTIONS

## Do Basestealers Improve With Age?

Suppose that you are watching a game, and there is a young player on first who is very fast, but who is 11-for-25 stealing bases so far this year. What is the announcer going to tell you?

Sure. The announcer is going to tell you that "that stolen base percentage is going to get a lot better as Charlie gets more experience, and learns to steal bases." But is it true? Can one in fact expect a player's stolen base percentage to improve substantially with experience?

I did two things to try to figure that out. First, I asked computer wizard David Pinto to retrieve for me the overall stolen base percentages, by age, of all major league players since 1980. Since 1980 there have been 8,392 stolen base attempts by 25-year-old players, of which 5,730 have been successful. That's 68.3%. The percentages, by age, are given below:

| Age 21 | 69.3% |
|--------|-------|
| Age 22 | 68.2% |
| Age 23 | 68.6% |
| Age 24 | 70.3% |
| Age 25 | 68.3% |
| Age 26 | 67.5% |
| Age 27 | 68.4% |
| Age 28 | 68.3% |
| Age 29 | 68.0% |
| Age 30 | 67.8% |
| Age 31 | 67.3% |
| Age 32 | 66.6% |
| Age 33 | 66.4% |
| Age 34 | 65.3% |
| Age 35 | 64.6% |
| Age 36 | 64.5% |

Before age 21 and after 36 we have less than 1,000 stolen base attempts, and thus erratic data, but the pattern within the stable-data range is extremely clear: **Stolen Base Percentages do NOT increase as players age. They decline.** Stolen base percentages from age 24 to 36 decline at a fairly steady rate of one-half of one percent per season.

More complete data on this study is given on page 229. One more note from that study: 79% of major league stolen bases are by players aged 30 or younger.

The other thing I did was, I formed a group of young players who had significant numbers of stolen base attempts early in their careers, but poor stolen base percentages. I generated several lists, but the one I wound up using was **the 40 players since 1946 who had the poorest career stolen base percentages at age 26 with a minimum of 60 stolen base attempts.** The two worst were a couple of Cleveland Indians from the 1970s, Buddy Bell and Duane Kuiper. Bell, who ran well as a young player, was 24-for-72 as a base stealer at age 26.

Of those 40 players, how many later developed into good base stealers? At the outside, four. **None** of the 40 players ever developed into a certified, Grade A base stealing threat. Not a single one of the forty players ever went on to steal 50 bases in a season, for example. Only one, Omar Vizquel, would ever steal 40 bases in a season.

However, arguably as many as four of the players did develop into good base stealers later in their careers. Vizquel, a 53% base stealer at age 26, has been a 77% base stealer since age 27, and has pilfered 78 flour sacks over the last two seasons. Junior Gilliam, a 55% base stealer through age 26, was successful 68% of the time the rest of his career, although his career high in stolen bases was just 26.

In addition to those, you could make an argument for two other guys, if you're a mind to. Robby Thompson, a 58% base stealer at age 26, has been a 66% swiper since then, although that percentage is based on only 61 successful steals in eight seasons. Bill Madlock, a poor percentage runner as a young player, was successful 70% of the time after age 27 and had one year (1979) when he stole 32 bases, although he never became a real base stealing threat.

With the exception of those four players, every player in the 40-man study either

a) stole less than 50 bases in his career after turning 27, or

b) had a stolen base percentage lower than 64% after that age.

A few guys, like Will Clark and Bobby Richardson, did become effective *percentage* runners as they aged, but with very limited attempts. A few other guys, like Alfredo Griffin and Lenny Randle, continued to run although their percentages were not good.

But 15 of the 40 players had career stolen base percentages no higher than 50% after age 27, and 27 of the 40 had stolen base percentages less than 60% after age 27.

The 40 players, as a group, *did* have better stolen base percentages after age 27 than before. But their collective stolen base percentage is lower than the age-level norm at every age where there is significant data. Whereas all players, as a group, have a stolen base percentage of 68% at age 30, these players had a stolen base percentage of 59% at age 30. At age 31, the norm for all players is 67%; for these players, 55%. At age 35, for all players, 65%; for these players, 48%.

In short, the conclusion could not be any more obvious. While there is a chance that a young player who is a poor percentage base stealer will later develop into a good base stealer, the odds against it are long—certainly at least five to one, and probably more like twenty to one.

—Bill James

A full list of the 40 players in the study is also given on page 229.

## When Will We See Another Triple Crown Winner?

Along with flirting with a .400 average for much of the 1997 season, Larry Walker came close to becoming the National League's first Triple Crown winner in 60 years (Joe Medwick did it last back in 1937). Walker led the National League in home runs with 49, he was second in batting average (.366) and he ranked third in runs batted in (130). But for the 30th year in a row, baseball went without a Triple Crown winner. . . or since Carl Yastrzemski of the 1967 Red Sox.

Why has baseball gone so long without a Triple Crown winner? One reason is expansion; it's obviously tougher to lead a 12- or 14-team league in a category than it is to lead an eight- or 10-team league. How much tougher? In an article in *The Baseball Book* a few years ago, Bill James concluded that "the expansion of the leagues from eight to fourteen teams, absent any other contributing causes, would cut the number of triple crown winners to less than one-third of what it previously was." That's a lot.

But there's more to it than just expansion. In the same 1992 article, Bill pointed out that the number of players leading their *teams* in all three Triple Crown categories has declined since the 1950s. It's true. This chart shows the number of Triple Crown winners by decade since 1901, and the percentage of teams in the decade which had "team Triple Crown" winners:

### Triple Crown Winners and Pct of Team Triple Crown Leaders

| Decade | League TC Winners | Pct of Teams w/ TC Leaders |
|--------|-------------------|----------------------------|
| 1901-09 | 2 | 27.1 |
| 1910-19 | 1 | 18.8 |
| 1920-29 | 2 | 27.5 |
| 1930-39 | 4 | 26.9 |
| 1940-49 | 2 | 23.8 |
| 1950-59 | 1 | 29.4 |
| 1960-69 | 2 | 26.8 |
| 1970-79 | 0 | 19.1 |
| 1980-89 | 0 | 15.0 |
| 1990-97 | 0 | 20.6 |

Except for the deadball-era teens, the percentage of team Triple Crown winners was consistently over 20 percent—usually *well* over it—until the 1970s. The percentage of team winners in the 1980s was the lowest in this century, and while the percentage has risen in the '90s, it's still a far cry from what fans were used to seeing from the 1920s through the 1960s. What happened? Here's Bill's take on the subject:

> In the 1930s, and to a lesser extent in the 1950s and 1960s, each team might have only two or three real hitters, and each team might have only one power hitter, if that. The competition for the league lead in home runs and RBI, realistically, might be among just three or four players.

> Players today *don't* specialize offensively, to the degree they did earlier. Rather than a cleanup-hitting first baseman, a .245-hitting shortstop and a basestealing outfielder, what we have now is a fleet-footed outfielder who is *also* a power hitter, and the .245 hitting shortstop might very well lead the team in home runs. And I can't really tell you why that is, other than simply that the distance between the good players and the average players isn't nearly as great as it used to be.

But Larry Walker's big 1997 season points out that there are still a number of players around who can hit for both great power and a big average, and thus threaten to win a Triple Crown. Indeed, a number of players have finished in the top five in their league in each of the Triple Crown categories during the 1990s:

## CLOSEST TO TRIPLE CROWN 1990s

| | Year | HR | RBI | Avg. | MISSED BY |
|---|---|---|---|---|---|
| Gary Sheffield | 1992 | 3rd | 5th | 1st | 2 HR, 9 RBI |
| Barry Bonds | 1993 | 1st | 1st | 4th | 34 pts |
| Albert Belle | 1994 | 3rd | 3rd | 2nd | 4 HR, 11 RBI, 2 pts |
| Frank Thomas | 1994 | 2nd | 3rd | 3rd | 2 HR, 11 RBI, 6 pts |
| Jeff Bagwell | 1994 | 2nd | 1st | 2nd | 4 HR, 26 pts |
| Dante Bichette | 1995 | 1st | 1st | 3rd | 28 pts |
| Ellis Burks | 1996 | 5th | 5th | 2nd | 7 HR, 22 RBI, 9 pts |
| Larry Walker | 1997 | 1st | 3rd | 2nd | 10 RBI, 6 pts |
| Mike Piazza | 1997 | 4th | 4th | 3rd | 9 HR, 16 RBI, 10 pts |

Barry Bonds and Dante Bichette each won two of the three "crowns" in this decade, while ranking fourth and third, respectively, in the other category. Jeff Bagwell was first or second in all three categories in 1994. The closest to winning a Triple Crown was probably Gary Sheffield in 1992. So it's possible that the Triple Crown drought will end this year, or soon thereafter. But if Bill James is right, we might never see another Ted Williams, who *always* seemed to be in contention for the Crown:

### Ted Williams—Triple Crown Contention

| Year | HR | RBI | Avg | Missed by |
|------|-----|-----|-----|------------------|
| 1941 | 1st | 4th | 1st | 5 RBI |
| 1942 | 1st | 1st | 1st | |
| 1946 | 2nd | 2nd | 2nd | 6 HR, 4 RBI, 11 pts |
| 1947 | 1st | 1st | 1st | |
| 1949 | 1st | 1st | 2nd | 0.2 pts |
| 1951 | 2nd | 2nd | 4th | 3 HR, 3 RBI, 26 pts |

The Splendid Splinter won two Triple Crowns outright, and missed a third in 1949 when George Kell edged him for the batting title on the last day of the season, .3429 to .3427. Williams missed another Triple Crown in 1941 by only five RBI, and he ranked in the top five in all three categories in two other seasons, 1946 and 1951. None of the modern players, great as they are, has been able to post a record like that. To win a Triple Crown these days, a player has to not only beat off *more* competition, in terms of the greater number of players due to expansion, but probably a deeper pool of Triple Crown-caliber hitters as well.

— Don Zminda

# What Are the Winningest Stats?

Which stats correlate best with winning? That's a question which has intrigued us for a long time, so we asked Brent Osland to study the statistics of every major league game over the last five seasons. Brent came up with a startling discovery: the team with the most runs *always* won!

Actually, Brent uncovered a little more than just that. For each major league game of the last five years, he compared the opposing teams' stats in a number of different categories. The chart shows the winning percentage for the team with the statistical advantage for that game in a number of different categories. Note that this is the team with the advantage in each category *for that game only*, not for the season.

## Winningest Stats—1993-97

| Advantage | Pct | W | L |
| --- | --- | --- | --- |
| Higher On-Base Plus Slugging Percentage | .852 | 8867 | 1545 |
| Higher On-Base Percentage | .824 | 8493 | 1816 |
| Higher Slugging Percentage | .820 | 8474 | 1854 |
| Higher Batting Average | .804 | 8256 | 2011 |
| Fewest Errors Per 9 Defensive Innings | .669 | 4847 | 2395 |
| Most SB Per 9 Offensive Innings | .653 | 4462 | 2368 |
| Higher HR Percentage (HR/PA) | .653 | 5604 | 2975 |
| Higher BB Percentage (BB/PA) | .623 | 6378 | 3852 |
| Higher SB Percentage | .576 | 4240 | 3123 |
| Most Pitcher K's Per 9 Defensive Innings | .543 | 5327 | 4477 |

If you're wondering why on-base plus slugging percentage (OPS) is such a highly regarded stat, here's a big reason: the team with the better OPS in a particular game winds up winning 85 percent of the time. Next come the individual components of OPS, on-base percentage (.824 winning percentage) and slugging percentage (.820), followed by higher batting average with a very impressive .804 winning percentage. It's possible that batting average has been derided as being an overrated stat for so long that now it's a bit *underrated*. The numbers show that if you outhit your opponents, you've got a heck of a chance to win. If you can hit with power and put players on base in other ways as well, your chances of winning are even greater.

OPS, on-base percentage and slugging percentage are hybrid stats comprised of a number of different statistics, so they have a built-in advantage over some of the other numbers listed here. Which is not to minimize their importance. For instance, the strong winning percentage recorded by the teams with more stolen bases is undoubtedly due in part to the fact that their stolen-base threats happened to be getting on base in that particular game. Home runs are important (.653 winning percentage), but they're obviously even more important if they come with men on base.

One stat listed here which should not be overlooked is the walk. This is one stat which is *not* a hybrid, and not really dependent on any other category. Yet the team with the higher walk percentage—just that, more walks per plate appearance than the opponent—wins the game 62 percent of the time. That's truly impressive, and it underscores the importance of having patient hitters, along with pitchers who can throw strikes.

One last comment: the team with the fewest errors per nine innings—the one with the higher fielding percentage, in other words—wins the game two-thirds of the time (.669 winning percentage). It ain't everything, but it's obviously important to have players who can hold onto the ball.

— Don Zminda

## How Important Is It to Score First?

Baseball people often talk about the importance of "jumping out in front" in a ballgame. How much difference does scoring the first run make? Here's how major league teams have fared during each of the last 10 seasons in games in which they scored the first run:

### Overall W-L When Scoring First—1988-97

| Year | W | L | Pct |
|---|---|---|---|
| 1988 | 1,406 | 692 | .670 |
| 1989 | 1,406 | 697 | .669 |
| 1990 | 1,408 | 697 | .669 |
| 1991 | 1,394 | 710 | .663 |
| 1992 | 1,426 | 680 | .677 |
| 1993 | 1,496 | 772 | .660 |
| 1994 | 1,090 | 509 | .682 |
| 1995 | 1,315 | 701 | .652 |
| 1996 | 1,469 | 797 | .648 |
| 1997 | 1,483 | 783 | .654 |
| **Total** | **13,893** | **7,038** | **.664** |

Over the last decade, major league teams have won nearly two-thirds of the games in which they happened to score first. In 1997, all 28 major league teams posted winning records in games in which they scored first:

### Team W-L When Scoring First—1997

| Team | W | L | Pct |
|---|---|---|---|
| Baltimore Orioles | 67 | 20 | .770 |
| Atlanta Braves | 73 | 23 | .760 |
| Los Angeles Dodgers | 63 | 21 | .750 |
| New York Yankees | 71 | 24 | .747 |
| San Francisco Giants | 56 | 22 | .718 |
| Florida Marlins | 63 | 26 | .708 |
| Seattle Mariners | 59 | 26 | .694 |
| Chicago White Sox | 57 | 27 | .679 |
| Detroit Tigers | 52 | 25 | .675 |
| Toronto Blue Jays | 51 | 25 | .671 |
| Cleveland Indians | 54 | 27 | .667 |
| Houston Astros | 62 | 32 | .660 |

| Team | W | L | Pct |
|------|------|------|------|
| Anaheim Angels | 55 | 29 | .655 |
| Colorado Rockies | 43 | 24 | .642 |
| Pittsburgh Pirates | 50 | 28 | .641 |
| Texas Rangers | 48 | 27 | .640 |
| Montreal Expos | 50 | 29 | .633 |
| Cincinnati Reds | 49 | 29 | .628 |
| St. Louis Cardinals | 49 | 30 | .620 |
| Boston Red Sox | 50 | 31 | .617 |
| New York Mets | 50 | 31 | .617 |
| Minnesota Twins | 49 | 31 | .613 |
| Chicago Cubs | 44 | 29 | .603 |
| San Diego Padres | 54 | 37 | .593 |
| Oakland Athletics | 44 | 32 | .579 |
| Milwaukee Brewers | 47 | 35 | .573 |
| Philadelphia Phillies | 38 | 31 | .551 |
| Kansas City Royals | 35 | 32 | .522 |
| **Total** | **1,483** | **783** | **.654** |

To put this in better perspective, the Atlanta Braves, the winningest team in baseball last year, had a .760 winning percentage (73-23) in games in which they scored first; when the other team scored, the Braves were 28-38 (.424) a difference of 336 percentage points. The team with the *worst* record in baseball, the Oakland Athletics, had a .579 winning percentage (44-32) in games in which they scored first; when the A's opponents put the first run across the plate, Oakland had a .244 winning percentage (21-65), a difference of 335 percentage points. This is typical. Over the last decade, the average difference in winning percentage was 328 points: .664 when scoring first, .336 when the other team scores fist.

During the last five seasons, only one team out of a possible 140 has had a losing record in games in which it scored first: the 1996 Tigers (53-109, .327). The Tigers that year were 33-42 (.440) when scoring first, 20-67 (.230) when the other team plated the first run. Scoring first wasn't a panacea for *that* hapless bunch, but it helped. Incidentally, we did this same study for the NFL and found virtually the same results: over the last three years, NFL clubs had a winning percentage of .660 when scoring first, just about the same as the MLB's .652 figure for the same period. If you put points on the board before the other guy, you're well on the way to victory.

— Don Zminda

## Which Teams Come From Behind?

In the next essay, we'll look at the 1997 teams that won the most games in their final at-bat (see page 90). Another stat often quoted by major league P.R. directors is "come-from-behind wins"—that is, victories in games in which a team was trailing at some point. Do the same teams show up at the top of both lists? Here's the list of 1997 come-from-behind (CFB) wins by team, along with the number of times each team recorded a CFB win in the seventh inning or later:

### Come-From-Behind Wins—1997

| Team | CFB Wins | CFB After 6 |
|------|----------|-------------|
| Mets | 47 | 19 |
| Giants | 46 | 15 |
| Rockies | 45 | 11 |
| Angels | 44 | 19 |
| Indians | 43 | 12 |
| Marlins | 43 | 19 |
| Orioles | 42 | 13 |
| Mariners | 41 | 11 |
| Pirates | 41 | 13 |
| Brewers | 39 | 8 |
| Red Sox | 38 | 15 |
| Royals | 38 | 11 |
| Rangers | 38 | 13 |
| Braves | 38 | 6 |
| Expos | 38 | 13 |
| Padres | 36 | 15 |
| Tigers | 34 | 10 |
| Athletics | 34 | 14 |
| Blue Jays | 34 | 11 |
| Yankees | 33 | 12 |
| Phillies | 33 | 10 |
| White Sox | 32 | 11 |
| Cubs | 32 | 10 |
| Dodgers | 32 | 11 |
| Cardinals | 32 | 8 |
| Reds | 31 | 7 |
| Astros | 30 | 9 |
| Twins | 29 | 4 |

There are a lot of similarities between the two lists. Bobby Valentine's Mets, who tied for the major league lead with 24 wins in their last at-bat, also had the most come-from-behind wins with 47. The Giants, who had the third-most wins in their final at-bat, had the second-most come-from-behind wins (46). The Angels also finished in the top five on both lists.

The Mets, Angels and Marlins each had 19 come-from-behind wins from the seventh inning on, and all three teams ranked highly in team wins in the final at-bat. That's a sign of resiliency in the late innings, a trait *not* shown by such high-profile teams as the Cardinals, Dodgers and White Sox, all of whom missed the playoffs last year. But one can get carried away attributing a trait like this to "character" or "team chemistry." For one thing, you have to be trailing in a game in order to come from behind and win, and many of the better teams simply don't put themselves in that position. For another, we looked at the data over a longer period of time, and this appears to be one of those categories, like one-run wins, that doesn't show much consistency from year to year. That leads one to think that luck is a big factor.

A come-from-behind win, especially in the late innings, is much more of a rare occurrence than you might think. This chart shows the composite MLB team won-lost records over the last five seasons when leading after each inning from the first through the eighth:

### MLB W-L Leading After Inn 1-8—1993-97

| Lead After | W | L | Pct |
|:---:|:---:|:---:|:---:|
| 1 | 3,468 | 1,625 | .681 |
| 2 | 5,081 | 2,015 | .716 |
| 3 | 6,037 | 2,014 | .750 |
| 4 | 6,755 | 1,841 | .786 |
| 5 | 7,293 | 1,631 | .817 |
| 6 | 7,813 | 1,307 | .857 |
| 7 | 8,285 | 953 | .897 |
| 8 | 8,875 | 479 | .949 |

The high won-lost percentage when leading after one inning underscores the importance of scoring first, a topic we discuss on page 86. With each passing inning, the chances of winning improve. Teams leading after five innings win more than 80 percent of the time; teams leading after eight have a winning percentage of .949, which means they win 19 out of every 20 games. It's tough to come from behind late in a game.

— Don Zminda

## Who Wins 'Em Late (and What Does It Mean)?

There are few things in baseball as dramatic as a game-winning rally in a team's final trip to the plate. After one of those breathless victories by the home nine, the announcer will often say something like, "That was the Shelbyvillians 18th victory this year in their final at-bat!" That might lead you to think that good old Shelbyville is a great clutch team. But if you're the skeptical type, as are we, you might ask yourself things like, "How does 18 wins in a team's final at-bat compare with other clubs?" and "How significant is this stat, anyway?"

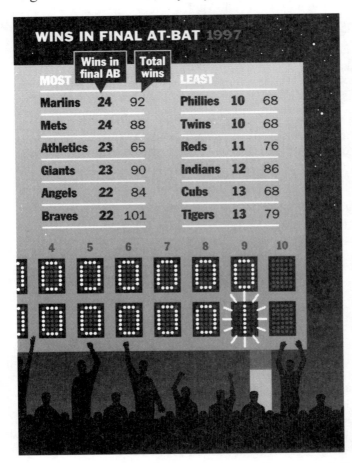

WINS IN FINAL AT-BAT 1997

| MOST | Wins in final AB | Total wins | LEAST | Wins in final AB | Total wins |
|---|---|---|---|---|---|
| Marlins | 24 | 92 | Phillies | 10 | 68 |
| Mets | 24 | 88 | Twins | 10 | 68 |
| Athletics | 23 | 65 | Reds | 11 | 76 |
| Giants | 23 | 90 | Indians | 12 | 86 |
| Angels | 22 | 84 | Cubs | 13 | 68 |
| Braves | 22 | 101 | Tigers | 13 | 79 |

Let's look at the data. The chart shows the 1997 teams with the most and least wins in their final at-bat, along with their total number of victories for the season. We're counting the stat the way major league teams do: a win in your final at-bat is any victory in which a club scores the run or runs which give it the lead for good, as long as the rally takes place in their final half-inning at-bat. This means that the winning rally could come in the bottom of the eighth, as well as in the ninth or extra innings.

At first glance it seems pretty significant that the World Champion Florida Marlins had the most wins in their final at-bat last year, along with the New York Mets. And indeed, the Marlins continued their late-inning heroics in the postseason, with two wins in their final at-bat in the Division Series against the Giants, plus two more in the World Series.

But Art Howe's Oakland Athletics, a last-place club, had only one less final at-bat victory than the Marlins did, and 10 of the 28 teams in the majors had at least 20 wins in their final at-bat. So it wasn't like the Marlins had a patent on this kind of win. In addition, we didn't show you how many wins the teams' *opponents* recorded in their final at-bat. The Marlins' opponents had 15 such wins, the Mets' and A's opponents had 16, the San Francisco Giants' opponents had 17, and so on. Looked at from a percentage basis, the best "final at-bat" team of 1997 was the Chicago White Sox, who had 18 victories in their final at-bat compared to only nine by their opponents, a .667 percentage. The White Sox, of course, didn't exactly cover themselves with glory last year.

And if you look at the list of the teams with the *fewest* wins in their final at-bat last year, you'll find a very big name: the American League champion Cleveland Indians. The Tribe, of course, got to the World Series last year with a string of final at-bat victories over the Yankees (a big one in Game 4) and the Baltimore Orioles (Games 3, 4 and 6). From the way people were talking during their postseason run, you got the impression that the Indians were doing this kind of thing all year. That was anything but the case.

We also looked at the teams which had the most wins in their final at-bat in this decade (top six). With the exception of the mighty 1995 Indians, who had a lot of wins in *every* kind of breakdown, it's not exactly a log of the most memorable nines of the '90s:

### Most Final At-Bat Victories—1990s

| Team | Year | Wins in Final AB | Season W-L |
|------|------|------------------|------------|
| Astros | 1992 | 30 | 81-81 |
| Cardinals | 1992 | 30 | 83-79 |
| White Sox | 1991 | 28 | 87-75 |
| Indians | 1995 | 27 | 100-44 |
| Phillies | 1991 | 27 | 77-85 |
| Astros | 1990 | 26 | 75-87 |

Apart from the '95 Tribe, the most interesting thing about this list is the presence of two more Art Howe teams (the 1992 and 1990 Astros) which, like the '97 Athletics, won a lot of games in their final at-bat but did little else of significance. Give Howe credit for the fact that whether his teams have a lot of talent or not, they're always battling in the late innings.

On the whole, however, this stat seems not worth the attention that announcers and media people sometimes give it. It's great to win a game in your final at-bat, of course, and winning a lot of these games is sometimes the mark of a scrappy, overachieving club. But as with one-run victories, clubs seldom continue to show such scrappiness from one year to the next. Of the top six teams in final at-bat victories in 1996 (including ties), only one was also in the top six in 1997: the Atlanta Braves, a team which just knows how to win, period.

— Don Zminda

A more complete listing for this category can be found on page 230.

## Who Does What the Most?

Just for fun, we thought we'd revive an old *Scoreboard* topic that used to be an annual feature in the early years of the book. If you've ever wondered who hit into the most forceouts during the course of the 1997 season or how often major league batters reached first on interference, wonder no more. Here's the scoop:

| Category | MLB Total | Leader | Total |
|---|---|---|---|
| Ground Outs | 33,495 | Mark Grudzielanek, Mon | 184 |
| Strikeouts | 29,937 | Jay Buhner, Sea | 175 |
| Singles | 27,944 | Tony Gwynn, SD | 152 |
| Fly Outs | 22,880 | Joe Carter, Tor | 134 |
| Runs Scored | 21,604 | Craig Biggio, Hou | 146 |
| Walks | 15,666 | Barry Bonds, SF | 145 |
| Popouts | 10,279 | Joe Carter, Tor | 90 |
| Doubles | 8,004 | Mark Grudzielanek, Mon | 54 |
| Line Outs | 6,327 | Nomar Garciaparra, Bos | 43 |
| Force Outs | 4,726 | Tom Goodwin, KC/Tex | 33 |
| Home Runs | 4,640 | Mark McGwire, Oak/StL | 58 |
| Ground into DP | 3,436 | Albert Belle, WSox | 26 |
| Stolen Bases | 3,308 | Brian Hunter, Det | 74 |
| Foul Pop Outs | 3,171 | Joe Carter, Tor | 39 |
| Game-Winning RBI | 2,142 | Tino Martinez, Yanks | 22 |
| Sacrifice Hits | 1,577 | Edgar Renteria, Fla | 19 |
| Caught Stealing | 1,564 | Kenny Lofton, Atl | 20 |
| Hit by Pitch | 1,449 | Craig Biggio, Hou | 34 |
| Sacrifice Flies | 1,383 | Tino Martinez, Yanks | 13 |
| 1B on Error | 1,379 | Alex Rodriguez, Sea | 12 |
| Intentional Walks | 1,169 | Barry Bonds, SF | 34 |
| Advance on Error | 1,035 | Ray Durham, WSox | 12 |
| Out Advancing | 919 | Brady Anderson, Bal | 8 |
| | | Jeff Cirillo, Mil | 8 |
| | | Raul Mondesi, LA | 8 |
| Triples | 883 | Delino DeShields, StL | 14 |
| Advance on Throw | 499 | Raul Mondesi, LA | 9 |
| Foul Fly Outs | 421 | Tom Goodwin, KC/Tex | 6 |
| | | Dave Martinez, WSox | 6 |
| Bunt Outs | 391 | Otis Nixon, Tor/LA | 20 |

| Category | MLB Total | Leader | Total |
|---|---|---|---|
| Line DPs | 342 | Joey Cora, Sea | 5 |
| | | Tony Gwynn, SD | 5 |
| | | Jeff Kent, SF | 5 |
| Double Steals | 264 | Delino DeShields, StL | 8 |
| 2B on Error | 239 | Mike Piazza, LA | 5 |
| Picked Off | 202 | Damion Easley, Det | 4 |
| | | Wilton Guerrero, LA | 4 |
| SB + Error | 183 | Brian Hunter, Det | 6 |
| Bunt Pop Out | 161 | Deion Sanders, Cin | 6 |
| Advance on Error on Pickoff Throw | 155 | Tony Womack, Pit | 7 |
| Advance-No Play | 139 | Derrick May, Phi | 4 |
| 1B on K+WP | 76 | Tony Womack, Pit | 3 |
| 1B on Failed FC | 75 | Damion Easley, Det | 3 |
| 1B on SH+Error | 68 | 8 tied with | 2 |
| Fly DP | 65 | Dave Martinez, WSox | 3 |
| Error on Foul Fly | 47 | Scott Brosius, Oak | 2 |
| | | Scott Spiezio, Oak | 2 |
| 1B on SH+FC | 38 | Brett Butler, LA | 2 |
| | | Kevin Foster, Cubs | 2 |
| 1B on Batter Obstruction | 30 | Jose Guillen, Pit | 2 |
| CS but Reached on Error | 30 | Carlos Baerga, Mets | 2 |
| 1B on Interference | 28 | 4 tied with | 3 |
| GDP on Bunt | 20 | Jon Lieber, Pit | 3 |
| 3B on Error | 17 | 17 tied with | 1 |
| 1B on K+PB | 15 | 15 tied with | 1 |
| Bunt Pop DP | 13 | 13 tied with | 1 |
| 1B/Ball Hits Runner | 11 | Mark Grace, Cubs | 2 |
| Sac Flies + Error | 8 | 8 tied with | 1 |
| 1B on K+Error | 5 | 5 tied with | 1 |
| Advance on Obstruction | 4 | 4 tied with | 1 |
| Line Triple Plays | 2 | Rich Amaral, Sea | 1 |
| | | Eddie Taubensee, Cin | 1 |
| Ground Triple Plays | 1 | Alex Gonzalez, Tor | 1 |
| Out on Obstruction | 1 | Tony Fernandez, Cle | 1 |

A few random comments:

1. Should Mark Grudzielanek's nickname be "Grudzy the Grounder-Outer?" (Well, he did hit a few doubles also.)

2. Who says Joe "Air" Carter isn't the same player he used to be? When we first published this data after the 1989 season, Joe Carter led the majors in popouts. Nine years later, he was still the hitter with the most "pop." In fact, he's getting better at it: 64 popouts in 1989, 90 popouts in 1997!

3. Joe led the league in fly outs and foul popouts as well. Gee, Joe, if you can't make the other team respect your ground game, they're gonna be blitzing and going to the nickel defense on every down. No wonder you only hit .234 last year. . .

4. Tip O' the Day to Gene Lamont: don't let Jon Lieber bunt! The Pirates righthander actually bunted into more double plays last year (three) than he had sacrifice hits (two).

5. Raul Mondesi must be the most aggressive baserunner in the game. Mondesi led the majors in both advancing on throws (nine) and times *out* advancing on the bases (eight, tied with Brady Anderson and Jeff Cirillo).

6. Just think how good Nomar Garciaparra's rookie season might have been if a few more of those line-drive outs had dropped in.

7. A few years ago, we did a *Scoreboard* study on what kind of players are most likely to reach first base on an error. The basic profile: righthanded hitter, good speed, hits the ball hard on the ground a lot. Alex Rodriguez, who fits that profile perfectly, led the majors by reaching first base 12 times on errors last year.

8. Delino DeShields' eight stolen bases on double steals were more than all but four *teams* recorded last year (in case you're wondering about the MLB total, there were 132 double steals last year, resulting in 264 stolen bases). The Cardinals had 10 double steals, most in the majors along with the Rockies and Astros, and DeShields was involved in eight of them.

9. Who says the Game-Winning RBI is a defunct stat? We still keep it, and Tino Martinez led the majors with 22 of them last year.

10. Is he swinging at pitches over his head, or is this an integral part of his offensive game? On three occasions last year, Tony Womack of the Pirates struck out, but managed to reach first safely on a wild pitch. Hmm. . . maybe Jon Lieber could try working on this play.

— Don Zminda

# Why Don't They Tag Up From First More Often?

It's standard, smart baserunning. On a fly ball with less than two out, the runner on first positions himself halfway between first and second. If the ball is not caught, the runner can advance easily to second and hopefully to third. But does this really make any sense? After all, major league outfielders drop fly balls about as often as Jerry Rice drops touchdown passes. Wouldn't runners on first be better off tagging up, at least on balls hit to the deeper parts of the outfield?

In order to answer the question, we looked at all fly outs with a runner on first only and less than two out. We did not want to include any other base situations, as the attempted advance of other runners and the defense's play on those runners confuse the issue. We want to focus only on those situations where the runner tagging from first is the only defensive concern. Here, then, are the results:

### Tagging From First—1993-97

| Team | Pct | Successful | Attempts |
|------|-----|------------|----------|
| Angels | 88.9 | 8 | 9 |
| Orioles | 60.0 | 3 | 5 |
| Red Sox | 100.0 | 1 | 1 |
| White Sox | 72.7 | 8 | 11 |
| Indians | 80.0 | 4 | 5 |
| Tigers | 93.8 | 15 | 16 |
| Royals | 80.0 | 4 | 5 |
| Brewers | 90.9 | 10 | 11 |
| Twins | 77.8 | 21 | 27 |
| Yankees | 76.5 | 13 | 17 |
| Athletics | 92.3 | 12 | 13 |
| Mariners | 100.0 | 3 | 3 |
| Rangers | 84.2 | 16 | 19 |
| Blue Jays | 100.0 | 11 | 11 |
| **AL Average** | **84.3** | **129** | **153** |
| Braves | 80.0 | 8 | 10 |
| Cubs | 77.8 | 7 | 9 |
| Reds | 80.0 | 8 | 10 |
| Rockies | 100.0 | 19 | 19 |
| Marlins | 77.8 | 7 | 9 |
| Astros | 100.0 | 4 | 4 |
| Dodgers | 100.0 | 9 | 9 |

| Team | Pct | Successful | Attempts |
|------|-----|------------|----------|
| Expos | 90.9 | 10 | 11 |
| Mets | 100.0 | 4 | 4 |
| Phillies | 100.0 | 6 | 6 |
| Pirates | 80.0 | 8 | 10 |
| Padres | 50.0 | 2 | 4 |
| Giants | 85.7 | 12 | 14 |
| Cardinals | 100.0 | 12 | 12 |
| **NL Average** | **88.5** | **116** | **131** |
| **MLB Average** | **86.3** | **245** | **284** |

(Note: Includes only fly balls to the outfield with less than two out and a runner on first only.)

As you can see, the success rate of the tag from first is extremely high. Despite this, it is rarely attempted. Over the past five years, there have been 13,343 fly balls to the outfield with a man on first only and less than two out. Only 284 times did the runner attempt to tag. That's only once every 47 opportunities! Tom Kelly's Twins led the way, with 27 attempts in these situations. The Red Sox, meanwhile, solidify their standing as the ultimate station-to-station team in the majors. They have only tagged from first once in the past five years!

If the runner on first is rarely thrown out attempting to tag, why don't teams try it more often? After all, most managers are content with a two-thirds success rate when stealing second. Why, then, are they reluctant to try something that is successful 86 percent of the time or more?

One reason is that many flyballs aren't hit deep enough for the runner to risk going to second. But another reason may be that conventional wisdom has forever dictated that the tag from first is not a wise play. Perhaps positioning the runner between first and second on a fly ball made sense in the Neanderthal days of baseball, when field conditions were poor and when there were few routine plays. But not any more. In 1997, major league outfielders caught 23,647 fly outs. They were charged with 96 errors on fly balls. Basically, an outfielder muffed a fly ball about once every 250 chances. Sure, this doesn't include misplays that turn into hits, but even if you include those, and even if it's Jose Canseco shagging flies, you can almost always plan on a fly ball being caught. Going halfway to second doesn't make sense if it lets you advance an extra base a couple of times a year, but prevents you from tagging up on numerous occasions. Indeed, wouldn't it be worthwhile to challenge outfielders more often?

—John Sasman

## Is the Straight Steal of Home a Lost Art?

A steal of home is an exciting and daring play, no doubt. Most steals of home, however, are on the back end of double steals. In these cases, with runners on first and third, the runner does not break for home until the catcher has thrown to second base. He then must beat the return throw to the catcher. Sure, it's risky, but it's altogether different than a *straight* steal of home. On a straight steal, the runner on third breaks for home when the pitcher starts his delivery. Just how rare is a straight steal of home?

Before we answer that question, let's take a look at all steals of home. In 1997, there were only 20 successful thefts of home plate. Seventy-three times the runner on third was caught at home. This makes for a very poor success rate of 21.5 percent. The major league average each of the past several years has been right around 20 percent. Again, however, this includes *all* steal attempts of home. If we remove the double steals and look at only those situations with runners on third, second and third, or the bases loaded, the percentage is even worse. In 1997, there were only two successful straight steals of home in 16 attempts. In the 1990s, there have been only 22 straight steals of home in 173 attempts (12.7 percent). Which players have pulled off the ultimate larceny? The list of all the players with at least one straight steal of home in the 1990s follows.

### Players with Straight Steals of Home—1990s

| Player | Steals | Attempts |
| --- | --- | --- |
| Marquis Grissom | 2 | 2 |
| Billy Hatcher | 2 | 2 |
| Jacob Brumfield | 2 | 3 |
| Lance Johnson | 2 | 5 |
| Rich Becker | 1 | 1 |
| Jerald Clark | 1 | 1 |
| Mike Difelice | 1 | 1 |
| Rex Hudler | 1 | 1 |
| Jeff Kent | 1 | 1 |
| Jeff King | 1 | 1 |
| Brian McRae | 1 | 1 |
| Paul Molitor | 1 | 1 |
| Juan Samuel | 1 | 1 |
| Reggie Sanders | 1 | 1 |
| Vince Coleman | 1 | 2 |
| Jon Nunnally | 1 | 2 |
| Gerald Williams | 1 | 2 |
| Kenny Lofton | 1 | 3 |

Most of these players are (or were) serious basestealing threats. It's clear that only the swiftest can pull off a straight steal of home. Mike Difelice, of course, is the most notable exception to that rule. His only major league steal came on April 17 last year when he swiped home. That increased his professional (major and minor league) total to six steals in seven years.

The list of players who have never succeeded on a straight steal attempt is rather lengthy and includes some surprising names: Dave Valle (0 for 1), Matt Nokes (0 for 2), Matt Williams (0 for 3) and Andres Galarraga (0 for 4). Galarraga, in fact, is second to Lance Johnson for most attempted straight steals of home in the 1990s. Evidently, the "Big Cat" would like to believe he has a little bit of cheetah in him.

Actually, we are not giving Galarraga, or anyone else for that matter, a fair shake concerning straight steals of home. Most of the outs, in fact, are botched suicide squeeze attempts. Two of the things our STATS reporters track are bunt attempts and pitchouts. Of the 151 times a runner was caught, 70 were when the batter attempted to bunt, but missed the pitch. Another 24 were on pitchouts. Only one of the successful attempts was on a failed bunt try. There certainly are many other instances when the batter missed the sign, leaving the oncoming runner high and dry. Obviously, when you remove these miscues, the success rate of the straight steal of home climbs.

Even so, it's safe to say there is no one in today's game who has mastered the art of the straight steal of home. Rod Carew, who perfected the skill on his way to seven steals of home in 1969 and 17 in his career, was probably the last practitioner. These days, consider yourself lucky if you ever see a straight steal of home. They are rarely attempted, and they rarely work.

—John Sasman

### In What Style Were Interleague Games Played?

For years, many of us acquired certain beliefs about the way in which the two major leagues played the game of baseball. The National League, we were told, emphasized speed on the basepaths and velocity on the mound. The American League, on the other hand, relied on power hitters and breaking-ball artists. Conventional wisdom dictated that these contrasting playing styles evolved due to differences as varied as the designated hitter, the predominance of certain playing surfaces, and even the way the umpires crouched behind home plate.

Well, for the first time in history last year, we had a chance to see how those perceived "differences" actually stacked up in extended interleague competition. To refresh your memory, the National League ended up with bragging rights, posting a winning percentage of .547 (117-97). And here's how the stats broke down in all games, depending on the kind of matchup:

| Stat<br>**Stats for All Games—1997** | AL vs AL | NL vs NL | NL @ AL | AL @ NL |
|---|---|---|---|---|
| Games | 1,025 | 1,027 | 107 | 107 |
| Runs/Gm | 9.9 | 9.2 | 9.7 | 9.0 |
| Home Runs/Gm | 2.2 | 1.9 | 2.1 | 2.1 |
| Walks/Gm | 7.0 | 6.9 | 6.9 | 6.4 |
| Strikeouts/Gm | 12.8 | 13.7 | 12.6 | 13.3 |
| Stolen Bases/Gm | 1.3 | 1.6 | 1.4 | 1.3 |
| SB Pct. | 67.7 | 68.7 | 67.4 | 61.8 |
| Sac Hits/Gm | 0.47 | 0.91 | 0.54 | 0.99 |
| Batting Average | .272 | .262 | .272 | .261 |
| On Base Percentage | .341 | .333 | .341 | .329 |
| Slugging Percentage | .429 | .408 | .428 | .418 |
| ERA | 4.61 | 4.20 | 4.45 | 4.11 |
| Time Of Game* | 2:57 | 2:48 | 2:53 | 2:49 |

*Nine-inning games only

The data presents some pretty interesting figures. For one thing, did you notice how closely the percentages corresponded when the games were played in the ballparks of one particular league? For instance, the batting average in games featuring two American League teams was .272 last year. When a National League team played in an AL ballpark, the combined average was again .272. In fact, you had to go all the way to one-thousandth decimal place (.27168 vs .27163) before finding a different digit. Similarly, the on-base percentage in both cases was .341, and there was only a one-point difference in slugging percentage.

While those averages in NL-NL and AL@NL matchups weren't *quite* as identical, they nevertheless mirrored each other closely. This phenomenon may be due in part to ballpark effects, although the more likely explanation is the presence or absence of the designated hitter. With the designated hitter available only in American League parks, the two leagues combined to hit 11 points lower when the AL visited the National League, just as the NL hit 10 points lower than the AL in all *intraleague* games.

Keep in mind, too, the sample sizes for interleague games were still relatively small, so we don't want to make sweeping generalizations. But it appears that the two leagues had an assimilating effect in the areas of power and speed. While the American League averaged 2.2 homers per game and the NL 1.9 in intraleague games, the loops combined to average 2.1 homers per game when facing each other. Similarly, while the AL attempted 2.0 stolen bases per game versus the NL rate of 2.3 when facing their own respective "families," they averaged a combined 2.1 attempts in interleague contests. It may be surprising, however, that the stolen-base success rate fell appreciably when the American League visited National League parks. We're not sure we can state with absolute certainty what all this says about the leagues' perceived playing styles, but again, based on the limited sample sizes, there doesn't *appear* to be a sizable difference. We'll likely learn more with another season of interleague play.

One last thing we noticed when looking at the numbers was how much faster the American League finished its games when taking on the NL. The average nine-inning game length in those games was roughly six and a half minutes shorter compared to AL-only tilts, although it was still about three minutes *longer* compared to NL contests. If the National League can teach the AL about accelerating the pace of its games, we won't complain.

—Jim Henzler

## Which Parks Change at Night?

For generations, Wrigley Field has been known as a good place to hit. Since it's considered easier to hit in the sunshine than it is under the lights, it was suspected that Wrigley's status as the last major league field without lights had something to do with its tendency to favor the hitters.

The Cubs have played occasional night games at Wrigley ever since lights were installed in 1988, and the results of those games have confirmed what many suspected: Wrigley, like most parks, doesn't favor the hitter to quite the same degree at night. In night games over the last three years, in fact, Wrigley has been one of the toughest places to hit at night in all of baseball (with a nightime run index of 89), despite the fact that it's still one of the *easiest* places to hit during the day (daytime run index of 115).

This year, for the first time, we calculated park indexes for each of the major league parks for both day and night games. Wrigley's schizophrenic nature was only one of several surprises. For example, we had expected Coors Field to remain atop the charts in most categories, but we didn't expect Edison International Field (formerly Anaheim Stadium) to surpass Coors as the easiest home-run park during the daytime. The chart to the left shows park indexes for the top three and bottom three parks for runs and home runs, both during the day and at night.

### BEST AND WORST PARK INDEXES 1995–97

**DAYTIME**

| BEST | RUNS | HOME RUNS | |
|---|---|---|---|
| Rockies | 161 | Angels | 161 |
| Athletics** | 116 | Rockies | 159 |
| Cubs | 115 | Padres | 127 |

| WORST | | | |
|---|---|---|---|
| Astros | 77 | Expos | 70 |
| Dodgers | 81 | Dodgers | 70 |
| Braves* | 82 | Astros | 72 |
| Padres | 82 | | |

**NIGHTTIME**

| BEST | RUNS | HOME RUNS | |
|---|---|---|---|
| Rockies | 152 | Rockies | 150 |
| Pirates | 117 | Tigers | 141 |
| Brewers | 117 | Giants | 121 |

| WORST | | | |
|---|---|---|---|
| Dodgers | 82 | Astros | 75 |
| White Sox | 86 | Dodgers | 82 |
| Astros | 86 | White Sox | 82 |

*1997 only.
**1996 and 1997 only.

There are a few more unexpected results to report. We hadn't expected domed stadiums to show any significant difference in play between day and night, but in fact, all four non-retractable domes (the Astrodome, the Kingdome, the Metrodome and Olympic Stadium) were better hitters' parks at night. The Metrodome's pattern was particularly odd: during the day, it boosted home runs but suppressed batting average and runs scored. At night, it was exactly the opposite: it decreased home runs, but inflated batting average and runs scored. This may lend credence to the argument that the Metrodome's air-conditioning system affects the way the ball carries, since it's likely that the system is used less fully at night.

### Day and Night Park Indexes for Domed Stadiums—1995-97

|  | —Day— | | —Night— | |
| --- | --- | --- | --- | --- |
|  | R | HR | R | HR |
| Astrodome | 77 | 72 | 86 | 75 |
| Kingdome | 95 | 104 | 99 | 107 |
| Metrodome | 92 | 113 | 111 | 98 |
| Olympic Stadium | 86 | 70 | 113 | 98 |

Some other individual parks exhibited odd day/night variations. At night, Tiger Stadium was second only to Coors Field as a home-run park, but during the day, it was dead average. What's more, it cut batting average so severely at night that it was actually a better overall hitters' park during the day, even without all the home runs. The winds at the Ballpark in Arlington seem to vary greatly from day to night. During the day, it helps righthanded hitters hit for both power and average, while hindering lefthanded hitters in both respects. Once the sun goes down, the pattern reverses itself, and the lefthanded swingers have a field day, er, night.

—Mat Olkin

A more complete listing for this category can be found on page 231.

# Which Park Is Best for Stolen Bases?

For years, the Atlanta Braves played their home games in one of the best hitters' parks in all of baseball. Whether it was the altitude, the visibility, the warm weather or whatever, Atlanta-Fulton County Stadium acquired a well-deserved reputation as a haven where batters loved to take their cuts.

That all changed in 1997. The number of runs scored in Braves home games diminished considerably last year, while home runs also showed a dramatic decrease. There's little doubt the move the Braves had made across the street, to Turner Field, played a significant role in changing the offensive dynamics in Atlanta.

Although the hitters' difficulties at Turner Field have received their share of attention, there is another, less obvious area which also suffered last year—stolen bases. After succeeding on 72 percent of stolen-base attempts in Atlanta in 1996, the Braves and their opponents could muster just a 64 percent rate there in '97.

STATS has been providing "Park Indexes" for a variety of statistical categories over a number of years. At first blush, stolen bases may not seem like a phase of the game that is subject to the variations caused by ballpark effects. But it is. To illustrate, we'll begin by looking at the stadiums which have been most harmful to baserunners:

## Lowest Stolen-Base Park Indexes—Current Stadiums

| Stadium (Years) | Home | Road | Index |
|---|---|---|---|
| Oakland-Alameda County Coliseum (1996-97) | .653 | .751 | 87 |
| Shea Stadium (1995-97) | .640 | .725 | 88 |
| Turner Field (1997) | .645 | .712 | 91 |
| Yankee Stadium (1995-97) | .663 | .727 | 91 |
| Fenway Park (1995-97) | .684 | .741 | 92 |
| Veterans Stadium (1995-97) | .677 | .728 | 93 |
| 3Com Park (1995-97) | .648 | .695 | 93 |
| Busch Stadium (1996-97) | .682 | .731 | 93 |
| Edison International Field of Anaheim (1995-97) | .636 | .659 | 96 |
| Ewing M. Kauffman Stadium (1995-97) | .672 | .690 | 97 |

The index is calculated by dividing the stolen-base success rate in a team's home games (including opponents) by the rate in its away contests. The lower the index is below 100, the greater effect the stadium has on depressing the percentage. We are excluding interleague games, and including only the years since 1995 or the last change to a ballpark's surface or dimensions, whichever occurred last.

By this definition, Oakland-Alameda County Coliseum is the most hazardous park to a base burglar's livelihood. It has increased the caught-stealing rate by roughly 13 percent over the past two years. Shea Stadium is a close second, continuing to afflict thieves as it plagued Vince Coleman.

You remember Coleman. When he was with the Cardinals, Coleman averaged over 90 stolen bases per year and succeeded on roughly 83 percent of his attempts. Moving to the Mets in 1991, he totaled just 99 steals over the next three seasons combined, and his success rate fell to 73 percent. Traded to Kansas City before the '94 campaign, he rebounded to pilfer 50 bases in 58 attempts (86 percent). The next year, however, Coleman again slumped to 26 steals and a 74-percent success rate before he was shipped off to Seattle in August.

All a coincidence? Probably not. Coleman's best seasons each had one thing in common—they occurred in a home ballpark with Astroturf. Artificial surface appears to be the greatest single factor in determining a park's stolen-base index. Between 1990 and 1995, Busch Stadium had a stolen base index of 108. Since installing grass in 1996, the index has plummeted to 93. The effect of grass in Kauffman Stadium hasn't been quite as dramatic, though it has lowered the stolen-base index from 101 between 1990 and 1994 to 97 since '95.

While Veterans Stadium is the only turf field appearing on the bottom 10 list, four of the five best parks for basestealers feature artificial surfaces:

**Highest Stolen-Base Park Indexes—Current Stadiums**

| Stadium (Years) | Home | Road | Index |
|---|---|---|---|
| Olympic Stadium (1995-97) | .802 | .696 | 115 |
| The Kingdome (1995-97) | .705 | .632 | 112 |
| County Stadium (1995-97) | .727 | .671 | 108 |
| Three Rivers Stadium (1995-97) | .724 | .674 | 107 |
| SkyDome (1995-97) | .709 | .664 | 107 |
| Dodger Stadium (1995-97) | .751 | .704 | 107 |
| Tiger Stadium (1997) | .724 | .689 | 105 |
| Comiskey Park (1995-97) | .693 | .675 | 103 |
| Cinergy Field (1995-97) | .752 | .734 | 103 |
| Wrigley Field (1995-97) | .709 | .693 | 102 |

Basestealers have been running wild in Olympic Stadium, succeeding on over 80 percent of their attempts since 1995. No other park is over 75 percent. While the troubles of the Montreal catchers, especially Darrin Fletcher, may have something to do with that, remember that the Expos have the same catchers in road contests, and the combined success rate is under 70 percent on the road. Again, the most likely explanation is that Olympic Stadium features turf.

We're not sure if we'll go so far as to recommend stolen bases as an effective offensive strategy, though if you're going to employ it anywhere, Montreal is the place. But please apply the brakes in Oakland.

—Jim Henzler

A more complete listing for this category can be found on page 232.

# III.  QUESTIONS ON OFFENSE

## Who's the Best Table-Setter?

There's nothing that ignites an offense better than a top-flight leadoff man: a guy who can tire opposing pitchers by forcing them to work deep counts, get on base, wreak havoc once he's on base and provide scores of RBI opportunities for teammates hitting behind him. In continuing a long-standing tradition, the *Baseball Scoreboard* rewards each season's most outstanding leadoff hitter with the "Slidin' Billy Trophy." The award is named for the legendary Slidin' Billy Hamilton, who, in the 19th century, first perfected the art of batting leadoff by racking up a career on-base percentage of .455. Hamilton scored 100 or more runs for 10 straight seasons during his career, and actually crossed the plate *192* times in a single year (1894).

Since a leadoff man's primary function is to score runs, it's only natural that his most important job is to get on base. The following chart identifies the players with the best OBPs last year while batting first.

| THE NUMBER-ONE MEN 1997 | OBP | AB | R | SB |
|---|---|---|---|---|
| F.P. Santangelo | .427 | 153 | 29 | 5 |
| Craig Biggio | .418 | 614 | 145 | 47 |
| Tim Raines | .417 | 214 | 45 | 8 |
| Walt Weiss | .417 | 114 | 24 | 3 |
| Kenny Lofton | .409 | 492 | 90 | 27 |
| Rickey Henderson | .399 | 388 | 79 | 44 |
| Brady Anderson | .398 | 550 | 94 | 18 |
| Derek Jeter | .394 | 427 | 81 | 16 |
| Jeff Blauser | .391 | 133 | 23 | 1 |
| Chuck Knoblauch | .390 | 608 | 116 | 62 |

Batting #1 only; minimum 100 plate appearances.

Felipe Alou's favorite utilityman, F.P. Santangelo, came out on top, compiling a phenomenal .427 OBP from the No. 1 slot. Santagelo batted over one hundred points higher when leading off last year (.307 compared to

.203 elsewhere). Part of his ability to get on base stemmed from his incredibly pronounced tendency to collide with pitched balls; he was plunked 25 times last year, including 10 times (one per 18.5 plate appearances) from the leadoff slot. We know you're willing to "take one for the team," F.P., but at this rate, Alou's going to have to wheel you to the plate in a body cast by next summer.

Although we're sure Santangelo would probably be clamoring for the trophy right now were he reading this, we can't bestow the award upon a player who only garnered about 150 at-bats in the leadoff slot. The following five players are this year's "Slidin' Billy" finalists:

**Brady Anderson.** One of the inspirations behind our mammoth computer simulation last year (see below), Anderson returns to the list of finalists, despite the fact that he slugged nowhere near the 50 home runs he bashed in 1996. With a .393 overall OBP, he had a great season, but the fact that he only scored 97 runs while sitting at the head of a good Orioles offense has to hurt his chances.

**Craig Biggio.** Although he's always been an upper-echelon leadoff man, Biggio raised his game a couple of notches last season, compiling career highs in on-base percentage (.415), slugging percentage (.501), and runs scored (146, tops in the majors in '97). Biggio's numbers look even more impressive when you consider that he resides in the Astrodome, one of the toughest hitters' parks in baseball. One final note: he can tell Santangelo a thing or two about getting plunked; Biggio was hit by a league-leading 34 pitches last season.

**Derek Jeter.** He may not be a *true* leadoff man—he spent about two-thirds of his time there last season—but Jeter proved he was dangerous nonetheless, compiling a .394 OBP at the top of the order while scoring 116 runs on the year. The Yanks used Tim Raines at the top of the order at year's end (who didn't do too badly himself, ranking third on the chart), but they might do well to return Jeter to the No. 1 slot in '98. After all, Raines can't play *forever*.

**Chuck Knoblauch.** Winner of the last two "Slidin' Billy" trophies, Knoblauch is threatening to monopolize the entire competition. Despite his All-Star-caliber season (117 runs, .390 overall OBP), his numbers pale in comparison to those of '96; both his batting average and on-base percentage are down by 50 or more points from his 1996 totals.

**Kenny Lofton.** The subject of Atlanta's "rent-a-center-fielder" strategy in 1997, Lofton wasn't quite able to live up to the grandiose expectations that were placed upon him at the start of the season. Still, he managed an outstanding .409 on-base percentage and scored 90 runs despite missing nearly a quarter of the season due to injury.

The uniqueness of 1996's competition—a home-run hitter (Anderson) vs. a prototypical leadoff man (Knoblauch)—inspired us to call upon Bill James' computer simulations to more accurately assess which player had a greater impact on his team's fortunes. (If you recall, Anderson lost out to Knoblauch in a scintillatingly-close contest.) However, this year, the field isn't close enough to warrant any extended studies. Although any general manager would salivate at the opportunity to acquire any one of the above players to head his team's lineup, we couldn't help but award the "Slidin' Billy" trophy to Craig Biggio in a landslide. Biggio's incredible numbers in a park that actually *hampered* his hitting ability earned him the well-deserved accolades. Congratulations, Craig, on a job well done!

—Kevin Fullam

A more complete listing for this category can be found on page 233.

## Who Created the Most Runs?

In the grand scheme of human history, it may not have had quite the same impact as the invention of the wheel or indoor plumbing, but modern baseball statistics just wouldn't be the same without the granddaddy of them all—Runs Created. That stat was itself created, as many of the most significant typically were, by Bill James. Bill still hasn't abandoned his search for a brighter lightbulb, developing even better ways to calculate realistic runs created totals. As a result, we can now present new runs created estimates which are the most accurate ever produced.

The new procedure to calculate runs created has been improved in a number of ways, the most important of which are:

- The formula now addresses the specific negative impact of batter strikeouts, in contrast to other outs.

- Each individual's runs created are now estimated in a "theoretical team" context.

- A batter's performance in two specific situations—hitting with runners in scoring position and the number of runners on base when he hits his home runs—are taken into account.

- A "reconciling stage" has been added to account for discrepancies which exist between the team total of runs scored and the sum of runs created by its individual players.

The primary goal of runs created is to determine, to the best of our ability, which individuals are responsible for each run a team scores. There's no doubt that the changes outlined above bring us closer to that goal. Perhaps we haven't yet arrived at the point where we can say with absolute certainty that Joe Homer was responsible for "x" amount of runs, but it's nevertheless clear that the new procedure is a sizable step forward in that direction.

That means that the runs created estimates for 1997 are more precise than for any previous year. Your leaders for last season appear on the following page:

Larry Walker obviously had a huge season, and his total of 158 runs created is an awesome sum. That mark has been exceeded just twice in the past 40 years, both times by Barry Bonds (162 in 1993 and 160 in 1996). Still, without the adjustments for situational hitting, Walker's total would have been even *higher*. Though he hit .364 with runners in scoring position, he clubbed all but 15 of his 49 homers with the bases empty. Based on his home-run-per-at-bat rate and the number of times Walker hit with men on base, we would have expected him to hit roughly 23 homers with at least one man on. Therefore, his account is debited about eight runs created.

**THE RUN MAKERS 1997**

Runs created

| | |
|---|---|
| Larry Walker | 158 |
| Frank Thomas | 150 |
| Ken Griffey Jr. | 148 |
| Craig Biggio | 147 |
| Jeff Bagwell | 142 |
| Tony Gwynn | 138 |
| Mike Piazza | 137 |
| Barry Bonds | 132 |
| Tim Salmon | 130 |
| Edgar Martinez | 127 |

Frank Thomas, on the other hand, was terrific with runners in scoring position, ranking second in the American League with a .417 batting average in those situations. In addition, he smacked more home runs than expected with runners on base. By the end of all the math, Thomas' runs created total improves from 139 to 150.

Not all players will have their runs created totals change as a result of their situational stats. Jeff Bagwell, for instance, had 142 runs created prior to figuring his situational stats and before the reconciliation stage with the Astro team totals. His final total is also 142. Likewise, Mike Piazza had 137 before, 137 after.

Now, perhaps you're wondering whether it's really appropriate to credit players for their performances in situations which are dependent to some extent on the abilities of their teammates. You might be arguing that you can't hit a two-run homer without a teammate first reaching base. True enough. But remember the goal of runs created—to determine as precisely as possible how many runs each individual generated. And as Bill has said, "You can do that more accurately using situational stats than not using them. We didn't put in biases of team context. We didn't give a player extra credit for batting lots of times with men in scoring position. We adjusted for *performance* in team context. If a player hits .350 with runners in scoring position, this causes his team to score more runs, which means that he has created more runs. If he hits most of his home runs with the bases empty (disproportional to his individual opportunities) this will mean that his team will score fewer runs, which will mean that he has, in fact, created fewer runs. And that's all that we're trying to measure."

—Jim Henzler

A more complete listing for this category can be found on page 234.

## Which Switch-Hitters Are Wasting Their Time?

In 1997, switch-hitting J.T. Snow hit .312 with 27 homers while batting lefthanded. He hit .188 with one homer in 133 at-bats while batting righthanded. Basically, he hit like Mo Vaughn as a lefty. Turned around, he hit like Benji Gil without the power, or David Howard without the average, or a poor man's Ozzie Guillen. Pretty scary, huh?

Suprisingly, Snow is not alone among his switch-hitting brethren. Many, in fact, show a notable lack of ambidexterity. Take a look at the switch-hitters with the largest differences between one side of the plate and the other. We'll use on-base percentage plus slugging percentage (OPS) as our measure:

### Largest OPS Platoon Differences, Switch-Hitters—1995-97

| Batter | OPS as LH | OPS as RH | Diff |
|---|---|---|---|
| J.T. Snow | .888 | .613 | .275 |
| Jose Valentin | .807 | .586 | .221 |
| Todd Hundley | .963 | .752 | .211 |
| Bernie Williams | .855 | 1.053 | .198 |
| Dave Hollins | .734 | .917 | .183 |
| Roberto Alomar | .920 | .756 | .164 |
| Chipper Jones | .905 | .754 | .151 |
| Gregg Jefferies | .721 | .860 | .139 |
| Walt Weiss | .778 | .662 | .116 |
| Carl Everett | .755 | .647 | .108 |

(minimum 1000 PA)

Why does this group continue to bat from both sides? Though many of these players are superstars, the dropoff from one side to the other is so dramatic, it's questionable if many of them are helping their teams. Take Todd Hundley, for instance. He has terrorized righthanders the last several years. Mike Piazza is the only catcher who can post numbers comparable to Hundley's against righties. Last year, however, Hundley hit .219 against lefties. In 1996, he hit only .196. Likewise, Roberto Alomar and Chipper Jones turn into mere mortals when hitting from the right side. Bernie Williams, meanwhile, is less effective as a lefthander, though his numbers are still very solid.

Of course, some of these players have viable excuses. Hampered by injuries most of last year, Alomar actually stopped switch-hitting midway through the season. In 1996, he hit lefties and righties equally well. Meanwhile, Snow was drilled in the face by a Randy Johnson pitch in spring training. Perhaps we should cut him a little slack if he's just a wee bit timid against lefties. Then again, his performance in 1997 was not any different than in 1996, when he managed a .199 average with just three homers hitting righthanded. And what's Walt Weiss' excuse? His slugging percentage as a righthander over the last three years is .299. That would be bad if he played in Dodger Stadium. In Coors Field, it's hardly better than most pitchers could do.

Should these players give up switch-hitting? After all, switch-hitting makes sense if it gives you a platoon advantage. If it doesn't, what's the point? Only seven players (among all hitters) have a larger platoon differential than Snow over the last three years. (Rich Becker has the largest, with an OPS of .366 higher against righties than lefties. Becker was a switch-hitter for several years, but now hits lefthanded exclusively.) Could Snow possibly hit any worse against lefties if he batted lefthanded against them? Would Hundley do worse than he's done? What do you lose if you give up switch-hitting and find out you can't hit lefties or righties? Nothing, if you couldn't hit against them in the first place.

While the benefits of switch-hitting for some of these players is questionable, there are others for whom it pays dividends. Kevin Stocker has the smallest platoon differential for switch-hitters. His OPS over the last three years is .661 hitting from the left side and .666 hitting from the right. While he is not exactly an offensive force, Stocker does edge out Brian McRae and Otis Nixon as the switch-hitter with the most consistent stroke from both sides of the plate.

—John Sasman

A more complete listing for this category can be found on page 236.

## Will Expansion Mean a Record-Breaking Year for the Hitters?

Conventional wisdom in baseball circles says that expansion is great for hitters. A quick look at the numbers seems to back up the theory: every time the majors have expanded since 1961, the level of offense has risen. However, there were often extenuating circumstances that came along with expansion—for example, the addition of great hitters' parks like Wrigley Field in Los Angeles (the home of the 1961 Angels) and Mile High Stadium in Denver, and the rules changes designed to help the hitter which baseball adopted in 1969. So does expansion *really* lead to more hitting? We examined this subject in the *Scoreboard* a few years ago, and with the leagues about to expand once more, we thought it a good time to revisit it.

Our 1994 expansion study used standard deviations to measure the spread between the best and worst ERA qualifiers—and the best and worst batting title qualifiers—in the seasons prior to major league expansion, and then during the expansion season itself. If the caliber of pitching was slipping due to expansion, one would expect the standard deviation for ERA to increase. Our numbers showed that it did, every time:

### ERA Qualifiers—Pre- and During Expansion

| Year | Mean ERA | Standard Deviation |
|------|----------|--------------------|
| 1960 | 3.56 | .53 |
| 1961 | 3.77 | .58 |
| 1962 | 3.71 | .65 |
| 1968 | 2.83 | .60 |
| 1969 | 3.35 | .68 |
| 1976 | 3.30 | .51 |
| 1977 | 3.77 | .67 |
| 1992 | 3.51 | .69 |
| 1993 | 3.97 | .77 |

But expansion means a lot of former minor league hitters *and* pitchers now wearing major league uniforms. Does the standard deviation for batting average qualifiers go up also? Here are the figures:

### Batting Average Qualifiers—Pre- and During Expansion

| Year | Mean BA | Standard Deviation |
|------|---------|--------------------|
| 1960 | .275 | .023 |
| 1961 | .281 | .028 |
| 1962 | .280 | .025 |

| 1968 | .262 | .028 |
|------|------|------|
| 1969 | .272 | .027 |
| 1976 | .272 | .029 |
| 1977 | .281 | .025 |
| 1992 | .274 | .027 |
| 1993 | .281 | .027 |

In the five previous expansions, the standard deviation among batting average qualifiers increased only once, when the AL expanded in 1961. Thus the numbers indicate that expansion causes pitching talent to thin out much more than hitting talent. Why would that be? As David Pinto, who prepared this data, wrote four years ago, "the simplest explanation supported by the data is that it is easier to find hitters than pitchers." Indeed, the standard deviations among batting title qualifiers range from about eight to 10 percent of the mean; ERA standard deviations are about twice that high (15-20 percent), a sign that the pitching talent is spread thinner. When the leagues expand, the spread between the best and worst pitchers gets even greater, and the hitters take advantage.

What will this mean in 1998, and in the next few years? Four years ago, we wrote:

> One last point: it's not going to get better anytime soon. The Census Bureau reports that in 1980, there were 30.5 million people in [the 18-to-24] age group, while in 1990 there were only 26.7 million, about one-sixth less. The Census Bureau does not expect a return to the 1980 level until 2010; even though baseball could heighten the search for talent in places like Latin America, Australia or Japan, we still figure to have at least another 15 years of higher diversity among players. Couple this with the likely expansion to 32 teams by the end of the century, and we could possibly be in for a decade of offense unmatched since the 1930s.

Our speculation that major league teams might "heighten the search for talent in places like Latin America, Australia or Japan" turned out to be right on the money, and so did our final prediction: "we could possibly be in for a decade of offense unmatched since the 1930s."

Barring something unforeseen—like rules changes to help the pitchers or perhaps a return to enforcing the rulebook strike zone—the next few years figure to be better than ever for the hitters. 1998 could finally see the fall of Maris' record, a .400 hitter, who knows? This should be some year, unless you're a pitcher.

— Don Zminda

## Is This Era Second(ary) to None?

We are living in the Golden Age of secondary average. Generations from now, our grandchildren may very well look back on this era with the same sense of wonder and awe that we reserve for the prolific stolen-base totals of the early 1900s or the remarkable power-pitching numbers of the mid-'60s. To refresh your memory, secondary average was introduced by Bill James in his *1986 Baseball Abstract*. It measures the offensive contributions that batting average doesn't—power, speed and plate discipline:

**Secondary Average** = (Total Bases - Hits + BB + SB - CS) / AB

Baseball's combined secondary average was .264 in 1997, meaning that four of the five highest marks in modern baseball history have occurred since 1994. Before '94, it had reached .250 on only two other occasions—1950 (.258) and 1987 (.267). And remember, caught-stealing totals weren't universally available prior to 1951, so the actual secondary average in 1950 was probably three or four points lower. In 1976, the majors' secondary average was just .211, and it stood at .229 as recently as '92. But then came expansion, and secondary average hasn't been below .246 since. Barry Bonds has helped lead the recent surge in secondary average. Last year he clubbed 40 homers, stole 37 bases and drew an eye-popping 145 walks. No wonder he led the majors with a secondary average of .620:

### Best Secondary Average—1997

| Player, Team | Avg |
|---|---|
| Barry Bonds, SF | .620 |
| Jeff Bagwell, Hou | .567 |
| Mark McGwire, Oak/StL | .565 |
| Larry Walker, Col | .535 |
| Jim Thome, Cle | .534 |
| Ray Lankford, StL | .516 |
| Ken Griffey Jr., Sea | .485 |
| Jay Buhner, Sea | .483 |
| Gary Sheffield, Fla | .477 |
| Todd Hundley, Mets | .472 |
| **MLB Average** | **.264** |

(minimum 250 PA)

With last year's performance, Bonds returned to the top spot he occupied every season between 1991 and 1993. In the three years between '94 and '96, his secondary average never fell below .561. His career average now stands at a robust .514—only two other legends can claim higher marks. There are also two other contemporaries who crack history's top five:

### Best Secondary Average—Career

| Player | Avg |
| --- | --- |
| Babe Ruth | .593 |
| Ted Williams | .552 |
| Barry Bonds | .514 |
| Frank Thomas | .501 |
| Mark McGwire | .489 |
| (minimum 1,500 PA) | |

If you want more evidence of the secondary nature of the current era, consider the Seattle Mariners. Led by Griffey (.485), Buhner (.483) and Edgar Martinez (.439), the Mariners in 1997 produced a *team* secondary average of .3244, edging the 1994 Tigers (.3241) for the best mark since 1900. Not everyone is getting with the program, however. The following group of players compiled the *lowest* secondary averages of 1997:

### Worst Secondary Average—1997

| Player, Team | Avg |
| --- | --- |
| Mariano Duncan, Yanks-Tor | .094 |
| Deivi Cruz, Det | .099 |
| Rey Ordonez, Mets | .107 |
| Gary DiSarcina, Ana | .109 |
| Rey Sanchez, Cubs-Yanks | .120 |
| Fernando Vina, Mil | .127 |
| Kirt Manwaring, Col | .128 |
| Joe Girardi, Yanks | .133 |
| Jorge Fabregas, Ana-WSox | .133 |
| Wilton Guerrero, LA | .137 |
| (minimum 250 PA) | |

We can cut these players *some* slack, since they all played demanding defensive positions. But you might wonder at what point their defense no longer compensates for meager offensive contributions. Mariano Duncan isn't going to win any Gold Gloves, and last year he hit an empty .236—no power, few stolen bases, and wretched strike-zone judgment. We know guys like Deivi Cruz and Rey Ordonez have lustrous defensive reputations. They'll need to keep polishing them, though, in order to justify retaining their spots in the lineup. After all, they're swimming against the tide of history.

—Jim Henzler

A more complete listing for this category can be found on page 237.

# Did the Rockies Show the Most "Heart" in 1997?

They fill the stadiums, send chills down the spines of even the most battle-hardened hurlers, cost opposing managers their jobs and sign the multi-million dollar contracts. *They* are the hitters who make their homes in the "heart" of the order, and many are among the best in the game. Important? You betcha'. Last season, the heart of baseball's order—players hitting in the 3, 4 or 5 positions—accounted for 50.1 percent (2,323 of 4,640) of all home runs hit and 43.5 percent (8,907 of 20,468) of all runs driven in. The following illustration shows which hearts beat the fastest in 1997:

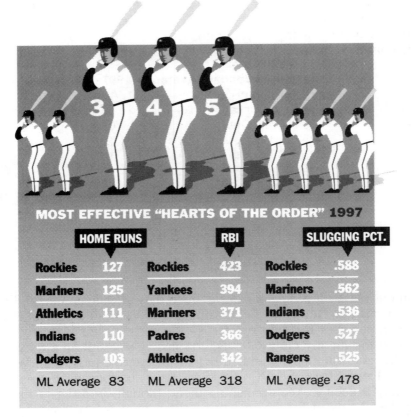

**MOST EFFECTIVE "HEARTS OF THE ORDER" 1997**

| HOME RUNS | | RBI | | SLUGGING PCT. | |
|---|---|---|---|---|---|
| Rockies | 127 | Rockies | 423 | Rockies | .588 |
| Mariners | 125 | Yankees | 394 | Mariners | .562 |
| Athletics | 111 | Mariners | 371 | Indians | .536 |
| Indians | 110 | Padres | 366 | Dodgers | .527 |
| Dodgers | 103 | Athletics | 342 | Rangers | .525 |
| ML Average | 83 | ML Average | 318 | ML Average | .478 |

Vital? Not necessarily. The Florida Marlins went to the World Series in 1997 with a heart of the order that ranked near the bottom in home runs,

RBI and slugging percentage. Still, you wouldn't want to have to win year-in and year-out with a weak heart. . . sooner or later the stress and strain on the pitching staff and defense would cause a collapse. Which hearts were the strongest? Here are our choices for the top five tickers of '97:

**1. Rockies.** Sorry, but we could no longer justify docking the trio of Larry Walker, Andres Galarraga and Dante Bichette for playing in Coors Field. Both Walker and Galarraga hit more homers *away* from the mile-high altitude last year, and Walker slugged his way to the National League MVP Award. The Rockies' .588 slugging percentage was the best figure by any heart this decade.

**2. Mariners.** The M's lost their top billing after back-to-back first-place finishes in this category. They, too, had the benefit of an MVP pumping life into the offense, but Ken Griffey Jr. had plenty of assistance from Edgar Martinez and Jay Buhner. Junior finished with the ninth-best single-season slugging percentage (.646) of all-time among hitters with at least 600 at-bats.

**3. Indians.** Goodbye, Albert Belle. Hello, Matt Williams and David Justice. Cleveland underwent a major heart transplant last year and came through the surgery with flying colors. The heart of the Indians' order produced *more* homers and a *higher* slugging percentage without Belle in '97 than it did with him in '96.

**4. Athletics.** The return of "Bash Brother" Jose Canseco wasn't exactly a triumphant one, but Mark McGwire more than compensated for Jose's sporadic body and bat. So, too, did Matt Stairs, who socked 17 homers from the No. 3 and 4 slots in the order. With McGwire, Canseco and Geronimo Berroa all gone, Oakland's heart may be up for a bypass in '98.

**5. Dodgers.** Only the hearts of the Rockies and Mariners produced more total bases than did the Dodgers' middle men (1,007). Mike Piazza, Eric Karros and Raul Mondesi put up AL-like offensive totals while playing half their games in one of the toughest hitters' parks in the NL.

As for the quietest heart of 1997, the Twins, Brewers and Phillies each made strong cases for needing a pacemaker. Minnesota gets the nod thanks to a complete absence of power; the Twins' heart hit just 44 home runs and slugged a paltry .413. No other heart hit fewer than 60 longballs. Even an entire *staff* of Brad Radkes would have had a tough time keeping Minnesota off the respirator with that kind of production.

—Tony Nistler

A more complete listing for this category can be found on page 238.

## Who Are the Real RBI Kings?

As if you needed any more proof that Ken Griffey Jr. was the Most Valuable Player in the American League last year, if not in all of baseball, we offer yet another exhibit of his extraordinary 1997 campaign. Not only did Junior lead the major leagues in RBI with 147, he also led the pack in making the most of each and every RBI opportunity. What do we mean by that? No other player in the bigs turned a greater percentage of his "RBI available" into actual RBI.

After some tinkering and some help from reader Bill Penn a few years ago, "RBI available" has come to be defined here as the number of RBI a hitter would accumulate if he homered every single time he stepped to the plate. Any at-bat with the bases loaded counts as four RBI available; a bases-empty at-bat counts as one. Simple. . . but we *do* throw in one curve. If a batter comes to the plate with men on base and draws a walk, is hit by a pitch or reaches first due to catcher's interference, we don't charge him with any RBI available for that at-bat *except* if one of those runners score. Why penalize a hitter for getting on base without using up an out?

When we put this concept into practice for the 1997 season, Griffey was clearly King Ken:

### Most RBI per Opportunity—1997

| Player, Team | RBI Available | RBI | Pct |
|---|---|---|---|
| Ken Griffey Jr., Sea | 999 | 147 | 14.7 |
| Frank Thomas, WSox | 889 | 125 | 14.1 |
| Jeff Bagwell, Hou | 961 | 135 | 14.1 |
| Juan Gonzalez, Tex | 952 | 131 | 13.8 |
| Mike Piazza, LA | 903 | 124 | 13.7 |
| Larry Walker, Col | 947 | 130 | 13.7 |
| Mark McGwire, Oak/StL | 902 | 123 | 13.6 |
| Andres Galarraga, Col | 1,043 | 140 | 13.4 |
| Ray Lankford, StL | 749 | 98 | 13.1 |
| Tino Martinez, Yanks | 1,089 | 141 | 13.0 |

(minimum 350 RBI available)

Not only did Junior drive in more runs than Andres Galarraga and Tino Martinez—the No. 2 and 3 RBI men in the major leagues—but he also did so with fewer opportunities available to him. Frank Thomas and Jeff Bagwell deserve accolades for their production; Thomas may well have led the league in RBI if not for the inconsistency at the top of the Chicago batting order last season, while Bagwell finished slightly ahead of both Mike Piazza and Larry Walker—the two players he finished *behind* in the National League MVP vote. And after wearing the crown of true RBI king in both 1995 and '96, Mark McGwire fell to seventh last year, but he and Juan Gonzalez share the distinction of being the only two players to finish in the top 10 in each of the last three seasons.

The other end of the spectrum always proves enlightening as well. Every year we list 10 players who *should* have posted bigger RBI totals given their RBI available and their position in the batting order. Here are our "underachievers" for 1997, each of whom spent most of the season hitting in the third through six spots in the order *and* had at least 800 RBI available:

### RBI "Underachievers"—1997

| Player, Team | RBI Available | RBI | Pct |
| --- | --- | --- | --- |
| Shawon Dunston, Cubs/Pit | 804 | 57 | 7.1 |
| Luis Gonzalez, Hou | 938 | 68 | 7.3 |
| Wil Cordero, Bos | 940 | 72 | 7.7 |
| Reggie Jefferson, Bos | 842 | 67 | 8.0 |
| Gary Gaetti, StL | 850 | 69 | 8.1 |
| Cal Ripken, Bal | 1,015 | 84 | 8.3 |
| Garret Anderson, Ana | 1,094 | 92 | 8.4 |
| Derek Bell, Hou | 843 | 71 | 8.4 |
| Bernard Gilkey, Mets | 913 | 78 | 8.5 |
| Dave Nilsson, Mil | 938 | 81 | 8.6 |

(minimum 800 RBI available)

Shawon Dunston's triumphant return to the North Siders in Chicago was short-lived, though he did pick up his production considerably when he moved on to Pittsburgh at the end of August. Both Luis Gonzalez and Derek Bell failed to shore up the Astros' cleanup spot, though in all fairness both probably shouldn't have been asked to hit No. 4 in the first place. The Red Sox were certainly hurt by the lack of production from Wil Cordero and Reggie Jefferson, and at least one of them won't be playing his home games in Boston in '98.

—Tony Nistler

A more complete listing for this category can be found on page 239.

### Who Went to the Moon—And Beyond—in 1997?

"Hey, Mark McGwire, can you top this?"

That's what Colorado's Andres Galarraga seemed to be saying when, on May 31 of last year, he connected for a mammoth, 530-foot homer off Florida's Kevin Brown, a moon shot that landed in a remote section of the upper deck in Florida's Pro Player Stadium. Could McGwire—he of the five 450-foot homers in 1996—match or top the Big Cat's big blast?

Less than a month later, McGwire delivered the answer: a resounding "yes!" On June 24, he blasted a 540-foot homer off a Seattle lefthander whom you might have heard something about—Randy Johnson. McGwire's shot stood up as the longest homer of 1997, and McGwire and Galarraga actually finished the season with the *six* longest homers in the majors:

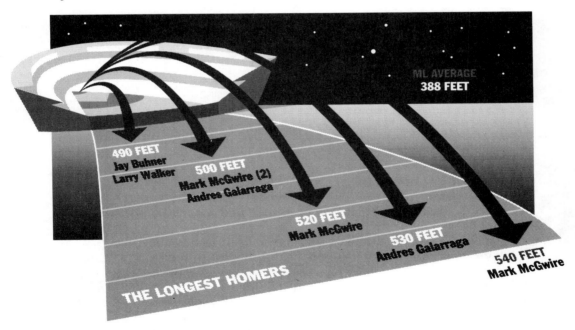

ML AVERAGE
**388 FEET**

**490 FEET**
Jay Buhner
Larry Walker

**500 FEET**
Mark McGwire (2)
Andres Galarraga

**520 FEET**
Mark McGwire

**530 FEET**
Andres Galarraga

**540 FEET**
Mark McGwire

THE LONGEST HOMERS

Apparently, when you have seasons as dominant as McGwire and Galarraga did in 1997, it doesn't matter *what pitcher* you face. McGwire hit his moon shot off Johnson, the 1995 American League Cy Young winner and a 20-game winner in '97. Galarraga victimized Brown, who simply won the 1996 NL ERA title, then added 16 wins and a no-hitter last year.

McGwire's 520-foot blast, MLB's third-longest last year, came against another pretty decent hurler, the Dodgers' Ramon Martinez.

Surprised that Allen Watson *isn't* among the pitchers who gave up mammoth homers last year? If you read last year's *Scoreboard*, you might remember that Watson suffered the ignominy of surrendering the two longest home runs of 1996. But Watson made a comeback of sorts in '97: the longest homer he allowed, by Seattle's Jay Buhner, traveled "only" 490 feet, tied for the league's seventh-longest moon shot.

Back to McGwire: in last year's essay, we looked forward to McGwire's August debut at that renowned home-run park, Colorado's Coors Field. Well, McGwire's July trade to the Cardinals delayed his Coors Field appearance by a week, but the wait was worth it. No, he didn't connect for a 500-footer in Denver, but fans of the moon shot couldn't complain: in the Cards' four-game series at Coors, McGwire had 16 at-bats and hit four home runs—each of them traveling at least 420 feet. McGwire made his Coors debut on September 5, and on the second pitch he had ever seen in the stadium, sent a Frank Castillo offering 480 feet, tied for 1997's ninth-longest blast. For good measure, he added a 460-footer off Castillo four innings later. We can hardly wait for St. Louis' return to Coors this April 7, 8 and 9. . .

One more note on McGwire, a tidbit that just has to be researched when a moon shot artist has a season like he did. All told, McGwire's 58 homers traveled a total of 24,340 feet, which computes to a mind-boggling 4.61 miles. We've heard of hitting the ball "a country mile," but 4.61 miles of home runs? Heck, that's almost four times as far as Barry Sanders ran in 1997!

What role did Coors Field play in the longest homers of 1997? Well, the three longest blasts of last season were hit in other parks, but of the 44 moon shots of at least 460 feet, 12 of them—the most in any stadium—were launched on Blake Street. National League MVP Larry Walker had three of the 12 Coors Field bombs, while McGwire had a pair. Meanwhile, Seattle's Kingdome, site of McGwire's 540-foot rocket, finished second to Coors with seven blasts of at least 460 feet. In case you're wondering, McGwire's was the only such homer hit against Johnson—in Seattle or anywhere else. Other than McGwire, no one hit a ball as far as 420 feet off the Big Unit last year.

—Ethan D. Cooperson

A more complete listing for this category can be found on page 241.

## Who Puts Their Team Ahead?

For San Francisco second baseman Jeff Kent, production and redemption went hand-in-hand in 1997. If you'll recall, we weren't too forgiving of Kent in this essay in last year's edition of the *Baseball Scoreboard*. Of course, neither the Mets nor the Indians were very forgiving, either, as both clubs sent him packing in 1996. Why were *we* so hard on him? Simple. Not only did Kent fail to drive in runs in general two years ago, but he also failed to drive in "clutch" runs—runs that gave his teams a lead. We've been espousing the virtues of what we call the "go-ahead RBI" for years now, and Kent logged just six of them during the 1996 campaign.

But Kent laughed all the way to the National League West pennant last year, putting all naysayers—including us—in their proper place. After producing just 55 ribbies the previous season, Kent knocked in 121 runs last year, and 33 of those RBI gave the Giants the lead in a given game. That put *him* among some pretty well-known names in 1997:

### Go-Ahead RBI Leaders—1997

| Player, Team | RBI |
| --- | --- |
| Jeff Bagwell, Hou | 46 |
| Ken Griffey Jr., Sea | 38 |
| Frank Thomas, WSox | 36 |
| Travis Fryman, Det | 34 |
| Andres Galarraga, Col | 34 |
| Tony Gwynn, SD | 34 |
| Tino Martinez, Yanks | 34 |
| Larry Walker, Col | 34 |
| Jeff Kent, SF | 33 |
| Mike Piazza, LA | 32 |
| Gary Sheffield, Fla | 32 |

While Kent's performance was perhaps the most surprising, Jeff Bagwell's was clearly the most impressive. Bagwell's 135 *total* RBI placed him behind Ken Griffey Jr., Tino Martinez and Andres Galarraga, but no one could match the 46 times he put Houston ahead. He may have come up empty in the divisional playoffs, but he more than deserved to push both Larry Walker and Mike Piazza for NL MVP honors. Bagwell's name also came up when we looked at the best go-ahead RBI *percentages* for '97. To calculate these, we divide a player's total go-ahead RBI by his "go-ahead opportunities," which we define as go-ahead RBI *plus* the number of times a player strands a go-ahead run in scoring position while using up an out, *except* if he executes a successful sacrifice bunt or ties the game with a sacrifice fly. Without further ado, here's the top 10:

### Best Go-Ahead RBI Percentage—1997

| Player, Team | Opp | RBI | Pct |
|---|---|---|---|
| Tony Gwynn, SD | 55 | 34 | 61.8 |
| Frank Thomas, WSox | 59 | 36 | 61.0 |
| David Justice, Cle | 41 | 25 | 61.0 |
| Shawn Green, Tor | 25 | 15 | 60.0 |
| Nomar Garciaparra, Bos | 45 | 26 | 57.8 |
| Jeff Bagwell, Hou | 80 | 46 | 57.5 |
| J.T. Snow, SF | 35 | 20 | 57.1 |
| Paul O'Neill, Yanks | 48 | 27 | 56.3 |
| Ken Griffey Jr., Sea | 68 | 38 | 55.9 |
| Ken Caminiti, SD | 48 | 26 | 54.2 |
| **MLB Avg** | | | **36.6** |

(minimum 50 total RBI)

Tony Gwynn capped an amazing five-year run by winning his fourth straight batting title. His .372 overall average was impressive enough, but it was nothing compared to his .459 mark with runners in scoring position. Kent may have fallen off this list, but teammate J.T. Snow certainly backed him up. Frank Thomas gave his team the lead again and again when he had the opportunity, but teammate Albert Belle finished with a go-ahead RBI percentage (36.5) that was below the league average. Still, Belle was far from the bottom of this category in 1997:

### Worst Go-Ahead RBI Percentage—1997

| Player, Team | Opp | RBI | Pct |
|---|---|---|---|
| Jose Vizcaino, SF | 39 | 7 | 17.9 |
| Darren Bragg, Bos | 25 | 5 | 20.0 |
| Joe Randa, Pit | 31 | 7 | 22.6 |
| Roberto Kelly, Min/Sea | 21 | 5 | 23.8 |
| Mike Lieberthal, Phi | 39 | 10 | 25.6 |

In the past, the list of trailers has included such names as Jay Bell, John Olerud, Dean Palmer, Todd Hundley, Tino Martinez and one Jeff Kent. Can guys like Bragg and Randa follow in their footsteps and find redemption in '98? Not likely, but then again, we were saying the same thing about Kent last year.

—Tony Nistler

A more complete listing for this category can be found on page 242.

### Who Are the Human Air Conditioners?

In 1998, Chicago Cub fans will find out exactly why they call this "The Windy City."

On your left (left field, that is), we present Henry Rodriguez, swinger-and-misser extraordinaire. In 1996, on his way to a National League-leading 160 Ks, Rodriguez swung and missed 396 times, most in the majors. In 1997, Henry missed 30 games for various reasons, but still ranked third in the NL in Ks (149) and fourth in the majors in swings that missed with 355.

On your right (right field), we present Sammy Sosa, the 1997 National League leader in strikeouts (174) and the major league leader in missed swings with 450. Oddly enough, Sammy also led the majors in missed swings in 1993 and 1995, which means that this year it must be Henry's turn. Welcome to Chicago, Hank, and thanks for cooling us off!

The Cubs, of course, added Rodriguez to their lineup this year *not* to cool off the Wrigley Field faithful with his whiffs, but to find the bleachers with his home runs. Which he can do. Indeed, all the players on the swing-and-miss leaders list hit more than 25 homers last year, including Sosa (36) and Rodriguez (26). Do that enough times, and people won't complain very much about your whiffs.

Then again, maybe they should. Consider that Mike Piazza hit 40 home runs last year, yet he swung and missed only 196 times. Barry Bonds also had 40 homers, yet he missed on only 170 swings all year. Most amazing of all was Frank Thomas, who hit 35 home runs but swung and missed only 127 times all season. Can you spell "complete hitter"?

Thomas missed on only 13.3 percent of his 957 swings last year, an amazing percentage for a power hitter. The other side of the coin is represented by the players with the *highest* percentage of missed swings:

| Batter, Team | Swings | Missed | Pct |
|---|---|---|---|
| **Highest Percentage of Swings that Missed—1997** | | | |
| Melvin Nieves, Det | 777 | 320 | 41.2 |
| Archi Cianfrocco, SD | 483 | 171 | 35.4 |
| Ernie Young, Oak | 375 | 129 | 34.4 |
| Jay Buhner, Sea | 1056 | 359 | 34.0 |
| Rick Wilkins, SF/Sea | 412 | 139 | 33.7 |
| Henry Rodriguez, Mon | 1068 | 355 | 33.2 |
| Yamil Benitez, KC | 383 | 125 | 32.6 |
| Reggie Sanders, Cin | 615 | 197 | 32.0 |
| Sammy Sosa, Cubs | 1419 | 450 | 31.7 |
| Jon Nunnally, KC/Cin | 510 | 161 | 31.6 |
| **MLB Average** | | | **20.4** |

(minimum 350 Swings)

Rodriguez and Sosa make this list as well, which includes some genuine stars like Jay Buhner along with struggling players like Ernie Young (.223 average last year) and Melvin Nieves (.228). Nieves, who fanned 157 times in only 359 at-bats last year, would surely have shattered the single-season record for Ks in a season with a little more playing time. Think the Cubs would be interested in him?

— Don Zminda

A more complete listing for this category can be found on page 243.

## Who's the Best Bunter?

Once upon a time, if you played in the major leagues, you knew how to bunt. Even the big-name sluggers might be called upon to lay down a sacrifice from time to time. As a case in point, we present the Astros' Jimmy Wynn, who in 1967 and '68 homered a total of 63 times, drove in 174 runs—and also laid down 11 sacrifice hits.

Nowadays, though, players just don't bunt as often, or, some would say, as successfully as their predecessors. Still we make sure, each year, to acknowledge the best bunters in the majors, both in sacrificing and in bunting for base hits. Without further ado, here are 1997's leaders in sacrifice bunt percentage:

### Top Sacrifice Bunt Percentage—1997

| Bunter, Team | SH | Att | Pct |
|---|---|---|---|
| Omar Vizquel, Cle | 16 | 16 | 1.000 |
| Kevin Foster, Cubs | 11 | 11 | 1.000 |
| Chan Ho Park, LA | 11 | 11 | 1.000 |
| Jeff Reboulet, Bal | 11 | 11 | 1.000 |
| Eric Young, Col/LA | 10 | 10 | 1.000 |
| Edgar Renteria, Fla | 19 | 20 | .950 |
| Deivi Cruz, Det | 14 | 15 | .933 |
| Rey Ordonez, Mets | 14 | 15 | .933 |
| Mickey Morandini, Phi | 12 | 13 | .923 |
| Mark Leiter, Phi | 10 | 11 | .909 |
| **MLB Average** | | | **.780** |

(minimum 10 attempts)

The Tribe's Omar Vizquel certainly fits most fans' description of a "good little ballplayer," and his sacrifice bunting prowess helps him fit the bill. Vizquel was perfect in 16 sacrifice bunt attempts, giving him the most sac hits without a failed attempt since John Valentin also went 16-for-16 back in 1993. And Vizquel's 1997 season is perhaps more impressive, as we raised the standards for perfection beginning with last year's *Scoreboard*. Now, if a hitter fouls off two bunt attempts and fails to sacrifice, he is charged with a failed sac attempt. Vizquel had no such failed attempts last year; he was *truly* a perfect sacrifice bunter.

Special mention should be made of Florida's Edgar Renteria, who topped the majors with 19 sac hits, failing to sacrifice only once. If not for a July 23 at-bat against Cincinnati's Mike Morgan, when Renteria fouled off two bunts before bunting through a 1-2 pitch, we might well be talking about one of the best sacrifice bunting seasons in a long time.

Interestingly, our top 10 list in bunts for base hits produces 10 different names than the ones on the sacrifice bunting leader board. It shouldn't be a shock to baseball fans to see Otis Nixon with the most base hit bunts:

**TOP BASE-HIT BUNTERS 1997**

| | HITS | ATTEMPTS | PCT. |
|---|---|---|---|
| Otis Nixon | 25 | 51 | .490 |
| Tom Goodwin | 16 | 23 | .696 |
| Kenny Lofton | 15 | 24 | .625 |
| Dave Hollins | 12 | 19 | .632 |
| Deion Sanders | 12 | 26 | .462 |
| Delino DeShields | 11 | 32 | .344 |
| Ray Durham | 10 | 20 | .500 |
| Jose Valentin | 9 | 10 | .900 |
| Wilton Guerrero | 9 | 15 | .600 |
| Tony Womack | 9 | 17 | .529 |
| ML Average | | | .529 |

As the chart shows, Nixon recorded the most bunt hits in the majors—but it took him quite a few tries to do it. In fact, the success rate among the leaders dropped off quite a bit from the previous year. Five of 1996's leaders in bunt hits had success rates of .700 or higher; among last year's leaders, only Jose Valentin—who went 9-for-10 for the second straight season—reached that plateau. Tom Goodwin, who posted 16 bunt singles, was arguably the best base-hit bunter in '97, finishing second in bunt singles and posting a success rate of .696, second among players with at least nine bunt hits.

As for Delino DeShields, we'd suggest that he try a different means of reaching base. It might have made sense for Delino to try 32 bunts for hits in 1996, when his overall on-base percentage was a mere .288. A .344 success rate on bunts wouldn't have looked so bad then. . . but last year, when DeShields had an OBP of .357, he actually fared *worse* when he bunted than when he swung away.

Every year we award the "STATS FlatBat" to the season's best bunter, one who succeeds in both sacrifice bunting *and* bunting for base hits. The finalists for the 1997 honor:

**Tom Goodwin**. He's perennially among the leaders in bunting for base hits, and he may have been the best in baseball in 1997. But Goodwin was a relatively disappointing 11-for-17 in sacrifices last year. Does he perhaps try harder when the bunt stands to help his batting average?

**Wilton Guerrero**. Guerrero tied for seventh in the majors in sacrifices, and tied for eighth in bunt hits. Did the corked bat help his bunting—or did it help lead to his five failed sacrifices?

**Kenny Lofton.** Last year's winner of the FlatBat had another stellar year bunting for base hits. But National League leadoff men aren't asked to sacrifice very often, and Lofton went just 2-for-3 in sac bunt attempts. His return to the American League next year should again give Lofton the chance to show he can handle *both* types of bunts.

**Otis Nixon.** Nixon's numbers were outstanding—though his success rates have dropped off somewhat in recent years. With Brett Butler out of the game, fans of the bunt have to be worried about the future of the craft once the 39-year-old Nixon hangs it up.

**Edgar Renteria**. What else to say? He went 19-for-20 in attempted sacrifices, and 7-for-11 on base hit bunts. Problem is. . .

**Omar Vizquel**. Vizquel matched Renteria's 7-for-11 when bunting for a base hit, and his 16-for-16 was slightly better, in terms of percentage, than Renteria.

The award has to go to Renteria or Vizquel, and Renteria's July 23 failed sacrifice turns out to cost him dearly. In a reversal of the World Series result, Vizquel edges Renteria for the 1997 STATS FlatBat. Kudos to Vizquel, our winner for the second time in five years.

—Ethan D. Cooperson

A more complete listing for this category can be found on page 245.

## How Important Is "Protection"?

We heard it again last spring, after the White Sox signed Albert Belle. "Now Frank Thomas will finally have some protection behind him," a lot of pundits were saying. "The other teams won't want to walk him with Albert hitting behind him. They'll have to pitch to him instead of pitching around him. Watch what kind of year he has."

Thomas *did* have a great year, but his stats were virtually identical to those he posted without Belle in 1996. Actually, his numbers *decreased* a little. In 1996, he hit 40 homers and had a .626 slugging percentage; in '97, he hit 35 homers and slugged .611. Thomas' intentional-walk total *did* drop from 26 in '96 to nine in '97, but his overall walk total remained the same, 109 each year. So it's hard to find any evidence that pitchers were challenging Thomas any more last year, or that having Belle behind him offered any benefit. "But that's because Albert wasn't having a great year," the Protectionists retort. And the argument continues.

Thomas' 1997 experiences, of course, neither prove nor disprove the "protection" theory; you can always find isolated examples that back one argument or another. A better approach is an empirical one which studies the performance of a good number of players. That's what we did in an essay on the protection theory in the 1994 *Scoreboard*. The data we examined back then indicated that a star player gets only a slight benefit from having another star hitting behind him. The data also showed that a superstar like Thomas generally received more substantial benefit from the presence of another superstar hitting right behind him, but not enough to explain an unusually good or bad season.

Would a study of 1997 data yield the same conclusions? We decided to find out. Let's begin with a group of "star" players, defined as anyone with at least 75 runs created in 1997 and 150 runs created for the 1995-97 three-year period. A total of 87 players met these criteria, about three per team. Here's the 1997 data on how these players performed with and without another star hitting behind them:

### Stars With and Without "Protection"—1997

| | PA | AB | HR/PA | BB/PA | Avg | OBP | Slg |
|---|---|---|---|---|---|---|---|
| Overall | 55,350 | 48,177 | .039 | .108 | .293 | .373 | .493 |
| Star Behind | 27,319 | 23,770 | .041 | .109 | .297 | .377 | .505 |
| Star not Behind | 28,031 | 24,407 | .036 | .106 | .289 | .369 | .482 |

(87 players; minimum 75 RC in 1997 and 150 RC in 1995-97)

Star players got slightly more benefit in this study than they did in our original study, which was based on players from the 1993 season. The biggest improvement was in the home-run rate, which was 14 percent higher when a second star was batting behind the first one. Over a 600-plate appearance season, a star player with a second star hitting behind him would hit about three more homers than a star who didn't have such "protection." That's not enough to define the difference between a good season and a great one, but it's a definite benefit.

Overall, star players had an on-base plus slugging percentage of .882 with another star behind them, .866 without them—a production increase of about two percent. Curiously, they walked at a higher rate with another star behind them than they did without them, which is the opposite of what you'd expect. It's also the opposite of what happened in 1993, so it could be a fluke. At any rate, there's nothing in this data to change what we wrote four years ago about protection to star players: "No big deal, in other words—certainly not enough to justify the talk about how 'important' this is to a hitter."

As we did in 1994, we also looked at how superstar players—defined as those with at least 100 runs created in 1997 and 200 RC over the last three seasons—performed with and without other superstars hitting behind them. Only 34 players met these criteria. Here's the data:

### Superstars With and Without "Protection"—1997

|  | PA | AB | HR/PA | BB/PA | Avg | OBP | Slg |
|---|---|---|---|---|---|---|---|
| Overall | 22,283 | 19,056 | .047 | .123 | .310 | .400 | .546 |
| Superstar Behind | 4,548 | 3,922 | .059 | .118 | .324 | .407 | .603 |
| Superstar not Behind | 17,735 | 15,134 | .044 | .124 | .306 | .398 | .531 |

(34 Players; minimum 100 RC in 1997 and 200 RC in 1995-97)

As in 1993, the benefits of having one superstar hitting behind another were more substantial. The home-run rate jumped 34 percent (it was 33 percent in '93), a difference of about nine home runs in a 600-plate appearance season. That's a lot. Slugging percentage was 72 points higher with a superstar offering protection, and OPS jumped 81 points from .929 to 1.010, an increase of nearly nine percent. The walk rate was lower with another superstar hitting next, but the difference was not nearly as great as it was in 1993. It may be that after several years of big home-run totals, pitchers are less reluctant to put a superstar on base with a walk—even with another superstar coming up next.

The Frank Thomas situation notwithstanding, there's no question that having one superstar hitting behind another offers definite benefits to the one coming up first. This makes perfect sense. As we wrote four years ago, "the benefit wouldn't seem to be enough to explain an unusually good or bad season," but it does help, especially in the home-run department. If you've only got one superstar in your lineup, a second one will indeed provide some "protection". . . and usually some additional home runs for the first one.

— Don Zminda

## When Do Home-Run Hitters Reach Their Peaks?

Last spring, I was part of an ongoing debate which raged for several weeks in my America Online column ("The Zee-Man Reports". . . check it out!), in John Hunt's fantasy baseball column in *Baseball Weekly* and on various Internet sites. The subject? The age at which position players usually reach their peak. For years there's been a consensus among sabermetricians that, as a group, position players reach their peak at about age 27, and almost certainly in the 26-28 age group. But some observers felt that modern players tend to peak later than that, and that the actual peak age is now closer to 30. Others thought that age 27 was still right as the peak age for overall offensive performance, but felt that peak age was different for more specialized skills like hitting home runs and stealing bases. These people felt that power hitters tend to peak later, with their best seasons more likely to take place at age 30 or older.

Not all players are home-run hitters, of course, so we decided to limit the study to players who had demonstrated a decent level of power during their careers. Only players whose careers had finished prior to 1997 were considered, and they needed to meet both of these criteria:

1. At least 100 home runs in their careers, *and*

2. At least two seasons with 20 or more homers.

A total of 305 players met both criteria, from Hank Aaron to Richie Zisk. That's a fairly good sample. We looked at the peak-year issue in two different ways. First, we simply noted the age at which each player had his peak home-run season. The peak season was based on highest home-run percentage (HR/AB) in a season in which the player batted at least 400 times. The chart on the following page shows the number of peak seasons at each age.

## PEAK HOME RUN SEASONS

| Age | Number of players | Pct. of total |
|---|---|---|
| 20 | 1 | 0.3% |
| 21 | 0 | 0.0% |
| 22 | 11 | 3.6% |
| 23 | 17 | 5.6% |
| 24 | 15 | 4.9% |
| 25 | 26 | 8.5% |
| 26 | 28 | 9.2% |
| 27 | 39 | 12.8% |
| 28 | 34 | 11.1% |
| 29 | 24 | 7.9% |
| 30 | 22 | 7.2% |
| 31 | 23 | 7.5% |
| 32 | 25 | 8.2% |
| 33 | 11 | 3.6% |
| 34 | 12 | 3.9% |
| 35 | 6 | 2.0% |
| 36 | 4 | 1.3% |
| 37 | 3 | 1.0% |
| 38 | 3 | 1.0% |
| 39 | 1 | 0.3% |

Age 27 wins again with 39 peak seasons out of the 305, followed by age 28 and then age 26. As a group, home-run hitters retain a good deal of their power up through age 32, but this data gives us no reason to think that sluggers reach their peak at a later age than hitters overall do. It's still age 27.

We also looked at the same group of players in a slightly different way. This time we took the 305 players and looked at their entire careers, rather than just their peak seasons. This chart shows the number of players active at each age level, the total number of home runs hit by those players at each age, the average number of homers hit by each player and the percentage of the grand total of 70,730 home runs hit by the group that were hit at each age level:

### Elite Home-Run Hitters

| Age | Players | HR | HR/Player | Pct |
|-----|---------|------|-----------|-----|
| 17 | 2 | 0 | 0 | 0.0 |
| 18 | 8 | 5 | 0.6 | 0.0 |
| 19 | 36 | 100 | 2.8 | 0.1 |
| 20 | 78 | 491 | 6.3 | 0.7 |
| 21 | 130 | 1,037 | 8.0 | 1.5 |
| 22 | 194 | 2,063 | 10.6 | 2.9 |
| 23 | 244 | 3,376 | 13.8 | 4.8 |
| 24 | 266 | 4,322 | 16.2 | 6.1 |
| 25 | 286 | 5,140 | 18.0 | 7.3 |
| 26 | 295 | 5,905 | 20.0 | 8.3 |
| 27 | 291 | 6,223 | 21.4 | 8.8 |
| 28 | 296 | 5,949 | 20.1 | 8.4 |
| 29 | 291 | 5,830 | 20.0 | 8.2 |
| 30 | 289 | 5,465 | 18.9 | 7.7 |
| 31 | 286 | 4,995 | 17.5 | 7.1 |
| 32 | 265 | 4,694 | 17.7 | 6.6 |
| 33 | 243 | 4,047 | 16.7 | 5.7 |
| 34 | 225 | 3,179 | 14.1 | 4.5 |
| 35 | 183 | 2,543 | 13.9 | 3.6 |
| 36 | 149 | 1,925 | 12.9 | 2.7 |
| 37 | 113 | 1,267 | 11.2 | 1.8 |
| 38 | 80 | 839 | 10.5 | 1.2 |
| 39 | 54 | 615 | 11.4 | 0.9 |
| 40+ | 82 | 720 | 8.8 | 1.0 |

(minimum 100 career HR and two 20-HR seasons)

Age 27 wins again, followed by age 28, age 26 and age 29. Again there's good production past age 30, but it can't match the production of ages 26-29.

Overall, this data continues to back the theory that, as a group, hitters reach their peak at age 27. Of necessity this study is based on players who have already retired, and it might be that with modern weight training and conditioning techniques, players of the present and future will push the peak age up a little, or at least extend the age at which sluggers retain most of their value. But until the data proves otherwise, we'll continue to believe that sluggers, like hitters all over, peak at age 27 more than any other age.

— Don Zminda

## How Do Runs Score?

Here's a quick question for you: Do more runs cross home plate as the result of home runs or singles? Another: How many runs are scored on groundouts during an average season? And a third: How many runs are plated as a direct result of errors? We could play this game all day, but you get the picture. This essay, an old *Scoreboard* staple which we're reviving this year, looks into the subject of how runs score—that is, the immediate action that causes the run to cross the plate. Without further ado, here's the data, along with the major league club that led in each category.

### How Runs Scored—1997

| Scoring Play | MLB Total | Team Leader |
|---|---|---|
| Home Run | 7,331 | Mariners 412 |
| Single | 6,235 | Rockies 282 |
| Double | 3,487 | Astros 158 |
| Sacrifice Fly | 1,380 | Yankees 70 |
| Error | 736 | Angels 38 |
| Ground Out | 601 | Reds 30 |
| Triple | 576 | Astros 33 |
| Force Out | 322 | Twins 23 |
| Walk | 313 | Yankees 26 |
| Wild Pitch | 246 | Astros 14 |
| Ground DP | 136 | Indians 10 |
| Passed Ball | 55 | Five with 4 |
| Hit by Pitch | 44 | Four with 4 |
| Sacrifice Hit | 41 | Dodgers 7 |
| 1B on Failed FC | 32 | Reds 4 |
| Balk | 24 | Mets 4 |
| Stolen Base | 19 | Five with 2 |
| Throw | 15 | Three with 2 |
| 1B on K+WP | 4 | Four with 1 |
| Caught Stealing | 2 | Tigers/Pirates 1 |
| 1B on K+PB | 2 | White Sox/Astros 1 |
| Strikeout | 1 | Rockies 1 |
| FC Ground DP | 1 | White Sox 1 |
| Out Advancing | 1 | Red Sox 1 |

Random comments:

1. More runs score as a result of home runs than anything else, followed by singles and doubles. About a third of all runs score as a result of homers, which makes sense because a homer with runners on base scores both the batter *and* the runners. Singles are a reasonably close second; nearly 63 percent of all runs scoring last year came home on either a home run or a single.

2. Triples are such a rarity in baseball these days that more runs scored on errors (736) and groundouts (601) last year than on three-baggers (576).

3. There were a total of 313 walks with the bases loaded last year. That seems like a lot, but in fact only a little over seven percent of all plate appearances with the bases loaded end in a walk. The New York Yankees were the masters of coaxing a walk with the bags juiced, drawing 26 bases on balls in just 220 plate appearances, a walk rate of 11.8 percent. David Pinto points out that for the last several years, the Yanks have had a great knack for drawing a walk with the bases loaded; just think of Wade Boggs walking to force in the winning run in the 10th inning of Game 4 of the 1996 World Series against the Braves. On the other hand the San Diego Padres had 167 PA with the bases loaded last year, and drew only six bases on balls, a walk percentage of just 3.6 percent.

4. Bill Russell loves the squeeze play, and the Dodgers scored seven times on squeeze bunts last year. No other team had more than three successful squeeze plays in 1997, and in fact, more runs scored on bases-loaded passed balls (55) and hit-by-pitches (44) than on squeeze bunts (41).

5. We May Not Be the Big Red Machine, But We Know How to Get Those Productive Outs: The Reds scored 30 runs on groundouts last year, more than any other team.

6. They know how to make a pitcher nervous: The Mets scored four times on balks last year, more than any other club.

— Don Zminda

# IV. QUESTIONS ON PITCHING

## Which Pitchers Have Misleading Earned Run Averages?

In last year's *Baseball Scoreboard*, we unveiled a new performance measure called "Predicted ERA." It was designed to identify pitchers whose earned run averages were misleading. Although ERA is one of the most reliable stats in terms of its predictive value from year to year, every once in a while, it tells us a little white lie. In order to understand how this happens, it's important to understand how the ERA works.

What it's *supposed* to measure is a pitcher's ability to keep runs off the scoreboard. It does this by measuring the end result—the actual number of earned runs that scored. But the number of runs itself is determined by an even more basic pitching skill—the ability to *get hitters out.*

There is a very precise relationship between a pitcher's ability to retire batters (i.e., to keep them off base and prevent them from hitting for power) and his ability to prevent runs from scoring. The former determines the latter.

Every once in a while, a combination of outside influences and random events disrupt this relationship. When this happens, the pitcher's ERA will temporarily stray from where it ought to be, given the pitcher's level of effectiveness in retiring hitters. Here is the key: in these rare cases, we find that the pitcher's ERA eventually will come back into line with his true level of ability. In other words, by independently measuring his ability to retire hitters, we can accurately predict whether his ERA will rise or fall in subsequent seasons.

Bill James' runs created formula demonstrates that the number of runs a team scores is determined by the product of two factors: the team's ability to put runners on base (measured by on-base percentage) and its ability to hit for power (slugging percentage). We reasoned that a pitcher's ability to prevent runs must be tied to the product of his opponent on-base and slugging percentages. Our research confirmed this, and we were able to devise a simple, straightforward method of predicting a pitcher's ERA.

(Opp. on-base pct.) * (Opp. slugging pct.) * 31 = **Predicted ERA**

In last year's *Scoreboard*, we demonstrated that when a pitcher's Predicted ERA differs from his actual ERA by a significant amount, the Predicted ERA is the better predictor of future performance about two-thirds of the time (using minimums of 100 innings pitched for starters and 50 for relievers). We then went on to list pitchers whose ERAs were expected to improve or decline in 1997. We're happy to say that those pitchers performed as we had predicted they would.

The five pitchers that we expected to improve were Bobby Ayala, Jason Grimsley, Jim Bullinger, Brad Clontz and Jim Abbott. Grimsley and Abbott didn't pitch last year, while Clontz came up two innings short of reaching our 50-inning cutoff (if he had pitched two more innings, we would have been able to say that we had anticipated the decline of his ERA). Ayala and Bullinger both made the cut, and in each case, their 1997 ERA was more in line with the previous season's Predicted ERA rather than its actual ERA.

We also listed five pitchers whose ERAs were expected to rise: Jim Poole, John Franco, Scott Radinsky, Mike Mohler and Dave Mlicki. In four of the five cases, the Predicted ERA was a better predictor than actual ERA, making it six-for-seven overall. So, without further ado, let's reveal this year's lists. The following pitchers ought to improve in 1998:

### Predicted ERA Furthest Below Actual ERA—1997

| Player, Team | Difference | ERA | |
| --- | --- | --- | --- |
| | | Actual | Predicted |
| Norm Charlton, Sea | -1.42 | 7.27 | 5.85 |
| Jose Bautista, Det/StL | -1.28 | 6.66 | 5.38 |
| Reggie Harris, Phi | -1.09 | 5.30 | 4.21 |
| Jose Lima, Hou | -0.99 | 5.28 | 4.29 |
| Doug Bochtler, SD | -0.98 | 4.77 | 3.79 |

(minimun 100 IP as starter or 50 IP as reliever)

Charlton and Bautista didn't pitch effectively by any measure, although Lima and Bochtler were more respectable than they might have seemed. Some more prominent pitchers who figure to improve are James Baldwin, Jaime Navarro and Tom Gordon.

These pitchers have been hiding behind their ERAs and soon will be exposed:

### Predicted ERA Furthest Above Actual ERA—1997

| Player, Team | Difference | ERA | |
| --- | --- | --- | --- |
| | | Actual | Predicted |
| Darren Hall, LA | +2.08 | 2.30 | 4.38 |
| Paul Quantrill, Tor | +2.02 | 1.94 | 3.97 |
| Mark Hutton, Fla/Col | +1.79 | 4.48 | 6.27 |
| Tony Fossas, StL | +1.28 | 3.83 | 5.11 |
| Ramon Tatis, Cubs | +1.27 | 5.34 | 6.61 |

Darren Hall was the luckiest of all—the Dodgers rewarded him with a two-year deal during the offseason, something they may come to regret. Quantrill's sub-2.00 ERA is pretty, but the fact that his opponents batted almost .300 against him is a sure sign that his prosperity will be short-lived. Others who lived on borrowed time last year were Jose Mesa, T.J. Mathews, Roger Bailey and Garrett Stephenson.

Of the 10 pitchers above, you can expect that the Predicted ERA will be the better predictor in the majority of cases this year. We're proud to say that it's performed that well in each of the last five years.

—Mat Olkin

A more complete listing for this category can be found on page 246.

## Whose Heater Is Hottest?

It was a great year for *the whiff* in 1997, with Philadelphia's Curt Schilling and Montreal's Pedro Martinez each surpassing the 300 mark in strikeouts. Yes, Schilling and Martinez both throw hard, but this essay *isn't* about pitch velocity—rather, we present the hurlers who fanned the most hitters per nine innings pitched. Martinez and Schilling both make the top 10, but as we see from the chart below, they're a good distance from the top of the list:

|  | Strikeouts | Innings pitched | Strikeouts per 9 innings pitched |
|---|---|---|---|
| Billy Wagner | 106 | 66.1 | 14.4 |
| Armando Benitez | 106 | 73.1 | 13.0 |
| Troy Percival | 72 | 52.0 | 12.5 |
| Randy Johnson | 291 | 213.0 | 12.3 |
| Trevor Hoffman | 111 | 81.1 | 12.3 |
| Russ Springer | 74 | 55.1 | 12.0 |
| Mark Wohlers | 92 | 69.1 | 11.9 |
| Ugueth Urbina | 84 | 64.1 | 11.8 |
| Perdro Martinez | 305 | 241.1 | 11.4 |
| Curt Schilling | 319 | 254.1 | 11.3 |

Minimum 50 innings pitched.

As usually happens, relievers dominate the chart; only three hurlers listed above are starters. But something not-so-usual happened in 1997: Billy Wagner. With his 14.4 Ks per nine innings, Wagner topped all MLB hurlers by a wide margin, and, in fact, posted the highest ratio in baseball history:

### Most Strikeouts per 9 Innings—All-Time

| Pitcher, Team | Year | K | IP | K/9 IP |
|---|---|---|---|---|
| Billy Wagner, Hou | 1997 | 106 | 66.1 | 14.4 |
| Rob Dibble, Cin | 1992 | 110 | 70.1 | 14.1 |
| Rob Dibble, Cin | 1991 | 124 | 82.1 | 13.6 |
| Armando Benitez, Bal | 1997 | 106 | 73.1 | 13.0 |
| Rob Dibble, Cin | 1989 | 141 | 99.0 | 12.8 |

(minimum 50 IP)

Just a minute here. In the history of America's pastime, we've had great strikeout pitchers like Nolan Ryan, Walter Johnson, Bob Gibson and Bob Feller, yet the all-time leader in whiffs per nine innings for a single season is. . . Billy Wagner? What's going on here? Well, look at the other names on the all-time list, Rob Dibble and Armando Benitez. Like Wagner, both are hard-throwing relievers in the modern era of one-batter specialists and one-inning closers. Clearly, the way to rack up overwhelming strikeout-per-nine-inning figures is to come into games and throw as hard as you can to just a handful of hitters. We don't expect the closer's role to change tremendously in the foreseeable future, so it's very possible that Wagner's 14.4 Ks per nine innings might not stay No. 1 for long.

Of course, two of the candidates to smash Wagner's mark are Wagner himself, as well as Benitez, whose 13.0 strikeouts per nine innings last year rank fourth all-time. Wagner is a rare lefthanded closer, and you might think that facing primarily righthanded hitters is a disadvantage for him. Not really. Forty-four percent of the righthanded at-bats against Wagner in '97 resulted in strikeouts, only slightly less than the 47 percent of lefthanded at-bats which ended with strike three. Wagner clearly is an equal-opportunity strikeout artist.

Benitez, meanwhile, will face a slight career change in the future. To date a setup man, Benitez is likely to become the O's closer this year. But his workload won't change that much: Benitez averaged just over one inning per appearance last year, which is normal for a closer. The difference is, now he'll be working the ninth inning instead of the eighth. Benitez will be just 25 next year, and certainly has some strikeouts in his future. Can he top Wagner's mark?

Randy Johnson led all starting pitchers with 12.3 Ks per nine innings last year, and Johnson's No. 4 ranking comes as no surprise: the Big Unit has finished no *lower* than fourth in this category for six straight seasons! While Martinez and Schilling got much of the attention for their 300-

strikeout seasons, consider this: tendinitis in his middle finger kept Johnson to "only" 213.0 innings last year, while Martinez worked 241.1. Prorate Johnson's strikeout rate over 240 innings, and he'd have 328 Ks. Figure Johnson's rate over the 254.1 innings Schilling worked, and he'd have set down a whopping 347 hitters on strikes.

Finally, two other interesting notes on pitchers' strikeouts per nine innings. Notice that the Astros' Russ Springer ranked sixth last year, at 12.0. At the other end of the scale, Anaheim's knuckleballing *Dennis* Springer ranked dead last in the majors, recording just 3.5 Ks per nine innings. No, the two Springers aren't related. . . But two guys who are related are brothers Alan and Andy Benes, and the numbers are almost eerie. Last year, Alan Benes recorded 8.9 strikeouts per nine innings—the same number Andy did. Not likely that one of them is the mailman's son.

—Ethan D. Cooperson

A more complete listing for this category can be found on page 248.

## Who Are the Best-Hitting Pitchers?

There was a time, not that long ago, when baseball had some pitchers who could hit. . . and we mean *hit*. A few examples:

- In 1955, Don Newcombe of the Dodgers hit .359 with seven homers, 23 RBI and a .632 slugging percentage in 117 at-bats.

- In 1965, Don Drysdale of the Dodgers hit .300 with seven homers, 19 RBI and a .508 slugging percentage in 130 at-bats (and don't forget he was playing in the Dodger Stadium of the 1960s, one of the toughest hitters' parks of all time).

- In a five-season stretch from 1964-68, Earl Wilson of the Red Sox and Tigers hit 29 homers and drove in 79 runs in only 444 at-bats. A lot of teams' cleanup hitters couldn't do that.

- In 1971, Catfish Hunter of the A's batted .350 with 12 RBI in 103 at-bats.

- In 1984, Rick Rhoden of the Pirates batted .333 with four homers in 84 at-bats.

ACTIVE PITCHERS WHO CAN HIT CAREER

| | AVG. | SLG |
|---|---|---|
| Allen Watson | .255 | .339 |
| Omar Olivares | .238 | .340 |
| Todd Stottlemyre | .230 | .279 |
| Tommy Greene | .221 | .310 |
| Bill Swift | .214 | .268 |

Minimum 150 career plate appearances.

You don't see performances like that much any more (though Orel Hershiser *did* bat .356 in 1993). Even the best-hitting moundsmen of the day (see chart) are a frustrating bunch for people who enjoy pitchers who can swing the bat. Allen Watson and Omar Olivares, the top two hitters in terms of batting average, were in the American League last year. Tommy Greene and Bill Swift hardly played because of injuries. Todd Stottlemyre of the Cardinals, at least, held up his end of the bargain by hitting .236 with a .333 on-base percentage and .345 slugging percentage. Not Newcombe, but not bad either. Actually, the player who may well be the best-hitting pitcher active today didn't make the leaders list because—this is typical—he's a relief pitcher who's also spent a lot of his career in the American League. But check out Dennis Cook's career batting line:

| | AB | H | 2B | 3B | HR | RBI | Avg | OBP | SLG |
|---|---|---|---|---|---|---|---|---|---|
| Dennis Cook | 105 | 29 | 2 | 1 | 2 | 9 | .276 | .296 | .371 |

In 1997, Cook came to bat only nine times, but had five hits, including a homer. Shades of Terry Forster, the portly reliever of a decade ago who retired with a career batting average of .397 (albeit in only 78 at-bats). Jim Leyland had such faith in Cook's hitting that he used him as a pinch-hitter twice last year. And to top off a perfect story, Cook came through with singles both times, and added a run scored and an RBI.

These moundsmen were the best-hitting pitchers of 1997:

**Best Hitting Pitchers—1997**

| Pitcher, Team | AVG | OBP | SLG | AB | R | H | 2B | 3B | HR | RBI | BB | SO |
|---|---|---|---|---|---|---|---|---|---|---|---|---|
| Armando Reynoso, Mets | .241 | .281 | .345 | 29 | 3 | 7 | 0 | 0 | 1 | 3 | 2 | 15 |
| Todd Stottlemyre, StL | .236 | .333 | .345 | 55 | 6 | 13 | 4 | 1 | 0 | 4 | 8 | 13 |
| John Smoltz, Atl | .228 | .307 | .266 | 79 | 10 | 18 | 3 | 0 | 0 | 4 | 9 | 22 |
| Tom Glavine, Atl | .222 | .310 | .222 | 63 | 6 | 14 | 0 | 0 | 0 | 7 | 7 | 13 |
| Andy Benes, StL | .218 | .246 | .255 | 55 | 4 | 12 | 2 | 0 | 0 | 5 | 1 | 14 |
| John Thomson, Col | .213 | .245 | .213 | 47 | 2 | 10 | 0 | 0 | 0 | 5 | 2 | 23 |
| Roger Bailey, Col | .210 | .234 | .226 | 62 | 9 | 13 | 1 | 0 | 0 | 2 | 2 | 15 |
| Jim Bullinger, Mon | .209 | .209 | .302 | 43 | 2 | 9 | 1 | 0 | 1 | 2 | 0 | 15 |
| Matt Morris, Stl | .205 | .256 | .233 | 73 | 4 | 15 | 2 | 0 | 0 | 6 | 5 | 36 |
| Dave Burba, Cin | .196 | .245 | .196 | 46 | 2 | 9 | 0 | 0 | 0 | 2 | 1 | 18 |

(minimum 30 PA in 1997)

Atlanta pitchers have a reputation for helping themselves with the bat, with good reason. John Smoltz and Tom Glavine not only hit for respectable averages, but drew 16 walks between them. Glavine added 17 sacrifice hits, the second-highest total in the majors, and Smoltz even stole a base!

— Don Zminda

A more complete listing for this category can be found on page 250.

## Which Starters Combine Quality With Quantity?

How do you determine who's the most consistent starting pitcher in baseball? Do you look at victory totals? Or does ERA truly tell the tale? Perhaps neither statistic is the best measure of starters' consistency. We like to consider starting pitchers' *quality start percentage*, or the percentage of their starts in which they work at least six innings while allowing no more than three earned runs. In essence, how frequently does the pitcher toss at least a *decent* game? Here are 1997's leaders:

| Highest Percentage Of Quality Starts—1997 | | | |
|---|---|---|---|
| Pitcher, Team | GS | QS | Pct |
| Kevin Brown, Fla | 33 | 27 | 81.8 |
| Greg Maddux, Atl | 33 | 27 | 81.8 |
| Pedro Martinez, Mon | 31 | 25 | 80.6 |
| Denny Neagle, Atl | 34 | 27 | 79.4 |
| Randy Johnson, Sea | 29 | 23 | 79.3 |
| Tom Glavine, Atl | 33 | 26 | 78.8 |
| Justin Thompson, Det | 32 | 25 | 78.1 |
| Andy Benes, StL | 26 | 20 | 76.9 |
| Roger Clemens, Tor | 34 | 26 | 76.5 |
| Darryl Kile, Hou | 34 | 26 | 76.5 |
| **MLB Average** | | | **49.4** |
| (minimum 20 GS) | | | |

So you thought 1997 was Greg Maddux' second consecutive off year? Apparently not. OK, Maddux didn't win the Cy Young, but his QS percentage of 81.8 was his highest since 1994, and tied Kevin Brown for the major league lead. Maddux, Brown and Pedro Martinez all threw quality starts in better than 80 percent of their starts; in the last three years, no other pitcher who made at least 20 starts reached that plateau.

Without question, the list above includes many of the names we'd expect to see. We've got both '97 Cy Young winners in Martinez and Roger Clemens, 20-game winners Denny Neagle and Randy Johnson, along with 19-game winners in Maddux and Darryl Kile. But what of Detroit's Justin Thompson? The 25-year-old lefty didn't get a single Cy Young vote, but he was awfully impressive in his first full year as a starter, winning 15 games and ranking fifth in the American League with a 3.02 ERA. Between late April and mid-June, Thompson enjoyed a string of 10 consecutive quality starts; he closed the season with 12 QS in 13 outings. And check this out for consistency: in his 32 starts, Thompson pitched at least six innings 29 times, and at least seven innings on 21 different occasions. If Thompson can just stay healthy, the Tigers should have themselves a workhorse—and an effective one—for the foreseeable future.

With Maddux tying for first in QS percentage, and Neagle and Tom Glavine ranking fourth and sixth, respectively, the Atlanta Braves are well represented on our list. But wait, there's more: Atlanta's John Smoltz just missed making the list, ranking 15th in the majors with a percentage of 71.4. Put it all together, and Braves starters had 114 quality starts in 162 games, a QS percentage of 70.4. Amazingly, only the top 16 pitchers in quality-start percentage could top Atlanta's *staff* percentage. As the years go on, we keep finding new ways of saluting these Atlanta hurlers.

Of course, the Braves' dominance on the hill starts with Maddux, and his quality-start numbers over the past five years illustrate his excellence. Not only does Maddux have the best QS percentage, but he's practically in a league all his own:

### Highest Percentage Of Quality Starts—1993-97

| Pitcher | GS | QS | Pct |
|---|---|---|---|
| Greg Maddux | 157 | 126 | 80.3 |
| Randy Johnson | 124 | 90 | 72.6 |
| Tom Glavine | 159 | 108 | 67.9 |
| Curt Schilling | 125 | 83 | 66.4 |
| David Cone | 127 | 84 | 66.1 |
| Kevin Brown | 150 | 98 | 65.3 |
| Denny Neagle | 129 | 84 | 65.1 |
| Kevin Appier | 154 | 98 | 63.6 |
| Roger Clemens | 144 | 91 | 63.2 |
| Andy Benes | 150 | 94 | 62.7 |
| Mike Mussina | 150 | 94 | 62.7 |

(minimum 100 GS)

Maddux gets it done start after start—and year after year, too. He has six straight top-10 finishes in QS percentage—most impressive when you consider that Kevin Brown is the only other hurler to rank in the top 10 in each of the last *two years*. It's high time we started associating monikers like "Meal Ticket" and "Automatic" with the Braves' righty.

—Ethan D. Cooperson

A more complete listing for this category can be found on page 252.

## How Costly Is a Blown Save?

In 1997, major league clubs recorded 1,139 saves in 1,706 opportunities, a success rate of 66.8 percent. This suggests that a late-inning lead is a precarious thing, and that a top closer should be worth his weight in gold. Yet if you've studied the essays in this book over the years, you know very well that:

a) A lot of blown saves occur not in the ninth inning, but much earlier.

b) Teams often blow a save opportunity but win the game anyway.

How often do major league teams blow saves—especially late in a contest—yet win the game anyway? This chart, which is an update of a study we first did in the 1993 *Scoreboard*, shows the 1997 team won-lost record, by inning, in games in which a save opportunity was blown:

| | W-L in Games with Blown Saves—1997 | | |
|---|---|---|---|
| **Inning** | **AL** | **NL** | **MLB** |
| 6 | 14-24 (.368) | 7-22 (.241) | 21-46 (.313) |
| 7 | 31-52 (.373) | 28-36 (.438) | 59-88 (.401) |
| 8 | 25-64 (.281) | 35-61 (.365) | 60-125 (.324) |
| 9 | 29-48 (.377) | 29-50 (.367) | 58-98 (.372) |
| 10+ | 2-4 (.333) | 2-5 (.286) | 4-9 (.308) |
| | **101-192 (.345)** | **101-174 (.367)** | **202-366 (.356)** |

As you can see, a blown save is hard to come back from, but not necessarily fatal. Major league teams won over one-third of the games in which they had a blown save last year. The winning percentage in games with ninth-inning blown saves was even higher at .372. When we did this study five years ago with results based on the 1992 season, the winning percentage in games with a ninth-inning blown save was only .260. The difference? Runs were more plentiful in 1997 (9.5 runs per game, on average) than they were in 1992 (8.2). It's easier to recover from a blown save— and easier to *blow* a save, for that matter—in an era of high-powered offense. Nonetheless, a blown save remains very costly, and when your bullpen blows the lead, you're usually going to lose the game.

Here are the team won-lost records for games with a ninth-inning blown save last year:

## W-L in Games with 9th-Inning Blown Saves—1997

| American League | W-L | National League | W-L |
|---|---|---|---|
| Anaheim | 0-5 | Atlanta | 1-3 |
| Baltimore | 0-1 | Chicago | 0-9 |
| Boston | 2-4 | Cincinnati | 4-2 |
| Chicago | 3-1 | Colorado | 3-5 |
| Cleveland | 1-3 | Florida | 4-4 |
| Detroit | 1-3 | Houston | 1-2 |
| Kansas City | 2-2 | Los Angeles | 4-5 |
| Milwaukee | 0-3 | Montreal | 0-4 |
| Minnesota | 3-3 | New York | 3-2 |
| New York | 3-6 | Philadelphia | 2-2 |
| Oakland | 5-3 | Pittsburgh | 2-2 |
| Seattle | 4-8 | San Diego | 2-1 |
| Texas | 2-2 | San Francisco | 3-3 |
| Toronto | 3-4 | St. Louis | 0-6 |

The Seattle Mariners, whose bullpen was so shaky that they traded top hitting prospect Jose Cruz Jr. in order to get some midseason relief help, had 12 blown saves in the ninth inning last year—more than any other team, by far. Yet the Mariner offense was so strong that the M's came back to win four of the 12 games. The Chicago Cubs weren't so resilient. The Cubbies had nine blown saves in the ninth inning, and they lost all nine games.

In actuality, the Cub bullpen last year, while not great, was probably not as bad as the team's top brass seemed to think. The Cubs had the same number of ninth-inning blown saves as the playoff-bound New York Yankees, who had Mariano Rivera closing games, and only one more than the World Champion Florida Marlins, who had the highly regarded Robb Nen. But because Cub hitters couldn't bail out their bullpen the way the Yankee and Marlin hitters bailed out their pens, the Cub front office may have overestimated the degree of their closer problem. As a result, they went out and signed Rod Beck, whose old club, the Giants, had six blown saves in the ninth inning last year. . . not much better than the Cubs.

The "Bullpen of the Year" award for 1997 has to go to the Baltimore Orioles—only 10 blown saves all year, just one of them in the ninth inning. The O's pen may not be so golden this year, since ace closer Randy Myers is now wearing a Toronto Blue Jay uniform.

— Don Zminda

A more complete listing for this category can be found on page 253.

## Who Gets the "Red Barrett Trophy"?

Each season, we award the "Red Barrett Trophy" to the pitcher who throws the fewest pitches in a nine-inning complete game. The award is named after Boston Braves pitcher Red Barrett, who reportedly needed only 58 pitches to complete a game back in 1944.

By the time Greg Maddux retires, the award may bear his name instead. Maddux sets the standard for efficiency among modern hurlers. Last year, he finished eighth in the National League in innings pitched while surpassing the 100-pitch mark only six times all season. His exceptional control resulted in only 14 unintentional walks in 232.2 innings, the lowest unintentional walk rate on record since IBB were first recorded in 1955. That broke his own record from the year before, when he'd issued 17 unintentional walks in 245 frames.

When the Cubs faced Maddux on July 22, they were instructed by manager Jim Riggleman to go after Maddux early in the count. It was a reasonable approach, given Maddux' penchant for throwing strikes and getting ahead in the count, but it simply didn't work. Maddux beat them 4-1, and needed only 78 pitches to do so. No other pitcher used so few pitches to complete a game last year:

### Fewest Pitches in a Nine-Inning Complete Game—1997

| Pitcher, Team | Date | Score | Opp | W/L | IP | H | ER | BB | K | #Pit |
|---|---|---|---|---|---|---|---|---|---|---|
| Greg Maddux, Atl | 7/22 | 4-1 | @Cubs | W | 9 | 5 | 1 | 0 | 6 | 78 |
| Joey Hamilton, SD | 8/1 | 8-2 | @Mon | W | 9 | 4 | 2 | 1 | 2 | 82 |
| Mike Grace, Phi | 9/2 | 5-0 | Yanks | W | 9 | 3 | 0 | 0 | 1 | 84 |
| Greg Maddux, Atl | 7/2 | 2-0 | @Yanks | W | 9 | 3 | 0 | 0 | 8 | 86 |
| Ricky Bones, KC | 8/19 | 9-2 | Bal | W | 9 | 7 | 2 | 0 | 1 | 88 |
| Greg Maddux, Atl | 6/27 | 7-1 | Phi | W | 9 | 6 | 1 | 0 | 8 | 90 |
| Sterling Hitchcock, SD | 8/15 | 5-1 | Cubs | W | 9 | 4 | 1 | 0 | 4 | 90 |
| Carlos Perez, Mon | 6/18 | 1-0 | @Bal | W | 9 | 8 | 0 | 0 | 2 | 92 |
| Jim Bullinger, Mon | 6/23 | 5-0 | Cin | W | 9 | 4 | 0 | 1 | 0 | 93 |
| Carlos Perez, Mon | 9/3 | 1-0 | Bos | W | 9 | 2 | 0 | 0 | 8 | 94 |

Maddux' remarkable 78-pitch effort is all the more astounding upon closer examination. The Braves' ace faced 31 batters, throwing a first-pitch strike to all but five. He needed only four pitches to retire the side in two separate innings, and threw only five pitches in a third frame. Of his 78 pitches, a total of 63—over 80 percent of them—were strikes.

At the other end of the spectrum lies Boston knuckleballer Tim Wakefield, who posted the highest single-game pitch count in the major leagues for the third time in five seasons. His 168-pitch outing against the Brewers on June 5 was the season's longest by a considerable margin. In 1996 he threw 162 pitches in a game to tie for the season high, and in 1993 he notched the highest pitch count of the last 10 years with a 172-pitch effort.

### Most Pitches in a Game—1997

| Pitcher, Team | Date | Score | Opp | W/L | IP | H | ER | BB | K | #Pit |
|---|---|---|---|---|---|---|---|---|---|---|
| Tim Wakefield, Bos | 6/5 | 2-1 | @Mil | W | 8.2 | 7 | 0 | 7 | 10 | 168 |
| Randy Johnson, Sea | 7/18 | 5-4 | KC | W | 9 | 9 | 4 | 3 | 16 | 154 |
| Dennis Springer, Ana | 5/23 | 12-2 | @Tor | W | 9 | 7 | 2 | 4 | 3 | 149 |
| Randy Johnson, Sea | 8/8 | 5-0 | WSox | W | 9 | 5 | 0 | 3 | 19 | 149 |
| Dennis Springer, Ana | 6/29 | 2-3 | @Sea | N/D | 8 | 4 | 2 | 4 | 5 | 145 |
| Kevin Appier, KC | 6/5 | 3-6 | Tex | N/D | 9 | 4 | 3 | 5 | 11 | 143 |
| Randy Johnson, Sea | 6/24 | 1-4 | Oak | L | 9 | 11 | 4 | 0 | 19 | 143 |
| Randy Johnson, Sea | 9/23 | 4-3 | Ana | W | 8 | 8 | 3 | 1 | 11 | 143 |
| Roger Clemens, Tor | 9/28 | 3-2 | Bos | N/D | 8.1 | 7 | 2 | 2 | 8 | 143 |
| Kevin Appier, KC | 5/26 | 1-2 | Oak | N/D | 9 | 5 | 0 | 1 | 10 | 141 |

Although Wakefield relies almost entirely on his knuckleball, it's clear that his arm does not respond well to such extreme use. Following his 168-pitch game last year, he posted a 7.54 ERA over his next seven starts before being temporarily exiled to the bullpen. He suffered a similar slump in '96 after tossing 162 pitches while working on only two days' rest—his ERA over his next five starts was a bloated 7.77. And his 172-pitch game in 1993 precipitated the most severe crisis of his career. In his next eight starts, he went 0-5 with a 7.59 ERA, before being sent first to the bullpen and later to the minors.

—Mat Olkin

A more complete listing for this category can be found on page 254.

## Which Pitchers Heat Up in the Cold?

On Saturday, April 12, 1997, the thermometer at Coors Field registered 28 degrees. Intermittent snow flurries fell as the wind lowered the wind-chill to 18 degrees. As the Rockies played the Montreal Expos that afternoon, two of the umpires wore ski masks on the field. Colorado starter Jamey Wright was the only one who didn't seem to feel the cold. Refusing even to wear a long-sleeved undershirt, he pitched seven innings, allowing four earned runs while defeating the Expos, 12-8. Wright's performance probably was sufficient to earn him recognition as a "cold-weather pitcher" in many people's eyes.

But does such an animal even exist? Conventional wisdom holds that cold weather generally favors *all* pitchers. The ball doesn't carry as well in the cold, it is said, and most of us recall all too well how it feels to hit one off the trademark on a cold day. Could it be that some individual pitchers are better able to exploit the advantages that cold weather affords a pitcher? Before we can answer that question, perhaps we should ask: what is the *nature* of the advantages that the cold weather provides? The chart below sheds some light on the subject:

### Starting Pitchers' Performance by Temperature—1993-97

| Temp | BB/9 IP | HR/9 IP | Opp. Avg | ERA |
|------|---------|---------|----------|-----|
| Below 50 | 3.73 | 0.85 | .260 | 4.34 |
| 50s | 3.60 | 0.99 | .268 | 4.54 |
| 60s | 3.25 | 1.01 | .264 | 4.28 |
| 70s | 3.21 | 1.03 | .270 | 4.49 |
| Above 79 | 3.21 | 1.12 | .275 | 4.68 |

As you can see, cold weather's main advantage—from the pitcher's point of view—is that it reduces home runs and, to a lesser extent, base hits. Although the opponents' batting average at temperatures below 50 degrees is 15 points lower than it is at temperatures over 80, much of that difference may be accounted for by the decrease in the rate of home runs allowed.

Oddly, cold weather seems to hurt a pitcher's control to a considerable extent. As you can see above, pitchers' control improves consistently as the temperature rises. Taken all together, cold weather seems to help the pitcher, although not to the extent we might have expected.

There still may be certain pitchers who are better able to survive the cold, however. Here are the starters with the best ERAs in temperatures under 50 degrees over the last five years (minimum five games started):

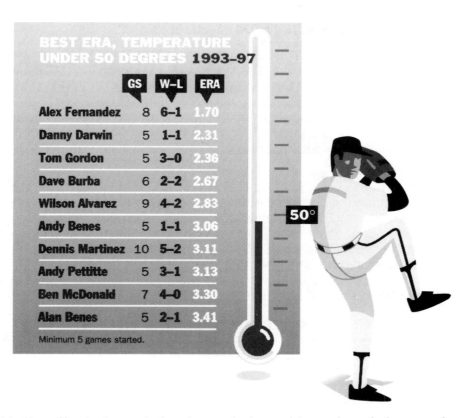

**BEST ERA, TEMPERATURE UNDER 50 DEGREES 1993–97**

| | GS | W–L | ERA |
|---|---|---|---|
| Alex Fernandez | 8 | 6–1 | 1.70 |
| Danny Darwin | 5 | 1–1 | 2.31 |
| Tom Gordon | 5 | 3–0 | 2.36 |
| Dave Burba | 6 | 2–2 | 2.67 |
| Wilson Alvarez | 9 | 4–2 | 2.83 |
| Andy Benes | 5 | 1–1 | 3.06 |
| Dennis Martinez | 10 | 5–2 | 3.11 |
| Andy Pettitte | 5 | 3–1 | 3.13 |
| Ben McDonald | 7 | 4–0 | 3.30 |
| Alan Benes | 5 | 2–1 | 3.41 |

Minimum 5 games started.

This list effectively explodes the myth that cold-weather pitchers are born and bred in northern climates. Alex Fernandez and Tom Gordon hail from Florida, while both Andy Pettitte and Ben McDonald are from Louisiana. Danny Darwin is a lifelong Texan. Wilson Alvarez and Dennis Martinez make their homes even further south—in Venezuela and Nicaragua, respectively. It's safe to say that the only pitchers on the list who threw snowballs as children are Dave Burba, from Ohio, and the Benes brothers, from Indiana. And the *worst* cold-weather pitcher? Milwaukee's Cal Eldred was born in Cedar Rapids, Iowa, and attended the University of Iowa. Despite all those years in the upper Midwest, Eldred has never grown acclimated to the cold. In six below-50 degree starts, he's posted a 7.84 ERA. Perhaps it's no coincidence that he now resides in Arizona.

—Mat Olkin

A more complete listing for this category can be found on page 255.

## Who Knows How to Handle Their Inheritance?

For 40-year-old southpaw Tony Fossas of the St. Louis Cardinals, 1997 wasn't exactly a banner season. The veteran reliever posted a 2-7 record, saw his ERA climb sharply for the second straight year (to 3.83), and allowed opposing hitters to rack up a scary .298 batting average. Cardinals manager Tony La Russa, however, didn't lose faith in Fossas—even during the second half of the year, when it seemed as if the lefty had shifted into batting-practice mode: opponents hit .374 against him after the All-Star break.

What did La Russa see in Fossas? Perhaps his uncanny ability to register outs in tough situations, particularly against dangerous lefthanded hitters. Fossas inherited a total of 60 runners last season, the ninth-highest figure in the majors, but allowed just six of them to score; his "IRS percentage" of 10.0 was the best in baseball. While he wasn't exactly the guy you'd want out there to start an inning—and he usually didn't last long enough to finish them—Fossas was effective within his tightly-defined role. Let's look at last season's top 10 hurlers in stranding baserunners:

**Lowest Percentage of Inherited Runners Scored—1997**

| Reliever, Team | IR | Scored | Pct |
|---|---|---|---|
| Tony Fossas, StL | 60 | 6 | 10.0 |
| Alan Embree, Atl | 43 | 6 | 14.0 |
| Mike Remlinger, Cin | 50 | 8 | 16.0 |
| Marc Wilkins, Pit | 31 | 5 | 16.1 |
| Terry Adams, Cubs | 43 | 7 | 16.3 |
| Anthony Telford, Mon | 53 | 10 | 18.9 |
| Scott Radinsky, LA | 56 | 11 | 19.6 |
| Jeff Nelson, Yanks | 53 | 11 | 20.8 |
| Buddy Groom, Oak | 72 | 15 | 20.8 |
| Armando Benitez, Bal | 57 | 12 | 21.1 |
| **MLB Totals** | **7,145** | **2,298** | **32.2** |

(mininum 30 IR)

Fossas had his share of difficulties last season, but few games blew up with him on the mound; in contrast, the average major league reliever would have allowed 19 of 60 inherited runners to cross the plate. Alan Embree was regarded as a throw-in when Cleveland sent him to Atlanta before the 1997 season in the Kenny Lofton/Marquis Grissom/Dave Justice trade, but the Braves reliever turned out to be much more effective than anyone could have anticipated. With Cleveland in '96, Embree allowed just five of 24 inherited runners to score (20.8 percent), but he topped that mark last year by posting the second-lowest IRS percentage in the majors. Admittedly, he was used in much the same manner as Fossas was, but he still played a valuable role in the Braves bullpen. Now if only Atlanta had also hung onto Lofton. . .

Which relief corps were the best at collectively stifling enemy scoring threats? Here's a list of last season's IRS percentages by team:

**Team Inherited-Runners Percentage—1997**

| AL Team | IR | Scored | Pct | NL Team | IR | Scored | Pct |
|---|---|---|---|---|---|---|---|
| Yankees | 245 | 62 | 25.3 | Dodgers | 217 | 49 | 22.6 |
| Orioles | 277 | 72 | 26.0 | Cardinals | 205 | 53 | 25.9 |
| Angels | 290 | 77 | 26.6 | Braves | 147 | 44 | 29.9 |
| Indians | 294 | 81 | 27.6 | Cubs | 291 | 88 | 30.2 |
| Blue Jays | 183 | 52 | 28.4 | Marlins | 184 | 58 | 31.5 |
| White Sox | 277 | 86 | 31.1 | Expos | 251 | 80 | 31.9 |
| Athletics | 386 | 121 | 31.4 | Giants | 333 | 117 | 35.1 |
| Brewers | 226 | 71 | 31.4 | Pirates | 247 | 87 | 35.2 |
| Rangers | 304 | 96 | 31.6 | Phillies | 204 | 72 | 35.3 |
| Twins | 285 | 91 | 31.9 | Rockies | 239 | 86 | 36.0 |
| Mariners | 269 | 92 | 34.2 | Reds | 246 | 89 | 36.2 |
| Tigers | 306 | 110 | 36.0 | Padres | 293 | 110 | 37.5 |
| Red Sox | 281 | 103 | 36.7 | Mets | 169 | 64 | 37.9 |
| Royals | 270 | 101 | 37.4 | Astros | 226 | 86 | 38.1 |
| **Average** | | | **31.2** | **Average** | | | **33.3** |

If you recall, in 1996 the Yankees finished *last* in the AL in IRS percentage, allowing a whopping 40.7 percent of their inherited runners to score. A year later, we find the Yanks at the top of the list, with relievers like Jeff Nelson (20.8), Mariano Rivera (23.5), and Graeme Lloyd (25.6) leading the way. Remember Jim Mecir? He allowed over half of his inherited runners to score in '96 (51.7), but cut that figure sharply last season (nine of 35, 25.7 percent).

Not surprisingly, teams with strong pitching staffs tended to have relievers who excelled in pressure situations; the top three clubs on the list in each league placed among the top five in ERA. However, it's important to remember that they *also* helped pad their IRS stats by rapidly shuffling their relief corps in and out of ballgames during critical situations.

—Kevin Fullam

A more complete listing for this category can be found on page 256.

## If You Hold the Fort, Will You Soon Be Closing the Gate?

The "hold"—a save situation inherited by a relief pitcher who records at least one out and then passes on the save situation to a subsequent reliever without relinquishing the lead—has been a STATS staple for years, so we won't spend a lot of time elaborating on it. The chart shows the 1997 leaders in holds, and it's a list of some of the top middle relievers in the game.

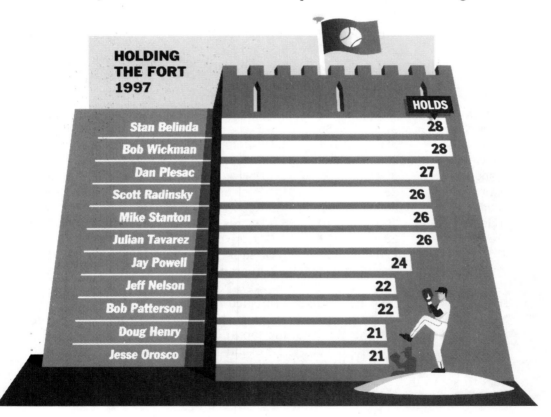

**HOLDING THE FORT 1997**

| | HOLDS |
|---|---|
| Stan Belinda | 28 |
| Bob Wickman | 28 |
| Dan Plesac | 27 |
| Scott Radinsky | 26 |
| Mike Stanton | 26 |
| Julian Tavarez | 26 |
| Jay Powell | 24 |
| Jeff Nelson | 22 |
| Bob Patterson | 22 |
| Doug Henry | 21 |
| Jesse Orosco | 21 |

As the title of this article suggests, many holds leaders are so good at their job that they get promoted to the role of closer within a year or two. The 1996 hold leader, Mariano Rivera, became the Yankees' closer last year when John Wetteland signed a free-agent contract with Texas. The No. 3 man in holds in '96, Jeff Shaw, became the Reds' closer last year when Jeff Brantley was injured. All he did was to lead the National League with 42 saves. In the past, relievers such as Rob Dibble, Duane Ward, Troy Percival and Ricky Bottalico have moved seamlessly from holds leaders to saves leaders.

Among the 1997 holds leaders, only Jay Powell of the Marlins seems to have much chance right now to be finishing games this year. Many of the '97 leaders—Stan Belinda, Dan Plesac, Mike Stanton and Doug Henry, to name four—have already had their chance at a closer's job, with only middling success. Still, you never know; Shaw entered the 1997 season with a career total of nine saves in seven years, and look what *he* did.

One interesting thing about the leaders list is that Dusty Baker's San Francisco Giants had *two* pitchers with more than 20 holds (Julian Tavarez and Doug Henry), a very rare feat. As a team the Giants had 85 holds, 10 more than any other team in the majors (the Dodgers were next with 75). Since 1991, only one other major league team has had more than 80 holds: the 1993 Giants, who were also managed by Baker. When Baker has a strong, deep bullpen, as he did in 1997, he's not afraid to use it. The 1997 team hold totals:

| American League | Holds | National League | Holds |
| --- | --- | --- | --- |
| Indians | 71 | Giants | 85 |
| Orioles | 68 | Dodgers | 75 |
| Tigers | 65 | Reds | 74 |
| Blue Jays | 63 | Rockies | 71 |
| Yankees | 62 | Pirates | 65 |
| White Sox | 62 | Cubs | 63 |
| Brewers | 57 | Marlins | 60 |
| Mariners | 56 | Cardinals | 48 |
| Angels | 55 | Padres | 43 |
| Twins | 52 | Mets | 43 |
| Red Sox | 51 | Braves | 43 |
| Athletics | 49 | Phillies | 38 |
| Rangers | 42 | Astros | 32 |
| Royals | 39 | Expos | 30 |

— Don Zminda

A more complete listing for this category can be found on page 257.

## Which Relievers Can Be Counted on to Convert?

In a game filled with "What have you done for me lately?" it's a shame that the lingering memory of the 1997 Baltimore Orioles' bullpen will be its 0-4 performance in the ALCS against Cleveland. Randy Myers couldn't get anyone out, Armando Benitez got whiplash from turning around to watch his offerings fly out of the park, and the Indians went home with another American League pennant. A shame, because it was an inglorious end to a glorious season for the Baltimore relief corps. As you can see from the chart below, both Myers and Benitez were nearly perfect when it came to either holding leads or closing the door in '97:

| Best Relief Conversion Percentage—1997 | | | | | |
|---|---|---|---|---|---|
| Pitcher, Team | Holds | Saves | SvOpp | TotOpp | Pct |
| Mike Munoz, Col | 19 | 2 | 2 | 21 | 100.0 |
| Randy Myers, Bal | 2 | 45 | 46 | 48 | 97.9 |
| Armando Benitez, Bal | 20 | 9 | 10 | 30 | 96.7 |
| Matt Karchner, WSox | 12 | 15 | 16 | 28 | 96.4 |
| Paul Assenmacher, Cle | 20 | 4 | 5 | 25 | 96.0 |
| Doug Jones, Mil | 0 | 36 | 38 | 38 | 94.7 |
| Mike Jackson, Cle | 14 | 15 | 17 | 31 | 93.5 |
| Scott Radinsky, LA | 26 | 3 | 5 | 31 | 93.5 |
| Mike Stanton, Yanks | 26 | 3 | 5 | 31 | 93.5 |
| Jay Powell, Fla | 24 | 2 | 4 | 28 | 92.9 |
| **ML Average** | | | | | **82.6** |

(minimum 20 total opp)

Editor Don Zminda coined the term "relief conversion percentage" two editions ago, and it's simply a measure of a pitcher's hold-plus-save percentage. We stand by it as an effective tool to compare the overall effectiveness of all relievers, whether they be "middlers," setup men or stoppers. As you can see, among relievers with at least 20 opportunities last year, only one was *more* effective at converting his hold-plus-save opportunities than the Oriole tandem. That one hurler was Mike Munoz, who held his own in the thin Colorado air. The dynamic duo in Baltimore converted an astounding 76 of 78 combined hold-plus-save situations. When you also consider that teammates Arthur Rhodes, Terry Mathews and Jesse Orosco were a combined 40 of 46, it's not hard to see why the O's led the American League East from wire to wire.

You'll notice that the guys who work the middle innings get their due in this approach, and that's precisely the intention. Along with Benitez and Munoz, "quarterbacks" Paul Assenmacher, Scott Radinsky, Mike Stanton and Jay Powell did an exceptional job of handing off the ball, and with Myers and Robb Nen changing uniforms in the offseason, Benitez and Powell may have earned themselves a closer's role in '98.

Not all relievers shared the same success, however. Many had fans covering their eyes and ducking for cover last season:

### Worst Relief Conversion Percentage—1997

| Pitcher, Team | Holds | Saves | SvOpp | TotOpp | Pct |
|---|---|---|---|---|---|
| Jim Corsi, Bos | 11 | 2 | 9 | 20 | 65.0 |
| Norm Charlton, Sea | 9 | 14 | 25 | 34 | 67.6 |
| Steve Reed, Col | 10 | 6 | 13 | 23 | 69.6 |
| Greg McMichael, Mets | 19 | 7 | 18 | 37 | 70.3 |
| Mike Timlin, Tor-Sea | 9 | 10 | 18 | 27 | 70.4 |
| T.J. Mathews, StL-Oak | 12 | 3 | 9 | 21 | 71.4 |
| Doug Brocail, Det | 16 | 2 | 9 | 25 | 72.0 |
| Mike Holtz, Ana | 14 | 2 | 8 | 22 | 72.7 |
| Mel Rojas, Cubs-Mets | 7 | 15 | 22 | 29 | 75.9 |
| Mike James, Ana | 12 | 7 | 13 | 25 | 76.0 |

Each year you'll find this list littered with closers who lost their jobs as the season wore on, and Norm Charlton, Mike Timlin and Mel Rojas all earned that ignominious distinction in 1997. STATS' headquarters is located just north of Chicago, so you can only imagine what Cubs fans in the office endured watching the much-heralded Rojas self-destruct.

As for team honors, we'll start at the bottom and work our way up. The worst figure of 1997 belongs to the Rangers at 75.8 percent (42 holds, 33 saves, 99 opps). Texas piled up 24 blown saves. As for the top spot, if you haven't guessed by now, the Orioles took home the team honors with a relief conversion percentage of 92.7 percent (68-59-137). They knocked the Indians out of the top spot for the first time in three seasons. But thanks to those very same Indians, that probably *won't* be what the '97 Orioles' bullpen will be remembered for.

—Tony Nistler

A more complete listing for this category can be found on page 258.

## Who Gets the Easy Saves—And Who Toughs It Out?

We all like to look at stats that detail a player's performance in clutch situations. We talk about batting averages with runners in scoring position, and in the late innings with the game on the line. But what about relief pitchers—in particular those late-inning specialists, the closers?

To some degree, every time a closer takes the ball and tries to nail down a victory, he faces a clutch situation. But let's face it—not all save opportunities are created equal. Whether you enter the game with the tying run on third base or with a three-run lead, you still can only earn one save, and thus the save statistic can be misleading. To gain more insight into closers' performances, we've divided save opportunities into three categories, based on the situation when the reliever enters the game:

**Easy Save:** First batter faced is not the tying run *and* the reliever pitches one inning or less. Example: Ugueth Urbina comes in to start the bottom of the ninth, with the Expos ahead by a 10-7 score. This is an Easy Save Opportunity.

**Tough Save:** The reliever comes in with the tying run anywhere on base. Example: With the Yankees clinging to a 3-2 lead, Mariano Rivera enters with a man on first and no outs in the ninth. This is considered a Tough Save Opportunity.

**Regular Save:** All save opportunities that fall into neither of the categories above are classified as Regular Save Opportunities.

You'd probably expect Tough Save Opportunities to be significantly more difficult to convert than Easy Save Opportunities. But you may be surprised at just how great the disparity is:

### League-Wide Save Conversions—1997

| | Easy | | | Regular | | | Tough | | |
|---|---|---|---|---|---|---|---|---|---|
| League | Sv | Op | Pct | Sv | Op | Pct | Sv | Op | Pct |
| AL | 268 | 297 | 90 | 223 | 356 | 63 | 77 | 208 | 37 |
| NL | 296 | 329 | 90 | 222 | 349 | 64 | 53 | 168 | 32 |
| **MLB Totals** | **564** | **626** | **90** | **445** | **705** | **63** | **130** | **376** | **35** |

The numbers are very similar to what they have been in recent years: Tough Saves were converted in about one-third of all opportunities, Regular Saves in just under two-thirds, and Easy Saves in 90 percent of all opportunities. Give a major league closer some room for error, and he should be money in the bank. Bring him in with the tying run on base, and boy, oh boy, does the going get a lot tougher.

OK, so how does this list break down for individual closers? Who doesn't choke when brought into a truly sticky situation? Here's the breakdown for each reliever who saw at least 25 save opportunities in 1997:

### Save Conversions by Major League Closers—1997

| Pitcher, Team | Easy | | | Regular | | | Tough | | | Total | | |
|---|---|---|---|---|---|---|---|---|---|---|---|---|
| | Sv | Op | Pct | Sv | Op | Pct | Sv | Op | Pct | Sv | Op | Pct |
| Randy Myers, Bal | 26 | 26 | 100 | 18 | 19 | 95 | 1 | 1 | 100 | 45 | 46 | 98 |
| Doug Jones, Mil | 25 | 26 | 95 | 9 | 9 | 100 | 2 | 3 | 67 | 36 | 38 | 95 |
| Troy Percival, Ana | 21 | 23 | 91 | 4 | 4 | 100 | 2 | 4 | 50 | 27 | 31 | 87 |
| Todd Jones, Det | 16 | 16 | 100 | 11 | 13 | 85 | 4 | 7 | 57 | 31 | 36 | 86 |
| Jeff Shaw, Cin | 23 | 23 | 100 | 16 | 21 | 76 | 3 | 5 | 60 | 42 | 49 | 86 |
| John Franco, Mets | 24 | 26 | 92 | 9 | 12 | 75 | 3 | 4 | 75 | 36 | 42 | 86 |
| Rich Loiselle, Pit | 18 | 19 | 95 | 9 | 11 | 82 | 2 | 4 | 50 | 29 | 34 | 85 |
| Ugueth Urbina, Mon | 7 | 8 | 88 | 12 | 13 | 92 | 8 | 11 | 73 | 27 | 32 | 84 |
| Trevor Hoffman, SD | 23 | 24 | 96 | 7 | 10 | 70 | 7 | 10 | 70 | 37 | 44 | 84 |
| John Wetteland, Tex | 23 | 25 | 92 | 7 | 8 | 88 | 1 | 4 | 25 | 31 | 37 | 84 |
| Dennis Eckersley, StL | 25 | 26 | 96 | 11 | 14 | 79 | 0 | 3 | 0 | 36 | 43 | 84 |
| Robb Nen, Fla | 26 | 30 | 87 | 8 | 11 | 73 | 1 | 1 | 100 | 35 | 42 | 83 |
| Ricky Bottalico, Phi | 17 | 17 | 100 | 14 | 18 | 78 | 3 | 6 | 50 | 34 | 41 | 83 |
| Mariano Rivera, Yanks | 28 | 28 | 100 | 13 | 21 | 62 | 2 | 3 | 67 | 43 | 52 | 83 |
| Mark Wohlers, Atl | 19 | 20 | 95 | 10 | 13 | 77 | 4 | 7 | 57 | 33 | 40 | 83 |
| Rod Beck, SF | 24 | 26 | 92 | 13 | 17 | 76 | 0 | 2 | 0 | 37 | 45 | 82 |
| H. Slocumb, Bos/Sea | 14 | 14 | 100 | 10 | 12 | 83 | 3 | 7 | 43 | 27 | 33 | 82 |
| Todd Worrell, LA | 25 | 26 | 96 | 10 | 18 | 56 | 0 | 0 | — | 35 | 44 | 80 |
| R. Hernandez, WSox/SF | 15 | 16 | 94 | 11 | 14 | 79 | 5 | 9 | 56 | 31 | 39 | 79 |
| Billy Wagner, Hou | 8 | 8 | 100 | 12 | 13 | 92 | 3 | 8 | 38 | 23 | 29 | 79 |
| Rick Aguilera, Min | 16 | 16 | 100 | 8 | 15 | 53 | 2 | 2 | 100 | 26 | 33 | 79 |
| Billy Taylor, Oak | 8 | 11 | 73 | 12 | 14 | 86 | 3 | 5 | 60 | 23 | 30 | 77 |
| Norm Charlton, Sea | 5 | 6 | 83 | 7 | 13 | 54 | 2 | 6 | 33 | 14 | 25 | 56 |

(minimum 25 save opportunities)

Of course, Randy Myers had an outstanding season in 1997, leading the majors with 45 saves while blowing only one save opportunity. But, as our chart reveals, only once was Myers called upon in a Tough Save situation; 44 of his 45 saves were of the Easy or Regular variety. Maybe Myers' season wasn't quite as impressive as one might think. Maybe, just maybe, the Orioles had something other than money in mind when they let Myers fly the coop after the season. The man who figures to replace him as the O's closer, Armando Benitez (who doesn't show up on our chart because of a limited number of save opportunities) was a perfect 3-for-3 in Tough Save chances in '97.

But let's not be too hard on Myers. Look at the numbers posted by Mariano Rivera and Jeff Shaw, who finished second and third in the majors, respectively, in total saves. Both Shaw and Rivera were perfect in Easy Save opportunities, but not nearly as effective when it came to Regular Save situations. Rivera was just 13-of-21 in Regular Save opportunities, and actually had a better percentage in Tough Save chances, in which he went 2-for-3.

The truly exceptional performers when it came to Tough Save situations were Montreal's Ugueth Urbina and San Diego's Trevor Hoffman. Urbina and Hoffman were the only closers to be handed at least 10 Tough Save opportunities, and each of them nailed it down at least 70 percent of the time—twice the major league success rate. To everyone who thinks that wise old veterans have a huge advantage in pressure situations, consider that Urbina and Hoffman were 23 and 29 last season, respectively, with a combined five seasons of big league experience. Maybe they simply didn't know enough to feel pressure with the game on the line.

Speaking of veterans, we have to mention the Dodgers' Todd Worrell. Of Worrell's 44 save opportunities, not one was of the Tough variety. As recently as two seasons ago, Worrell was a perfect 5-for-5 in Tough Save chances, tied for the most Tough Saves in the majors. But in 1997, L.A. skipper Bill Russell made sure to keep Worrell out of such hairy situations. And judging from how bad Worrell's season was—he had a 5.28 ERA and blew *eight* Regular Save opportunities—who knows how many more saves Worrell would have blown had Russell given him some Tough Save chances?

—Ethan D. Cooperson

A more complete listing for this category can be found on page 259.

## Which Reliever Is Best at Preventing Runs?

In last year's *Baseball Scoreboard* we introduced a new statistic, "Runs Prevented," which uses "run expectation" to measure the performance of relief pitchers. Run expectation, calculated by John Thorn and Pete Palmer in the classic book *The Hidden Game of Baseball*, tells us how many runs are expected to score, on average, for the rest of an inning given the runners on base and the number of outs remaining. For instance, with runners on first and third and nobody out, a team should score, on average, 1.64 runs the rest of its half of the inning. The run expectation for each of the 24 potential combinations of outs and runners on base, according to Thorn and Palmer, are listed below.

### Run Expectation (or "Runs Prevented Value")

| Runners | Number of Outs | | |
| --- | --- | --- | --- |
| | 0 | 1 | 2 |
| None | .45 | .25 | .10 |
| 1st | .78 | .48 | .21 |
| 2nd | 1.07 | .70 | .35 |
| 3rd | 1.28 | .90 | .38 |
| 1st & 2nd | 1.38 | .89 | 46 |
| 2nd & 3rd | 1.95 | 1.37 | .66 |
| Full | 2.25 | 1.55 | .80 |

What, you ask, does this have to do with relief pitching? Well, since a relief pitcher often takes the mound—and heads for the showers—with runners on base, the run expectation figures can be used to measure his performance more accurately than most conventional statistics. Here's how: we calculate the difference between (i) the run expectation when the pitcher enters the game (the "Initial RP Value"), and (ii) the run expectation when he leaves the game (the "End RP Value"), accounting for (iii) the runs that score and errors that are made (which increase run expectation) when he is on the mound. The result of this calculation is Runs Prevented, a holistic statistic that is more accurate for relievers than ERA (which is affected by what the next pitcher does with the runners left behind), or inherited/stranded runners (which does not distinguish between where the runners are, or how many outs remain), or holds or saves (which are only awarded when the pitcher's team is ahead).

A pitcher's Runs Prevented are calculated inning by inning (the run expectation resets at 0.45 at the beginning of each half-inning), and over the course of a season the reliever accumulates positive or negative RP totals with each appearance. At the end of the season, the average pitcher should have an RP total of zero, which means that he allowed as many runners to advance and score as we expected. Accordingly, better pitchers will have positive scores, and below-average pitchers will have negative scores. (Because Thorn and Palmer's run expectation figures were derived using data from 1961-1977, the average pitcher in these homer-happy times will score slightly below zero; in 1997, of 248 of 420 pitchers with relief innings finished with negative RP values.)

For those of you who like formulas, here it is: Runs Prevented = Initial RP Value - Runs Scored + Error RP Value (i.e., the amount the run expectation increased due to an error) - Final RP Value.

For those of you who learn better by example, here's a simple look at how it works: Mike Stanton enters the game with a runner on third and one out (Initial RP Value = 0.90). He whiffs one batter, receives his pat on the bottom from Joe Torre, and heads for the showers. The runner is still on third, but with two outs, the run expectation for the rest of the inning has dropped to 0.38 (Final RP Value). Stanton therefore has a Runs Prevented total of 0.52 for the game (0.90 - 0.38).

That's a pretty easy example. Try this one for size: Antonio Osuna takes the mound against the Giants with runners on first and third with nobody out (Initial RP Value = 1.64). He strikes out Barry Bonds and Jeff Kent, and then J.T. Snow grounds the ball to Eric Young, who promptly launches it over Eric Karros' head, so that instead of an inning-ending groundout, the Giants have runners on second and third with two outs and a run in. The run expectation for the rest of the inning should be zero, but instead it's 1.66: 1.00 for the run that scored, plus the 0.66 run expectation for the runners on 2nd & 3rd with two outs. In other words, the error increased the run expectation for the inning by 1.66 runs. Osuna then takes matters into his own hands, and strikes out Stan Javier to end the inning. Osuna's RP total for the inning is 2.30: 1.64 (Initial RP Value) - 1.00 (the run that scored) + 1.66 (the increase in run expectation due to Young's error) - 0 (Final RP Value).

Now let's cut to the chase: Who were the best relievers at preventing runs in 1997?

### Highest Run Prevented Totals—1997

| Pitcher, Team | Runs Prevented |
|---|---|
| Paul Quantrill, Tor | 21.8 |
| Jeff Shaw, Cin | 20.5 |
| Mariano Rivera, Yanks | 19.8 |
| Doug Jones, Mil | 19.5 |
| Jose Mesa, Cle | 18.2 |
| Randy Myers, Bal | 17.4 |
| Roberto Hernandez, WSox/SF | 16.8 |
| Arthur Rhodes, Bal | 16.1 |
| Greg McMichael, Mets | 15.6 |
| Antonio Osuna, LA | 15.2 |

Paul Quantrill?? His name certainly doesn't appear on many lists with the likes of Mariano Rivera, Randy Myers and Roberto Hernandez. On the other hand, the righthander posted a stellar 1.94 ERA while hurling 88 innings over 77 appearances, serving as a solid workhouse in the Toronto bullpen. Quantrill also stranded 39 of the 55 runners he inherited, and while these figures might not seem spectacular, remember that not all inherited runners are valued equally. As the run expectation figures show, a runner on third with nobody out has a much higher probability of scoring than does a runner on first with two out. Quantrill's high ranking shows that he got his teammates out of some mighty tough jams.

In addition, stranding an inherited runner does not necessarily mean that the reliever is doing his job; if the pitcher is taken out of the game before the inherited runner scores, the runner is counted as "stranded," regardless of whether he has advanced on the basepaths. Take the case of Tony Fossas: in 1997, he stranded 54 of 60 inherited runners to lead the NL with an efficiency rating of 90 percent. However, Fossas often left those same runners for the next guy, as La Russa often used the veteran lefty for only one or two batters per game. Runs Prevented was more indicative of Fossas's value: he finished tied for 101st among all pitchers who threw in relief, with 1.9 Runs Prevented.

Randy Myers deserves special mention for amassing his 17.4 Runs Prevented in just 59.2 innings; he led the majors in 1997 with 0.29 Runs Prevented per inning pitched (RP/IP). Hats off also to the four pitchers who repeated from the 1996 Runs Prevented top 10 list:

- Jeff Shaw finished eighth in Runs Prevented in 1996, and kept going strong in 1997 after taking over for injured Cincinnati closer Jeff

Brantley. Shaw's 94.2 innings pitched, 2.38 ERA and 18 of 25 inherited runners stranded all contributed to his fine showing.

• Mariano Rivera dropped to third last season after leading the pack in 1996 with 27.7 Runs Prevented. Rivera's much-publicized early-season troubles were not responsible for the decline; instead, Rivera's promotion to closer simply cut down his innings (from 107.2 to 71.2), and thereby his opportunities to prevent more runs. (In fact, Rivera prevented *more* runs per inning pitched in 1997 than he did in 1996.)

• Roberto Hernandez survived a late-season switch in leagues and roles, posting good numbers as both a closer and set-up man to follow his third-place finish from 1996.

• In 1996, Antonio Osuna finished ninth in the majors with 14.3 Runs Prevented, and in 1997 the Dodgers sent him to Albuquerque to start the season. He quickly made it back to the big club, however, and improved to 15.2 Runs Prevented for the 1997 campaign. Maybe Bill Russell will finally figure out that this guy should be his closer—or maybe this year he'll send poor Antonio to Bakersfield.

—Steve Schulman

*Steven Schulman, the creator of the Runs Prevented system, is a SABR member and a private attorney practicing in Washington, D.C.*

A more complete listing for this category can be found on page 260.

## Which Pitchers "Scored" the Highest in 1997?

There were some eyebrows raised when the Toronto Blue Jays signed Roger Clemens to a lucrative, long-term contract in December 1996. After all, here was a pitcher who, at the time, hadn't won more than 11 games in any of his previous four seasons. Who was just one game over .500 during the same period. And who, forebodingly, had turned 34 years of age during the prior campaign, hardly the age at which to expect a rebirth. Yet the Jays signed Clemens to an extended contract worth mega-millions. Was someone in the front office drinking too much Labatt's, or what?

Well, as it turned out, Clemens proved Toronto GM Gord Ash a very sober evaluator of talent. We all know Clemens ended up capturing the American League Cy Young Award. And he did so while demonstrating that he can still be as dominating in his mid-30s as he was in his early 20s.

Need proof? You've come to the right place. Bill James developed a system about a decade ago in which he attempted to quantify a pitcher's single-game performance based upon a statistic called "game score." The system was designed with the intention of imparting, in a single number, how effective the pitcher had been in his start. Usually, a game score of 90 means he had been awesome, a score of 50 normally means he was average, and a score of 10 conveys that he was awful. We won't bog you down with the details of exactly how these figues are calculated, but for a complete definition, please consult the glossary on page 273. Without further ado, there were only 10 games last season in which the starter produced a score of 93 or higher. Clemens' performance on September 7 tops the list:

### Highest Game Scores—1997

| Pitcher, Team | Date | Opp | W/L | IP | H | R | ER | BB | K | Score |
|---|---|---|---|---|---|---|---|---|---|---|
| Roger Clemens, Tor | 9/7 | Tex | W | 9.0 | 2 | 0 | 0 | 0 | 14 | 97 |
| Mike Mussina, Bal | 5/30 | Cle | W | 9.0 | 1 | 0 | 0 | 0 | 10 | 95 |
| Francisco Cordova, Pit | 7/12 | Hou | ND | 9.0 | 0 | 0 | 0 | 2 | 10 | 95 |
| Kevin Brown, Fla | 6/10 | @ SF | W | 9.0 | 0 | 0 | 0 | 0 | 7 | 94 |
| David Wells, Yanks | 7/30 | Oak | W | 9.0 | 3 | 0 | 0 | 3 | 16 | 94 |
| Alex Fernandez, Fla | 4/10 | @ Cubs | W | 9.0 | 1 | 0 | 0 | 0 | 8 | 93 |
| Alan Benes, StL | 5/16 | @ Atl | ND | 9.0 | 1 | 0 | 0 | 3 | 11 | 93 |
| Pedro Martinez, Mon | 6/14 | Det | W | 9.0 | 3 | 0 | 0 | 2 | 14 | 93 |
| Pedro Martinez, Mon | 7/13 | @ Cin | W | 9.0 | 1 | 0 | 0 | 1 | 9 | 93 |
| Randy Johnson, Sea | 8/8 | WSox | W | 9.0 | 5 | 0 | 0 | 3 | 19 | 93 |

Clemens' two-hit, 14-strikeout, zero-walk gem against the Rangers was arguably the most dominating performance of the year. It even outscored the only no-hitter of 1997, Kevin Brown's masterpiece against the Giants, as well as Francisco Cordova's partial no-hitter versus the Astros. Clemens also produced the highest game score of 1996, another 97, when he struck out 20 men and shut out the Tigers on September 18. Sound familiar? Remember when Clemens fanned 20 Seattle Mariners way back in 1986? That performance also generated a game score of 97.

All told, Clemens produced seven starts last year which scored at 80 or above, and another 13 which tallied at least a 70. His average for the season was a sparkling 67.9. Still, that mark doesn't rate as the best in baseball. That distinction belongs to the reigning National League Cy Young winner, and the man now being asked to assume the role Clemens once filled with the Red Sox, Pedro Martinez:

### Highest Average Game Scores—1997

| Pitcher | Team |
|---|---|
| Pedro Martinez, Mon | 70.8 |
| Roger Clemens, Tor | 67.9 |
| Randy Johnson, Sea | 67.8 |
| Curt Schilling, Phi | 63.6 |
| Greg Maddux, Atl | 62.9 |
| (minimum 15 GS) | |

Martinez had only three starts all season which scored under 50. That's remarkable, considering the *average* game score by an NL starter was 50.8. The average was appreciably lower in the AL—47.8—so Pedro's standard, in such a context, was roughly equivalent to Clemens' mark.

So much for the sublime performances of 1997. How about the ridiculous? While the century mark hasn't been reached since Nolan Ryan scored a 101 in his last no-hitter against the Blue Jays in 1991, there were seven cases last year alone in which a starter posted a sub-zero outing:

### Lowest Game Scores—1997

| Pitcher, Team | Date | Opp | W/L | IP | H | R | ER | BB | K | Score |
|---|---|---|---|---|---|---|---|---|---|---|
| Pat Rapp, Fla | 4/22 | @ Col | L | 2.2 | 13 | 10 | 10 | 2 | 0 | −10 |
| David Wells, Yanks | 8/19 | @ Ana | L | 3.0 | 10 | 11 | 11 | 3 | 3 | −5 |
| Jaime Navarro, WSox | 8/22 | @ Tex | L | 3.0 | 10 | 11 | 10 | 3 | 1 | −5 |
| Scott Erickson, Bal | 7/6 | @ Det | L | 4.1 | 10 | 12 | 11 | 4 | 3 | −4 |
| Ken Hill, Tex | 7/10 | @ Sea | L | 4.1 | 11 | 10 | 10 | 4 | 1 | −2 |
| Dave Burba, Cin | 4/7 | @ Col | L | 3.1 | 10 | 10 | 10 | 3 | 2 | −1 |
| Jaime Navarro, WSox | 7/31 | @ Ana | ND | 4.2 | 11 | 11 | 10 | 2 | 1 | −1 |

As you can see, Coors Field is still a dangerous place for pitchers to toil. Their game scores can *implode* in a hurry there. Pat Rapp was the sacrificial lamb on April 22, and you might ask why. Florida was idle the day before, and the Marlins had used only two relief pitchers over the previous three days. So why did Jim Leyland ask Rapp to absorb that kind of punishment? Still, for the strange handling of a pitcher, not much can top Terry Bevington's use of Jaime Navarro. On occasion, Bevington seemed less reluctant to egg Albert Belle's house than to remove Navarro from a game. The two starts you see above are just the tip of the iceberg. In addition to the -5 and -1 outings that are listed, Navarro also twirled game scores of 7, 8 and 9. If you needed more reasons for Bevington's departure, those are five good ones.

Navarro was also involved in arguably the worst pitching "duel" of the decade, when he hooked up with Jason Dickson on July 31. The White Sox struck for nine runs in the first two innings, eight of them coming at the expense of Dickson. But Navarro couldn't stand the prosperity. By the time Navarro was finally lifted in the fifth, he was responsible for 11 runs, the game was tied, and *neither* pitcher would be saddled with the loss.

**Worst Pitchers Duel Since 1987**

| Pitcher, Team | Date | W/L | IP | H | R | ER | BB | K | Score | Total |
|---|---|---|---|---|---|---|---|---|---|---|
| Jason Dickson, Ana | 7/31/97 | ND | 1.2 | 7 | 8 | 8 | 4 | 1 | 6 | 5 |
| Jaime Navarro, WSox | | ND | 4.2 | 11 | 11 | 10 | 2 | 1 | −1 | |

Dickson's game score of 6 lifted the duo's combined total to 5, easily the worst combined mark since 1987. The next-lowest total over the past 11 seasons? Ironically, it was generated by a pair of potential Hall of Famers. On June 26, 1987, Tommy John allowed six hits and eight runs in 1.1 innings of work. His opponent also allowed eight runs while coughing up nine hits over 2.1 innings. They each produced game scores of 8, and their combined total of 16 lasted as the mark of futility for over 10 years. John's opponent that day? None other than Roger Clemens. Baseball can sure be a humbling game, can't it?

—Jim Henzler

A more complete listing for this category can be found on page 261.

## How Bad Was Navarro?

Along with superstar Albert Belle, righthander Jaime Navarro was supposed to be one of the key free-agent signings of the 1996-97 offseason that would help catapult the Chicago White Sox into championship contention. After watching him post a couple of stellar seasons right across town for the Cubs, the Sox lured Navarro over to Comiskey with a four-year, $20-million deal last winter.

Belle was certainly a disappointment, as his HR production fell off by 40 percent and he failed to help create the feared one-two power combo with fellow slugger Frank Thomas that Chicago had hoped for. But Navarro *completely* crumbled, posting a 9-14 mark with a 5.79 ERA. As the season wore on, Navarro's problems continued to grow; after the All-Star break, opponents hit .348 against him with a .524 slugging percentage.

Despite all his troubles on the mound, though, White Sox manager Terry Bevington continued to start Navarro every fifth day, in part because he didn't have too many other options. . . but probably also because the Sox didn't want to admit that one of their "prize acquisitions" had turned out to be a major flop. Navarro wound up totaling over 200 innings during the season, which piqued our interest; how unusual was it for a hurler to be given that heavy a workload despite the fact that he was struggling immensely on the mound?

To analyze this question, we searched our database for those hurlers since 1901 with the highest ERAs, with a minimum of 200 innings pitched. Here's what we found:

### Worst ERAs—1901-97

| Year Player, Team | ERA | ER | IP |
|---|---|---|---|
| 1931 Pat Caraway, WSox | 6.22 | 152 | 220.0 |
| 1930 Guy Bush, Cubs | 6.20 | 155 | 225.0 |
| 1936 Buck Ross, A's | 5.83 | 130 | 200.2 |
| 1939 Jack Kramer, Browns | 5.83 | 137 | 211.2 |
| 1939 Vern Kennedy, Det/Browns | 5.80 | 137 | 212.2 |
| 1997 Jaime Navarro, WSox | 5.79 | 135 | 209.2 |
| 1936 Gordon Rhodes, A's | 5.74 | 138 | 216.1 |
| 1982 Matt Keough, Oak | 5.72 | 133 | 209.1 |
| 1930 Ray Benge, Phils | 5.70 | 143 | 225.2 |
| 1950 Herm Wehmeier, Cin | 5.67 | 145 | 230.0 |

(minimum 200 IP)

Pretty exclusive group, huh? Seven of the 10 highest ERAs on this leader board were turned in by pre-1940 hurlers. Quite a different game back then, wasn't it? Pitch counts were an unheard-of concept, relief specialists were virtually non-existent—and it was *even* quite commonplace for fans to wear suits and ties to the games. (Horrors. . .) Navarro's 5.79 ERA was the highest mark posted by a 200-inning hurler since the immortal Jack Kramer spun a 5.83 figure in 1939—a span of 58 years.

However, when you examine it more closely, Navarro's record isn't *quite* as bad as it seems. The average AL pitcher posted a 4.56 ERA last season; when we adjusted Navarro's numbers for league context (dividing his ERA by the AL average), Navarro dropped to 145th on the leader board. Like the previous list, this chart was dominated by turn-of-the-century players. In the interest of space, let's restrict it to post-1980 performances. (For the curious, the highest "ERA Index" in history was posted by Jack Neagle in 1884. Neagle compiled a 5-23 mark for three teams that season, posting a 5.94 ERA and a 1.83 index.)

### Worst ERA Indexes—1980-97

| Year | Player, Team | ERA | Lg ERA | Index |
|------|--------------|-----|--------|-------|
| 1980 | Dennis Lamp, Cubs | 5.20 | 3.61 | 1.44 |
| 1982 | Matt Keough, Oak | 5.72 | 4.08 | 1.40 |
| 1988 | Bert Blyleven, Min | 5.43 | 3.98 | 1.37 |
| 1983 | Frank Viola, Min | 5.49 | 4.08 | 1.35 |
| 1986 | Rick Mahler, Atl | 4.88 | 3.73 | 1.31 |
| 1984 | Jim Clancy, Tor | 5.12 | 4.00 | 1.28 |
| 1997 | Jaime Navarro, WSox | 5.79 | 4.56 | 1.27 |
| 1991 | Dave Stewart, Oak | 5.18 | 4.09 | 1.26 |
| 1980 | Mike Torrez, Bos | 5.08 | 4.04 | 1.26 |
| 1989 | Kevin Gross, Phi | 4.38 | 3.50 | 1.25 |

(minimum 200 innings pitched)

Lamp's season in 1980 was truly a pitcher's nightmare; Lamp posted a 10-14 record, surrendered 11.5 hits/9 IP, and compiled a less than impressive 83:82 strikeout/walk ratio. At a glance, you wouldn't have thought Kevin Gross' 11-12, 4.38 season in 1989 would have been *that* bad. However, his ERA index of 1.25 was one of the worst figures of the last two decades. He led the NL in earned runs allowed that season (with 98) in a very strong pitcher's season. After adjusting for the context of his league, his campaign was almost as bad as Navarro's was in '97.

Navarro's season was one of the most disastrous pitching campaigns in recent memory—and one of the key reasons why Chicago GM Ron Schueler felt they couldn't compete down the stretch with the Indians for the AL Central title last year (leading to the subsequent trading of Harold Baines, Roberto Hernandez and Wilson Alvarez). But it wasn't as *un*common as you might have originally thought. . . which is probably small consolation for White Sox fans.

—Kevin Fullam

A more complete listing for this category can be found on page 262.

# V. QUESTIONS ON DEFENSE

## Who's Best in the Infield Zone?

"That shortstop sure botched that one." "True, but most other shortstops wouldn't have even *gotten* to that ball." The preceding exchange predates fielder's gloves or outfield fences, and it rages on even today because its resolution turns on a question that baseball's traditional statistics fail to address—specifically, "Would another shortstop have gotten to that ball?"

STATS, Inc. has developed the "zone rating" in an attempt to shed some light on this issue. It's based on the simple idea of assigning each defensive player a "zone" and counting how many balls are hit into that zone. Comparing this total to the number of outs a player records can help us to figure out which players prevent the most balls from going through.

### INFIELD ZONE RATINGS 1997

| POSITION | BALLS IN ZONE | | OUTS | ZONE RATING | ML AVG. |
|---|---|---|---|---|---|
| FIRST BASE | Jeff King | 309 | 298 | .964 | .869 |
| SECOND BASE | Mike Lansing | 425 | 402 | .946 | .899 |
| THIRD BASE | Jeff Cirillo | 416 | 369 | .887 | .800 |
| SHORTSTOP | Gary DiSarcina | 445 | 440 | .989 | .940 |

Minimum 1,000 innings played at each position.

STATS reporters record the distance and direction of every batted ball, providing the raw information that's used to generate zone ratings. For the purposes of the zone rating, the number of "outs" a player is credited with includes all balls fielded cleanly and turned into outs within his zone, plus balls turned into outs outside the zone, plus double plays (since a double play results in two outs. First basemen do not receive credit for participating in a double play). For the purposes of calculating the number of balls hit into an infielder's zone, all ground balls hit within the zone are counted, line drives are counted only if they land in the zone, and pop flies are ignored. Here are the 1997 leaders at each infield position (minimum 1,000 innings played):

### First Basemen—1997 Zone Ratings

| Player, Team | Rtg |
| --- | --- |
| Jeff King, KC | .964 |
| Tony Clark, Det | .931 |
| Rafael Palmeiro, Bal | .901 |
| Wally Joyner, SD | .896 |
| Mark Grace, Cubs | .896 |
| **Worst** | |
| Mo Vaughn, Bos | .754 |

Tony Clark is the only surprise here, but the former college hoops player apparently has retained his superior ball-handling skills. Jeff King's fine showing doesn't surprise us, since he's proven to be capable of holding his own at third base or even at second.

### Second Basemen—1997 Zone Ratings

| Player, Team | Rtg |
| --- | --- |
| Mike Lansing, Mon | .946 |
| Eric Young, Col/LA | .939 |
| Jeff Kent, SF | .933 |
| Craig Biggio, Hou | .930 |
| Mickey Morandini, Phi | .920 |
| **Worst** | |
| Damion Easley, Det | .802 |

Mike Lansing rebounded from three years of below-average zone ratings to post the major league's best mark at second base. Meanwhile, Craig Biggio made an even more remarkable recovery after finishing last in '96.

### Third Basemen—1997 Zone Ratings

| Player, Team | Rtg |
| --- | --- |
| Jeff Cirillo, Mil | .887 |
| Edgardo Alfonzo, Mets | .876 |
| Gary Gaetti, StL | .860 |
| Travis Fryman, Det | .845 |
| Scott Rolen, Phi | .842 |
| **Worst** | |
| Dave Hollins, Ana | .741 |

Dave Hollins plummets to last place after leading major league third basemen in zone rating in 1996; perhaps he had trouble adjusting to Anaheim's grass after playing most of his career on turf. Jeff Cirillo is an unheralded defensive standout in Milwaukee, while Edgardo Alfonzo's glove has drawn raves ever since the former middle infielder was installed at third.

### Shortstops—1997 Zone Ratings

| Player, Team | Rtg |
|---|---|
| Gary DiSarcina, Ana | .989 |
| Royce Clayton, StL | .988 |
| Omar Vizquel, Cle | .981 |
| Edgar Renteria, Fla | .971 |
| Deivi Cruz, Det | .965 |
| **Worst** | |
| Greg Gagne, LA | .903 |

Youngsters Edgar Renteria and Deivi Cruz made the list for the first time this year, joining veteran defensive stalwarts Gary DiSarcina, Royce Clayton and Omar Vizquel. Shortstop is a young man's position, and we expect to see Renteria and Cruz remain on this list for years to come. Greg Gagne's diminishing range is evident both in his major league-worst zone rating and his assists-per-game; the latter plunged by 18 percent last season.

Here are the major league leaders over the last three years (minimum 1,000 innings played):

### 1995-97 Infield Zone Rating Leaders

| Player | Rtg | Player | Rtg |
|---|---|---|---|
| **First Base** | | **Third Base** | |
| Jeff King | .969 | Jeff Branson | .882 |
| John Jaha | .929 | Jeff Cirillo | .862 |
| Jeff Conine | .920 | Scott Brosius | .860 |
| **Second Base** | | **Shortstop** | |
| Keith Lockhart | .947 | David Howard | .992 |
| Mark McLemore | .944 | Cal Ripken | .979 |
| Jody Reed | .943 | Royce Clayton | .973 |

—Mat Olkin

A more complete listing for this category can be found on page 263.

## Who Can Turn the Pivot?

Last year, something rather unusual happened to Los Angeles second baseman Wilton Guerrero. He was expected to contend for National League Rookie of the Year honors, and in mid-August, it seemed that he was living up to everyone's expectations. In 100 games, he was batting .292 and had committed only four errors. On August 18, the Dodgers' record was 10 games over .500, and they trailed the Giants by just two games in the NL West Division race. Despite all of this, Los Angeles GM Fred Claire decided that Guerrero had to be replaced and acquired Eric Young to play second base.

To call the move highly unusual would be putting it lightly; Guerrero had become one of the few players in recent memory to lose his job while batting close to .300. What had motivated Claire to replace a player who was, at first glance, performing quite competently? When asked why he'd made the move, Claire offered a rather unexpected justification: he explained that the Dodgers' performance *on the double play* had been unsatisfactory.

We now can confirm that Claire's eyes hadn't been lying to him. It's clear that Guerrero—a converted shortstop whose previous experience at the keystone consisted of a half-season of Triple-A ball—had been the most inept second baseman in the majors when it came to the double-play pivot.

We define a double-play opportunity as any situation with a runner on first and less than two out where the second baseman records a putout at second base (triple plays are excluded). In those situations, the better second basemen will go on to complete the double play upwards of 60 percent of the time. Last year, Guerrero had 35 opportunities to make the DP pivot (almost all of which came before he lost his job to Eric Young), and succeeded in getting the second out only 14 times. His dismal 40 percent success rate was easily the worst in the majors for any second baseman with 30 or more opportunities.

Here are the second basemen who made good on the *highest* percentage of their double-play opportunities last year:

### Best Pivot Men—1997

| Player, Team | DP | Opp | Pct |
|---|---|---|---|
| Damion Easley, Det | 56 | 80 | .700 |
| Bret Boone, Cin | 44 | 63 | .698 |
| Carlos Baerga, Mets | 52 | 80 | .650 |
| Mark Lemke, Atl | 35 | 54 | .648 |
| Delino DeShields, StL | 50 | 79 | .633 |
| Scott Spiezio, Oak | 50 | 80 | .625 |
| Jeff Kent, SF | 58 | 93 | .624 |
| John Valentin, Bos | 40 | 65 | .615 |
| Mike Lansing, Mon | 50 | 82 | .610 |
| Ray Durham, WSox | 48 | 80 | .600 |
| Jeff Frye, Bos | 36 | 60 | .600 |
| Mark McLemore, Tex | 36 | 60 | .600 |

(minimum 50 opportunities)

Several of the players listed above joined new teams last year, and in almost every single case, their expertise on the twin-killing made a measurable impact on the ERA of their team's pitching staff. In fact, the man at the top of the list, Damion Easley, took over at second base for the Tigers, the team that enjoyed the biggest drop in team ERA last year. Justin Thompson surely had a lot to do with the Detroit staff's revival, but even his efforts cannot completely account for the massive 1.82-run decline.

Many others on the list joined teams that experienced a drop in ERA. Carlos Baerga took over as the Mets' second baseman, and the team ERA went down by over a quarter of a run. Delino DeShields went to St. Louis, and for all the Cardinals' problems last year, their pitching staff actually improved, shaving nine points off the staff ERA. Jeff Kent went to San Francisco, where the Giants' ERA dropped by almost one-third of a run, and John Valentin moved to second base for the Red Sox, who saw their ERA drop by 13 points—even without Roger Clemens. Oakland rookie Scott Spiezio was the only member of the top 10 who wasn't able to help his pitchers improve, although that was an admittedly difficult assignment, considering the state of the A's staff last year. Still, his performance was laudable, especially for a player who'd played third base almost exclusively in the minors.

Here are the game's best pivot men over the last six seasons:

### Best Pivot Men—1992-97

| Player | DP | Opp | Pct |
|---|---|---|---|
| Jeff Kent | 175 | 264 | .663 |
| Bret Boone | 210 | 318 | .660 |
| Carlos Garcia | 198 | 317 | .625 |
| Jody Reed | 178 | 285 | .625 |
| Luis Alicea | 198 | 320 | 619 |
| Pat Kelly | 135 | 220 | .614 |
| Mark Lemke | 196 | 322 | .609 |
| Mark McLemore | 163 | 268 | .608 |
| Chuck Knoblauch | 254 | 419 | .606 |
| Brent Gates | 131 | 217 | .604 |

(minimum 210 opportunities)

For the second year in a row, Milwaukee's Fernando Vina just misses topping this list. Although he barely misses qualifying—coming up only 14 opportunities short—his DP percentage would lap the rest of the field. Over the last six years, Vina has turned 149 double plays in 196 opportunities for a fantastic 76 percent success rate, nearly 100 points better than current leader Jeff Kent. Vina suffered a broken ankle last April that sidelined him for 77 games; had it not been for the injury, he likely would have come out on top of *both* of the above lists. In the time that he did play last year, he produced 31 twin-killings in 40 opportunities for a .775 percentage.

—Mat Olkin

A more complete listing for this category can be found on page 265.

## Which Catchers Catch Thieves?

It isn't easy to evaluate the defensive abilities of catchers; they don't really have any measurable range on the field, and without some extensive statistical analysis, it's difficult to tell who handles pitchers well. . . and who doesn't. But one critical defensive strength that has always been simple to gauge is a backstop's throwing prowess. Nothing demoralizes an offense quite like having a catcher gun down an overzealous basestealer to prematurely stifle a promising rally.

What catchers exterminated the highest percentages of basestealers last season? Let's take a look at the best-and worst-throwing catchers:

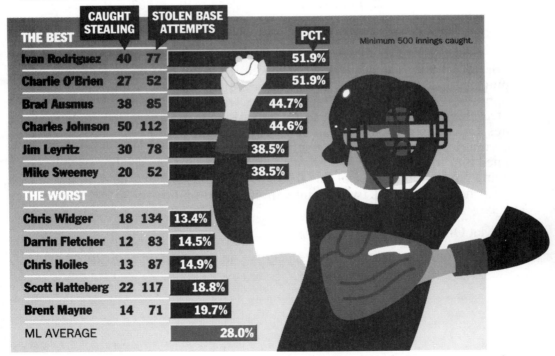

| THE BEST | CAUGHT STEALING | STOLEN BASE ATTEMPTS | PCT. |
|---|---|---|---|
| Ivan Rodriguez | 40 | 77 | 51.9% |
| Charlie O'Brien | 27 | 52 | 51.9% |
| Brad Ausmus | 38 | 85 | 44.7% |
| Charles Johnson | 50 | 112 | 44.6% |
| Jim Leyritz | 30 | 78 | 38.5% |
| Mike Sweeney | 20 | 52 | 38.5% |
| **THE WORST** | | | |
| Chris Widger | 18 | 134 | 13.4% |
| Darrin Fletcher | 12 | 83 | 14.5% |
| Chris Hoiles | 13 | 87 | 14.9% |
| Scott Hatteberg | 22 | 117 | 18.8% |
| Brent Mayne | 14 | 71 | 19.7% |
| ML AVERAGE | | | 28.0% |

Minimum 500 innings caught.

For the third straight season, Ivan Rodriguez of the Texas Rangers posted the major leagues' highest caught-stealing percentage. While we'd say that Pudge's arm isn't his only defensive strength, it's certainly the one that's gotten him the most attention—as well as an ongoing streak of six consecutive Gold Gloves. The real story behind the plate last year, though, was veteran backstop Charlie O'Brien.

Two years ago, O'Brien posted the lowest caught-stealing percentage in the majors, nabbing only eight of 79 basestealers with the Braves for a mark of 10.1 percent. When you post those kind of numbers and lug around a lifetime batting average of .222, it's a pretty clear sign that your baseball days are numbered. However, O'Brien's arm rebounded sharply in 1996 (33.3 percent caught-stealing rate) after latching on with the Toronto Blue Jays, and he finished just a hair behind Rodriguez in the race for the ML's *top* CS percentage last season. Bionic implants? Quicksand on the basepaths? There's no question that O'Brien was aided by the move from Atlanta to Toronto; he spent much of his time in 1997 catching Roger Clemens as opposed to the Braves' Greg Maddux in the early '90s, and Clemens has always done a much better job at holding baserunners than his NL counterpart.

Although Florida's Charles Johnson is known throughout the league as having one of the strongest cannons in the game, players still feel compelled to run against him. Johnson faced 112 baserunning challenges last season—the eighth-highest total in the majors—and Marlin opponents paid the price, suffering 50 casualties. Only Pittsburgh's Jason Kendall (51) threw out more basestealers.

Basestealers might have challenged Johnson, but that's *nothing* compared to the havoc they wreaked upon Montreal last year. Expo catchers Chris Widger and Darrin Fletcher finished one-two on the trailers board in 1997, as they faced a frightening total of *217* stolen-base attempts during the season. With the Widger/Fletcher duo turning only 13.8 percent of them into outs, there wasn't much reason for Montreal opponents to curtail their running. . . and they certainly didn't. Widger was a rookie, and Fletcher's never had a quality arm, but manager Felipe Alou is probably as much to blame. Like Maddux, Alou prefers to ignore baserunners and have his pitchers concentrate on retiring hitters. That isn't bad advice, but it makes it tough on his catchers.

—Kevin Fullam

A more complete listing for this category can be found on page 266.

## Who's Best in the Outfield Zone?

Fielding percentages have their place in the world of baseball defensive analysis, but they're just one piece in what is truly a very large and complex puzzle. The problem with these statistics is that they fail to reward players who cover lots of outfield territory and take risks in the field. If an outfielder can't reach a drive, it's not scored an error—it's a hit. As we said in last year's *Scoreboard*: "You can put Cecil Fielder in center field and he may register a 1.000 fielding percentage, but he'll probably only snare the 10 fly balls a season that are hit directly to him."

One alternative method to evaluate an outfielder's defensive contributions involves the concept of "zone ratings." By measuring the number of outs recorded by a player in relation to the number of balls that are hit into his defensive area, zone ratings can paint a more accurate picture as to which fielders cover the most ground—and which ones help send their pitchers' ERAs skyrocketing by turning would-be outs into hits. Here are last season's zone-rating leaders at each outfield spot (minimum 1,000 innings), starting in left:

### Left Field—1997 Zone Ratings

| Player, Team | Zone Rating |
| --- | --- |
| Ron Gant, StL | .845 |
| B.J. Surhoff, Bal | .834 |
| Henry Rodriguez, Mon | .823 |
| Barry Bonds, SF | .799 |
| Albert Belle, WSox | .799 |
| **MLB Average** | **.798** |
| **Trailer** | |
| Dante Bichette, Col | .733 |

Surprised by the name at the top of the list? We sure were. Ron Gant? The same Ron Gant who got his leg smashed up in a vicious dirt bike accident four years ago? Gant's bat suffered a major slide last season, as he hit just .229 and struck out in nearly a third of his at-bats. But the left fielder (whose glove isn't exactly, uh, highly regarded) attempted to make up for his poor performance at the plate by running full steam in the outfield.

As for this year's trailer. . . well, we knew Dante Bichette couldn't escape our wrath for long. Bichette, who was the 1996 "trailer" on the *right*-field leader board, posted a .733 zone rating to take the (dis)honor in left field this time around, finishing just percentage points behind Gregg Jefferies of the Philadelphia Phillies.

### Center Field—1997 Zone Ratings

| Player, Team | Zone Rating |
| --- | --- |
| Brian Hunter, Det | .850 |
| Kenny Lofton, Atl | .837 |
| Brian McRae, Cubs-Mets | .835 |
| Steve Finley, SD | .833 |
| Otis Nixon, Tor-LA | .832 |
| **MLB Average** | **.814** |
| Trailer | |
| Brady Anderson, Bal | .769 |

Brian Hunter, who placed fifth in zone ratings in 1996, rose to the top of the charts after a stellar performance last season. Between Hunter's blazing speed in center and Bobby Higginson's cannon arm in left, the Tigers have built quite a cornerstone on outfield defense.

The Orioles' Brady Anderson, on the other hand, might have been hampered in the field by a cracked rib he suffered in spring training. Anderson has never had good zone ratings throughout his career, but his .769 mark last season was the worst in the majors among regular center fielders.

### Right Field—1997 Zone Ratings

| Player, Team | Zone Rating |
| --- | --- |
| Sammy Sosa, Cubs | .852 |
| Tim Salmon, Ana | .848 |
| Manny Ramirez, Cle | .842 |
| Raul Mondesi, LA | .835 |
| Jay Buhner, Sea | .822 |
| **MLB Average** | **.814** |
| Trailer | |
| Larry Walker, Col | .726 |

Sammy Sosa made his way up to the top of yet another fielding chart. His combination of speed and arm strength has turned him into one of the top defensive outfielders in baseball. Larry Walker is viewed as having good speed—he stole 33 bases in '97—but his zone rating was markedly below average. In his defense, however, Coors Field is such a spacious park that every Colorado outfielder is going to appear worse than he actually is. In 1996, Rockie Quinton McCracken posted a *.665* rating in center—meaning one of every *three* balls hit to center during his watch turned into hits. Maybe there's hope for Dante yet. . .

—Kevin Fullam

A more complete listing for this category can be found on page 267.

## Which Outfielders Know How to Hold 'Em?

**M**ost of us have seen football games where a receiver darts across the field, prepares to extend himself for a catch. . . and then pulls up short at the last moment after catching a whiff of a menacing onrushing linebacker. Whether or not the linebacker actually pummels the receiver is inconsequential—just the mere *threat* of contact sometimes is enough to deter the player from his intended course. Well, the same holds true for those cannon-armed outfielders; after watching a guy like Sammy Sosa rifle the ball back to the infield a few times, most runners tend to sober up pretty quickly on the basepaths.

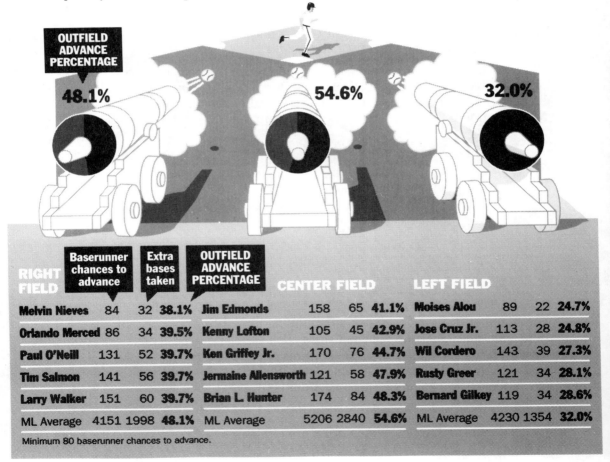

**OUTFIELD ADVANCE PERCENTAGE**

48.1%    54.6%    32.0%

| RIGHT FIELD | Baserunner chances to advance | Extra bases taken | OUTFIELD ADVANCE PERCENTAGE | CENTER FIELD | | | | LEFT FIELD | | | |
|---|---|---|---|---|---|---|---|---|---|---|---|
| Melvin Nieves | 84 | 32 | 38.1% | Jim Edmonds | 158 | 65 | 41.1% | Moises Alou | 89 | 22 | 24.7% |
| Orlando Merced | 86 | 34 | 39.5% | Kenny Lofton | 105 | 45 | 42.9% | Jose Cruz Jr. | 113 | 28 | 24.8% |
| Paul O'Neill | 131 | 52 | 39.7% | Ken Griffey Jr. | 170 | 76 | 44.7% | Wil Cordero | 143 | 39 | 27.3% |
| Tim Salmon | 141 | 56 | 39.7% | Jermaine Allensworth | 121 | 58 | 47.9% | Rusty Greer | 121 | 34 | 28.1% |
| Larry Walker | 151 | 60 | 39.7% | Brian L. Hunter | 174 | 84 | 48.3% | Bernard Gilkey | 119 | 34 | 28.6% |
| ML Average | 4151 | 1998 | 48.1% | ML Average | 5206 | 2840 | 54.6% | ML Average | 4230 | 1354 | 32.0% |

Minimum 80 baserunner chances to advance.

One of the most commonly debated points in the subject of baseball field-ing is the belief that strong-armed outfielders don't tally as many assists as they normally would—because few runners care to test their speed against such intimidating opposition. Because of this, we created the "outfield ad-vance" a few years ago. An advance is credited whenever a runner takes an extra base on a hit to that particular outfielder. For example, if a batter lines a single to right field with a runner on first base, the right fielder is charged with an advance if the runner goes to third. Usually, center field-ers have the worst advance percentages, while left fielders have the best ones. Why? Well, the longer the distance that the fielder has to throw the ball, the more likely the chance that the opposing runners will test his arm. The chart on the previous page lists the top five advance percentages at each outfield position.

Sosa, normally a mainstay on the right-field chart, just missed the cutoff in 1997. His 41.1 advance percentage placed him sixth behind Larry Walker. However, there's no evidence whatsoever that his arm is slipping; he gunned down 16 baserunners last season to lead all major league right fielders. Let's take a look at last year's assist leaders:

### Outfield Assist Leaders—1997

| Right Field | | Center Field | | Left Field | |
|---|---|---|---|---|---|
| Sammy Sosa, Cubs | 16 | Steve Finley, SD | 10 | Bernard Gilkey, Mets | 17 |
| Tim Salmon, Ana | 15 | Darren Bragg, Bos | 9 | Bobby Higginson, Det | 12 |
| Gary Sheffield, SD | 14 | Jim Edmonds, Ana | 9 | Marty Cordova, Min | 12 |
| | | Ken Griffey Jr., Sea | 9 | Brady Anderson, Bal | 12 |
| | | Damon Mashore, Oak | 9 | | |

It was definitely a tough year for center fielders throughout the majors. The Padres' Steve Finley was the only one to rack up double-digit assist totals. . . and his 10 assists wouldn't have even placed among the top three on last year's chart! One has to be impressed with the arm of the Athletics' Damon Mashore, however. Despite playing only 71 games in center field, Mashore still managed to throw out nine baserunners to rank among the game's best.

Once again, we decided to track the players who rated the best in advance percentage over the past three seasons—since it's based as much on repu-tation as on anything else. Here's what we found:

### Outfield Advance Percentage Leaders—1995-97

| Right Field | Pct | Center Field | Pct | Left Field | Pct |
|---|---|---|---|---|---|
| Orlando Merced | 37.6 | Jim Edmonds | 45.1 | Bobby Higginson | 23.9 |
| Larry Walker | 39.9 | Brian L. Hunter | 47.4 | Rusty Greer | 28.6 |
| Sammy Sosa | 42.4 | Kenny Lofton | 48.3 | Barry Bonds | 29.8 |
| **Trailer** | | **Trailer** | | **Trailer** | |
| Troy O'Leary | 57.4 | Quinton McCracken | 64.1 | Ron Gant | 39.3 |

(minimum 200 baserunner chances to advance)

Surprise, surprise. . . long-time STATS whipping boy Dante Bichette finally managed to break out of the "trailer" spot in right field. Of course, that's partly because he slid over to left field last season, where his arm received much more respect than it had in the past (36.0 advance percentage in '97 compared to league average of 32.0 for left fielders).

It wasn't too much of a surprise to see Bobby Higginson at the top of the left-field chart; after all, he gunned down 17 baserunners last season to tie for the league lead. However, check out the size of the gap between him and his closest competitors. Impressed? Higginson posted a 32.2 advance percentage this past year (29 of 90), which means that he actually managed an outrageous 18.4 percentage over the previous two seasons (25 of 136)! Maybe the Tigers should cue up the old "Jaws" theme on the loudspeakers next year when Higginson has the ball with a greedy baserunner on the move. . .

— Kevin Fullam

A more complete listing for this category can be found on page 269.

## Which Fielders Have the Best "Defensive Batting Average"?

One thing we have tried to do here at STATS, Inc., is increase the understanding of defensive ability. Our efforts have resulted in the creation of such tools as zone ratings, pivot ratings and outfield arm ratings. "Defensive batting average" is an attempt to use those tools, along with fielding percentage, to create one number that will identify the top defensive players in the infield and outfield. At the same time, that number should be easy to understand.

The formulas are complex, so we'll spare you a detailed discussion here. But the end result is that the pertinent ratings at a position are scaled so they read like batting averages. A .300 fielder is very good, while a .200 fielder is very bad. In other words, Red Sox first baseman Mo Vaughn's defensive batting average will look like Mets shortstop Rey Ordonez' batting average, and vice versa. We weigh different factors at each position, taking into account the most important skills needed there. A breakdown:

| Pos | Weighting |
|-----|-----------|
| 1B | Zone Rating 75%, Fielding Pct. 25% |
| 2B | Zone Rating 60%, Pivot Pct. 25%, Fielding Pct. 15% |
| 3B | Zone Rating 60%, Fielding Pct. 40% |
| SS | Zone Rating 80%, Fielding Pct. 20% |
| LF | Zone Rating 65%, OF Hold Pct. 20%, Fielding Pct. 15% |
| CF | Zone Rating 55%, OF Hold Pct. 30%, Fielding Pct. 15% |
| RF | Zone Rating 50%, OF Hold Pct. 35%, Fielding Pct. 15% |

We'll take a look at the five best and the single worst defensive batting averages at each position in 1997. Players needed 900 innings at an infield position or 800 innings at an outfield position to qualify.

| First Baseman, Team | Zone | FPct | DBA |
|---------------------|------|------|-----|
| Jeff King, KC | .334 | .308 | .328 |
| Tony Clark, Det | .313 | .283 | .306 |
| Jeff Conine, Fla | .310 | .271 | .301 |
| Wally Joyner, SD | .291 | .309 | .295 |
| Mark Grace, Cubs | .291 | .301 | .293 |
| **Worst** | | | |
| Mo Vaughn, Bos | .200 | .236 | .209 |

In his first season as an everyday first baseman, Jeff King posted the highest DBA in baseball. This wasn't a huge surprise, however, because King had a DBA of .356 when he played first base for the Pirates in 1996. Wally Joyner and Mark Grace made the top five in 1996 as well, while American League Gold Glove winner Rafael Palmeiro of the Orioles just missed making this list at .290. National League Gold Glover J.T. Snow of the Giants ranked in the middle of the pack at .266. Mo Vaughn and the White Sox' Frank Thomas usually duel for last place, with Vaughn's knee injury slowing him down enough to let him come out on top, er, bottom.

| Second Baseman, Team | Zone | Pivot | FPct | DBA |
|---|---|---|---|---|
| Mike Lansing, Mon | .310 | .284 | .300 | .302 |
| Bret Boone, Cin | .284 | .316 | .346 | .301 |
| Ryne Sandberg, Cubs | .320 | .235 | .287 | .294 |
| Scott Spiezio, Oak | .290 | .290 | .315 | .294 |
| Jeff Kent, SF | .300 | .289 | .263 | .292 |
| **Worst** | | | | |
| Joey Cora, Sea | .214 | .260 | .234 | .228 |

Bret Boone was nearly flawless in the field, but Mike Lansing had the superior range to win the defensive batting crown at second base. NL Gold Glove winner Craig Biggio of the Astros escaped the basement this year, ranking eighth at .284. His AL counterpart, Chuck Knoblauch of the Twins, also finished at .284. Joey Cora had a surprising year with the bat, but his last-place finish in DBA was more expected. His lack of range makes him an annual contender for the dishonor; he also had the worst DBA at second base in 1995.

| Third Baseman, Team | Zone | FPct | DBA |
|---|---|---|---|
| Jeff Cirillo, Mil | .333 | .294 | .317 |
| Gary Gaetti, StL | .314 | .319 | .316 |
| Edgardo Alfonzo, Mets | .325 | .300 | .315 |
| Travis Fryman, Det | .304 | .318 | .309 |
| Matt Williams, Cle | .295 | .305 | .299 |
| **Worst** | | | |
| Dave Hollins, Ana | .232 | .228 | .230 |

Defending champion Scott Brosius of the Athletics would have repeated as the leader with a .324 DBA, but a knee injury kept him a few innings shy of qualifying. Thus the title went to Jeff Cirillo, who had the best zone rating among third basemen. Matt Williams is the first Gold Glover to make the top five at his position, but NL winner Ken Caminiti of the Padres wasn't close with a DBA of .265. Dave Hollins is a liability at third base, with limited range and an erratic arm.

| Shortstop, Team | Zone | FPct | DBA |
|---|---|---|---|
| Omar Vizquel, Cle | .305 | .314 | .307 |
| Gary DiSarcina, Ana | .312 | .284 | .306 |
| Rey Ordonez, Mets | .303 | .306 | .303 |
| Royce Clayton, StL | .311 | .267 | .302 |
| Alex Gonzalez, Tor | .287 | .315 | .293 |
| **Worst** | | | |
| Shawon Dunston, Cubs-Pit | .207 | .254 | .217 |

We can't question the Gold Glove selections at shortstop. The two winners, Omar Vizquel and Rey Ordonez, were .300 defenders across the board. Not so fortunate was Shawon Dunston, who had easily the worst zone rating at the position and finished 28 points behind the Dodgers' Greg Gagne, the next-worst qualifier at shortstop. Dunston hit .300 with a career-high 32 steals, so his defense is probably the reason he was finding few nibbles as a free agent in the offseason.

| Left Fielder, Team | Zone | OF Arm | FPct | DBA |
|---|---|---|---|---|
| B.J. Surhoff, Bal | .307 | .292 | .309 | .304 |
| Marty Cordova, Min | .297 | .250 | .306 | .289 |
| Henry Rodriguez, Mon | .299 | .243 | .288 | .287 |
| Bobby Higginson, Det | .296 | .281 | .250 | .286 |
| Barry Bonds, SF | .283 | .292 | .283 | .285 |
| **Worst** | | | | |
| Al Martin, Pit | .225 | .274 | .203 | .232 |

Like King at first base, B.J. Surhoff adapted to a new position with ease. He led all left fielders in DBA in his first season of more than 100 games in the outfield, after posting a .275 DBA at third base in 1996. Barry Bonds was the only left fielder to win a Gold Glove in 1997, and we won't quibble with his selection. Al Martin's woeful range made him an easy repeater as the game's worst left fielder.

| Center Fielder, Team | Zone | OF Arm | FPct | DBA |
|---|---|---|---|---|
| Mike Cameron, WSox | .334 | .275 | .266 | .306 |
| Brian Hunter, Det | .307 | .298 | .295 | .302 |
| Kenny Lofton, Atl | .296 | .321 | .264 | .299 |
| Damon Buford, Tex | .298 | .288 | .292 | .294 |
| Lance Johnson, Mets/Cubs | .315 | .296 | .211 | .294 |
| **Worst** | | | | |
| Ray Lankford, StL | .258 | .268 | .209 | .254 |

Not only does Mike Cameron look like a future 25-25 player, but he was the best center fielder in the game during his rookie season. Only Lance Johnson came within 20 points of Cameron's zone batting average. Of the three center fielders to win Gold Gloves, California's Jim Edmonds (.293) and Seattle's Ken Griffey Jr. (.284) almost made the list. The Yankees' Bernie Williams (.277) wasn't as close.

| Right Fielder, Tm | Zone | OF Arm | FPct | DBA |
|---|---|---|---|---|
| Orlando Merced, Tor | .300 | .303 | .293 | .300 |
| Tim Salmon, Ana | .299 | .309 | .263 | .297 |
| Sammy Sosa, Cubs | .301 | .294 | .276 | .295 |
| Raul Mondesi, LA | .289 | .289 | .300 | .291 |
| Paul O'Neill, Yanks | .274 | .312 | .289 | .289 |
| **Worst** | | | | |
| Jose Guillen, Pit | .218 | .253 | .247 | .234 |

Orlando Merced has made the top five for four years running, and also led right fielders in DBA in 1995. Sosa has been on this list for the last three seasons, while O'Neill was on top of it in 1996. Raul Mondesi was the only right fielder to win a Gold Glove last year, and the selection seems justified. Jose Guillen, who idolizes and works out with Mondesi, jumped from Class A to the majors last year and brought with him a reputation for a cannon arm. He didn't live up to that billing as a rookie.

Now that we've covered each position, it's time for a long-standing STATS tradition, the awarding of STATS Gold Gloves. Unlike the real thing, popularity and reputation won't help you here. Our choices are based on DBAs, other defensive statistics and general observations.

**Catcher:** Ivan Rodriguez, Rangers (AL), and Charles Johnson, Marlins (NL). True, we don't have DBAs for catchers. But we're correcting our past omissions of STATS Gold Glove catchers by picking two this year.

The decisions were pretty easy. Rodriguez led the majors by throwing out 56 percent of basestealers, while Johnson ranked third at 47 percent, played errorless ball and committed just one passed ball. Rodriguez and Johnson also won the major league Gold Gloves.

**First Base:** Jeff King, Royals (AL), and Wally Joyner, Padres (NL). With the highest DBA in the game, King wins a STATS Gold Glove in his first full season as a first baseman. Joyner gets the edge over Florida's Jeff Conine because he led major league first basemen in fielding percentage and had a solid zone rating.

**Second Base:** Chuck Knoblauch, Twins (AL), and Bret Boone, Reds (NL). Knoblauch has solid skills across the board and is capable of making the spectacular play. Boone is losing his hitting ability, but he's the most surehanded middle infielder in the game.

**Third Base:** Jeff Cirillo, Brewers (AL), and Edgardo Alfonzo, Mets (NL). The underrated Cirillo fielded more balls cleanly than any major league third baseman and started more double plays from the hot corner than anyone in the AL. The similarly underappreciated Alfonzo brings middle-infield skills and sound instincts to third base.

**Shortstop:** Omar Vizquel, Indians (AL), and Rey Ordonez, Mets (NL). As we said earlier, we have no qualms with the major league Gold Glove winners. Both are steady and spectacular.

**Left Field:** B.J. Surhoff, Orioles (AL), and Barry Bonds, Giants (NL). Surhoff had no problem adjusting from third base, leading regular AL left fielders in zone rating and fielding percentage. When a left fielder wins a Gold Glove in real life, that's saying something. And in Bonds' case, we'll say it was deserved.

**Center Field:** Jim Edmonds, Angels (AL), and Steve Finley, Padres (NL). Edmonds' highlight-reel catches and strong arm were impossible to ignore. The NL doesn't have a leading candidate—and didn't give a Gold Glove to a center fielder—but we went with Finley, who's solid even if his arm doesn't scare baserunners.

**Right Field:** Tim Salmon, Angels (AL), and Sammy Sosa, Cubs. Salmon and Sosa both made a few too many errors for our liking, but they more than made up for it with their other skills. Each led their league's right fielders in assists, and they both have above-average range.

—Jim Callis

A more complete listing for this category can be found on page 270.

### Which First Basemen Are the Best at Starting Double Plays?

It is widely held that lefthanded first basemen enjoy an advantage over righthanded first-sackers. A southpaw gains a particular advantage on a throw to second base, a play which requires a righthanded thrower to perform a 180-degree turn before completing. The righthander's handicap on such a play always has been obvious, and in the *Historical Baseball Abstract,* Bill James noted that the advantages of a lefthanded first baseman were recognized as far back as the 1870s.

Although the issue of whether lefthanded first basemen are superior fielders *overall* is beyond the scope of this essay, we hope to shed some light on the question of whether lefthanded first basemen are more adept at starting double plays. The 3-6-3 or 3-6-1 double play requires a strong, accurate throw by the first baseman, and it stands to reason that since lefthanders make that throw more efficiently, they ought to start more double plays than their righthanded counterparts.

We undertook to study the issue on the basis of double plays started *per opportunity.* We defined an "opportunity" as any situation where the double play was in order, and the first baseman fielded a grounder and threw to second base for a forceout. Then we looked at data from the last three years, separating the lefties from the righties to see which group started more double plays per opportunity. The results of the study stunned us:

**First Basemen's Double Plays Started per Opportunity—1995-97**

|  | Pct. |
| --- | --- |
| Lefthanded Throwers | 33.3 |
| Righthanded Throwers | 38.1 |
| **MLB Average** | **36.3** |

It's tough to make sense of that. Could it be an aberration? Probably not; the study included 1,431 opportunities. Lefties started 183 double plays in 549 opportunities, 26 fewer than the righthanders would have turned in that many chances. We can't fathom any legitimate reason to think that lefthanders actually suffer a *dis*advantage on throws to second, so we're quite willing to entertain the possibility that our methods are too limited to reveal their true advantage. One influence is the fact that righthanded throwers take the "safe" out at first more often than lefthanders do (as you can see in the table on the following page, which lists unassisted putouts at first base). Since righties opt out of some of the tougher DP chances, this artificially inflates their success rate. The impact of this is minor, however, and it serves to explain only a small part of the difference between righthanders' and lefthanders' respective DP success rates.

**First Basemen—1995-97**

| Throws | DP Opp | DP | Pct. | PO at 1B | Pct. |
|--------|--------|-----|------|----------|------|
| Left   | 549    | 183 | 33.3 | 19       | 3.5  |
| Right  | 882    | 336 | 38.1 | 43       | 4.9  |

Another problem may involve our definition of an "opportunity." Due to the limitations of our data, we were not able to charge a first baseman with an opportunity when he fielded a ball with the double play in order but failed to record an out anywhere. Theoretically, righthanded first basemen may have artificially improved their DP success percentage rate by failing to get *either* runner. Our research suggests that righthanded first basemen *are* slightly more prone to throwing errors, but the difference only amounts

**FIRST BASEMAN**

**LEADING FIRST BASEMEN IN STARTING DOUBLE PLAYS 1995–97**

*Throws lefthanded. Minimum 15 opportunities.

| | DP | Opportunities | PCT. |
|---|----|----|------|
| David Segui* | 14 | 19 | 73.7% |
| Carlos Delgado | 9 | 15 | 60.0% |
| Jeff Conine | 11 | 20 | 55.0% |
| Jeff King | 23 | 43 | 53.5% |
| Wally Joyner* | 22 | 42 | 52.4% |
| Andres Galarraga | 30 | 60 | 50.0% |
| Mo Vaughn | 21 | 42 | 50.0% |
| John Jaha | 12 | 25 | 48.0% |
| Tino Martinez | 24 | 54 | 44.4% |
| Greg Colbrunn | 14 | 36 | 38.9% |
| ML Average | | | 36.3% |

to about one additional throwing error per season (3.1 throwing errors per 1,350 innings for righties and 2.2 per 1,350 for lefties). We're skeptical that this effect would be large enough to make much of an impact on the double-play rates listed above.

It's a minor relief to note that the runaway leader in starting the double plays (shown in the illustration on the previous page) *is* a lefty—David Segui.

Out of the top 10, Wally Joyner—a perennial Gold Glove candidate—is the only other lefthanded thrower apart from Segui. Jeff King's experience at third base seems to come in handy, and former catcher Carlos Delgado has retained his throwing accuracy.

The list of the *worst* DP-starters has a few surprises, although we aren't completely shocked to find that Cecil Fielder's 2-for-16 showing brings up the rear (so to speak). St. Louis' John Mabry has the second-worst percentage with only four twin killings in 29 opportunities; obviously, this doesn't bode well for the Cardinals' present plan to convert him into a third baseman. The next three men on the list are lefthanded throwers: Mark Grace (8-51, .157), Will Clark (6-35, .171) and Fred McGriff (6-24, .250).

It's a shock to find four-time Gold Glove-winner Mark Grace ending up with the third-worst mark. Although he's reputed to have a good arm, his reputation mainly rests on his soft hands and his ability to scoop low throws. Perhaps his inability to throw to second has escaped notice simply because the play occurs so infrequently.

According to our figures, the first baseman's ability to start the double play can have a small but significant impact. The average first baseman faces about 16 double-play opportunities per year, and an exceptional fielder may initiate two or three more double plays than the average first baseman. The difference between one of the best and one of the worst may be in the range of six or seven DPs per year. Last year, 22 of 28 major league teams turned between 130 and 170 double plays, so a margin of six or seven seems pretty significant within that 40-DP range.

—Mat Olkin

A more complete listing for this category can be found on page 272.

## Which Players Cleaned up at the Awards Banquet?

Forget the Oscars or the Emmys. The Golden Globes or the Grammys don't have a thing on us. The ESPYs? Don't give 'em a second thought. *We've* got the premier awards banquet in town, and this year the extravaganza is bigger and better than ever. For the last nine years, we've been handing out our annual awards, and our past honorees have included some of the top names in the game. Our unique honors include the esteemed FlatBat (best bunter), the coveted Slidin' Billy Trophy (best leadoff man), the much-publicized Hottest Heater Award (most K/9 IP) and the control artist's prize, the Red Barrett Trophy (for the fewest pitches in a nine-inning game). We also award STATS Gold Gloves; the concept is hardly original, but the approach—namely, rewarding consistent excellence over flashiness—certainly is. And new this year we'll also present the past winners in the categories of Go-Ahead RBI, Holds and Best-Throwing Catchers. Without further adieu, we present your host, self-admitted baseball junkie Billy Crystal!

### STATS FlatBat

The STATS FlatBat goes to the game's best bunter. To get the nod, a player must be able to bunt for a base hit as well as a sacrifice, and he must do both often and effectively. Here are the annual winners:

| Year | Player | Year | Player |
|------|--------|------|--------|
| 1989 | Brett Butler | 1994 | Kenny Lofton |
| 1990 | Brett Butler | 1995 | Otis Nixon |
| 1991 | Steve Finley | 1996 | Kenny Lofton |
| 1992 | Brett Butler | 1997 | Omar Vizquel |
| 1993 | Omar Vizquel |  |  |

Omar Vizquel keeps this honor in Cleveland for the fourth time in the last five seasons. The Tribe shortstop laid down seven bunts for base hits, and was a remarkable 16-for-16 when it came to moving teammates over with a sacrifice bunt. All that, and not a bad fielder to boot (as you'll see later in the show)!

### Slidin' Billy Trophy

In 1894, Slidin' Billy Hamilton hit .404 and set a major league record by scoring 192 runs. Those certainly sound like the numbers of the consummate leadoff hitter to us. In his honor, the Slidin' Billy Trophy goes to the top leadoff hitter each season. His 192 runs may be out of reach in this day and age, but the following players have done Hamilton proud, nonetheless.

| Year | Player | Year | Player |
|------|--------|------|--------|
| 1989 | Rickey Henderson | 1994 | Kenny Lofton |
| 1990 | Rickey Henderson | 1995 | Chuck Knoblauch |
| 1991 | Paul Molitor | 1996 | Chuck Knoblauch |
| 1992 | Brady Anderson | 1997 | Craig Biggio |
| 1993 | Lenny Dykstra | | |

The story of the Houston offense last year began with Craig Biggio reaching base and Jeff Bagwell driving him in. That story was played out over and over and over again, helping the Astros earn a trip to the postseason. For his part, Biggio crossed the plate 146 times, the highest total since Rickey Henderson scored that many for the 1985 Yankees.

## Go-Ahead RBI Leaders

The game-winning RBI may have gone the way of platform shoes and bell-bottoms (oh wait, those things are *back*, aren't they?), but in its place we advocated the "go-ahead RBI" back in 1989. Here are the players who have led the league in RBI that put their team ahead at any point in a game, even if their team failed to hold the lead:

| Year | Player | RBI | Year | Player | RBI |
|------|--------|-----|------|--------|-----|
| 1989 | Pedro Guerrero | 40 | 1994 | Jeff Bagwell | 36 |
| 1990 | Joe Carter | 36 | 1995 | Barry Bonds | 38 |
| 1991 | Fred McGriff | 37 | 1996 | Dante Bichette | 35 |
| 1992 | Carlos Baerga | 42 | 1997 | Jeff Bagwell | 46 |
| 1993 | Albert Belle | 36 | | | |

We just told you the story of the Houston offense in '97, and here's how the other half of the "Killer Bs" fared. Bagwell finished a close third in the vote for National League MVP, and without him the 'Stros may have been fighting to stay out of the NL Central cellar instead of fighting for a spot in the postseason.

## Hottest Heater

It doesn't take a genius to know that the best way to get to strike three is with sheer heat. The winner of each year's "Hottest Heater" award is the pitcher with the highest strikeout rate:

| Year | Pitcher | K/9 | Year | Pitcher | K/9 |
|------|---------|-----|------|---------|-----|
| 1989 | Rob Dibble | 12.8 | 1994 | Bobby Ayala | 12.1 |
| 1990 | Rob Dibble | 12.5 | 1995 | Roberto Hernandez | 12.7 |
| 1991 | Rob Dibble | 13.6 | 1996 | Randy Johnson | 12.5 |
| 1992 | Rob Dibble | 14.1 | 1997 | Billy Wagner | 14.4 |
| 1993 | Duane Ward | 12.2 | | | |

The Astros cleaned up at our banquet in 1997! Billy Wagner fanned 106 batters in 66 1/3 innings last year, setting a major league record by averaging an amazing 14.4 strikeouts per nine innings pitched.

## Red Barrett Trophy

In 1944, Red Barrett threw a complete game using only 58 pitches. We can't even imagine that happening today! The pitcher who uses the fewest pitches in a nine-inning game each season receives the Red Barrett Trophy as a testament to his efficiency:

| Year | Pitcher | #Pitches | Year | Pitcher | #Pitches |
|------|---------|----------|------|---------|----------|
| 1989 | Frank Viola | 85 | 1994 | Bobby Munoz | 80 |
| 1990 | Bob Tewksbury | 76 | 1995 | Greg Maddux | 88 |
| 1991 | Chris Bosio | 82 | 1996 | Bob Wolcott | 79 |
| 1992 | John Smiley | 80 | 1997 | Greg Maddux | 78 |
| 1993 | Tom Glavine | 79 | | | |

The incomparable Greg Maddux may have been thwarted for the second straight year in his efforts to add another Cy Young Award to his already overstuffed mantle, but he *did* pick up this piece of hardware. Mr. Efficiency threw 90 or fewer pitches in three different complete-game efforts in '97, including that award-winning 78-pitch outing on July 22 at Wrigley Field at the expense of his former employers.

## Hold Leader

Saves get all the press, but most closers would never have the chance to steal the headlines without someone holding down the fort. If you're unsure about the definition of a hold, consult the glossary. If you're unsure about the leaders in holds over the past nine years, consult the list on the-following page:

| Year | Pitcher | Holds | Year | Pitcher | Holds |
|------|---------|-------|------|---------|-------|
| 1989 | Rick Honeycutt | 24 | 1994 | Mel Rojas | 19 |
| 1990 | Barry Jones | 30 | 1995 | Troy Percival | 29 |
| 1991 | Mark Eichhorn | 25 | 1996 | Mariano Rivera | 27 |
| 1992 | Duane Ward | 25 | 1997 | Stan Belinda | 28 |
|      | Todd Worrell | 25 |      | Bob Wickman | 28 |
| 1993 | Mike Jackson | 34 |      |         |       |

Over the years, the winners of this honor have usually parlayed their success at holding the fort into the job of closing the door. That probably *won't* be the case for either Stan Belinda or Bob Wickman, but both should remain stalwart "middlers" for years to come.

## Best-Throwing Catchers

Who are those masked men? You know, the ones with the cannons for arms and scopes for eyes? Wonder no more as we unmask the annual leaders in caught-stealing percentage:

| Year | Catcher | CS% | Year | Catcher | CS% |
|------|---------|-----|------|---------|-----|
| 1989 | Damon Berryhill | 44.6 | 1994 | Tom Pagnozzi | 46.8 |
| 1990 | Ron Karkovice | 50.0 | 1995 | Ivan Rodriguez | 43.7 |
| 1991 | Gil Reyes | 50.6 | 1996 | Ivan Rodriguez | 48.9 |
| 1992 | Ivan Rodriguez | 49.0 | 1997 | Ivan Rodriguez | 51.9 |
| 1993 | Steve Lake | 54.5 |      |         |     |

Can you blame us if we were considering renaming this award in honor of Ivan Rodriguez? The Texas wonder nailed 40 of 77 thieves last season, and has improved upon his league-leading figure in each of the last the past three seasons.

## STATS Gold Gloves

Defense continues to be one of the most challenging things to measure in all of baseball. We continue to present our objective findings, however, while maintaining a healthy—and necessary—dose of subjectivity. With that in mind, we turn to the portion of the show where we hand out the STATS Gold Gloves. We don't automatically award them to the most exciting performers or the guys with the best reputations—we're more concerned with finding the players who cover their positions with the greatest efficiency. The winners:

## Catcher

| Year | American | National |
|------|----------|----------|
| 1997 | Ivan Rodriguez | Charles Johnson |

We realized that we had been ignoring catchers when giving out our Gold Gloves, but we corrected that oversight this year. The choices were easy; Ivan Rodriguez led the majors in throwing out basestealers, while Charles Johnson ranked third and didn't make an error.

## First Base

| Year | American | National | Year | American | National |
|------|----------|----------|------|----------|----------|
| 1989 | Don Mattingly | Will Clark | 1994 | Don Mattingly | Jeff Bagwell |
| 1990 | Mark McGwire | Sid Bream | 1995 | Wally Joyner | Jeff Bagwell |
| 1991 | Don Mattingly | Mark Grace | 1996 | Rafael Palmeiro | Mark Grace |
| 1992 | Wally Joyner | Mark Grace | 1997 | Jeff King | Wally Joyner |
| 1993 | Don Mattingly | Mark Grace | | | |

Wally Joyner becomes the first first sacker to win our coveted Gold Glove in both leagues, helping solidify the Padres both at the plate and in the field. Rafael Palmeiro won the American League's Gold Glove, but we gave Jeff King the prize in his first full season at the position. King boasted the highest defensive batting average in all of baseball in '97 (see page 191).

## Second Base

| Year | American | National | Year | American | National |
|------|----------|----------|------|----------|----------|
| 1989 | Harold Reynolds | Ryne Sandberg | 1994 | Jody Reed | Mickey Morandini |
| 1990 | Billy Ripken | Ryne Sandberg | 1995 | Carlos Baerga | Jody Reed |
| 1991 | Mike Gallego | Ryne Sandberg | 1996 | Fernando Vina | Bret Boone |
| 1992 | Carlos Baerga | Ryne Sandberg | 1997 | Chuck Knoblauch | Bret Boone |
| 1993 | Harold Reynolds | Robby Thompson | | | |

The Twins will miss more than just Chuck Knoblauch's leadoff skills. Bret Boone's bat *really* sputtered, but he clearly didn't take his hitting woes into the field.

### Third Base

| Year | American | National | Year | American | National |
|------|----------|----------|------|----------|----------|
| 1989 | Gary Gaetti | Tim Wallach | 1994 | Wade Boggs | Matt Williams |
| 1990 | Gary Gaetti | Charlie Hayes | 1995 | Travis Fryman | Charlie Hayes |
| 1991 | Wade Boggs | Steve Buechele | 1996 | Robin Ventura | Ken Caminiti |
| 1992 | Robin Ventura | Terry Pendleton | 1997 | Jeff Cirillo | Edgardo Alfonzo |
| 1993 | Robin Ventura | Matt Williams | | | |

Thanks to a spring-training accident that ripped apart his ankle, Robin Ventura didn't get the chance to defend his AL crown, but Jeff Cirillo carried the torch admirably. Cirillo led all AL third basemen in double plays started. Edgardo Alfonzo hit .315 and won our Gold Glove Award, with all the fanfare of an Al Gore visit.

### Shortstop

| Year | American | National | Year | American | National |
|------|----------|----------|------|----------|----------|
| 1989 | Ozzie Guillen | Ozzie Smith | 1994 | Gary DiSarcina | Barry Larkin |
| 1990 | Ozzie Guillen | Ozzie Smith | 1995 | Gary DiSarcina | Kevin Stocker |
| 1991 | Cal Ripken | Ozzie Smith | 1996 | Omar Vizquel | Greg Gagne |
| 1992 | Cal Ripken | Ozzie Smith | 1997 | Omar Vizquel | Rey Ordonez |
| 1993 | Ozzie Guillen | Ozzie Smith | | | |

Omar Vizquel has made the postseason his personal playground—who can forget his unbelievable diving stop to help save Game 6 of the World Series for the Indians?—but he hasn't fared too badly during the regular season, either. Since Ozzie Smith's retirement, the NL has become a revolving door, but Rey Ordonez has the skills to stay put for quite some time.

### Left Field

| Year | American | National | Year | American | National |
|------|----------|----------|------|----------|----------|
| 1989 | Rickey Henderson | Barry Bonds | 1994 | Tony Phillips | Moises Alou |
| 1990 | Rickey Henderson | Barry Bonds | 1995 | Garret Anderson | Luis Gonzalez |
| 1991 | Dan Gladden | Bernard Gilkey | 1996 | Tony Phillips | Bernard Gilkey |
| 1992 | Greg Vaughn | Barry Bonds | 1997 | B.J. Surhoff | Barry Bonds |
| 1993 | Greg Vaughn | Barry Bonds | | | |

After a three-year hiatus, Barry Bonds returned to the top spot for the NL in left field. As for B.J. Surhoff, the switch from third base was seamless—he led all regular AL left fielders in fielding percentage and zone rating.

## Center Field

| Year | American | National | Year | American | National |
|---|---|---|---|---|---|
| 1989 | Devon White | Eric Davis | 1994 | Devon White | Marquis Grissom |
| 1990 | Gary Pettis | Lenny Dykstra | 1995 | Jim Edmonds | Marquis Grissom |
| 1991 | Devon White | Brett Butler | 1996 | Kenny Lofton | Steve Finley |
| 1992 | Devon White | Darrin Jackson | 1997 | Jim Edmonds | Steve Finley |
| 1993 | Kenny Lofton | Darren Lewis | | | |

Jim Edmonds made one highlight catch after another to win his second STATS Gold Glove in three years. The NL didn't pass out a Gold Glove to a center fielder this year, but we'll give ours to the steady Steve Finley.

## Right Field

| Year | American | National | Year | American | National |
|---|---|---|---|---|---|
| 1989 | Jesse Barfield | Andre Dawson | 1994 | Paul O'Neill | Reggie Sanders |
| 1990 | Jesse Barfield | Tony Gwynn | 1995 | Tim Salmon | Reggie Sanders |
| 1991 | Joe Carter | Larry Walker | 1996 | Paul O'Neill | Sammy Sosa |
| 1992 | Mark Whiten | Larry Walker | 1997 | Tim Salmon | Sammy Sosa |
| 1993 | Paul O'Neill | Tony Gwynn | | | |

Sammy Sosa continues to play stellar defense. . . and the bleacher bums at Wrigley Field continue to worship him for it. Paul O'Neill? Tim Salmon? Paul O'Neill? Tim Salmon? This year our hardware goes to Salmon. Salmon gunned down 15 baserunners from his right-field post in 1997.

Goodnight, everyone. . . and thanks for tuning in. As always, you were wonderful, Mr. Crystal.

—Tony Nistler

## What Do the Readers Have to Say?

The *Scoreboard* generates lots of letters from our readers, so for the second year in a row, we thought we'd use the last essay to highlight some of the more interesting questions and comments we've received from you "*Scoreboard*-watchers":

Jim Petty writes to us via America Online:

*On one of the various message boards on AOL we got into a little argument over Mike Hargrove's lineups. Some of the people were saying Hargrove tinkers with the lineup and it was hurting the Indians. I and a few others were saying it wasn't. Hargrove has a lineup for facing righthanders, one against lefties and one against tough lefties. All the rest of the lineup changes could be attributed to injuries, slumps or resting Sandy Alomar. . . But it does bring up an interesting question: how many different lineups does a team use in a year, and is there any correlation between the number of lineups and W-L records?*

Interesting question. We provide data on managers each year in our other publications, the *STATS Major League Handbook*, and the number of starting lineups used is one of the subjects listed. Hargrove used 109 different starting lineups last year. That seems like a lot, but it was average for an American League skipper, ranking seventh in the league. The AL skippers who used different starting lineups the most were two guys stuck with losing clubs, Tom Kelly of the Twins (139 different lineups) and Art Howe of the A's (133). The manager who used the *fewest* lineups was Lou Piniella of the Mariners (84), whose team made the playoffs. This suggests a correlation between losing and lineup tinkering, but the relationship isn't really that strong. In the National League, Larry Dierker used the third-most lineups last year (131), and his team won a division. An even better example is Joe Torre with the 1996 Yankees; he used the second-most lineups in the American League that year (131), and his team won a World Series championship. Some guys just like to tinker. Though this is not meant to be a comprehensive study, it nevertheless provides evidence of little correlation.

Brian K. Snell of South Bend, IN, writes:

*While I was looking up something else in the '97 Handbook, I noticed that the National League had a really bad year, fielding-wise, compared to the AL. This intrigued me, so I started researching earlier seasons. . . Every single season the AL was at least as good as, if not better, in fielding percentage. In five of the six seasons, the NL had substantially more errors per game, and in four of the six seasons allowed more unearned runs per game.*

This is interesting, and something we hadn't noticed. Look at errors per game over the last five years:

**Errors per Game—1993-97**

|     | 1993 | 1994 | 1995 | 1996 | 1997 |
|-----|------|------|------|------|------|
| AL  | 1.42 | 1.45 | 1.36 | 1.39 | 1.38 |
| NL  | 1.65 | 1.50 | 1.53 | 1.57 | 1.48 |

Brian offers several theories as to why there would be more errors in the NL, such as the fact that you can't hide a bad fielder at DH, the increased number of stolen-base attempts leading to more errors, poorer field surfaces compared to the newer AL parks, and perhaps stricter official scoring. Your guess is as good as ours at this point, but it's an interesting phenomenon, isn't it?

David Smyth of Riverwoods, IL, always sends us a long, detailed letter full of insightful comments about subjects covered in the *Scoreboard*. Here's what he says about last year's essay, "Who Gets the Green Light on 3-and-0?"

*The idea of having the real good hitters swing at 3-0 cripple pitches more often might be OK except for one thing: pitchers aren't stupid and batters don't wear masks up there. These hitters simply aren't going to get fat 3-0 pitches as often, which essentially equalizes the gain/loss ratio. There is one and only one good reason to occasionally swing at the 3-0 pitch: to keep the pitchers honest.*

True enough; if Frank Thomas or Mike Piazza is up with a 3-0 count, not many pitchers are going to lay the ball down the middle just to avoid giving up a walk. But interestingly, the percentage of 3-0 swings has risen fairly steadily in recent years, especially in the American League. In 1991, the average AL hitter swung at a 3-and-0 strike (that is, any 3-0 pitch that was not called ball four by the umpire) about 15 percent of the time. By 1997, the swing percentage had risen to a little over 20 percent. NL figures fluctuated more, but the trend was still upward; the NL swing percentage was 13 percent in 1992, 18 percent in 1996 with some dips before and after. While hitters are still taking the 3-0 pitch the vast majority of the time, managers seem to be a lot less reluctant to give the hitter the green light than they used to be.

Donald Ketchek of Rochester, NY, comments:

*In a lot of the new statistical equations, a walk is given equal weight to a single. Yet every baseball fan knows that when runners are on base, a walk and a single are not equal. And since moving runners around the bases until they score is the object of the offense, can't we better measure a player's offensive ability if we more accurately measure the value of a walk and a single?*

Donald did his own calculations over a sample of 20 major league games, and found that for a batter and any runners who were on base at the time, each walk was worth 0.829 bases, while each single was worth 1.275 bases, a pretty big difference.

He's right, of course, but the best measuring sticks *do* account for the fact that singles are more valuable than walks. For instance, Pete Palmer's Linear Weights formula estimates that each walk is worth .33 runs, while each single is worth .47 runs, which is over 40 percent more. Bill James' runs created formulas begin by multiplying times on base (which is mostly hits plus walks) by total bases—effectively giving significantly more weight to singles than walks, since they're counted in both factors of the equation while walks are counted only once. The same goes for on-base plus slugging; since singles are a component of both on-base *and* slugging percentage while walks are a component only of on-base percentage, the result is again a much heavier weighting for singles. Still, it would be good to calculate the exact run value of a walk vs. a single using actual major league data, and perhaps we'll get to that in a future edition of the book.

Finally, our colleague Rob Neyer passed along an e-mail message from Matt Tiemeyer of Wichita, KS, who wrote:

*I was checking the K.C. box score this morning, and saw that the beleaguered Mike Macfarlane was 2-for-2 against Tom Gordon. This got me to thinking, since Gordon shackled the rest of the lineup for most of the evening: Has anyone ever run the numbers on catchers' averages against pitchers they've caught versus their overall average?*

Yes, we've done this, though we did it a little differently from the way Matt suggested. Last April, after Terry Steinbach had a big game against his ex-teammates from Oakland, ace programmer Stefan Kretschmann calculated how catchers performed against guys they had caught. He separated their plate appearances into the times they batted against the pitcher prior to getting a chance to catch him as a teammate, and then the PAs after they'd worked as a batterymate to the pitcher. Here's the data:

**Catchers Hitting Versus Pitchers They've Caught—1987-97**

|  | AB | Avg | OBP | SLG |
|---|---|---|---|---|
| Before catching pitcher | 9,199 | .248 | .310 | .377 |
| After catching pitcher | 6,553 | .259 | .333 | .409 |

Having previously caught a pitcher seems to be an advantage to a catcher. The differences were more extreme for Steinbach: he batted .257 and slugged .403 before catching a pitcher, but he batted .299 and slugged .425 after catching these same pitchers. A little first-hand knowledge pays off!

— Don Zminda

# APPENDIX

Each Appendix has two pieces of information to help reference it to its corresponding essay. The "Title" matches the title in the Table of Contents, and the "Page" refers to the page number of the corresponding essay. Most appendices will be accompanied by a brief explanation describing the order of the list as well as any minimum requirements used. Also note that in some appendices, we could not include every team for players who played with more than one club in 1997. In those cases, the player is listed with the last team he played for.

The team abbreviation following a player's name refers to the team with which he accumulated all or most of his playing time. Here are the abbreviations for current franchises:

| American League Teams | | National League Teams | |
|---|---|---|---|
| Bal | Baltimore Orioles | Atl | Atlanta Braves |
| Bos | Boston Red Sox | Cubs | Chicago Cubs |
| Cal | California Angels | Cin | Cincinnati Reds |
| WSox | Chicago White Sox | Col | Colorado Rockies |
| Cle | Cleveland Indians | Fla | Florida Marlins |
| Det | Detroit Tigers | Hou | Houston Astros |
| KC | Kansas City Royals | LA | Los Angeles Dodgers |
| Mil | Milwaukee Brewers | Mon | Montreal Expos |
| Min | Minnesota Twins | Mets | New York Mets |
| Yanks | New York Yankees | Phi | Philadelphia Phillies |
| Oak | Oakland Athletics | Pit | Pittsburgh Pirates |
| Sea | Seattle Mariners | StL | St. Louis Cardinals |
| Tex | Texas Rangers | SD | San Diego Padres |
| Tor | Toronto Blue Jays | SF | San Francisco Giants |

# Boston Red Sox: Was Garciaparra the Best Rookie Shortstop Ever? (p. 9)

## Most Runs Created

| Rookie Shortstops (min 130 previous AB) | | | Shortstops | | |
|---|---|---|---|---|---|
| Player, Team | Year | RC | Player, Team | Year | RC |
| Herman Long, KC | 1889 | 127 | Oyster Burns, Bal | 1887 | 153 |
| Nomar Garciaparra, Bos | 1997 | 117 | Hughie Jennings, Bal | 1895 | 147 |
| Jimmy Cooney, Chi | 1890 | 110 | Alex Rodriguez, Sea | 1996 | 147 |
| Joe Sewell, Cle | 1921 | 110 | Bill Dahlen, Chi | 1894 | 146 |
| Frank Fennelly, Was-Cin | 1884 | 107 | Hughie Jennings, Bal | 1896 | 144 |
| Gene DeMontreville, Was | 1896 | 104 | Billy Shindle, Phi | 1890 | 143 |
| Ed McKean, Cle | 1887 | 103 | Arky Vaughan, Pit | 1935 | 142 |
| Dick Howser, KC | 1961 | 102 | Monte Ward, Bro | 1890 | 140 |
| Tom Tresh, Yanks | 1962 | 102 | Ed McKean, Cle | 1894 | 138 |
| Johnny Pesky, RSox | 1942 | 97 | Honus Wagner, Pit | 1905 | 136 |
| Freddy Parent, RSox | 1901 | 93 | Robin Yount, Mil | 1982 | 136 |
| Jim Canavan, Cin-Mil | 1891 | 92 | Ed McKean, Cle | 1895 | 134 |
| Bill Keister, Bal | 1899 | 92 | Bill Dahlen, Chi | 1896 | 134 |
| Harvey Kuenn, Det | 1953 | 92 | Luke Appling, WSox | 1936 | 134 |
| Ollie Beard, Cin | 1889 | 91 | Jack Glasscock, Ind | 1889 | 133 |
| Stan Rojek, Pit | 1948 | 88 | George Davis, NYG | 1897 | 133 |
| Donie Bush, Det | 1909 | 85 | Honus Wagner, Pit | 1901 | 133 |
| Vern Stephens, Browns | 1942 | 85 | Arky Vaughan, Pit | 1936 | 132 |
| Cal Ripken, Bal | 1982 | 85 | Hughie Jennings, Bal | 1898 | 131 |
| Charlie Hollocher, Cubs | 1918 | 84 | Honus Wagner, Pit | 1908 | 131 |
| Glenn Wright, Pit | 1924 | 84 | Lou Boudreau, Cle | 1948 | 130 |
| Derek Jeter, Yanks | 1996 | 83 | Joe Cronin, Was | 1930 | 129 |
| Topper Rigney, Det | 1922 | 79 | Alan Trammell, Det | 1987 | 129 |
| Ron Hansen, Bal | 1960 | 79 | Honus Wagner, Pit | 1904 | 128 |
| Al Dark, Braves | 1948 | 78 | Vern Stephens, RSox | 1949 | 128 |
| Ernie Banks, Cubs | 1954 | 78 | Herman Long, KC | 1889 | 127 |
| Pat Listach, Mil | 1992 | 78 | Herman Long, Bos | 1891 | 127 |
| Frank Scheibeck, Tol | 1890 | 77 | Cecil Travis, Was | 1941 | 127 |
| Billy Klaus, Bos | 1955 | 76 | Honus Wagner, Pit | 1903 | 126 |
| Alfredo Griffin, Tor | 1979 | 76 | Arky Vaughan, Pit | 1934 | 126 |
| Arky Vaughan, Pit | 1932 | 75 | Joe Sewell, Cle | 1923 | 125 |
| Bob Allen, Phi | 1890 | 74 | Cal Ripken, Bal | 1991 | 125 |
| Red Kress, Browns | 1928 | 74 | Phil Rizzuto, Yanks | 1950 | 124 |
| George Wright, Bos | 1876 | 73 | John McGraw, Bal | 1893 | 123 |
| John Peters, Chi | 1876 | 72 | Ernie Banks, Cubs | 1958 | 123 |
| Mark Koenig, Yanks | 1926 | 72 | Joe Cronin, Was | 1931 | 122 |
| Sonny Jackson, Hou | 1966 | 71 | Joe Cronin, Bos | 1938 | 122 |
| Tommy Corcoran, Pit | 1890 | 70 | Herman Long, Bos | 1893 | 121 |
| Joe Sullivan, Was | 1893 | 70 | Hughie Jennings, Bal | 1894 | 121 |
| Wid Conroy, Mil | 1901 | 70 | Honus Wagner, Pit | 1907 | 121 |
| Phil Rizzuto, Yanks | 1941 | 70 | Ernie Banks, Cubs | 1959 | 121 |
| Chico Carrasquel, WSox | 1950 | 70 | Sam Wise, Bos | 1887 | 120 |
| Bobby Grich, Bal | 1972 | 70 | Ed McKean, Cle | 1890 | 120 |
| Dave Bancroft, Phils | 1915 | 69 | Herman Long, Bos | 1892 | 120 |
| Rabbit Maranville, Braves | 1913 | 68 | Ed McKean, Cle | 1893 | 120 |
| Buddy Kerr, NYG | 1944 | 68 | Ernie Banks, Cubs | 1957 | 120 |
| Monte Cross, Pit | 1895 | 67 | Travis Fryman, Det | 1993 | 120 |
| Charlie Babb, NYG | 1903 | 67 | Pee Wee Reese, Bro | 1949 | 119 |
| Ike Davis, WSox | 1925 | 67 | Monte Ward, NYG | 1887 | 118 |
| Solly Hemus, Cards | 1951 | 67 | Rico Petrocelli, Bos | 1969 | 118 |

# Chicago White Sox: Is The Big Hurt Unique? (p. 11)

## On-Base and Slugging Percentage Leaders—By Era
### (minimum 2500 PA)

| Era | OBP Leader | | Slg Leader | |
|---|---|---|---|---|
| 1876-1900 | John McGraw | .465 | Dan Brouthers | .520 |
| | Billy Hamilton | .458 | Sam Thompson | .506 |
| | Bill Joyce | .435 | Dave Orr | .502 |
| | Jesse Burkett | .433 | Ed Delahanty | .499 |
| | Joe Kelley | .428 | Joe Kelley | .492 |
| | Willie Keeler | .426 | Roger Connor | .486 |
| | Dan Brouthers | .424 | Jake Stenzel | .480 |
| | Cupid Childs | .418 | Willie Keeler | .477 |
| | Jake Stenzel | .408 | Jesse Burkett | .470 |
| | Ed Delahanty | .408 | Bill Joyce | .467 |
| **Era** | **OBP Leader** | | **Slg Leader** | |
| 1901-1919 | Ty Cobb | .434 | Ty Cobb | .516 |
| | Joe Jackson | .420 | Joe Jackson | .509 |
| | Tris Speaker | .418 | Gavy Cravath | .478 |
| | Eddie Collins | .417 | Tris Speaker | .476 |
| | Roy Thomas | .403 | Mike Donlin | .465 |
| | Frank Chance | .397 | Honus Wagner | .462 |
| | Honus Wagner | .392 | Sam Crawford | .453 |
| | Benny Kauff | .389 | Nap Lajoie | .451 |
| | Mike Donlin | .389 | Benny Kauff | .450 |
| | Roger Bresnahan | .386 | George Sisler | .444 |
| **Era** | **OBP Leader** | | **Slg Leader** | |
| 1920-1945 | Babe Ruth | .482 | Babe Ruth | .708 |
| | Ted Williams | .481 | Ted Williams | .642 |
| | Rogers Hornsby | .453 | Lou Gehrig | .632 |
| | Lou Gehrig | .447 | Rogers Hornsby | .621 |
| | Tris Speaker | .441 | Hank Greenberg | .617 |
| | Eddie Collins | .436 | Jimmie Foxx | .609 |
| | Ty Cobb | .431 | Joe DiMaggio | .607 |
| | Harry Heilmann | .431 | Johnny Mize | .588 |
| | Jimmie Foxx | .428 | Harry Heilmann | .558 |
| | Max Bishop | .423 | Ken Williams | .547 |
| **Era** | **OBP Leader** | | **Slg Leader** | |
| 1946-1960 | Ted Williams | .482 | Ted Williams | .631 |
| | Ferris Fain | .424 | Willie Mays | .585 |
| | Mickey Mantle | .422 | Stan Musial | .576 |
| | Stan Musial | .421 | Mickey Mantle | .568 |
| | Eddie Stanky | .419 | Hank Aaron | .560 |
| | Jackie Robinson | .409 | Ernie Banks | .557 |
| | Elmer Valo | .408 | Duke Snider | .554 |
| | Luke Appling | .402 | Frank Robinson | .552 |
| | Ralph Kiner | .398 | Eddie Mathews | .549 |
| | Minnie Minoso | .397 | Ralph Kiner | .548 |

| Era | OBP Leader | | Slg Leader | |
| --- | --- | --- | --- | --- |
| 1961-1976 | Mickey Mantle | .418 | Hank Aaron | .552 |
| | Joe Morgan | .400 | Mickey Mantle | .539 |
| | Frank Robinson | .392 | Dick Allen | .539 |
| | Ken Singleton | .389 | Willie Mays | .537 |
| | Bernie Carbo | .388 | Frank Robinson | .531 |
| | Carl Yastrzemski | .387 | Willie McCovey | .530 |
| | Rod Carew | .384 | Willie Stargell | .529 |
| | Willie McCovey | .383 | Harmon Killebrew | .511 |
| | Pete Rose | .381 | Roberto Clemente | .507 |
| | Harmon Killebrew | .380 | Reggie Jackson | .503 |
| Era | OBP Leader | | Slg Leader | |
| 1977-1997 | Frank Thomas | .452 | Frank Thomas | .600 |
| | Edgar Martinez | .423 | Mike Piazza | .576 |
| | Wade Boggs | .420 | Albert Belle | .566 |
| | Jeff Bagwell | .409 | Ken Griffey Jr. | .562 |
| | Jim Thome | .408 | Juan Gonzalez | .557 |
| | Barry Bonds | .408 | Mark McGwire | .556 |
| | Rickey Henderson | .406 | Barry Bonds | .551 |
| | Gene Tenace | .404 | Larry Walker | .542 |
| | Rod Carew | .403 | Jim Thome | .541 |
| | Mike Piazza | .398 | Mike Schmidt | .537 |

# Detroit Tigers: Can They Continue to Improve? (p. 15)

## Biggest Improvements

| Team | Year 1 | Pct | Year 2 | Pct | Change | Year 3 | Pct | Change |
|------|--------|-----|--------|-----|--------|--------|-----|--------|
| Giants | 1902 | .353 | 1903 | .604 | .251 | 1904 | .697 | .093 |
| Brewers | 1901 | .350 | 1902 | .570 | .220 | 1903 | .468 | −.102 |
| Red Sox | 1945 | .461 | 1946 | .675 | .214 | 1947 | .539 | −.136 |
| Braves | 1935 | .248 | 1936 | .461 | .213 | 1937 | .520 | .059 |
| Phillies | 1904 | .342 | 1905 | .546 | .204 | 1906 | .464 | −.082 |
| Orioles | 1988 | .335 | 1989 | .537 | .202 | 1990 | .472 | −.065 |
| Phillies | 1961 | .305 | 1962 | .503 | .198 | 1963 | .537 | .034 |
| Giants | 1992 | .444 | 1993 | .636 | .191 | 1994 | .478 | −.158 |
| Cardinals | 1913 | .340 | 1914 | .529 | .189 | 1915 | .471 | −.058 |
| Pirates | 1917 | .331 | 1918 | .520 | .189 | 1919 | .511 | −.009 |
| Athletics | 1946 | .318 | 1947 | .506 | .188 | 1948 | .545 | .039 |
| Senators | 1911 | .416 | 1912 | .599 | .183 | 1913 | .584 | −.015 |
| Reds | 1937 | .364 | 1938 | .547 | .183 | 1939 | .630 | .083 |
| Phillies | 1928 | .283 | 1929 | .464 | .181 | 1930 | .338 | −.126 |
| Red Sox | 1911 | .510 | 1912 | .691 | .181 | 1913 | .527 | −.164 |
| Braves | 1952 | .418 | 1953 | .597 | .179 | 1954 | .578 | −.019 |
| Braves | 1990 | .401 | 1991 | .580 | .179 | 1992 | .605 | .025 |
| Athletics | 1979 | .333 | 1980 | .512 | .179 | 1981 | .587 | .075 |
| Athletics | 1908 | .444 | 1909 | .623 | .179 | 1910 | .680 | .057 |
| Cubs | 1966 | .364 | 1967 | .540 | .176 | 1968 | .519 | −.021 |
| Giants | 1953 | .455 | 1954 | .630 | .175 | 1955 | .519 | −.111 |
| Orioles | 1902 | .365 | 1903 | .537 | .172 | 1904 | .609 | .072 |
| Senators | 1904 | .252 | 1905 | .424 | .172 | 1906 | .367 | −.057 |
| Cubs | 1917 | .481 | 1918 | .651 | .171 | 1919 | .536 | −.115 |
| Rangers | 1973 | .352 | 1974 | .522 | .170 | 1975 | .488 | −.034 |
| Cardinals | 1903 | .314 | 1904 | .484 | .170 | 1905 | .377 | −.107 |
| White Sox | 1918 | .460 | 1919 | .629 | .169 | 1920 | .623 | −.006 |
| Tigers | 1933 | .487 | 1934 | .656 | .169 | 1935 | .616 | −.040 |
| Reds | 1960 | .435 | 1961 | .604 | .169 | 1962 | .605 | .001 |
| Mets | 1968 | .451 | 1969 | .617 | .167 | 1970 | .512 | −.105 |
| Phillies | 1992 | .432 | 1993 | .599 | .167 | 1994 | .470 | −.129 |
| Tigers | 1960 | .461 | 1961 | .623 | .162 | 1962 | .528 | −.095 |
| Cubs | 1905 | .601 | 1906 | .763 | .162 | 1907 | .704 | −.059 |
| Senators | 1909 | .276 | 1910 | .437 | .161 | 1911 | .416 | −.021 |
| Brewers | 1977 | .414 | 1978 | .574 | .160 | 1979 | .590 | .016 |
| Tigers | 1996 | .327 | 1997 | .488 | .160 | 1998 | — | — |
| Highlanders | 1908 | .331 | 1909 | .490 | .159 | 1910 | .583 | .093 |
| White Sox | 1976 | .398 | 1977 | .556 | .158 | 1978 | .441 | −.115 |
| Cubs | 1983 | .438 | 1984 | .596 | .158 | 1985 | .478 | −.118 |
| Braves | 1913 | .457 | 1914 | .614 | .157 | 1915 | .546 | −.068 |
| Browns | 1905 | .353 | 1906 | .510 | .157 | 1907 | .454 | −.056 |
| Dodgers | 1944 | .409 | 1945 | .565 | .156 | 1946 | .615 | .050 |
| Browns | 1939 | .279 | 1940 | .435 | .156 | 1941 | .455 | .020 |
| Reds | 1918 | .531 | 1919 | .686 | .154 | 1920 | .536 | −.150 |
| Terriers | 1914 | .411 | 1915 | .565 | .154 | 1916 | Did not field a team | |
| Rangers | 1985 | .385 | 1986 | .537 | .152 | 1987 | .463 | −.074 |
| White Sox | 1989 | .429 | 1990 | .580 | .152 | 1991 | .537 | −.043 |
| Senators | 1944 | .416 | 1945 | .565 | .149 | 1946 | .494 | −.071 |
| Phillies | 1945 | .299 | 1946 | .448 | .149 | 1947 | .403 | −.045 |
| Athletics | 1943 | .318 | 1944 | .468 | .149 | 1945 | .347 | −.121 |

# Minnesota Twins: What Might Have Been for Molitor? (p. 20)

## Career Projections for a "Healthy" Paul Molitor

| Year | Team | G | AB | H | 2B | 3B | HR | R | RBI | SB | Avg |
|------|------|------|-------|------|-----|-----|-----|------|------|-----|------|
| 1978 | Mil | 125 | 521 | 142 | 26 | 4 | 6 | 73 | 45 | 30 | .273 |
| 1979 | Mil | 140 | 584 | 188 | 27 | 16 | 9 | 88 | 62 | 33 | .322 |
| 1980 | Mil | 155 | 628 | 191 | 40 | 3 | 13 | 113 | 52 | 47 | .304 |
| 1981 | Mil | 105 | 412 | 110 | 18 | 0 | 3 | 74 | 31 | 16 | .267 |
| 1982 | Mil | 160 | 666 | 201 | 26 | 8 | 19 | 136 | 71 | 41 | .302 |
| 1983 | Mil | 152 | 608 | 164 | 28 | 6 | 15 | 95 | 47 | 41 | .270 |
| 1984 | Mil | 155 | 625 | 175 | 29 | 5 | 13 | 97 | 51 | 32 | .280 |
| 1985 | Mil | 140 | 576 | 171 | 28 | 3 | 10 | 93 | 48 | 21 | .297 |
| 1986 | Mil | 155 | 645 | 182 | 35 | 9 | 13 | 92 | 81 | 30 | .282 |
| 1987 | Mil | 155 | 611 | 215 | 54 | 7 | 21 | 150 | 99 | 59 | .352 |
| 1988 | Mil | 154 | 609 | 190 | 34 | 6 | 13 | 115 | 60 | 41 | .312 |
| 1989 | Mil | 155 | 615 | 194 | 35 | 4 | 11 | 84 | 56 | 27 | .315 |
| 1990 | Mil | 155 | 629 | 179 | 41 | 9 | 18 | 96 | 68 | 27 | .285 |
| 1991 | Mil | 158 | 665 | 216 | 32 | 13 | 17 | 133 | 75 | 19 | .325 |
| 1992 | Mil | 158 | 609 | 195 | 36 | 7 | 12 | 89 | 89 | 31 | .320 |
| 1993 | Tor | 160 | 636 | 211 | 37 | 5 | 22 | 121 | 111 | 22 | .332 |
| 1994 | Tor | 115 | 454 | 155 | 30 | 4 | 14 | 86 | 75 | 20 | .341 |
| 1995 | Tor | 130 | 525 | 142 | 31 | 2 | 15 | 63 | 60 | 12 | .270 |
| 1996 | Min | 161 | 660 | 225 | 41 | 8 | 9 | 99 | 113 | 18 | .341 |
| 1997 | Min | 135 | 538 | 164 | 32 | 4 | 10 | 63 | 89 | 11 | .305 |
| Totals | | 2923 | 11816 | 3610 | 660 | 123 | 263 | 1960 | 1383 | 578 | .306 |

# Oakland Athletics: How Small Was Aaron's Win Total? (p. 25)

## Fewest Wins By A Team Leader
### (excluding 1981 and 1994 strike seasons)

| Year | Team | Leader | W |
|------|------|--------|---|
| 1987 | Cleveland Indians | Phil Niekro, Tom Candiotti, Scott Bailes | 7 |
| 1996 | Detroit Tigers | Omar Olivares | 7 |
| 1911 | Boston Beaneaters | Buster Brown | 8 |
| 1919 | Philadelphia Phillies | Lee Meadows | 8 |
| 1928 | Philadelphia Phillies | Ray Benge | 8 |
| 1945 | Philadelphia Phillies | Andy Karl, Dick Barrett | 8 |
| 1953 | St. Louis Browns | Marlin Stuart | 8 |
| 1965 | New York Mets | Al Jackson, Jack Fisher | 8 |
| 1969 | San Diego Padres | Joe Niekro, Al Santorini | 8 |
| 1988 | Baltimore Orioles | Dave Schmidt, Jeff Ballard | 8 |
| 1995 | St. Louis Cardinals | Rich DeLucia | 8 |
| 1996 | Oakland Athletics | John Wasdin | 8 |
| 1903 | St. Louis Cardinals | Three Finger Brown, Chappie McFarland | 9 |
| 1906 | St. Louis Cardinals | Fred Beebe | 9 |
| 1919 | Philadelphia Athletics | Walt Kinney, Jing Johnson | 9 |
| 1927 | Philadelphia Phillies | Jack Scott | 9 |
| 1937 | St. Louis Browns | Jim Walkup | 9 |
| 1939 | St. Louis Browns | Jack Kramer, Vern Kennedy | 9 |
| 1941 | Philadelphia Phillies | Tommy Hughes, Johnny Podgajny | 9 |
| 1945 | Boston Braves | Jim Tobin | 9 |
| 1948 | Chicago White Sox | Bill Wight, Joe Haynes | 9 |
| 1954 | Philadelphia Athletics | Arnie Portocarrero | 9 |
| 1957 | Kansas City Athletics | Tom Morgan, Virgil Trucks | 9 |
| 1963 | Washington Senators | Claude Osteen | 9 |
| 1973 | Texas Rangers | Jim Bibby | 9 |
| 1974 | San Diego Padres | Dan Spillner, Dave Freisleben, Larry Hardy, Bill Greif | 9 |
| 1979 | Toronto Blue Jays | Tom Underwood | 9 |
| 1985 | Cleveland Indians | Bert Blyleven, Neal Heaton | 9 |
| 1985 | San Francisco Giants | Scott Garrelts | 9 |
| 1986 | Chicago Cubs | Scott Sanderson, Lee Smith | 9 |
| 1988 | Atlanta Braves | Rick Mahler | 9 |
| 1996 | Philadelphia Phillies | Curt Schilling | 9 |
| 1997 | Colorado Rockies | Darren Holmes, Roger Bailey | 9 |
| 1997 | Oakland Athletics | Aaron Small | 9 |

## Seattle Mariners: Will Griffey Shatter the Home-Run Record? (p. 27)

### Percentage Chance to Reach Career Milestones

| Player | Age | Current H | HR | RBI | Home Runs 500 | 600 | 700 | 756 | 800 | Hits 3000 | 4000 | 4257 | RBI 2000 | 2298 |
|---|---|---|---|---|---|---|---|---|---|---|---|---|---|---|
| Mark McGwire | 33 | 1201 | 387 | 983 | 94% | 63% | 27% | 15% | 8% | — | — | — | 1% | — |
| Barry Bonds | 32 | 1750 | 374 | 1094 | 91% | 39% | 12% | 3% | — | 13% | — | — | 12% | — |
| Ken Griffey Jr | 27 | 1389 | 294 | 872 | 88% | 66% | 38% | 27% | 20% | 24% | — | — | 35% | 17% |
| Juan Gonzalez | 27 | 1045 | 256 | 790 | 78% | 41% | 20% | 13% | 7% | 10% | — | — | 30% | 14% |
| Albert Belle | 30 | 1188 | 272 | 867 | 56% | 24% | 7% | — | — | 10% | — | — | 19% | 5% |
| Frank Thomas | 29 | 1261 | 257 | 854 | 53% | 23% | 6% | — | — | 18% | — | — | 23% | 8% |
| Sammy Sosa | 28 | 1035 | 207 | 642 | 41% | 18% | 4% | — | — | 5% | — | — | 9% | — |
| Rafael Palmeiro | 32 | 1792 | 271 | 958 | 36% | 10% | — | — | — | 21% | — | — | 8% | — |
| Jay Buhner | 32 | 1053 | 253 | 795 | 35% | 11% | — | — | — | — | — | — | 1% | — |
| Jose Canseco | 32 | 1470 | 351 | 1107 | 35% | 1% | — | — | — | — | — | — | — | — |
| Mo Vaughn | 29 | 960 | 190 | 637 | 33% | 13% | — | — | — | 8% | — | — | 7% | — |
| Jim Thome | 26 | 617 | 133 | 386 | 31% | 14% | 3% | — | — | — | — | — | 1% | — |
| Larry Walker | 30 | 1100 | 202 | 673 | 29% | 9% | — | — | — | 3% | — | — | — | — |
| Jeff Bagwell | 29 | 1112 | 187 | 724 | 24% | 6% | — | — | — | 7% | — | — | 13% | 1% |
| Fred McGriff | 33 | 1622 | 339 | 1007 | 21% | — | — | — | — | 4% | — | — | — | — |
| Tino Martinez | 29 | 852 | 157 | 570 | 19% | 3% | — | — | — | 3% | — | — | 9% | — |
| Matt Williams | 31 | 1249 | 279 | 837 | 19% | — | — | — | — | — | — | — | — | — |
| Vinny Castilla | 29 | 674 | 124 | 365 | 18% | 4% | — | — | — | 2% | — | — | — | — |
| Tim Salmon | 28 | 782 | 153 | 503 | 16% | 1% | — | — | — | 5% | — | — | 5% | — |
| Manny Ramirez | 25 | 590 | 109 | 372 | 15% | 2% | — | — | — | 12% | — | — | 3% | — |
| Eric Karros | 29 | 891 | 154 | 535 | 12% | — | — | — | — | 1% | — | — | — | — |
| Gary Sheffield | 28 | 1048 | 180 | 621 | 10% | — | — | — | — | — | — | — | — | — |
| Alex Rodriguez | 21 | 435 | 64 | 228 | 9% | — | — | — | — | 18% | — | — | 1% | — |
| A. Galarraga | 36 | 1752 | 288 | 1051 | 9% | — | — | — | — | — | — | — | — | — |
| Cecil Fielder | 33 | 1216 | 302 | 940 | 8% | — | — | — | — | — | — | — | — | — |
| Raul Mondesi | 26 | 690 | 100 | 329 | 6% | — | — | — | — | 15% | — | — | — | — |
| Mike Piazza | 28 | 854 | 168 | 533 | 6% | — | — | — | — | — | — | — | — | — |
| Ellis Burks | 32 | 1378 | 209 | 744 | 5% | — | — | — | — | — | — | — | — | — |
| Ryan Klesko | 26 | 447 | 100 | 300 | 5% | — | — | — | — | — | — | — | — | — |
| Dean Palmer | 28 | 729 | 163 | 482 | 4% | — | — | — | — | — | — | — | — | — |
| Joe Carter | 37 | 2083 | 378 | 1382 | 2% | — | — | — | — | — | — | — | — | — |
| Jim Edmonds | 27 | 533 | 91 | 294 | 2% | — | — | — | — | — | — | — | — | — |
| Tony Gwynn | 37 | 2780 | 107 | 973 | — | — | — | — | — | 97% | — | — | — | — |
| Cal Ripken | 36 | 2715 | 370 | 1453 | — | — | — | — | — | 95% | — | — | 1% | — |
| Wade Boggs | 39 | 2800 | 109 | 933 | — | — | — | — | — | 49% | — | — | — | — |
| Roberto Alomar | 29 | 1659 | 113 | 653 | — | — | — | — | — | 28% | — | — | — | — |
| C. Knoblauch | 28 | 1197 | 43 | 391 | — | — | — | — | — | 23% | — | — | — | — |
| Craig Biggio | 31 | 1470 | 116 | 545 | — | — | — | — | — | 16% | — | — | — | — |
| Travis Fryman | 28 | 1176 | 149 | 679 | — | — | — | — | — | 14% | — | — | 3% | — |
| Harold Baines | 38 | 2561 | 339 | 1423 | — | — | — | — | — | 14% | — | — | — | — |
| Mark Grace | 33 | 1691 | 104 | 742 | — | — | — | — | — | 13% | — | — | — | — |
| Chipper Jones | 25 | 502 | 74 | 307 | — | — | — | — | — | 10% | — | — | 4% | — |
| Bobby Bonilla | 34 | 1810 | 262 | 1061 | — | — | — | — | — | 9% | — | — | — | — |
| Garret Anderson | 25 | 487 | 36 | 234 | — | — | — | — | — | 9% | — | — | — | — |
| M. Grissom | 30 | 1242 | 101 | 458 | — | — | — | — | — | 8% | — | — | — | — |
| Bernie Williams | 28 | 927 | 100 | 469 | — | — | — | — | — | 8% | — | — | — | — |
| Derek Jeter | 23 | 385 | 20 | 155 | — | — | — | — | — | 8% | — | — | — | — |
| N. Garciaparra | 23 | 230 | 34 | 114 | — | — | — | — | — | 7% | — | — | — | — |
| Carlos Baerga | 28 | 1231 | 114 | 623 | — | — | — | — | — | 6% | — | — | — | — |
| Kenny Lofton | 30 | 1047 | 44 | 309 | — | — | — | — | — | 5% | — | — | — | — |
| D. DeShields | 28 | 1063 | 49 | 350 | — | — | — | — | — | 4% | — | — | — | — |
| Brian McRae | 29 | 1102 | 70 | 405 | — | — | — | — | — | 4% | — | — | — | — |
| Ivan Rodriguez | 25 | 948 | 88 | 417 | — | — | — | — | — | 4% | — | — | — | — |
| Ray Durham | 25 | 446 | 28 | 169 | — | — | — | — | — | 3% | — | — | — | — |
| Edgar Renteria | 21 | 304 | 9 | 83 | — | — | — | — | — | 3% | — | — | — | — |
| Jay Bell | 31 | 1369 | 104 | 553 | — | — | — | — | — | 2% | — | — | — | — |
| John Olerud | 28 | 1064 | 131 | 573 | — | — | — | — | — | 1% | — | — | — | — |
| Rusty Greer | 28 | 573 | 67 | 294 | — | — | — | — | — | 1% | — | — | — | — |

# Atlanta Braves: How Good Is the Glavine/Maddux/Smoltz Trio? (p. 39)

## Top Starting Threesomes (minimum 15 GS by each pitcher each year)

| Pitchers | Team | Years | W |
|---|---|---|---|
| Lemon (172), Wynn (163), Garcia (138) | Cleveland Indians | 1949-57 | 473 |
| Mathewson (215), Wiltse (122), Ames (100) | New York Giants | 1905-12 | 437 |
| Mathewson (191), McGinnity (151), Taylor (93) | New York Giants | 1902-08 | 435 |
| Plank (141), Coombs (115), Bender (110) | Philadelphia Athletics | 1906-12 | 366 |
| Rixey (136), Donohue (119), Luque (108) | Cincinnati Reds | 1922-29 | 363 |
| Grove (152), Earnshaw (98), Walberg (94) | Philadelphia Athletics | 1928-33 | 344 |
| Cuellar (125), McNally (111), Palmer (106) | Baltimore Orioles | 1969-74 | 342 |
| Mathewson (147), McGinnity (112), Wiltse (80) | New York Giants | 1904-08 | 339 |
| Drysdale (124), Koufax (110), Podres (95) | Los Angeles Dodgers | 1958-65 | 329 |
| Lemon (128), Wynn (112), Feller (85) | Cleveland Indians | 1949-54 | 325 |
| Lemon (128), Garcia (104), Feller (85) | Cleveland Indians | 1949-54 | 317 |
| Spahn (121), Burdette (107), Buhl (89) | Milwaukee Braves | 1955-61 | 317 |
| Mullin (125), Killian (95), Donovan (95) | Detroit Tigers | 1904-09 | 315 |
| Raschi (111), Reynolds (99), Lopat (97) | New York Yankees | 1948-53 | 307 |
| Wynn (112), Garcia (104), Feller (85) | Cleveland Indians | 1949-54 | 301 |
| Bush (103), Malone (101), Root (96) | Chicago Cubs | 1928-33 | 300 |
| Mathewson (147), Wiltse (80), Taylor (73) | New York Giants | 1904-08 | 300 |
| Plank (116), Waddell (107), Bender (76) | Philadelphia Athletics | 1903-07 | 299 |
| Gooden (119), Darling (93), Fernandez (78) | New York Mets | 1984-90 | 290 |
| Glavine (116), Smoltz (100), Avery (72) | Atlanta Braves | 1990-96 | 288 |
| McGregor (102), Flanagan (95), Martinez (87) | Baltimore Orioles | 1978-85 | 284 |
| Alexander (143), Mayer (69), Rixey (60) | Philadelphia Phillies | 1913-17 | 272 |
| McGinnity (112), Wiltse (80), Taylor (73) | New York Giants | 1904-08 | 265 |
| Coveleski (104), Bagby (104), Morton (53) | Cleveland Indians | 1916-20 | 261 |
| Morris (103), Petry (78), Wilcox (77) | Detroit Tigers | 1979-84 | 258 |
| Osteen (99), Sutton (90), Singer (69) | Los Angeles Dodgers | 1967-72 | 258 |
| Young (117), Dinneen (85), Winter (50) | Boston Pilgrims | 1902-06 | 252 |
| Saberhagen (92), Gubicza (84), Leibrandt (76) | Kansas City Royals | 1984-89 | 252 |
| Brown (102), Reulbach (79), Pfiester (63) | Chicago Cubs | 1906-09 | 244 |
| Brown (101), Reulbach (72), Overall (70) | Chicago Cubs | 1907-10 | 243 |
| Mathewson (114), McGinnity (77), Ames (51) | New York Giants | 1905-08 | 242 |
| Maddux (89), Glavine (80), Smoltz (72) | Atlanta Braves | 1993-97 | 241 |
| Seaver (87), Matlack (75), Koosman (75) | New York Mets | 1972-76 | 237 |
| Cicotte (93), Williams (75), Faber (67) | Chicago White Sox | 1916-20 | 235 |
| Walsh (97), White (71), Smith (67) | Chicago White Sox | 1907-10 | 235 |
| Nichols (101), Stivetts (81), Staley (52) | Boston Beaneaters | 1892-94 | 234 |
| Tesreau (84), Mathewson (80), Marquard (70) | New York Giants | 1912-15 | 234 |
| Cicotte (85), Russell (74), Scott (71) | Chicago White Sox | 1913-17 | 230 |
| Marichal (107), Perry (83), Bolin (40) | San Francisco Giants | 1964-69 | 230 |
| Hubbell (79), Schumacher (76), Melton (75) | New York Giants | 1937-42 | 230 |
| Root (93), Bush (71), Blake (65) | Chicago Cubs | 1926-30 | 229 |
| Flanagan (82), McGregor (75), Palmer (69) | Baltimore Orioles | 1978-82 | 226 |
| Grove (108), Earnshaw (67), Mahaffey (50) | Philadelphia Athletics | 1930-33 | 225 |
| Brown (93), Reulbach (78), Lundgren (54) | Chicago Cubs | 1905-08 | 225 |
| Scott (81), Knepper (75), Ryan (68) | Houston Astros | 1983-88 | 224 |
| Tannehill (82), Chesbro (70), Leever (66) | Pittsburgh Pirates | 1899-1902 | 218 |
| Newhouser (80), Trout (69), Trucks (68) | Detroit Tigers | 1942-48 | 217 |
| Mullin (85), Summers (67), Willett (65) | Detroit Tigers | 1908-11 | 217 |
| Leonard (78), Gura (76), Splittorff (63) | Kansas City Royals | 1978-82 | 217 |
| Grove (108), Walberg (59), Mahaffey (50) | Philadelphia Athletics | 1930-33 | 217 |
| Mathewson (114), Taylor (52), Ames (51) | New York Giants | 1905-08 | 217 |

## Chicago Cubs: Can Rodriguez and Sosa Set the Combined Strikeout Record? (p. 42)

### Most Strikeouts by Teammates

| Year | Team | K | Players |
|------|------|-----|---------|
| 1975 | Phillies | 331 | Mike Schmidt (180), Greg Luzinski (151) |
| 1986 | Mariners | 329 | Jim Presley (172), Danny Tartabull (157) |
| 1991 | Tigers | 326 | Rob Deer (175), Cecil Fielder (151) |
| 1987 | Rangers | 322 | Pete Incaviglia (168), Larry Parrish (154) |
| 1987 | Brewers | 319 | Rob Deer (186), Dale Sveum (133) |
| 1968 | Athletics | 314 | Reggie Jackson (171), Rick Monday (143) |
| 1986 | Athletics | 301 | Jose Canseco (175), Dave Kingman (126) |
| 1997 | Tigers | 301 | Melvin Nieves (157), Tony Clark (144) |
| 1986 | Rangers | 299 | Pete Incaviglia (185), Larry Parrish (114) |
| 1990 | Yankees | 298 | Jesse Barfield (150), Roberto Kelly (148) |
| 1992 | Rangers | 297 | Dean Palmer (154), Juan Gonzalez (143) |
| 1969 | Phillies | 296 | Larry Hisle (152), Dick Allen (144) |
| 1997 | Mariners | 296 | Jay Buhner (175), Ken Griffey Jr. (121) |
| 1970 | Giants | 295 | Bobby Bonds (189), Dick Dietz (106) |
| 1989 | Royals | 295 | Bo Jackson (172), Danny Tartabull (123) |
| 1992 | Tigers | 295 | Cecil Fielder (151), Travis Fryman (144) |
| 1987 | Royals | 294 | Bo Jackson (158), Danny Tartabull (136) |
| 1970 | Padres | 292 | Nate Colbert (150), Cito Gaston (142) |
| 1984 | Red Sox | 290 | Tony Armas (156), Mike Easler (134) |
| 1987 | Athletics | 288 | Jose Canseco (157), Mark McGwire (131) |
| 1997 | Cardinals | 287 | Ron Gant (162), Ray Lankford (125) |
| 1965 | Phillies | 286 | Dick Allen (150), Dick Stuart (136) |
| 1996 | Tigers | 285 | Melvin Nieves (158), Tony Clark (127) |
| 1996 | Blue Jays | 285 | Ed Sprague (146), Carlos Delgado (139) |
| 1984 | Phillies | 284 | Juan Samuel (168), Mike Schmidt (116) |
| 1996 | Rangers | 283 | Dean Palmer (145), Kevin Elster (138) |
| 1977 | Red Sox | 282 | Butch Hobson (162), Jim Rice (120) |
| 1990 | Expos | 281 | Andres Galarraga (169), Larry Walker (112) |
| 1982 | Mets | 279 | Dave Kingman (156), George Foster (123) |
| 1996 | Expos | 279 | Henry Rodriguez (160), Shane Andrews (119) |
| 1966 | Cubs | 278 | Byron Browne (143), Adolfo Phillips (135) |
| 1972 | Giants | 277 | Dave Kingman (140), Bobby Bonds (137) |
| 1987 | Mariners | 276 | Jim Presley (157), Phil Bradley (119) |
| 1997 | Red Sox | 276 | Mo Vaughn (154), Wil Cordero (122) |
| 1988 | Brewers | 275 | Rob Deer (153), Dale Sveum (122) |
| 1990 | Athletics | 274 | Jose Canseco (158), Mark McGwire (116) |
| 1969 | Reds | 273 | Lee May (142), Tony Perez (131) |
| 1970 | Phillies | 271 | Larry Hisle (139), Deron Johnson (132) |
| 1973 | Phillies | 271 | Mike Schmidt (136), Greg Luzinski (135) |
| 1987 | Indians | 271 | Cory Snyder (166), Joe Carter (105) |
| 1996 | Rockies | 271 | Andres Galarraga (157), Ellis Burks (114) |
| 1996 | Mets | 271 | Todd Hundley (146), Bernard Gilkey (125) |
| 1973 | Giants | 270 | Bobby Bonds (148), Dave Kingman (122) |
| 1993 | Angels | 270 | Tim Salmon (135), Chili Davis (135) |
| 1989 | Brewers | 269 | Rob Deer (158), Glenn Braggs (111) |
| 1968 | Pirates | 268 | Donn Clendenon (163), Willie Stargell (105) |
| 1986 | Blue Jays | 268 | Jesse Barfield (146), Lloyd Moseby (122) |
| 1991 | Athletics | 268 | Jose Canseco (152), Mark McGwire (116) |
| 1997 | Cubs | 268 | Sammy Sosa (174), Ryne Sandberg (94) |
| 1983 | White Sox | 267 | Ron Kittle (150), Greg Luzinski (117) |
| 1990 | Tigers | 267 | Cecil Fielder (182), Tony Phillips (85) |
| 1993 | Tigers | 267 | Mickey Tettleton (139), Travis Fryman (128) |

# Cincinnati Reds: How Good a Leadoff Man Is Deion? (p. 44)

## Runs per Inning by Leadoff Hitters—1997
### (minimum 300 PA)

| Player, Team | R/Inn. | R | Inn. Batting 1/2 | Avg | OBP |
|---|---|---|---|---|---|
| Biggio, Hou | .210 | 92 | 439 | .288 | .387 |
| Jeter, Yanks | .197 | 76 | 386 | .315 | .373 |
| Phillips T, Ana | .190 | 66 | 347 | .269 | .377 |
| Knoblauch, Min | .188 | 75 | 399 | .290 | .373 |
| Lofton, Atl | .187 | 60 | 321 | .330 | .416 |
| Garciaparra, Bos | .186 | 76 | 408 | .304 | .324 |
| Cora, Sea | .186 | 70 | 376 | .303 | .364 |
| Easley, Det | .186 | 57 | 307 | .258 | .343 |
| Durham, WSox | .183 | 74 | 405 | .291 | .350 |
| Henderson, SD-Oak | .182 | 58 | 319 | .235 | .374 |
| Glanville, Cubs | .180 | 55 | 306 | .284 | .321 |
| Young E, Col-LA | .177 | 74 | 418 | .284 | .364 |
| Johnson L, Mets-Cubs | .174 | 47 | 270 | .310 | .367 |
| McRae, Cubs-Mets | .169 | 63 | 372 | .231 | .314 |
| Hunter, Det | .169 | 76 | 451 | .243 | .309 |
| Goodwin T, KC-Tex | .167 | 60 | 360 | .262 | .323 |
| Erstad, Ana | .166 | 57 | 344 | .285 | .333 |
| Hamilton, SF | .166 | 53 | 320 | .245 | .344 |
| DeShields, StL | .165 | 63 | 381 | .297 | .353 |
| Grudzielanek, Mon | .161 | 58 | 360 | .275 | .302 |
| Anderson, Bal | .159 | 63 | 395 | .279 | .377 |
| Nixon, Tor-LA | .158 | 61 | 386 | .248 | .321 |
| Womack, Pit | .157 | 61 | 389 | .261 | .305 |
| Offerman, KC | .148 | 38 | 256 | .300 | .361 |
| Sanders, Cin | .147 | 46 | 313 | .283 | .330 |
| Grissom, Cle | .143 | 45 | 315 | .273 | .333 |

# Florida Marlins: Is the Champs' Fire Sale Unprecedented? (p. 49)

## Most Regulars Relinquished—World Series Champions

| Year | Team | No. | Players |
|------|------|-----|---------|
| 1972 | Oakland Athletics | 4 | Larry Brown, Dave Duncan, Mike Epstein, Bob Locker |
| 1980 | Philadelphia Phillies | 3 | Randy Lerch, Greg Luzinski, Bob Walk |
| 1948 | Cleveland Indians | 3 | Wally Judnich, Ed Klieman, Eddie Robinson |
| 1918 | Boston Red Sox | 3 | Sam Agnew, Walt Kinney, Dutch Leonard |
| 1914 | Boston Braves | 3 | Charlie Deal, Les Mann, Possum Whitted |
| 1986 | New York Mets | 2 | Ray Knight, Kevin Mitchell |
| 1984 | Detroit Tigers | 2 | Howard Johnson, Dave Rozema |
| 1981 | Los Angeles Dodgers | 2 | Bobby Castillo, Davey Lopes |
| 1964 | St. Louis Cardinals | 2 | Roger Craig, Charlie James |
| 1962 | New York Yankees | 2 | Jim Coates, Bill Skowron |
| 1947 | New York Yankees | 2 | Bobo Newsom, Aaron Robinson |
| 1931 | St. Louis Cardinals | 2 | Burleigh Grimes, Chick Hafey |
| 1909 | Pittsburgh Pirates | 2 | Bill Abstein, Vic Willis |
| 1987 | Minnesota Twins | 1 | Mike Smithson |
| 1985 | Kansas City Royals | 1 | Joe Beckwith |
| 1982 | St. Louis Cardinals | 1 | Steve Mura |
| 1979 | Pittsburgh Pirates | 1 | Bruce Kison |
| 1978 | New York Yankees | 1 | Sparky Lyle |
| 1977 | New York Yankees | 1 | Mike Torrez |
| 1976 | Cincinnati Reds | 1 | Tony Perez |
| 1974 | Oakland Athletics | 1 | Catfish Hunter |
| 1970 | Baltimore Orioles | 1 | Tom Phoebus |
| 1968 | Detroit Tigers | 1 | Ray Oyler |
| 1965 | Los Angeles Dodgers | 1 | Dick Tracewski |
| 1963 | Los Angeles Dodgers | 1 | Larry Sherry |
| 1959 | Los Angeles Dodgers | 1 | Don Zimmer |
| 1956 | New York Yankees | 1 | Tom Morgan |
| 1955 | Brooklyn Dodgers | 1 | Don Hoak |
| 1953 | New York Yankees | 1 | Vic Raschi |
| 1951 | New York Yankees | 1 | Spec Shea |
| 1949 | New York Yankees | 1 | Cuddles Marshall |
| 1946 | St. Louis Cardinals | 1 | Johnny Beazley |
| 1945 | Detroit Tigers | 1 | Rudy York |
| 1940 | Cincinnati Reds | 1 | Billy Myers |
| 1938 | New York Yankees | 1 | Myril Hoag |
| 1937 | New York Yankees | 1 | Tony Lazzeri |
| 1934 | St. Louis Cardinals | 1 | Tex Carleton |
| 1933 | New York Giants | 1 | Kiddo Davis |
| 1932 | New York Yankees | 1 | Ed Wells |
| 1930 | Philadelphia Athletics | 1 | Jack Quinn |
| 1929 | Philadelphia Athletics | 1 | Sammy Hale |
| 1928 | New York Yankees | 1 | Joe Dugan |
| 1926 | St. Louis Cardinals | 1 | Rogers Hornsby |
| 1923 | New York Yankees | 1 | Carl Mays |
| 1922 | New York Giants | 1 | Johnny Rawlings |
| 1921 | New York Giants | 1 | George Burns |
| 1915 | Boston Red Sox | 1 | Tris Speaker |
| 1913 | Philadelphia Athletics | 1 | Jimmy Walsh |
| 1903 | Boston Pilgrims | 1 | Long Tom Hughes |

## Houston Astros: Is Bagwell/Biggio the Best Modern Batting Duo? (p. 52)

### Top Batting Duos in Percentage of Team's Offense

| Year | Team | Team R | Pct | Players (RC) |
|------|------|--------|-----|--------------|
| 1965 | Chicago Cubs | 635 | 39.5 | Billy Williams (131), Ron Santo (120) |
| 1917 | Detroit Tigers | 639 | 39.4 | Ty Cobb (144), Bobby Veach (108) |
| 1937 | St. Louis Cardinals | 789 | 38.8 | Joe Medwick (163), Johnny Mize (143) |
| 1972 | Chicago White Sox | 566 | 38.7 | Dick Allen (123), Carlos May (96) |
| 1948 | St. Louis Cardinals | 742 | 38.5 | Stan Musial (177), Enos Slaughter (109) |
| 1906 | St. Louis Browns | 559 | 38.1 | George Stone (127), Charlie Hemphill (86) |
| 1901 | Chicago Orphans | 578 | 38.1 | Topsy Hartsel (126), Danny Green (94) |
| 1989 | San Francisco Giants | 699 | 38.1 | Will Clark (141), Kevin Mitchell (125) |
| 1959 | Milwaukee Braves | 724 | 37.8 | Hank Aaron (143), Eddie Mathews (131) |
| 1963 | Milwaukee Braves | 677 | 37.5 | Hank Aaron (146), Eddie Mathews (108) |
| 1901 | Philadelphia Phillies | 668 | 37.4 | Ed Delahanty (132), Elmer Flick (118) |
| 1908 | St. Louis Cardinals | 372 | 37.4 | Red Murray (80), Ed Konetchy (59) |
| 1928 | Boston Braves | 631 | 37.2 | Rogers Hornsby (135), Lance Richbourg (100) |
| 1997 | Houston Astros | 777 | 37.2 | Craig Biggio (147), Jeff Bagwell (142) |
| 1965 | San Francisco Giants | 682 | 37.1 | Willie Mays (139), Willie McCovey (114) |
| 1904 | Cleveland Bronchos | 647 | 37.1 | Nap Lajoie (129), Elmer Flick (111) |
| 1932 | New York Giants | 755 | 37.1 | Mel Ott (143), Bill Terry (137) |
| 1911 | Detroit Tigers | 831 | 37.1 | Ty Cobb (172), Sam Crawford (136) |
| 1968 | Atlanta Braves | 514 | 37.0 | Hank Aaron (95), Felipe Alou (95) |
| 1927 | New York Yankees | 976 | 36.8 | Lou Gehrig (182), Babe Ruth (177) |
| 1968 | Houston Astros | 510 | 36.7 | Jimmy Wynn (97), Rusty Staub (90) |
| 1946 | St. Louis Cardinals | 712 | 36.7 | Stan Musial (152), Enos Slaughter (109) |
| 1918 | Philadelphia Athletics | 413 | 36.6 | George Burns (88), Tilly Walker (63) |
| 1941 | Philadelphia Phillies | 501 | 36.5 | Nick Etten (96), Danny Litwhiler (87) |
| 1909 | Detroit Tigers | 666 | 36.5 | Ty Cobb (138), Sam Crawford (105) |
| 1964 | Chicago Cubs | 649 | 36.4 | Ron Santo (122), Billy Williams (114) |
| 1916 | Cleveland Indians | 630 | 36.3 | Tris Speaker (136), Jack Graney (93) |
| 1947 | Boston Red Sox | 720 | 36.3 | Ted Williams (161), Johnny Pesky (100) |
| 1994 | San Francisco Giants | 504 | 36.1 | Barry Bonds (104), Matt Williams (78) |
| 1933 | Philadelphia Phillies | 607 | 36.1 | Chuck Klein (138), Spud Davis (81) |
| 1907 | Detroit Tigers | 696 | 35.9 | Ty Cobb (133), Sam Crawford (117) |
| 1928 | New York Yankees | 894 | 35.9 | Babe Ruth (165), Lou Gehrig (156) |
| 1965 | Houston Colt .45s | 569 | 35.9 | Jimmy Wynn (104), Joe Morgan (100) |
| 1969 | San Francisco Giants | 713 | 35.8 | Willie McCovey (140), Bobby Bonds (115) |
| 1908 | Pittsburgh Pirates | 585 | 35.7 | Honus Wagner (131), Fred Clarke (78) |
| 1912 | Detroit Tigers | 720 | 35.7 | Ty Cobb (148), Sam Crawford (109) |
| 1949 | St. Louis Cardinals | 766 | 35.6 | Stan Musial (155), Enos Slaughter (118) |
| 1963 | Chicago Cubs | 570 | 35.6 | Billy Williams (105), Ron Santo (98) |
| 1984 | Montreal Expos | 593 | 35.6 | Tim Raines (113), Gary Carter (98) |
| 1944 | Brooklyn Dodgers | 690 | 35.5 | Dixie Walker (124), Augie Galan (121) |
| 1905 | St. Louis Browns | 508 | 35.4 | George Stone (103), Bobby Wallace (77) |
| 1968 | Boston Red Sox | 614 | 35.3 | Carl Yastrzemski (121), Ken Harrelson (96) |
| 1979 | San Diego Padres | 603 | 35.3 | Dave Winfield (125), Gene Tenace (88) |
| 1916 | Chicago White Sox | 601 | 35.3 | Joe Jackson (115), Eddie Collins (97) |
| 1969 | Oakland Athletics | 740 | 35.3 | Reggie Jackson (138), Sal Bando (123) |
| 1925 | St. Louis Cardinals | 828 | 35.3 | Rogers Hornsby (158), Jim Bottomley (134) |
| 1944 | Chicago Cubs | 701 | 35.2 | Bill Nicholson (132), Phil Cavarretta (115) |
| 1961 | New York Yankees | 827 | 35.2 | Mickey Mantle (157), Roger Maris (134) |
| 1942 | New York Giants | 675 | 35.1 | Mel Ott (124), Johnny Mize (113) |
| 1923 | New York Yankees | 824 | 35.1 | Babe Ruth (193), Whitey Witt (96) |

# New York Mets: How Weak Was Ordonez? (p. 63)

## Worst Relative OPS—1920-97 (minimum 350 PA)

| Year | Player, Team | OPS | Lg OPS | OPS/Lg OPS |
|------|--------------|-----|--------|------------|
| 1979 | Mario Mendoza, Sea | .466 | .743 | .627 |
| 1977 | Rob Picciolo, Oak | .475 | .735 | .646 |
| 1933 | Jim Levey, Browns | .477 | .732 | .651 |
| 1937 | Del Young, Phils | .465 | .714 | .652 |
| 1977 | Tom Veryzer, Det | .485 | .735 | .659 |
| 1985 | George Wright, Tex | .483 | .733 | .660 |
| 1936 | Skeeter Newsome, A's | .531 | .784 | .677 |
| 1994 | Matt Walbeck, Min | .530 | .779 | .680 |
| 1997 | Rey Ordonez, Mets | .510 | .743 | .686 |
| 1989 | John Shelby, LA | .466 | .678 | .688 |
| 1995 | Pat Listach, Mil | .531 | .771 | .688 |
| 1963 | Bob Lillis, Hou | .466 | .669 | .696 |
| 1984 | Bob Boone, Cal | .504 | .724 | .696 |
| 1933 | Art Scharein, Browns | .513 | .732 | .701 |
| 1929 | Tommy Thevenow, Phils | .550 | .783 | .702 |
| 1982 | Doug Flynn, Tex-Mon | .504 | .716 | .704 |
| 1973 | Tim Johnson, Mil | .502 | .710 | .707 |
| 1970 | Dal Maxvill, StL | .510 | .721 | .707 |
| 1979 | Nelson Norman, Tex | .526 | .743 | .708 |
| 1928 | Bucky Harris, Was | .526 | .741 | .710 |
| 1937 | Leo Durocher, Cards | .507 | .714 | .711 |
| 1967 | Jerry Grote, Mets | .479 | .673 | .711 |
| 1931 | Tommy Thevenow, Pit | .513 | .721 | .712 |
| 1953 | Billy Hunter, Browns | .512 | .720 | .712 |
| 1993 | Mike Felder, Sea | .531 | .745 | .712 |
| 1932 | Rabbit Warstler, RSox | .535 | .750 | .713 |
| 1922 | Walter Barbare, Braves | .537 | .753 | .713 |
| 1936 | Chile Gomez, Phils | .515 | .722 | .714 |
| 1969 | Dal Maxvill, StL | .492 | .688 | .714 |
| 1940 | Bobby Mattick, Cubs | .502 | .702 | .715 |
| 1971 | Bobby Wine, Mon | .489 | .683 | .716 |
| 1979 | Tom Veryzer, Cle | .533 | .743 | .718 |
| 1973 | Larry Bowa, Phi | .501 | .698 | .718 |
| 1974 | Dave Roberts, SD | .497 | .693 | .718 |
| 1968 | Hal Lanier, SF | .461 | .641 | .719 |
| 1930 | Hod Ford, Cin | .581 | .808 | .719 |
| 1987 | Wayne Tolleson, Yanks | .547 | .759 | .721 |
| 1928 | Doc Farrell, Braves | .534 | .741 | .721 |
| 1997 | Mariano Duncan, Yanks-Tor | .554 | .768 | .722 |
| 1983 | Jim Sundberg, Tex | .526 | .728 | .722 |
| 1983 | Jose Oquendo, Mets | .504 | .698 | .722 |
| 1970 | Dick Green, Oak | .507 | .701 | .723 |
| 1928 | Wally Gerber, Browns-RSox | .536 | .741 | .723 |
| 1972 | Enzo Hernandez, SD | .492 | .680 | .724 |
| 1988 | Billy Ripken, Bal | .518 | .715 | .725 |
| 1932 | Wally Gilbert, Cin | .526 | .724 | .726 |
| 1990 | Alfredo Griffin, LA | .512 | .704 | .727 |
| 1977 | Frank Duffy, Cle | .535 | .735 | .727 |
| 1971 | Dave Concepcion, Cin | .496 | .683 | .727 |
| 1984 | Dick Schofield, Cal | .527 | .724 | .728 |

# Philadelphia Phillies: Will Their Second-Half Revival Carry Over?
# (p. 65)

## Best Second-Half Surges—1951-97

| Year | Team | Before | After | Change | Overall | Next Year | Change |
|------|------|--------|-------|--------|---------|-----------|--------|
| 1997 | Philadelphia Phillies | .282 | .571 | .289 | .420 | — | — |
| 1979 | Los Angeles Dodgers | .387 | .623 | .236 | .488 | .564 | .077 |
| 1995 | New York Mets | .362 | .587 | .224 | .479 | .438 | −.041 |
| 1996 | Boston Red Sox | .424 | .636 | .213 | .525 | .481 | −.043 |
| 1995 | Florida Marlins | .358 | .566 | .208 | .469 | .494 | .025 |
| 1986 | Oakland Athletics | .378 | .583 | .206 | .469 | .500 | .031 |
| 1973 | Cleveland Indians | .357 | .563 | .205 | .438 | .478 | .040 |
| 1984 | New York Yankees | .439 | .638 | .198 | .537 | .602 | .065 |
| 1952 | Philadelphia Phillies | .467 | .658 | .192 | .565 | .539 | −.026 |
| 1975 | Baltimore Orioles | .482 | .662 | .180 | .566 | .543 | −.023 |
| 1993 | Atlanta Braves | .562 | .740 | .178 | .642 | .596 | −.045 |
| 1994 | San Francisco Giants | .438 | .615 | .177 | .478 | .465 | −.013 |
| 1983 | Chicago White Sox | .519 | .694 | .175 | .611 | .457 | −.154 |
| 1995 | New York Yankees | .455 | .628 | .174 | .549 | .568 | .019 |
| 1991 | Philadelphia Phillies | .395 | .568 | .173 | .481 | .432 | −.049 |
| 1977 | New York Yankees | .543 | .714 | .171 | .617 | .613 | −.004 |
| 1984 | Pittsburgh Pirates | .381 | .551 | .170 | .463 | .354 | −.109 |
| 1991 | Atlanta Braves | .494 | .663 | .169 | .580 | .605 | .025 |
| 1962 | Philadelphia Phillies | .424 | .592 | .169 | .503 | .537 | .034 |
| 1956 | Detroit Tigers | .447 | .615 | .168 | .532 | .506 | −.026 |
| 1954 | Milwaukee Braves | .500 | .667 | .167 | .578 | .552 | −.026 |
| 1981 | Kansas City Royals | .400 | .566 | .166 | .485 | .556 | .070 |
| 1966 | Minnesota Twins | .471 | .636 | .166 | .549 | .562 | .012 |
| 1981 | Chicago Cubs | .288 | .451 | .163 | .369 | .451 | .082 |
| 1981 | Toronto Blue Jays | .276 | .438 | .162 | .349 | .481 | .132 |
| 1994 | Kansas City Royals | .517 | .679 | .161 | .557 | .486 | −.070 |
| 1951 | New York Giants | .544 | .705 | .161 | .624 | .597 | −.027 |
| 1979 | Oakland Athletics | .266 | .426 | .161 | .333 | .512 | .179 |
| 1988 | San Diego Padres | .443 | .603 | .160 | .516 | .549 | .034 |
| 1970 | Houston Astros | .414 | .573 | .160 | .488 | .488 | .000 |
| 1987 | Chicago White Sox | .400 | .558 | .158 | .475 | .441 | −.034 |
| 1989 | San Diego Padres | .477 | .635 | .158 | .549 | .463 | −.086 |
| 1964 | St. Louis Cardinals | .494 | .651 | .157 | .574 | .497 | −.077 |
| 1951 | Philadelphia Athletics | .377 | .532 | .156 | .455 | .513 | .058 |
| 1958 | Pittsburgh Pirates | .468 | .623 | .156 | .545 | .506 | −.039 |
| 1977 | Texas Rangers | .511 | .667 | .156 | .580 | .537 | −.043 |
| 1986 | St. Louis Cardinals | .419 | .573 | .155 | .491 | .586 | .096 |
| 1974 | Pittsburgh Pirates | .479 | .632 | .154 | .543 | .571 | .028 |
| 1955 | Baltimore Orioles | .295 | .447 | .152 | .370 | .448 | .078 |
| 1980 | Baltimore Orioles | .538 | .690 | .152 | .617 | .562 | −.055 |
| 1953 | Detroit Tigers | .321 | .471 | .150 | .390 | .442 | .052 |
| 1981 | Minnesota Twins | .304 | .453 | .149 | .376 | .370 | −.006 |
| 1976 | California Angels | .402 | .547 | .144 | .469 | .457 | −.012 |
| 1994 | Toronto Blue Jays | .442 | .586 | .144 | .478 | .389 | −.089 |
| 1989 | Toronto Blue Jays | .483 | .627 | .144 | .549 | .531 | −.019 |
| 1989 | Chicago White Sox | .364 | .507 | .143 | .429 | .580 | .152 |
| 1987 | Milwaukee Brewers | .494 | .636 | .142 | .562 | .537 | −.025 |
| 1969 | California Angels | .383 | .522 | .139 | .441 | .531 | .090 |
| 1966 | Chicago White Sox | .447 | .584 | .137 | .512 | .549 | .037 |
| 1973 | New York Mets | .452 | .588 | .137 | .509 | .438 | −.071 |

# Pittsburgh Pirates: How Important Is It to Grow Your Own Players? (p. 68)

## Most Homegrown Regulars—1997

| Team | Grown | W-L |
|------|-------|-----|
| Pirates | 12 | 79-83 |
| Braves | 10 | 101-61 |
| Dodgers | 10 | 88-74 |
| Brewers | 10 | 78-83 |
| Twins | 10 | 68-94 |
| Angels | 9 | 84-78 |
| Athletics | 8 | 65-97 |
| Blue Jays | 8 | 76-86 |
| Indians | 7 | 86-75 |
| Tigers | 7 | 79-83 |
| Expos | 7 | 78-84 |
| Phillies | 7 | 68-94 |
| Cardinals | 7 | 73-89 |
| Red Sox | 6 | 78-84 |
| Cubs | 6 | 68-94 |
| White Sox | 6 | 80-81 |
| Astros | 6 | 84-78 |
| Orioles | 5 | 98-64 |
| Marlins | 5 | 92-70 |
| Royals | 5 | 67-94 |
| Mets | 5 | 88-74 |
| Mariners | 5 | 90-72 |
| Rangers | 5 | 77-85 |
| Reds | 4 | 76-86 |
| Rockies | 4 | 83-79 |
| Yankees | 4 | 96-66 |
| Giants | 4 | 90-72 |
| Padres | 3 | 76-86 |

# St. Louis Cardinals: Will They Bounce Back After Crashing? (p. 70)

## First-Place Teams Below .500 in Year 2

| Year | Team | Year 1 | Year2 | Year 3 |
|------|------|--------|-------|--------|
| 1876 | Chicago White Stockings | 52-14 | 26-33 | 30-30 |
| 1884 | New York Metropolitans | 75-32 | 44-64 | 53-82 |
| 1884 | Providence Grays | 84-28 | 53-57 | — |
| 1884 | St. Louis Maroons | 92-19 | 36-72 | 43-79 |
| 1889 | New York Giants | 83-43 | 63-68 | 71-61 |
| 1890 | Brooklyn Bridegrooms | 86-43 | 61-76 | 95-59 |
| 1890 | Louisville Colonels | 87-43 | 54-84 | 62-89 |
| 1914 | Philadelphia Athletics | 99-53 | 43-109 | 36-117 |
| 1916 | Brooklyn Dodgers | 94-60 | 70-81 | 57-69 |
| 1917 | Chicago White Sox | 100-54 | 57-67 | 88-52 |
| 1918 | Boston Red Sox | 75-51 | 66-71 | 72-81 |
| 1931 | St. Louis Cardinals | 101-53 | 72-82 | 82-71 |
| 1933 | Washington Senators | 99-53 | 66-86 | 67-86 |
| 1940 | Detroit Tigers | 90-64 | 75-79 | 73-81 |
| 1948 | Boston Braves | 91-62 | 75-79 | 83-71 |
| 1950 | Philadelphia Phillies | 91-63 | 73-81 | 87-67 |
| 1960 | Pittsburgh Pirates | 95-59 | 75-79 | 93-68 |
| 1963 | Los Angeles Dodgers | 99-63 | 80-82 | 97-65 |
| 1964 | New York Yankees | 99-63 | 77-85 | 70-89 |
| 1964 | St. Louis Cardinals | 93-69 | 80-81 | 83-79 |
| 1966 | Baltimore Orioles | 97-63 | 76-85 | 91-71 |
| 1966 | Los Angeles Dodgers | 95-67 | 73-89 | 76-86 |
| 1969 | Atlanta Braves | 93-69 | 76-86 | 82-80 |
| 1970 | Cincinnati Reds | 102-60 | 79-83 | 95-59 |
| 1970 | Minnesota Twins | 98-64 | 74-86 | 77-77 |
| 1971 | San Francisco Giants | 90-72 | 69-86 | 88-74 |
| 1972 | Pittsburgh Pirates | 96-59 | 80-82 | 88-74 |
| 1973 | New York Mets | 82-79 | 71-91 | 82-80 |
| 1978 | Los Angeles Dodgers | 95-67 | 79-83 | 92-71 |
| 1979 | California Angels | 88-74 | 65-95 | 51-59 |
| 1980 | Kansas City Royals | 97-65 | 50-53 | 90-72 |
| 1981 | Cincinnati Reds | 66-42 | 61-101 | 74-88 |
| 1981 | Oakland Athletics | 64-45 | 68-94 | 74-88 |
| 1982 | California Angels | 93-69 | 70-92 | 81-81 |
| 1982 | St. Louis Cardinals | 92-70 | 79-83 | 84-78 |
| 1983 | Chicago White Sox | 99-63 | 74-88 | 85-77 |
| 1983 | Los Angeles Dodgers | 91-71 | 79-83 | 95-67 |
| 1984 | Chicago Cubs | 96-65 | 77-84 | 70-90 |
| 1985 | Kansas City Royals | 91-71 | 76-86 | 83-79 |
| 1985 | Los Angeles Dodgers | 95-67 | 73-89 | 73-89 |
| 1985 | St. Louis Cardinals | 101-61 | 79-82 | 95-67 |
| 1986 | Boston Red Sox | 95-66 | 78-84 | 89-73 |
| 1986 | California Angels | 92-70 | 75-87 | 75-87 |
| 1986 | Houston Astros | 96-66 | 76-86 | 82-80 |
| 1987 | St. Louis Cardinals | 95-67 | 76-86 | 86-76 |
| 1988 | Los Angeles Dodgers | 94-67 | 77-83 | 86-76 |
| 1989 | Chicago Cubs | 93-69 | 77-85 | 77-83 |
| 1990 | Cincinnati Reds | 91-71 | 74-88 | 90-72 |
| 1992 | Oakland Athletics | 96-66 | 68-94 | 51-63 |
| 1992 | Pittsburgh Pirates | 96-66 | 75-87 | 53-61 |
| 1993 | Philadelphia Phillies | 97-65 | 54-61 | 69-75 |
| 1993 | Toronto Blue Jays | 95-67 | 55-60 | 56-88 |
| 1994 | Chicago White Sox | 67-46 | 68-76 | 85-77 |
| 1994 | Montreal Expos | 74-40 | 66-78 | 88-74 |
| 1996 | San Diego Padres | 91-71 | 76-86 | — |
| 1996 | St. Louis Cardinals | 88-74 | 73-89 | — |
| 1996 | Texas Rangers | 90-72 | 77-85 | — |

# San Diego Padres: Is Gwynn the Best of All Time Relative to His League? (p. 72)

## Highest Career Batting Averages Relative to League (minimum 3000 PA)

| Player (Seasons) | Avg | Lg Avg | Avg/Lg Avg |
|---|---|---|---|
| Ty Cobb (1905-1928) | .366 | .265 | 1.384 |
| Joe Jackson (1908-1920) | .356 | .260 | 1.371 |
| Dave Orr (1883-1890) | .342 | .253 | 1.353 |
| Pete Browning (1882-1894) | .340 | .254 | 1.335 |
| Tony Gwynn (1982-1997) | .340 | .256 | 1.324 |
| Ted Williams (1939-1960) | .344 | .262 | 1.315 |
| Nap Lajoie (1896-1916) | .338 | .260 | 1.298 |
| Dan Brouthers (1879-1904) | .341 | .264 | 1.295 |
| Rogers Hornsby (1915-1937) | .358 | .277 | 1.295 |
| Tris Speaker (1907-1928) | .345 | .267 | 1.289 |
| Tip O'Neill (1883-1892) | .326 | .254 | 1.284 |
| Stan Musial (1941-1963) | .331 | .259 | 1.277 |
| Rod Carew (1967-1985) | .328 | .257 | 1.276 |
| Mike Donlin (1899-1914) | .333 | .262 | 1.270 |
| Honus Wagner (1897-1917) | .327 | .260 | 1.260 |
| Willie Keeler (1892-1910) | .341 | .271 | 1.257 |
| Wade Boggs (1982-1997) | .331 | .264 | 1.254 |
| Ed Delahanty (1888-1903) | .346 | .277 | 1.251 |
| Roberto Clemente (1955-1972) | .317 | .254 | 1.250 |
| Eddie Collins (1906-1930) | .333 | .266 | 1.250 |
| Billy Hamilton (1888-1901) | .344 | .276 | 1.248 |
| Cap Anson (1876-1897) | .329 | .266 | 1.238 |
| Frank Thomas (1990-1997) | .330 | .267 | 1.235 |
| Jesse Burkett (1890-1905) | .337 | .273 | 1.235 |
| George Stone (1903-1910) | .301 | .244 | 1.234 |
| Lefty O'Doul (1919-1934) | .349 | .284 | 1.230 |
| Tony Oliva (1962-1976) | .304 | .247 | 1.230 |
| Sam Thompson (1885-1906) | .331 | .270 | 1.225 |
| Harry Heilmann (1914-1932) | .342 | .279 | 1.223 |
| Sam Crawford (1899-1917) | .309 | .253 | 1.222 |
| Babe Ruth (1914-1935) | .342 | .280 | 1.220 |
| George Sisler (1915-1930) | .340 | .279 | 1.218 |
| Benny Kauff (1912-1920) | .311 | .255 | 1.218 |
| Matty Alou (1960-1974) | .307 | .252 | 1.216 |
| King Kelly (1878-1893) | .309 | .255 | 1.212 |
| Joe Medwick (1932-1948) | .324 | .267 | 1.211 |
| Kirby Puckett (1984-1995) | .318 | .263 | 1.211 |
| Paul Waner (1926-1945) | .333 | .276 | 1.207 |
| Lou Gehrig (1923-1939) | .340 | .282 | 1.207 |
| Bill Terry (1923-1936) | .341 | .283 | 1.206 |
| Manny Mota (1962-1982) | .304 | .252 | 1.206 |
| Mark Grace (1988-1997) | .310 | .257 | 1.204 |
| Jim O'Rourke (1876-1904) | .310 | .258 | 1.203 |
| Joe DiMaggio (1936-1951) | .325 | .270 | 1.203 |
| Elmer Flick (1898-1910) | .313 | .261 | 1.201 |
| Ginger Beaumont (1899-1910) | .311 | .259 | 1.200 |
| Ed Swartwood (1881-1892) | .299 | .250 | 1.199 |
| Hank Aaron (1954-1976) | .305 | .255 | 1.198 |
| Dale Mitchell (1946-1956) | .312 | .262 | 1.193 |
| Jackie Robinson (1947-1956) | .311 | .261 | 1.192 |

# Do Basestealers Improve With Age? (p. 78)

## Stolen-Base Percentage By Age— Since 1980

| Age | SB | SBA | Pct. |
|---|---|---|---|
| 18 | 3 | 3 | 100.0 |
| 19 | 36 | 57 | 63.2 |
| 20 | 170 | 258 | 65.9 |
| 21 | 843 | 1216 | 69.3 |
| 22 | 1591 | 2333 | 68.2 |
| 23 | 3270 | 4768 | 68.6 |
| 24 | 4681 | 6660 | 70.3 |
| 25 | 5730 | 8392 | 68.3 |
| 26 | 6532 | 9677 | 67.5 |
| 27 | 6455 | 9437 | 68.4 |
| 28 | 5621 | 8221 | 68.3 |
| 29 | 4783 | 7034 | 68.0 |
| 30 | 3892 | 5744 | 67.8 |
| 31 | 3376 | 5015 | 67.3 |
| 32 | 2535 | 3804 | 66.6 |
| 33 | 1913 | 2881 | 66.4 |
| 34 | 1421 | 2175 | 65.3 |
| 35 | 984 | 1523 | 64.6 |
| 36 | 766 | 1187 | 64.5 |
| 37 | 573 | 858 | 66.8 |
| 38 | 386 | 538 | 71.8 |
| 39 | 155 | 241 | 64.3 |
| 40 | 122 | 179 | 68.2 |
| 41 | 59 | 101 | 58.4 |
| 42 | 20 | 34 | 58.8 |
| 43 | 3 | 8 | 37.5 |
| 44 | 11 | 12 | 91.7 |
| 45 | 3 | 4 | 75.0 |

## Worst Stolen-Base Percentages Through Age 26—Since 1946 (minimum 60 SBA)

| | Career SB% | |
|---|---|---|
| | Through 26 | After 26 |
| Buddy Bell | 33% | 50% |
| Duane Kuiper | 45% | 39% |
| Curt Flood | 48% | 63% |
| Pete Rose | 48% | 60% |
| Chet Lemon | 48% | 32% |
| Rick Bosetti | 48% | — |
| Dion James | 48% | 71% |
| Bob Bailey | 50% | 51% |
| Bobby Richardson | 50% | 74% |
| Don Kessinger | 51% | 57% |
| Alfredo Griffin | 51% | 63% |
| Lenny Randle | 52% | 62% |
| Jose Oquendo | 52% | 62% |
| Will Clark | 53% | 64% |
| Nellie Fox | 53% | 44% |
| Omar Vizquel | 53% | 79% |
| Mike Jorgensen | 54% | 64% |
| Dick McAuliffe | 54% | 49% |
| Tom Brunansky | 55% | 45% |
| Ed Yost | 55% | 50% |
| Sixto Lezcano | 55% | 50% |
| Jim Gilliam | 55% | 68% |
| Junior Felix | 55% | — |
| Yastrzemski | 55% | 61% |
| Harvey Kuenn | 56% | 54% |
| Oscar Gamble | 56% | 57% |
| Marvell Wynne | 56% | 64% |
| Mike Edwards | 56% | 50% |
| Jim Wohlford | 56% | 58% |
| Warren Cromartie | 56% | 61% |
| Paul Householder | 56% | 33% |
| Rick Burleson | 57% | 47% |
| Larry Herndon | 57% | 67% |
| Dave Parker | 57% | 58% |
| Pedro Garcia | 57% | — |
| Jack Clark | 57% | 52% |
| Robby Thompson | 58% | 66% |
| Wally Moon | 58% | 56% |
| Bill Madlock | 58% | 70% |
| Derrel Thomas | 58% | 64% |

# Who Wins 'Em Late (and What Does It Mean)? (p. 90)

## Wins in Final At-Bat—Listed Alphabetically

| Team | W in Final AB | Total W |
|---|---|---|
| Anaheim Angels | 22 | 84 |
| Atlanta Braves | 22 | 101 |
| Baltimore Orioles | 16 | 98 |
| Boston Red Sox | 19 | 78 |
| Chicago Cubs | 13 | 68 |
| Chicago White Sox | 18 | 80 |
| Cincinnati Reds | 11 | 76 |
| Cleveland Indians | 12 | 86 |
| Colorado Rockies | 18 | 83 |
| Detroit Tigers | 13 | 79 |
| Florida Marlins | 24 | 92 |
| Houston Astros | 18 | 84 |
| Kansas City Royals | 15 | 67 |
| Los Angeles Dodgers | 20 | 88 |
| Milwaukee Brewers | 15 | 78 |
| Minnesota Twins | 10 | 68 |
| Montreal Expos | 17 | 78 |
| New York Mets | 24 | 88 |
| New York Yankees | 20 | 96 |
| Oakland Athletics | 23 | 65 |
| Philadelphia Phillies | 10 | 68 |
| Pittsburgh Pirates | 19 | 79 |
| San Diego Padres | 20 | 76 |
| San Francisco Giants | 23 | 90 |
| Seattle Mariners | 14 | 90 |
| St. Louis Cardinals | 19 | 73 |
| Texas Rangers | 21 | 77 |
| Toronto Blue Jays | 14 | 76 |

# Which Parks Change at Night? (p. 102)

## Day and Night Park Indexes

| Stadium (Years) | Runs | | | Home Runs | | |
|---|---|---|---|---|---|---|
| | Day | Night | Overall | Day | Night | Overall |
| Edison International Field of Anaheim (1995-1997) | 108 | 96 | 100 | 161 | 107 | 120 |
| Oriole Park at Camden Yards (1995-1997) | 92 | 98 | 96 | 108 | 110 | 110 |
| Fenway Park (1995-1997) | 105 | 103 | 104 | 92 | 95 | 94 |
| Comiskey Park (1995-1997) | 94 | 86 | 89 | 76 | 82 | 80 |
| Jacobs Field (1995-1997) | 105 | 92 | 96 | 80 | 89 | 86 |
| Tiger Stadium (1997) | 102 | 100 | 101 | 89 | 141 | 118 |
| Ewing M. Kauffman Stadium (1995-1997) | 95 | 99 | 98 | 97 | 93 | 94 |
| County Stadium (1995-1997) | 93 | 117 | 108 | 73 | 96 | 88 |
| Hubert H. Humphrey Metrodome (1995-1997) | 92 | 111 | 105 | 113 | 98 | 103 |
| Yankee Stadium (1995-1997) | 110 | 93 | 98 | 109 | 99 | 102 |
| Oakland-Alameda County Coliseum (1996-1997) | 116 | 97 | 105 | 109 | 94 | 98 |
| The Kingdome (1995-1997) | 95 | 99 | 98 | 104 | 107 | 107 |
| The Ballpark in Arlington (1995-1997) | 106 | 111 | 110 | 103 | 109 | 108 |
| SkyDome (1995-1997) | 88 | 106 | 99 | 88 | 105 | 98 |
| Turner Field (1997) | 82 | 102 | 97 | 79 | 88 | 84 |
| Wrigley Field (1995-1997) | 115 | 89 | 106 | 125 | 98 | 119 |
| Cinergy Field (1995-1997) | 99 | 100 | 100 | 101 | 95 | 97 |
| Coors Field (1995-1997) | 161 | 152 | 156 | 159 | 150 | 154 |
| Pro Player Stadium (1995-1997) | 101 | 87 | 91 | 81 | 88 | 86 |
| The Astrodome (1995-1997) | 77 | 86 | 83 | 72 | 75 | 74 |
| Dodger Stadium (1995-1997) | 81 | 82 | 81 | 70 | 82 | 78 |
| Olympic Stadium (1995-1997) | 86 | 113 | 104 | 70 | 98 | 88 |
| Shea Stadium (1995-1997) | 87 | 90 | 90 | 80 | 93 | 89 |
| Veterans Stadium (1995-1997) | 107 | 101 | 103 | 100 | 100 | 100 |
| Three Rivers Stadium (1995-1997) | 92 | 117 | 108 | 102 | 108 | 106 |
| Qualcomm Stadium (1996-1997) | 82 | 93 | 90 | 127 | 104 | 112 |
| 3Com Park (1995-1997) | 88 | 101 | 95 | 78 | 121 | 96 |
| Busch Stadium (1996-1997) | 92 | 99 | 96 | 84 | 101 | 94 |

# Which Park Is Best for Stolen Bases? (p. 104)

## Stolen-Base Indexes—Current Stadiums

| Stadium (Years) | Home | Road | Index |
|---|---|---|---|
| Olympic Stadium (1995-1997) | .802 | .696 | 115 |
| The Kingdome (1995-1997) | .705 | .632 | 112 |
| County Stadium (1995-1997) | .727 | .671 | 108 |
| Three Rivers Stadium (1995-1997) | .724 | .674 | 107 |
| SkyDome (1995-1997) | .709 | .664 | 107 |
| Dodger Stadium (1995-1997) | .751 | .704 | 107 |
| Tiger Stadium (1997) | .724 | .689 | 105 |
| Comiskey Park (1995-1997) | .693 | .675 | 103 |
| Cinergy Field (1995-1997) | .752 | .734 | 103 |
| Wrigley Field (1995-1997) | .709 | .693 | 102 |
| Hubert H. Humphrey Metrodome (1995-1997) | .719 | .704 | 102 |
| Pro Player Stadium (1995-1997) | .645 | .638 | 101 |
| Oriole Park at Camden Yards (1995-1997) | .719 | .714 | 101 |
| The Astrodome (1995-1997) | .709 | .706 | 100 |
| Qualcomm Stadium (1996-1997) | .702 | .703 | 100 |
| Coors Field (1995-1997) | .701 | .709 | 99 |
| The Ballpark in Arlington (1995-1997) | .612 | .620 | 99 |
| Jacobs Field (1995-1997) | .708 | .727 | 97 |
| Ewing M. Kauffman Stadium (1995-1997) | .672 | .690 | 97 |
| Edison International Field of Anaheim (1995-1997) | .636 | .659 | 96 |
| Busch Stadium (1996-1997) | .682 | .731 | 93 |
| 3Com Park (1995-1997) | .648 | .695 | 93 |
| Veterans Stadium (1995-1997) | .677 | .728 | 93 |
| Fenway Park (1995-1997) | .684 | .741 | 92 |
| Yankee Stadium (1995-1997) | .663 | .727 | 91 |
| Turner Field (1997) | .645 | .712 | 91 |
| Shea Stadium (1995-1997) | .640 | .725 | 88 |
| Oakland-Alameda County Coliseum (1996-1997) | .653 | .751 | 87 |

# Who's the Best Table-Setter? (p. 108)

## Both Leagues — Listed Alphabetically
## (minimum 100+ PA Batting Leadoff in 1997)

| Player, Team | OBP | AB | R | H | BB | HBP | SB |
|---|---|---|---|---|---|---|---|
| Anderson B, Bal | .398 | 550 | 94 | 161 | 79 | 18 | 18 |
| Biggio, Hou | .418 | 614 | 145 | 191 | 83 | 34 | 47 |
| Blauser, Atl | .391 | 133 | 23 | 40 | 16 | 5 | 1 |
| Butler B, LA | .381 | 292 | 45 | 89 | 36 | 0 | 13 |
| Castillo L, Fla | .304 | 210 | 20 | 50 | 20 | 0 | 15 |
| Clayton, StL | .285 | 175 | 29 | 43 | 10 | 0 | 5 |
| Cora, Sea | .350 | 551 | 101 | 162 | 47 | 5 | 6 |
| Cummings, Phi | .373 | 192 | 22 | 58 | 23 | 0 | 2 |
| DeShields, StL | .353 | 474 | 74 | 136 | 49 | 3 | 48 |
| Durham, WSox | .329 | 448 | 77 | 120 | 39 | 4 | 20 |
| Erstad, Ana | .318 | 138 | 18 | 36 | 13 | 0 | 5 |
| Everett, Mets | .294 | 211 | 31 | 51 | 14 | 2 | 12 |
| Garciaparra, Bos | .342 | 683 | 122 | 209 | 35 | 6 | 22 |
| Glanville, Cubs | .344 | 248 | 40 | 78 | 11 | 0 | 8 |
| Goodwin T, Tex | .302 | 233 | 40 | 52 | 26 | 1 | 16 |
| Grissom, Cle | .312 | 354 | 46 | 88 | 31 | 4 | 15 |
| Grudzielanek, Mon | .295 | 457 | 51 | 118 | 18 | 7 | 17 |
| Hamilton, SF | .350 | 446 | 74 | 120 | 57 | 0 | 14 |
| Henderson, Ana | .399 | 388 | 79 | 99 | 89 | 5 | 44 |
| Hunter B, Det | .332 | 641 | 109 | 172 | 63 | 1 | 71 |
| Javier, SF | .350 | 132 | 21 | 32 | 19 | 4 | 6 |
| Jefferies, Phi | .313 | 166 | 24 | 41 | 15 | 1 | 4 |
| Jeter, Yanks | .394 | 427 | 81 | 137 | 47 | 6 | 16 |
| Johnson L, Cubs | .369 | 396 | 59 | 121 | 41 | 0 | 20 |
| Knoblauch, Min | .390 | 608 | 116 | 178 | 84 | 16 | 62 |
| Lofton, Atl | .409 | 492 | 90 | 163 | 64 | 2 | 27 |
| Loretta, Mil | .317 | 131 | 16 | 34 | 10 | 1 | 2 |
| Mashore, Oak | .370 | 261 | 49 | 66 | 45 | 4 | 3 |
| McDonald, Oak | .351 | 226 | 44 | 59 | 32 | 0 | 13 |
| McLemore, Tex | .355 | 268 | 39 | 71 | 36 | 2 | 4 |
| McRae, Mets | .304 | 397 | 52 | 94 | 34 | 5 | 8 |
| Nixon, LA | .330 | 473 | 66 | 120 | 57 | 0 | 50 |
| Offerman, KC | .366 | 350 | 47 | 108 | 32 | 0 | 9 |
| Otero, Phi | .336 | 134 | 16 | 33 | 18 | 0 | 0 |
| Phillips T, Ana | .389 | 448 | 82 | 125 | 81 | 2 | 12 |
| Raines, Yanks | .417 | 214 | 45 | 72 | 33 | 0 | 8 |
| Reese, Cin | .280 | 148 | 20 | 32 | 12 | 1 | 4 |
| Roberts, Cle | .348 | 291 | 51 | 90 | 17 | 2 | 13 |
| Sanders D, Cin | .327 | 460 | 51 | 125 | 33 | 6 | 55 |
| Santangelo, Mon | .427 | 153 | 29 | 47 | 22 | 10 | 5 |
| Stewart S, Tor | .370 | 165 | 24 | 48 | 18 | 4 | 10 |
| Veras, SD | .335 | 226 | 35 | 50 | 35 | 4 | 11 |
| Vina, Mil | .311 | 322 | 37 | 88 | 12 | 7 | 8 |
| Vizquel, Cle | .369 | 129 | 19 | 37 | 18 | 0 | 9 |
| Weiss, Col | .417 | 114 | 24 | 31 | 28 | 1 | 3 |
| White D, Fla | .313 | 190 | 26 | 45 | 18 | 5 | 8 |
| Williams G, Mil | .283 | 144 | 21 | 36 | 6 | 1 | 6 |
| Womack, Pit | .326 | 636 | 83 | 176 | 43 | 3 | 59 |
| Young E, LA | .358 | 565 | 98 | 157 | 67 | 7 | 43 |
| AL Avg | .349 | 681 | 111 | 188 | 72 | 7 | 32 |
| NL Avg | .345 | 676 | 102 | 183 | 69 | 8 | 36 |
| MLB Avg | .347 | 1357 | 213 | 371 | 141 | 15 | 68 |

# Who Created the Most Runs? (p. 111)

In the chart below, **RC** stands for Runs Created, and **OW%** stands for Offensive Winning Percentage.

### Both Leagues — Listed Alphabetically
### (minimum 350 PA in 1997)

| Player, Team | RC | OW% | Player, Team | RC | OW% | Player, Team | RC | OW% |
|---|---|---|---|---|---|---|---|---|
| Alfonzo, Mets | 104 | .721 | Castilla, Col | 113 | .682 | Galarraga, Col | 118 | .715 |
| Alicea, Ana | 68 | .592 | Cedeno D, Tex | 51 | .509 | Gant, StL | 67 | .495 |
| Allensworth, Pit | 46 | .442 | Cirillo, Mil | 100 | .610 | Garcia C, Tor | 21 | .129 |
| Alomar R, Bal | 77 | .659 | Clark T, Det | 117 | .679 | Garciaparra, Bos | 117 | .618 |
| Alomar S, Cle | 78 | .624 | Clark W, Tex | 70 | .660 | Giambi, Oak | 94 | .637 |
| Alou, Fla | 100 | .675 | Clayton, StL | 59 | .361 | Giles, Cle | 66 | .592 |
| Anderson B, Bal | 112 | .662 | Conine, Fla | 51 | .465 | Gilkey, Mets | 77 | .534 |
| Anderson G, Ana | 85 | .498 | Coomer, Min | 78 | .548 | Girardi, Yanks | 45 | .373 |
| Ausmus, Hou | 51 | .438 | Cora, Sea | 92 | .574 | Glanville, Cubs | 56 | .449 |
| Baerga, Mets | 55 | .440 | Cordero, Bos | 71 | .450 | Gomez, SD | 48 | .309 |
| Bagwell, Hou | 142 | .787 | Cordova, Min | 45 | .396 | Gonzalez A, Tor | 43 | .307 |
| Baines, Bal | 72 | .583 | Cruz D, Det | 37 | .236 | Gonzalez J, Tex | 104 | .671 |
| Becker, Min | 64 | .514 | Cruz Jr, Tor | 62 | .543 | Gonzalez L, Hou | 68 | .459 |
| Bell D, Hou | 63 | .482 | Damon, KC | 67 | .505 | Goodwin T, Tex | 63 | .356 |
| Bell J, KC | 95 | .584 | Daulton, Fla | 73 | .662 | Grace, Cubs | 102 | .680 |
| Belle, WSox | 91 | .498 | Davis C, KC | 92 | .653 | Green S, Tor | 72 | .604 |
| Berroa, Bal | 86 | .542 | Davis R, Sea | 60 | .505 | Greene W, Cin | 78 | .585 |
| Bichette, Col | 94 | .639 | Delgado C, Tor | 96 | .636 | Greer, Tex | 116 | .687 |
| Biggio, Hou | 147 | .789 | DeShields, StL | 98 | .635 | Griffey Jr, Sea | 148 | .762 |
| Blauser, Atl | 104 | .712 | DiSarcina, Ana | 42 | .204 | Grissom, Cle | 73 | .437 |
| Boggs, Yanks | 48 | .503 | Dunston, Pit | 62 | .490 | Grudzielanek, Mon | 68 | .388 |
| Bonds, SF | 132 | .786 | Durham, WSox | 75 | .399 | Guerrero W, LA | 41 | .423 |
| Bonilla, Fla | 93 | .619 | Easley, Det | 84 | .534 | Guillen J, Pit | 53 | .392 |
| Boone B, Cin | 38 | .266 | Edmonds, Ana | 85 | .603 | Guillen O, WSox | 50 | .323 |
| Bordick, Bal | 39 | .196 | Erstad, Ana | 100 | .648 | Gwynn, SD | 138 | .801 |
| Bragg, Bos | 63 | .410 | Everett, Mets | 62 | .518 | Hamilton, SF | 69 | .557 |
| Brogna, Phi | 68 | .467 | Fabregas, WSox | 35 | .296 | Hammonds, Bal | 60 | .542 |
| Brosius, Oak | 24 | .095 | Fernandez, Cle | 51 | .433 | Hatteberg, Bos | 45 | .456 |
| Buford, Tex | 36 | .294 | Fielder, Yanks | 51 | .484 | Hayes, Yanks | 36 | .328 |
| Buhner, Sea | 96 | .594 | Finley, SD | 82 | .548 | Henderson, Ana | 67 | .583 |
| Burks, Col | 83 | .693 | Flaherty, SD | 48 | .408 | Higginson, Det | 113 | .699 |
| Burnitz, Mil | 88 | .616 | Franco J, Mil | 60 | .478 | Hill, SF | 56 | .523 |
| Cameron, WSox | 65 | .586 | Frye, Bos | 56 | .497 | Hollins, Ana | 85 | .536 |
| Caminiti, SD | 93 | .688 | Fryman, Det | 82 | .485 | Hundley, Mets | 86 | .711 |
| Canseco, Oak | 56 | .480 | Gaetti, StL | 52 | .356 | Hunter B, Det | 90 | .466 |
| Carter, Tor | 76 | .415 | Gagne, LA | 51 | .349 | Huskey, Mets | 62 | .490 |

| Player, Team | RC | OW% | Player, Team | RC | OW% | Player, Team | RC | OW% |
|---|---|---|---|---|---|---|---|---|
| Javier, SF | 72 | .618 | Meares, Min | 60 | .475 | Servais, Cubs | 43 | .408 |
| Jefferies, Phi | 60 | .476 | Merced, Tor | 48 | .465 | Sheffield, Fla | 88 | .685 |
| Jefferson, Bos | 69 | .528 | Molitor, Min | 84 | .567 | Snow, SF | 105 | .699 |
| Jeter, Yanks | 88 | .479 | Mondesi, LA | 100 | .623 | Sorrento, Sea | 63 | .489 |
| Johnson C, Fla | 59 | .519 | Morandini, Phi | 75 | .512 | Sosa, Cubs | 86 | .489 |
| Johnson L, Cubs | 66 | .614 | Mueller, SF | 59 | .568 | Spiezio, Oak | 60 | .367 |
| Jones A, Atl | 54 | .468 | Nieves, Det | 56 | .527 | Sprague, Tor | 50 | .316 |
| Jones C, Atl | 107 | .658 | Nilsson, Mil | 77 | .502 | Stairs, Oak | 74 | .707 |
| Joyner, SD | 83 | .677 | Nixon, LA | 72 | .430 | Steinbach, Min | 43 | .304 |
| Justice, Cle | 118 | .766 | O'Leary, Bos | 78 | .572 | Stevens, Tex | 68 | .569 |
| Karros, LA | 91 | .544 | O'Neill, Yanks | 123 | .732 | Stocker, Phi | 55 | .401 |
| Kelly R, Sea | 59 | .574 | Offerman, KC | 54 | .460 | Surhoff, Bal | 86 | .580 |
| Kendall, Pit | 78 | .608 | Olerud, Mets | 114 | .738 | Thomas, WSox | 150 | .831 |
| Kent, SF | 88 | .554 | Ordonez R, Mets | 24 | .170 | Thome, Cle | 113 | .733 |
| King, KC | 94 | .575 | Orie, Cubs | 55 | .559 | Tucker, Atl | 74 | .569 |
| Klesko, Atl | 81 | .629 | Palmeiro R, Bal | 94 | .533 | Valentin J, Bos | 95 | .592 |
| Knoblauch, Min | 110 | .632 | Palmer, KC | 71 | .462 | Valentin J, Mil | 61 | .420 |
| Lankford, StL | 104 | .748 | Phillips T, Ana | 93 | .597 | Vaughn G, SD | 44 | .429 |
| Lansing, Mon | 87 | .579 | Piazza, LA | 137 | .816 | Vaughn M, Bos | 111 | .722 |
| Lawton, Min | 76 | .571 | Ramirez, Cle | 100 | .647 | Veras, SD | 68 | .461 |
| Lemke, Atl | 35 | .336 | Randa, Pit | 72 | .620 | Vizcaino, SF | 69 | .444 |
| Leyritz, Tex | 61 | .555 | Reese, Cin | 31 | .241 | Vizquel, Cle | 68 | .401 |
| Lieberthal, Phi | 62 | .498 | Renteria, Fla | 66 | .371 | Walker L, Col | 158 | .851 |
| Lofton, Atl | 86 | .656 | Ripken C, Bal | 82 | .467 | Weiss, Col | 62 | .587 |
| Lopez J, Atl | 73 | .659 | Roberts, Cle | 58 | .499 | White R, Mon | 70 | .438 |
| Loretta, Mil | 54 | .439 | Rodriguez A, Sea | 100 | .610 | Williams B, Yanks | 105 | .708 |
| Mabry, StL | 47 | .466 | Rodriguez H, Mon | 74 | .575 | Williams G, Mil | 50 | .268 |
| Martin A, Pit | 72 | .634 | Rodriguez I, Tex | 97 | .595 | Williams M, Cle | 86 | .511 |
| Martinez D, WSox | 73 | .522 | Rolen, Phi | 109 | .696 | Wilson D, Sea | 77 | .529 |
| Martinez E, Sea | 127 | .755 | Salmon, Ana | 130 | .722 | Womack, Pit | 86 | .525 |
| Martinez T, Yanks | 121 | .685 | Sandberg, Cubs | 61 | .523 | Young E, LA | 89 | .524 |
| McGriff, Atl | 82 | .549 | Sanders D, Cin | 55 | .445 | Zeile, LA | 84 | .542 |
| McGwire, StL | 119 | .726 | Santangelo, Mon | 48 | .494 | | | |
| McRae, Mets | 68 | .433 | Segui, Mon | 74 | .628 | | | |

# Which Switch-Hitters Are Wasting Their Time? (p. 114)

## Largest OPS Platoon Differences, Switch-Hitters—1995-97
### (minimum 1000 PA and active in 1997)

| Player | OPS as LH | OPS as RH | Diff |
|---|---|---|---|
| J.T. Snow | .887 | .612 | .275 |
| Jose Valentin | .807 | .586 | .221 |
| Todd Hundley | .963 | .751 | .212 |
| Bernie Williams | .855 | 1.053 | .198 |
| Dave Hollins | .734 | .917 | .183 |
| Roberto Alomar | .920 | .756 | .164 |
| Chipper Jones | .905 | .754 | .150 |
| Gregg Jefferies | .721 | .860 | .139 |
| Walt Weiss | .778 | .663 | .115 |
| Carl Everett | .755 | .647 | .108 |
| Bobby Bonilla | .857 | .957 | .100 |
| Eddie Murray | .801 | .717 | .083 |
| Joey Cora | .756 | .832 | .076 |
| Mickey Tettleton | .867 | .792 | .075 |
| Mark Lemke | .632 | .706 | .075 |
| Ken Caminiti | .920 | .993 | .073 |
| Quilvio Veras | .736 | .664 | .072 |
| Bip Roberts | .735 | .665 | .070 |
| Tony Clark | .852 | .784 | .068 |
| Melvin Nieves | .783 | .717 | .066 |
| Mark McLemore | .737 | .675 | .062 |
| Carlos Baerga | .745 | .691 | .055 |
| Luis Alicea | .750 | .704 | .045 |
| Tony Phillips | .802 | .843 | .041 |
| Chili Davis | .893 | .932 | .039 |
| Brent Gates | .672 | .635 | .037 |
| Ruben Sierra | .711 | .747 | .036 |
| Tim Raines | .831 | .801 | .030 |
| Jose Offerman | .768 | .794 | .026 |
| Jose Vizcaino | .697 | .673 | .024 |
| Omar Vizquel | .732 | .709 | .023 |
| Mark Whiten | .790 | .769 | .020 |
| Ray Durham | .730 | .710 | .020 |
| David Segui | .840 | .858 | .018 |
| Terry Pendleton | .705 | .687 | .017 |
| Devon White | .756 | .770 | .014 |
| Stan Javier | .741 | .750 | .009 |
| Otis Nixon | .686 | .678 | .008 |
| Brian McRae | .760 | .767 | .007 |
| Kevin Stocker | .661 | .666 | .005 |

## Is This Era Second(ary) to None? (p. 118)

### Both Leagues — Listed Alphabetically
### (minimum 340 PA in 1997)

| Player, Team | SA | Player, Team | SA | Player, Team | SA | Player, Team | SA |
|---|---|---|---|---|---|---|---|
| Alfonzo, Mets | .249 | Duncan, Tor | .094 | Jefferson, Bos | .198 | Phillips T, Ana | .313 |
| Alicea, Ana | .330 | Dunston, Pit | .216 | Jeter, Yanks | .245 | Piazza, LA | .408 |
| Allensworth, Pit | .222 | Durham, WSox | .233 | Johnson B, SF | .242 | Ramirez, Cle | .349 |
| Alomar R, Bal | .279 | Easley, Det | .364 | Johnson C, Fla | .344 | Randa, Pit | .246 |
| Alomar S, Cle | .259 | Edmonds, Ana | .325 | Johnson L, Cubs | .237 | Reese, Cin | .191 |
| Alou, Fla | .338 | Erstad, Ana | .289 | Jones A, Atl | .348 | Renteria, Fla | .164 |
| Anderson B, Bal | .334 | Everett, Mets | .262 | Jones C, Atl | .337 | Ripken C, Bal | .224 |
| Anderson G, Ana | .163 | Fabregas, WSox | .133 | Joyner, SD | .266 | Roberts, Cle | .183 |
| Ausmus, Hou | .200 | Fernandez, Cle | .191 | Justice, Cle | .424 | Rodriguez A, Sea | .305 |
| Baerga, Mets | .150 | Fielder, Yanks | .291 | Karros, LA | .303 | Rodriguez H, Mon | .324 |
| Bagwell, Hou | .567 | Finley, SD | .313 | Kelly R, Sea | .250 | Rodriguez I, Tex | .241 |
| Baines, Bal | .277 | Flaherty, SD | .189 | Kendall, Pit | .265 | Rolen, Phi | .339 |
| Becker, Min | .298 | Franco J, Mil | .272 | Kent, SF | .319 | Salmon, Ana | .380 |
| Bell D, Hou | .260 | Frye, Bos | .215 | King, KC | .398 | Sanchez, Yanks | .120 |
| Bell J, KC | .300 | Fryman, Det | .266 | Klesko, Atl | .332 | Sandberg, Cubs | .208 |
| Belle, WSox | .300 | Gaetti, StL | .233 | Knoblauch, Min | .342 | Sanders D, Cin | .256 |
| Berroa, Bal | .319 | Gagne, LA | .158 | Lankford, StL | .516 | Sanders R, Cin | .410 |
| Bichette, Col | .257 | Galarraga, Col | .368 | Lansing, Mon | .280 | Santangelo, Mon | .277 |
| Biggio, Hou | .388 | Gant, StL | .291 | Lawton, Min | .339 | Santiago, Tor | .196 |
| Blauser, Atl | .316 | Garcia C, Tor | .154 | Lemke, Atl | .171 | Segui, Mon | .325 |
| Boggs, Yanks | .238 | Garciaparra, Bos | .298 | Lewis M, SF | .235 | Servais, Cubs | .161 |
| Bonds, SF | .620 | Giambi, Oak | .306 | Leyritz, Tex | .277 | Sheffield, Fla | .477 |
| Bonilla, Fla | .301 | Gil, Tex | .151 | Lieberthal, Phi | .290 | Snow, SF | .414 |
| Boone B, Cin | .210 | Giles, Cle | .385 | Lofton, Atl | .239 | Sorrento, Sea | .352 |
| Bordick, Bal | .143 | Gilkey, Mets | .295 | Lopez J, Atl | .336 | Sosa, Cubs | .315 |
| Bragg, Bos | .255 | Girardi, Yanks | .133 | Loretta, Mil | .213 | Spiers, Hou | .388 |
| Brogna, Phi | .258 | Glanville, Cubs | .160 | Mabry, StL | .186 | Spiezio, Oak | .238 |
| Brosius, Oak | .196 | Gomez, SD | .169 | Manwaring, Col | .128 | Sprague, Tor | .256 |
| Buford, Tex | .227 | Gonzalez A, Tor | .249 | Martin A, Pit | .326 | Stairs, Oak | .429 |
| Buhner, Sea | .483 | Gonzalez J, Tex | .355 | Martinez D, WSox | .248 | Stanley, Yanks | .363 |
| Burks, Col | .403 | Gonzalez L, Hou | .253 | Martinez E, Sea | .439 | Steinbach, Min | .235 |
| Burnitz, Mil | .437 | Goodwin T, Tex | .213 | Martinez T, Yanks | .411 | Stevens, Tex | .263 |
| Butler B, LA | .178 | Grace, Cubs | .301 | Mashore, Oak | .265 | Stocker, Phi | .200 |
| Cameron, WSox | .375 | Green S, Tor | .291 | Matheny, Mil | .144 | Strange, Mon | .275 |
| Caminiti, SD | .401 | Greene W, Cin | .376 | McCracken, Col | .249 | Surhoff, Bal | .267 |
| Canseco, Oak | .374 | Greer, Tex | .354 | McGriff, Atl | .294 | Thomas, WSox | .470 |
| Carter, Tor | .240 | Griffey Jr, Sea | .485 | McGwire, StL | .565 | Thome, Cle | .534 |
| Castilla, Col | .312 | Grissom, Cle | .228 | McLemore, Tex | .189 | Tucker, Atl | .261 |
| Cedeno D, Tex | .192 | Grudzielanek, Mon | .171 | McRae, Mets | .269 | Valentin J, Bos | .299 |
| Cirillo, Mil | .243 | Guerrero V, Mon | .237 | Meares, Min | .175 | Valentin J, Mil | .255 |
| Clark T, Det | .381 | Guerrero W, LA | .137 | Merced, Tor | .285 | Vaughn G, SD | .341 |
| Clark W, Tex | .295 | Guillen J, Pit | .177 | Molitor, Min | .227 | Vaughn M, Bos | .408 |
| Clayton, StL | .224 | Guillen O, WSox | .141 | Mondesi, LA | .330 | Veras, SD | .236 |
| Conine, Fla | .309 | Gwynn, SD | .260 | Morandini, Phi | .203 | Vina, Mil | .127 |
| Coomer, Min | .184 | Hamelin, Det | .371 | Morris, Cin | .150 | Vizcaino, SF | .169 |
| Cora, Sea | .232 | Hamilton, SF | .239 | Mueller, SF | .262 | Vizquel, Cle | .244 |
| Cordero, Bos | .202 | Hammonds, Bal | .338 | Nieves, Det | .315 | Walker L, Col | .535 |
| Cordova, Min | .272 | Hatteberg, Bos | .269 | Nilsson, Mil | .283 | Weiss, Col | .290 |
| Cruz D, Det | .099 | Hayes, Yanks | .255 | Nixon, LA | .247 | White R, Mon | .274 |
| Cruz Jr, Tor | .367 | Henderson, Ana | .427 | O'Leary, Bos | .238 | Williams B, Yanks | .373 |
| Cummings, Phi | .242 | Higginson, Det | .359 | O'Neill, Yanks | .331 | Williams G, Mil | .175 |
| Curtis, Yanks | .338 | Hill, SF | .229 | Offerman, KC | .191 | Williams M, Cle | .295 |
| Damon, KC | .212 | Hoiles, Bal | .322 | Olerud, Mets | .357 | Wilson D, Sea | .240 |
| Daulton, Fla | .405 | Hollins, Ana | .267 | Oliver, Cin | .223 | Womack, Pit | .246 |
| Davis C, KC | .415 | Hundley, Mets | .472 | Ordonez R, Mets | .107 | Young D, StL | .222 |
| Davis R, Sea | .290 | Hunter B, Det | .269 | Orie, Cubs | .264 | Young E, LA | .281 |
| Delgado C, Tor | .383 | Huskey, Mets | .276 | Palmeiro R, Bal | .345 | Young K, Pit | .309 |
| DeShields, StL | .320 | Javier, SF | .286 | Palmer, KC | .264 | Zeile, LA | .341 |
| DiSarcina, Ana | .109 | Jefferies, Phi | .258 | Perez N, Col | .224 | **MLB Avg** | **.264** |

## Did the Rockies Show the Most "Heart" in 1997? (p. 120)

### American League—Sorted by Most RBI in 1997

| Team | Avg | HR | RBI | Slg | Main 3-4-5 Hitters |
|------|-----|-----|-----|-----|--------------------|
| New York | .302 | 94 | 394 | .512 | Williams B, Martinez T, Fielder |
| Seattle | .297 | 125 | 371 | .562 | Griffey Jr, Martinez E, Buhner |
| Oakland | .273 | 111 | 342 | .510 | Canseco, McGwire, Berroa |
| Anaheim | .291 | 80 | 339 | .476 | Hollins, Salmon, Salmon |
| Cleveland | .296 | 110 | 339 | .536 | Thome, Williams M, Justice |
| Texas | .307 | 97 | 330 | .525 | Greer, Gonzalez J, Clark W |
| Detroit | .270 | 86 | 329 | .469 | Fryman, Clark T, Hamelin |
| Chicago | .290 | 80 | 328 | .482 | Thomas, Belle, Baines |
| Baltimore | .270 | 87 | 316 | .460 | Palmeiro R, Berroa, Ripken C |
| Kansas City | .272 | 81 | 315 | .458 | Bell J, King, Davis C |
| Boston | .300 | 83 | 306 | .490 | Vaughn M, Jefferson, Cordero |
| Minnesota | .272 | 44 | 274 | .413 | Molitor, Steinbach, Coomer |
| Toronto | .243 | 72 | 268 | .439 | Cruz Jr., Carter, Sprague |
| Milwaukee | .263 | 64 | 257 | .432 | Cirillo, Nilsson, Burnitz |
| **AL Avg** | **.282** | **87** | **322** | **.483** | |

### National League—Sorted by Most RBI in 1997

| Team | Avg | HR | RBI | Slg | Main 3-4-5 Hitters |
|------|-----|-----|-----|-----|--------------------|
| Colorado | .322 | 127 | 423 | .588 | Walker L, Galarraga, Bichette |
| San Diego | .297 | 76 | 366 | .485 | Gwynn, Caminiti, Joyner |
| San Francisco | .269 | 95 | 340 | .500 | Bonds, Kent, Snow |
| Atlanta | .283 | 78 | 336 | .471 | Jones C, McGriff, Klesko |
| Los Angeles | .305 | 103 | 328 | .527 | Piazza, Karros, Mondesi |
| New York | .281 | 80 | 323 | .476 | Olerud, Hundley, Gilkey |
| Chicago | .279 | 65 | 299 | .450 | Grace, Sosa, Dunston |
| Houston | .262 | 70 | 298 | .447 | Bagwell, Gonzalez L, Bell D |
| Florida | .266 | 65 | 298 | .445 | Sheffield, Bonilla, Alou |
| Pittsburgh | .274 | 63 | 287 | .451 | Martin A, Young K, Randa |
| Montreal | .273 | 82 | 286 | .474 | White R, Segui, Rodriguez H |
| St. Louis | .258 | 79 | 285 | .446 | McGwire, Lankford, Gaetti |
| Philadelphia | .255 | 60 | 266 | .420 | Jefferies, Rolen, Brogna |
| Cincinnati | .266 | 66 | 264 | .441 | Stynes, Perez E, Greene W |
| **NL Avg** | **.278** | **79** | **314** | **.473** | |

# Who Are the Real RBI Kings? (p. 122)

## Both Leagues — Sorted by RBI Percentage
### (minimum 500 RBI opportunities in 1997)

| Player, Team | Opp | RBI | Pct | Player, Team | Opp | RBI | Pct |
|---|---|---|---|---|---|---|---|
| Ken Griffey Jr, Sea | 915 | 120 | 13.1 | Matt Williams, Cle | 981 | 89 | 9.1 |
| Mark McGwire, Oak-StL | 832 | 109 | 13.1 | Steve Finley, SD | 883 | 80 | 9.1 |
| Juan Gonzalez, Tex | 881 | 115 | 13.1 | Butch Huskey, Mets | 760 | 68 | 8.9 |
| Andres Galarraga, Col | 969 | 125 | 12.9 | Wally Joyner, SD | 752 | 67 | 8.9 |
| Larry Walker, Col | 889 | 113 | 12.7 | Jeff Conine, Fla | 640 | 57 | 8.9 |
| Frank Thomas, WSox | 827 | 104 | 12.6 | Troy O'Leary, Bos | 792 | 70 | 8.8 |
| Jeff Bagwell, Hou | 880 | 107 | 12.2 | B.J. Surhoff, Bal | 839 | 74 | 8.8 |
| Tino Martinez, Yanks | 1017 | 120 | 11.8 | Joe Carter, Tor | 932 | 82 | 8.8 |
| Ray Lankford, StL | 697 | 82 | 11.8 | Fred McGriff, Atl | 900 | 79 | 8.8 |
| Jay Buhner, Sea | 896 | 105 | 11.7 | Dean Palmer, Tex-KC | 860 | 75 | 8.7 |
| David Justice, Cle | 781 | 89 | 11.4 | Glenallen Hill, SF | 632 | 55 | 8.7 |
| Jim Thome, Cle | 756 | 85 | 11.2 | Travis Fryman, Det | 933 | 81 | 8.7 |
| Dante Bichette, Col | 908 | 102 | 11.2 | Javy Lopez, Atl | 635 | 55 | 8.7 |
| Kevin Young, Pit | 555 | 62 | 11.2 | Ron Coomer, Min | 786 | 68 | 8.7 |
| Matt Stairs, Oak | 583 | 64 | 11.0 | Roberto Kelly, Min-Sea | 555 | 48 | 8.6 |
| Mike Piazza, LA | 830 | 91 | 11.0 | Todd Zeile, LA | 869 | 75 | 8.6 |
| Tim Salmon, Ana | 946 | 103 | 10.9 | Greg Vaughn, SD | 596 | 51 | 8.6 |
| Chili Davis, KC | 763 | 83 | 10.9 | Manny Ramirez, Cle | 879 | 75 | 8.5 |
| Todd Hundley, Mets | 710 | 77 | 10.8 | Russ Davis, Sea | 657 | 56 | 8.5 |
| Jeff King, KC | 879 | 94 | 10.7 | Jeffrey Hammonds, Bal | 599 | 51 | 8.5 |
| Tony Clark, Det | 871 | 93 | 10.7 | Eric Karros, LA | 1000 | 85 | 8.5 |
| J.T. Snow, SF | 799 | 85 | 10.6 | Jason Giambi, Oak | 800 | 68 | 8.5 |
| Moises Alou, Fla | 899 | 95 | 10.6 | Charles Johnson, Fla | 675 | 57 | 8.4 |
| Barry Bonds, SF | 817 | 86 | 10.5 | G. Berroa, Oak-Bal | 877 | 74 | 8.4 |
| Vinny Castilla, Col | 905 | 95 | 10.5 | Bobby Bonilla, Fla | 923 | 77 | 8.3 |
| Ryan Klesko, Atl | 725 | 76 | 10.5 | Jim Leyritz, Ana-Tex | 627 | 52 | 8.3 |
| Henry Rodriguez, Mon | 702 | 73 | 10.4 | Chipper Jones, Atl | 955 | 79 | 8.3 |
| Jeff Kent, SF | 981 | 101 | 10.3 | Nomar Garciaparra, Bos | 968 | 80 | 8.3 |
| Mike Stanley, Bos-Yanks | 567 | 58 | 10.2 | Charlie Hayes, Yanks | 595 | 49 | 8.2 |
| Paul O'Neill, Yanks | 915 | 93 | 10.2 | Darren Daulton, Phi-Fla | 632 | 52 | 8.2 |
| Melvin Nieves, Det | 573 | 58 | 10.1 | Jim Edmonds, Ana | 780 | 64 | 8.2 |
| Jose Canseco, Oak | 625 | 63 | 10.1 | Bob Hamelin, Det | 501 | 41 | 8.2 |
| Paul Sorrento, Sea | 746 | 75 | 10.1 | Cecil Fielder, Yanks | 613 | 50 | 8.2 |
| Edgar Martinez, Sea | 847 | 85 | 10.0 | Mike Cameron, WSox | 566 | 46 | 8.1 |
| Sandy Alomar, Cle | 725 | 72 | 9.9 | Raul Mondesi, LA | 936 | 76 | 8.1 |
| Rafael Palmeiro, Bal | 980 | 96 | 9.8 | Chad Curtis, Cle-Yanks | 572 | 46 | 8.0 |
| Bob Higginson, Det | 823 | 80 | 9.7 | Chris Hoiles, Bal | 500 | 40 | 8.0 |
| Ellis Burks, Col | 641 | 62 | 9.7 | Harold Baines, WSox-Bal | 704 | 56 | 8.0 |
| Bernie Williams, Yanks | 859 | 83 | 9.7 | Roberto Alomar, Bal | 642 | 51 | 7.9 |
| Sammy Sosa, Cubs | 1028 | 99 | 9.6 | Bernard Gilkey, Mets | 868 | 68 | 7.8 |
| John Olerud, Mets | 800 | 77 | 9.6 | Rondell White, Mon | 857 | 67 | 7.8 |
| Tony Gwynn, SD | 923 | 88 | 9.5 | Dave Hollins, Ana | 911 | 71 | 7.8 |
| Jeromy Burnitz, Mil | 767 | 73 | 9.5 | Dan Wilson, Sea | 796 | 62 | 7.8 |
| Carlos Delgado, Tor | 750 | 71 | 9.5 | Scott Rolen, Phi | 874 | 68 | 7.8 |
| Willie Greene, Cin | 774 | 73 | 9.4 | Dave Nilsson, Mil | 864 | 67 | 7.8 |
| Andruw Jones, Atl | 649 | 61 | 9.4 | Brian S. Giles, Cle | 598 | 46 | 7.7 |
| Jose Cruz Jr, Sea-Tor | 588 | 55 | 9.4 | Brian Johnson, Det-SF | 507 | 39 | 7.7 |
| Lee Stevens, Tex | 678 | 63 | 9.3 | Scott Hatteberg, Bos | 552 | 42 | 7.6 |
| Gary Sheffield, Fla | 661 | 61 | 9.2 | Garret Anderson, Ana | 1029 | 78 | 7.6 |
| Mo Vaughn, Bos | 781 | 72 | 9.2 | Paul Molitor, Min | 832 | 63 | 7.6 |
| Mike Lieberthal, Phi | 727 | 67 | 9.2 | Jay Bell, KC | 887 | 67 | 7.6 |
| Albert Belle, WSox | 1068 | 98 | 9.2 | Alex Rodriguez, Sea | 890 | 67 | 7.5 |
| Ken Caminiti, SD | 770 | 70 | 9.1 | David Segui, Mon | 667 | 50 | 7.5 |

| Player, Team | Opp | RBI | Pct | Player, Team | Opp | RBI | Pct |
|---|---|---|---|---|---|---|---|
| Brady Anderson, Bal | 842 | 63 | 7.5 | Damon Buford, Tex | 568 | 31 | 5.5 |
| Rico Brogna, Phi | 871 | 65 | 7.5 | Tony Fernandez, Cle | 613 | 33 | 5.4 |
| Carl Everett, Mets | 630 | 47 | 7.5 | Bret Boone, Cin | 669 | 36 | 5.4 |
| Edgardo Alfonzo, Mets | 765 | 57 | 7.5 | Brad Ausmus, Hou | 670 | 36 | 5.4 |
| Darin Erstad, Ana | 794 | 59 | 7.4 | Delino DeShields, StL | 750 | 40 | 5.3 |
| Damion Easley, Det | 785 | 58 | 7.4 | Rich Becker, Min | 648 | 34 | 5.2 |
| Will Clark, Tex | 626 | 46 | 7.3 | Bip Roberts, KC-Cle | 613 | 32 | 5.2 |
| Marty Cordova, Min | 586 | 43 | 7.3 | Jermaine Allensworth, Pit | 537 | 28 | 5.2 |
| J. Fabregas, Ana-WSox | 590 | 43 | 7.3 | Eric Young, Col-LA | 845 | 44 | 5.2 |
| Shawn Green, Tor | 626 | 45 | 7.2 | Tony Phillips, WSox-Ana | 758 | 39 | 5.1 |
| Cal Ripken, Bal | 958 | 67 | 7.0 | Al Martin, Pit | 639 | 32 | 5.0 |
| Ron Gant, StL | 718 | 50 | 7.0 | John Flaherty, SD | 705 | 35 | 5.0 |
| Jeff Blauser, Atl | 790 | 55 | 7.0 | Royce Clayton, StL | 867 | 43 | 5.0 |
| Jeff Cirillo, Mil | 863 | 60 | 7.0 | Dmitri Young, StL | 507 | 25 | 4.9 |
| Jose Guillen, Pit | 777 | 54 | 6.9 | Jose Offerman, KC | 609 | 30 | 4.9 |
| Craig Biggio, Hou | 808 | 56 | 6.9 | R. Henderson, SD-Ana | 530 | 26 | 4.9 |
| Rusty Greer, Tex | 896 | 62 | 6.9 | Jason Kendall, Pit | 735 | 36 | 4.9 |
| Pat Meares, Min | 696 | 48 | 6.9 | Johnny Damon, KC | 697 | 34 | 4.9 |
| Derek Bell, Hou | 769 | 53 | 6.9 | Domingo Cedeno, Tex | 520 | 25 | 4.8 |
| Ivan Rodriguez, Tex | 858 | 59 | 6.9 | Rey Ordonez, Mets | 522 | 25 | 4.8 |
| Wil Cordero, Bos | 873 | 60 | 6.9 | Omar Vizquel, Cle | 841 | 40 | 4.8 |
| Gary Gaetti, StL | 788 | 54 | 6.9 | F.P. Santangelo, Mon | 507 | 24 | 4.7 |
| Scott Spiezio, Oak | 833 | 57 | 6.8 | Julio Franco, Cle-Mil | 655 | 31 | 4.7 |
| Reggie Jefferson, Bos | 804 | 55 | 6.8 | Chris Gomez, SD | 811 | 38 | 4.7 |
| Joe Randa, Pit | 673 | 46 | 6.8 | Quilvio Veras, SD | 796 | 37 | 4.6 |
| Ryne Sandberg, Cubs | 677 | 46 | 6.8 | Joey Cora, Sea | 778 | 36 | 4.6 |
| Matt Lawton, Min | 686 | 46 | 6.7 | Chuck Knoblauch, Min | 854 | 39 | 4.6 |
| Stan Javier, SF | 686 | 45 | 6.6 | L. Johnson, Mets-Cubs | 561 | 25 | 4.5 |
| Mike Lansing, Mon | 781 | 51 | 6.5 | Kenny Lofton, Atl | 696 | 31 | 4.5 |
| Mark Grace, Cubs | 821 | 53 | 6.5 | John Mabry, StL | 564 | 25 | 4.4 |
| Joe Oliver, Cin | 513 | 33 | 6.4 | Ray Durham, WSox | 885 | 39 | 4.4 |
| John Valentin, Bos | 858 | 55 | 6.4 | Jose Vizcaino, SF | 840 | 37 | 4.4 |
| Benito Santiago, Tor | 504 | 32 | 6.3 | Scott Brosius, Oak | 752 | 33 | 4.4 |
| Joe Girardi, Yanks | 652 | 41 | 6.3 | Tony Womack, Pit | 835 | 36 | 4.3 |
| Dave Martinez, WSox | 751 | 47 | 6.3 | Brian McRae, Cubs-Mets | 749 | 32 | 4.3 |
| Mark Lewis, SF | 515 | 32 | 6.2 | Deivi Cruz, Det | 640 | 27 | 4.2 |
| Marquis Grissom, Cle | 843 | 51 | 6.0 | Luis Alicea, Ana | 569 | 24 | 4.2 |
| Jeff Frye, Bos | 613 | 37 | 6.0 | Alex Gonzalez, Tor | 617 | 26 | 4.2 |
| Michael Tucker, Atl | 763 | 46 | 6.0 | Wilton Guerrero, LA | 524 | 22 | 4.2 |
| Orlando Merced, Tor | 516 | 31 | 6.0 | Doug Glanville, Cubs | 646 | 27 | 4.2 |
| Derek Jeter, Yanks | 953 | 57 | 6.0 | Kevin Stocker, Phi | 718 | 29 | 4.0 |
| Jose Valentin, Mil | 753 | 45 | 6.0 | Edgar Renteria, Fla | 897 | 36 | 4.0 |
| S. Dunston, Cubs-Pit | 757 | 45 | 5.9 | Wade Boggs, Yanks | 518 | 20 | 3.9 |
| Greg Gagne, LA | 763 | 45 | 5.9 | Brian L. Hunter, Det | 898 | 34 | 3.8 |
| Bill Mueller, SF | 598 | 35 | 5.9 | Gary DiSarcina, Ana | 872 | 33 | 3.8 |
| Mark Loretta, Mil | 623 | 36 | 5.8 | M. Duncan, Yanks-Tor | 505 | 19 | 3.8 |
| Ozzie Guillen, WSox | 732 | 42 | 5.7 | Gerald Williams, Mil | 806 | 30 | 3.7 |
| Mike Bordick, Bal | 785 | 45 | 5.7 | Tom Goodwin, KC-Tex | 835 | 31 | 3.7 |
| Carlos Baerga, Mets | 734 | 42 | 5.7 | Mickey Morandini, Phi | 792 | 29 | 3.7 |
| Walt Weiss, Col | 582 | 33 | 5.7 | Otis Nixon, Tor-LA | 772 | 28 | 3.6 |
| Kevin Orie, Cubs | 547 | 31 | 5.7 | Mark Lemke, Atl | 524 | 19 | 3.6 |
| Terry Steinbach, Min | 691 | 39 | 5.6 | Kirt Manwaring, Col | 512 | 18 | 3.5 |
| Gregg Jefferies, Phi | 680 | 38 | 5.6 | Pokey Reese, Cin | 537 | 18 | 3.4 |
| Luis Gonzalez, Hou | 865 | 48 | 5.5 | Mark Grudzielanek, Mon | 883 | 28 | 3.2 |
| Darren Bragg, Bos | 757 | 42 | 5.5 | R. Sanchez, Cubs-Yanks | 504 | 12 | 2.4 |
| Scott Servais, Cubs | 577 | 32 | 5.5 | Deion Sanders, Cin | 601 | 10 | 1.7 |
| Darryl Hamilton, SF | 654 | 36 | 5.5 | **MLB Avg** | | | **8.0** |
| Ed Sprague, Tor | 748 | 41 | 5.5 | | | | |

# Who Went to the Moon—And Beyond— in 1997? (p. 124)

## Both Leagues — 1997 Longest Home Runs Listed by Distance

| Dis | Batter, Team | Pitcher, Team | Date | Site |
|---|---|---|---|---|
| 540 | McGwire, Oak | Johnson R, Sea | 6/24 | @Sea |
| 530 | Galarraga, Col | Brown, Fla | 5/31 | @Fla |
| 520 | McGwire, StL | Martinez R, LA | 9/16 | @StL |
| 500 | McGwire, StL | Saunders, Fla | 8/22 | @Fla |
| 500 | McGwire, StL | Navarro, WSox | 9/2 | @StL |
| 500 | Galarraga, Col | Olivares, Sea | 8/28 | @Col |
| 490 | Walker L, Col | Oquist, Oak | 8/31 | @Col |
| 490 | Buhner, Sea | Watson, Ana | 9/23 | @Sea |
| 480 | Conine, Fla | Holmes, Col | 6/7 | @Col |
| 480 | Piazza, LA | Holmes, Col | 9/26 | @Col |
| 480 | McGwire, StL | Castillo F, Col | 9/5 | @Col |
| 480 | Vaughn G, SD | Ruffcorn, Phi | 4/4 | @SD |
| 480 | Canseco, Oak | Rodriguez F, Min | 7/19 | @Oak |
| 470 | Walker L, Col | Cordova, Pit | 8/2 | @Pit |
| 470 | Buhner, Sea | Rusch, KC | 7/19 | @Sea |
| 470 | Johnson M, Pit | Fernandez A, Fla | 5/16 | @Pit |
| 470 | Walker L, Col | Ashby, SD | 7/10 | @Col |
| 470 | Griffey Jr, Sea | Drabek, WSox | 8/10 | @Sea |
| 470 | Ramirez, Cle | Mohler, Oak | 8/22 | @Oak |
| 470 | Ventura, WSox | Ayala, Sea | 8/9 | @Sea |
| 460 | Sosa, Cubs | Estes, SF | 5/18 | @Cubs |
| 460 | Griffey Jr, Sea | Dickson, Ana | 5/20 | @Ana |
| 460 | McGwire, Oak | Tewksbury, Min | 5/25 | @Min |
| 460 | Piazza, LA | Foulke, SF | 6/4 | @LA |
| 460 | Vaughn M, Bos | Lidle, Mets | 6/13 | @Mets |
| 460 | Buhner, Sea | Finley, Ana | 6/27 | @Sea |
| 460 | Sosa, Cubs | Petkovsek, StL | 7/11 | @Cubs |
| 460 | Thome, Cle | Ritchie, Min | 7/12 | @Min |
| 460 | Reed J, Col | Astacio, LA | 7/14 | @Col |
| 460 | Canseco, Oak | Jackson M, Cle | 7/25 | @Cle |
| 460 | Griffey Jr, Sea | Cruz, WSox | 8/8 | @Sea |
| 460 | McGwire, StL | Nen, Fla | 8/22 | @Fla |
| 460 | Hammonds, Bal | Plunk, Cle | 9/15 | @Bal |
| 460 | McGwire, StL | Bohanon, Mets | 8/13 | @StL |
| 460 | Walker L, Col | Valdes I, LA | 9/26 | @Col |
| 460 | Burks, Col | Remlinger, Cin | 8/27 | @Col |
| 460 | Thome, Cle | Spoljaric, Sea | 8/21 | @Sea |
| 460 | Griffey Jr, Sea | Woodard, Mil | 8/12 | @Sea |
| 460 | Vaughn G, SD | Leiter A, Fla | 9/9 | @SD |
| 460 | Jefferson, Bos | Radke, Min | 5/7 | @Bos |
| 460 | Sanders R, Cin | Bailey R, Col | 8/26 | @Col |
| 460 | Galarraga, Col | Cloude, Sea | 8/29 | @Col |
| 460 | Jones A, Atl | Avery, Bos | 8/31 | @Bos |
| 460 | McGwire, StL | Castillo F, Col | 9/5 | @Col |

## Who Puts Their Team Ahead? (p. 126)

In the chart below, **Tot RBI** is a player's Total RBI for the season; **GA RBI** is the number of times the player drove in the go-ahead run; **GA Opp** is the number of times a player drove in the go-ahead run plus the number of times he made an out and stranded the go-ahead run in scoring position; **DI%** is the percentage of times a player drove in the go-ahead run divided by his opportunities (**GA Opp**).

### Both Leagues — Listed Alphabetically
### (minimum 75 total RBI in 1997)

| Player, Team | Tot RBI | GA RBI | GA Opp | DI% | Player, Team | Tot RBI | GA RBI | GA Opp | DI% |
|---|---|---|---|---|---|---|---|---|---|
| Alomar S, Cle | 83 | 16 | 34 | 47.1 | Justice, Cle | 101 | 25 | 41 | 61.0 |
| Alou, Fla | 115 | 16 | 36 | 44.4 | Karros, LA | 104 | 30 | 65 | 46.2 |
| Anderson G, Ana | 92 | 20 | 52 | 38.5 | Kent, SF | 121 | 33 | 84 | 39.3 |
| Bagwell, Hou | 135 | 46 | 80 | 57.5 | King, KC | 112 | 25 | 59 | 42.4 |
| Bell J, KC | 92 | 27 | 67 | 40.3 | Klesko, Atl | 84 | 19 | 46 | 41.3 |
| Belle, WSox | 116 | 23 | 63 | 36.5 | Lankford, StL | 98 | 24 | 57 | 42.1 |
| Berroa, Bal | 90 | 25 | 54 | 46.3 | Lieberthal, Phi | 77 | 10 | 39 | 25.6 |
| Bichette, Col | 118 | 13 | 40 | 32.5 | Martinez E, Sea | 108 | 20 | 46 | 43.5 |
| Biggio, Hou | 81 | 20 | 37 | 54.1 | Martinez T, Yanks | 141 | 34 | 76 | 44.7 |
| Bonds, SF | 101 | 25 | 54 | 46.3 | McGriff, Atl | 97 | 26 | 77 | 33.8 |
| Bonilla, Fla | 96 | 16 | 47 | 34.0 | McGwire, StL | 123 | 22 | 58 | 37.9 |
| Brogna, Phi | 81 | 15 | 47 | 31.9 | Molitor, Min | 89 | 25 | 67 | 37.3 |
| Buhner, Sea | 109 | 23 | 56 | 41.1 | Mondesi, LA | 87 | 19 | 47 | 40.4 |
| Burks, Col | 82 | 7 | 27 | 25.9 | Nilsson, Mil | 81 | 21 | 52 | 40.4 |
| Burnitz, Mil | 85 | 22 | 43 | 51.2 | O'Leary, Bos | 80 | 16 | 41 | 39.0 |
| Caminiti, SD | 90 | 26 | 48 | 54.2 | O'Neill, Yanks | 117 | 27 | 48 | 56.3 |
| Carter, Tor | 102 | 29 | 63 | 46.0 | Olerud, Mets | 102 | 26 | 57 | 45.6 |
| Castilla, Col | 113 | 15 | 30 | 50.0 | Palmeiro R, Bal | 110 | 27 | 61 | 44.3 |
| Cirillo, Mil | 82 | 22 | 52 | 42.3 | Palmer, KC | 86 | 16 | 41 | 39.0 |
| Clark T, Det | 117 | 21 | 52 | 40.4 | Piazza, LA | 124 | 32 | 68 | 47.1 |
| Coomer, Min | 85 | 17 | 38 | 44.7 | Ramirez, Cle | 88 | 18 | 43 | 41.9 |
| Davis C, KC | 90 | 19 | 41 | 46.3 | Ripken C, Bal | 84 | 24 | 62 | 38.7 |
| Delgado C, Tor | 91 | 20 | 43 | 46.5 | Rodriguez A, Sea | 84 | 16 | 48 | 33.3 |
| Edmonds, Ana | 80 | 22 | 50 | 44.0 | Rodriguez H, Mon | 83 | 17 | 35 | 48.6 |
| Erstad, Ana | 77 | 16 | 39 | 41.0 | Rodriguez I, Tex | 77 | 15 | 34 | 44.1 |
| Finley, SD | 92 | 21 | 49 | 42.9 | Rolen, Phi | 92 | 23 | 55 | 41.8 |
| Fryman, Det | 102 | 34 | 64 | 53.1 | Salmon, Ana | 129 | 26 | 62 | 41.9 |
| Galarraga, Col | 140 | 34 | 71 | 47.9 | Snow, SF | 104 | 20 | 35 | 57.1 |
| Garciaparra, Bos | 98 | 26 | 45 | 57.8 | Sorrento, Sea | 80 | 14 | 36 | 38.9 |
| Giambi, Oak | 81 | 14 | 36 | 38.9 | Sosa, Cubs | 119 | 27 | 76 | 35.5 |
| Gilkey, Mets | 78 | 12 | 40 | 30.0 | Surhoff, Bal | 88 | 15 | 36 | 41.7 |
| Gonzalez J, Tex | 131 | 25 | 64 | 39.1 | Thomas, WSox | 125 | 36 | 59 | 61.0 |
| Grace, Cubs | 78 | 18 | 49 | 36.7 | Thome, Cle | 102 | 19 | 43 | 44.2 |
| Greene W, Cin | 91 | 24 | 63 | 38.1 | Valentin J, Bos | 77 | 20 | 44 | 45.5 |
| Greer, Tex | 87 | 29 | 63 | 46.0 | Vaughn M, Bos | 96 | 21 | 49 | 42.9 |
| Griffey Jr, Sea | 147 | 38 | 68 | 55.9 | Walker L, Col | 130 | 34 | 63 | 54.0 |
| Gwynn, SD | 119 | 34 | 55 | 61.8 | White R, Mon | 82 | 22 | 66 | 33.3 |
| Higginson, Det | 101 | 14 | 40 | 35.0 | Williams B, Yanks | 100 | 20 | 58 | 34.5 |
| Hollins, Ana | 85 | 24 | 49 | 49.0 | Williams M, Cle | 105 | 22 | 56 | 39.3 |
| Hundley, Mets | 86 | 18 | 48 | 37.5 | Zeile, LA | 90 | 17 | 44 | 38.6 |
| Huskey, Mets | 81 | 18 | 45 | 40.0 | **MLB Totals** | **20468** | **4225** | **11556** | **36.6** |
| Jones C, Atl | 111 | 29 | 71 | 40.8 | | | | | |
| Joyner, SD | 83 | 13 | 37 | 35.1 | | | | | |

# Who Are the Human Air Conditioners? (p. 128)

The table below shows swings missed (**Sw**) as a **%** of total pitches swung at (**Pit**).

## Both Leagues — Listed Alphabetically
### (minimum 350 PA in 1997)

| Player, Team | Sw | Pit | % | Player, Team | Sw | Pit | % | Player, Team | Sw | Pit | % |
|---|---|---|---|---|---|---|---|---|---|---|---|
| Alfonzo, Mets | 110 | 928 | 12 | Carter, Tor | 295 | 1380 | 21 | Frye, Bos | 74 | 683 | 11 |
| Alicea, Ana | 108 | 713 | 15 | Castilla, Col | 331 | 1222 | 27 | Fryman, Det | 187 | 1157 | 16 |
| Allensworth, Pit | 133 | 729 | 18 | Cedeno D, Tex | 178 | 725 | 25 | Gaetti, StL | 258 | 997 | 26 |
| Alomar R, Bal | 78 | 764 | 10 | Cirillo, Mil | 157 | 1052 | 15 | Gagne, LA | 265 | 979 | 27 |
| Alomar S, Cle | 139 | 864 | 16 | Clark T, Det | 361 | 1205 | 30 | Galarraga, Col | 325 | 1241 | 26 |
| Alou, Fla | 187 | 1017 | 18 | Clark W, Tex | 122 | 725 | 17 | Gant, StL | 302 | 1002 | 30 |
| Anderson B, Bal | 192 | 1084 | 18 | Clayton, StL | 225 | 1093 | 21 | Garcia C, Tor | 107 | 644 | 17 |
| Anderson, Ana | 185 | 1113 | 17 | Conine, Fla | 155 | 792 | 20 | Garciaparr., Bos | 271 | 1305 | 21 |
| Ausmus, Hou | 142 | 775 | 18 | Coomer, Min | 217 | 1014 | 21 | Giambi, Oak | 135 | 935 | 14 |
| Baerga, Mets | 121 | 785 | 15 | Cora, Sea | 68 | 1000 | 7 | Giles, Cle | 72 | 671 | 11 |
| Bagwell, Hou | 273 | 1156 | 24 | Cordero, Bos | 267 | 1065 | 25 | Gilkey, Mets | 202 | 940 | 21 |
| Baines, Bal | 111 | 780 | 14 | Cordova, Min | 215 | 857 | 25 | Girardi, Yanks | 118 | 694 | 17 |
| Becker, Min | 222 | 856 | 26 | Cruz D, Det | 124 | 762 | 16 | Glanville, Cubs | 104 | 846 | 12 |
| Bell D, Hou | 237 | 959 | 25 | Cruz Jr, Tor | 259 | 836 | 31 | Gomez, SD | 167 | 965 | 17 |
| Bell J, KC | 223 | 1174 | 19 | Cummings, Phi | 139 | 649 | 21 | Gonzalez A, Tor | 199 | 799 | 25 |
| Belle, WSox | 215 | 1145 | 19 | Curtis, Yanks | 105 | 669 | 16 | Gonzalez J, Tex | 292 | 1086 | 27 |
| Berroa, Bal | 294 | 1103 | 27 | Damon, KC | 140 | 872 | 16 | Gonzalez, Hou | 117 | 1035 | 11 |
| Bichette, Col | 216 | 1147 | 19 | Daulton, Fla | 124 | 752 | 16 | Goodwin T, Tex | 137 | 969 | 14 |
| Biggio, Hou | 207 | 1097 | 19 | Davis C, KC | 205 | 933 | 22 | Grace, Cubs | 87 | 987 | 9 |
| Blauser, Atl | 184 | 945 | 19 | Davis R, Sea | 203 | 828 | 25 | Green S, Tor | 228 | 872 | 26 |
| Boggs, Yanks | 43 | 580 | 7 | Delgado C, Tor | 309 | 1127 | 27 | Greene W, Cin | 262 | 917 | 29 |
| Bonds, SF | 170 | 950 | 18 | DeShields, StL | 107 | 917 | 12 | Greer, Tex | 159 | 1125 | 14 |
| Bonilla, Fla | 229 | 1158 | 20 | DiSarcina, Ana | 92 | 881 | 10 | Griffey Jr, Sea | 275 | 1286 | 21 |
| Boone B, Cin | 172 | 822 | 21 | Duncan, Tor | 181 | 709 | 26 | Grissom, Cle | 185 | 1044 | 18 |
| Bordick, Bal | 96 | 866 | 11 | Dunston, Pit | 182 | 947 | 19 | Grudziela., Mon | 206 | 1233 | 17 |
| Bragg, Bos | 191 | 997 | 19 | Durham, WSox | 169 | 1133 | 15 | Guerrero, Mon | 134 | 646 | 21 |
| Brogna, Phi | 263 | 1100 | 24 | Easley, Det | 189 | 969 | 20 | Guerrero W, LA | 118 | 691 | 17 |
| Brosius, Oak | 178 | 944 | 19 | Edmonds, Ana | 175 | 982 | 18 | Guillen J, Pit | 237 | 987 | 24 |
| Buford, Tex | 167 | 740 | 23 | Erstad, Ana | 189 | 952 | 20 | Guillen O, WSox | 70 | 808 | 9 |
| Buhner, Sea | 359 | 1056 | 34 | Everett, Mets | 241 | 892 | 27 | Gwynn, SD | 80 | 994 | 8 |
| Burks, Col | 169 | 835 | 20 | Fabrega., WSox | 86 | 607 | 14 | Hamelin, Det | 138 | 593 | 23 |
| Burnitz, Mil | 215 | 931 | 23 | Fernandez, Cle | 98 | 771 | 13 | Hamilton, SF | 81 | 841 | 10 |
| Butler B, LA | 57 | 626 | 9 | Fielder, Yanks | 227 | 813 | 28 | Hammonds, Bal | 170 | 747 | 23 |
| Cameron, WSox | 170 | 721 | 24 | Finley, SD | 211 | 1073 | 20 | Hatteberg, Bos | 105 | 598 | 18 |
| Caminiti, SD | 255 | 1022 | 25 | Flaherty, SD | 145 | 810 | 18 | Hayes, Yanks | 143 | 678 | 21 |
| Canseco, Oak | 208 | 761 | 27 | Franco J, Mil | 174 | 873 | 20 | Henderson, Ana | 110 | 750 | 15 |

| Player, Team | Sw | Pit | % | Player, Team | Sw | Pit | % | Player, Team | Sw | Pit | % |
|---|---|---|---|---|---|---|---|---|---|---|---|
| Higginson, Det | 151 | 974 | 16 | McCracken, Col | 92 | 599 | 15 | Santangel., Mon | 137 | 718 | 19 |
| Hill, SF | 215 | 812 | 26 | McGriff, Atl | 218 | 1040 | 21 | Santiago, Tor | 166 | 702 | 24 |
| Hoiles, Bal | 177 | 646 | 27 | McGwire, StL | 313 | 1002 | 31 | Segui, Mon | 159 | 867 | 18 |
| Hollins, Ana | 236 | 1164 | 20 | McLemore, Tex | 87 | 576 | 15 | Servais, Cubs | 127 | 711 | 18 |
| Hundley, Mets | 240 | 914 | 26 | McRae, Mets | 147 | 1097 | 13 | Sheffield, Fla | 149 | 834 | 18 |
| Hunter B, Det | 190 | 1155 | 16 | Meares, Min | 163 | 786 | 21 | Snow, SF | 182 | 1039 | 18 |
| Huskey, Mets | 215 | 881 | 24 | Merced, Tor | 118 | 649 | 18 | Sorrento, Sea | 200 | 825 | 24 |
| Javier, SF | 126 | 843 | 15 | Molitor, Min | 171 | 1005 | 17 | Sosa, Cubs | 450 | 1419 | 32 |
| Jefferies, Phi | 65 | 786 | 8 | Mondesi, LA | 285 | 1124 | 25 | Spiers, Hou | 89 | 505 | 18 |
| Jefferson, Bos | 207 | 967 | 21 | Morandini, Phi | 158 | 1100 | 14 | Spiezio, Oak | 110 | 901 | 12 |
| Jeter, Yanks | 234 | 1319 | 18 | Morris, Cin | 64 | 549 | 12 | Sprague, Tor | 202 | 967 | 21 |
| Johnson C, Fla | 238 | 928 | 26 | Mueller, SF | 101 | 713 | 14 | Stairs, Oak | 155 | 647 | 24 |
| Johnson, Cubs | 56 | 654 | 9 | Nieves, Det | 320 | 777 | 41 | Stanley, Yanks | 165 | 692 | 24 |
| Jones A, Atl | 249 | 827 | 30 | Nilsson, Mil | 141 | 1032 | 14 | Steinbach, Min | 274 | 960 | 29 |
| Jones C, Atl | 181 | 1072 | 17 | Nixon, LA | 132 | 1034 | 13 | Stevens, Tex | 234 | 855 | 27 |
| Joyner, SD | 112 | 822 | 14 | O'Leary, Bos | 161 | 864 | 19 | Stocker, Phi | 155 | 983 | 16 |
| Justice, Cle | 156 | 937 | 17 | O'Neill, Yanks | 151 | 1036 | 15 | Strange, Mon | 146 | 652 | 22 |
| Karros, LA | 268 | 1242 | 22 | Offerman, KC | 95 | 812 | 12 | Surhoff, Bal | 135 | 993 | 14 |
| Kelly R, Sea | 150 | 699 | 21 | Olerud, Mets | 106 | 865 | 12 | Thomas, WSox | 127 | 957 | 13 |
| Kendall, Pit | 107 | 885 | 12 | Oliver, Cin | 149 | 734 | 20 | Thome, Cle | 233 | 965 | 24 |
| Kent, SF | 315 | 1166 | 27 | Ordonez, Mets | 81 | 610 | 13 | Tucker, Atl | 269 | 1037 | 26 |
| King, KC | 182 | 1032 | 18 | Orie, Cubs | 127 | 714 | 18 | Valentin J, Bos | 145 | 1002 | 14 |
| Klesko, Atl | 248 | 924 | 27 | Palmeiro R, Bal | 237 | 1200 | 20 | Valentin J, Mil | 222 | 994 | 22 |
| Knoblauch, Min | 106 | 1139 | 9 | Palmer, KC | 281 | 1158 | 24 | Vaughn G, SD | 243 | 794 | 31 |
| Lankford, StL | 326 | 1065 | 31 | Phillips T, Ana | 204 | 1041 | 20 | Vaughn M, Bos | 331 | 1058 | 31 |
| Lansing, Mon | 192 | 1109 | 17 | Piazza, LA | 196 | 1025 | 19 | Veras, SD | 131 | 1088 | 12 |
| Lawton, Min | 123 | 822 | 15 | Ramirez, Cle | 212 | 1144 | 19 | Vizcaino, SF | 129 | 1078 | 12 |
| Lemke, Atl | 93 | 567 | 16 | Randa, Pit | 118 | 732 | 16 | Vizquel, Cle | 109 | 1086 | 10 |
| Lewis M, SF | 126 | 654 | 19 | Reese, Cin | 146 | 726 | 20 | Walker L, Col | 222 | 1091 | 20 |
| Leyritz, Tex | 178 | 762 | 23 | Renteria, Fla | 264 | 1304 | 20 | Weiss, Col | 72 | 646 | 11 |
| Lieberthal, Phi | 161 | 873 | 18 | Ripken C, Bal | 147 | 1098 | 13 | White R, Mon | 270 | 1096 | 25 |
| Lofton, Atl | 107 | 851 | 13 | Roberts, Cle | 130 | 870 | 15 | Williams, Yanks | 144 | 887 | 16 |
| Lopez J, Atl | 221 | 820 | 27 | Rodriguez, Sea | 186 | 1126 | 17 | Williams G, Mil | 262 | 1159 | 23 |
| Loretta, Mil | 91 | 777 | 12 | Rodriguez, Mon | 355 | 1068 | 33 | Williams M, Cle | 322 | 1240 | 26 |
| Mabry, StL | 182 | 787 | 23 | Rodriguez I, Tex | 239 | 1238 | 19 | Wilson D, Sea | 163 | 969 | 17 |
| Manwaring, Col | 128 | 652 | 20 | Rolen, Phi | 274 | 1137 | 24 | Womack, Pit | 236 | 1370 | 17 |
| Martin A, Pit | 197 | 837 | 24 | Salmon, Ana | 343 | 1334 | 26 | Young D, StL | 160 | 680 | 24 |
| Martinez, WSox | 86 | 894 | 10 | Sanchez, Yanks | 80 | 621 | 13 | Young E, LA | 94 | 969 | 10 |
| Martinez E, Sea | 116 | 941 | 12 | Sandberg, Cubs | 189 | 816 | 23 | Young K, Pit | 183 | 701 | 26 |
| Martinez, Yanks | 168 | 1099 | 15 | Sanders D, Cin | 138 | 844 | 16 | Zeile, LA | 166 | 956 | 17 |
| Matheny, Mil | 145 | 635 | 23 | Sanders R, Cin | 197 | 615 | 32 | MLB Avg | | | 20 |

## Who's the Best Bunter? (p. 130)

The following table shows: **SH** = Sac Hits, **FSH** = Failed Sac Hits; and **BH**= Bunt Hits, **FBH** = Failed Bunt Hits.

### Both Leagues — Listed Alphabetically
### (minimum 12 bunts in play)

| Batter, Team | SH | FSH | % | BH | FBH | % | Batter, Team | SH | FSH | % | BH | FBH | % |
|---|---|---|---|---|---|---|---|---|---|---|---|---|---|
| Alicea, Ana | 4 | 3 | 57 | 5 | 0 | 100 | Javier, SF | 2 | 1 | 67 | 3 | 6 | 33 |
| Allensworth, Pit | 9 | 0 | 100 | 3 | 4 | 43 | Jeter, Yanks | 8 | 0 | 100 | 4 | 2 | 67 |
| Alomar R, Bal | 7 | 4 | 64 | 3 | 2 | 60 | Kile, Hou | 10 | 5 | 67 | 0 | 0 | — |
| Astacio, Col | 11 | 4 | 73 | 0 | 0 | — | Lemke, Atl | 8 | 3 | 73 | 1 | 0 | 100 |
| Beech, Phi | 11 | 3 | 79 | 0 | 0 | — | Lewis D, LA | 7 | 1 | 88 | 4 | 5 | 44 |
| Bordick, Bal | 12 | 2 | 86 | 2 | 0 | 100 | Loaiza, Pit | 8 | 4 | 67 | 2 | 0 | 100 |
| Buford, Tex | 3 | 2 | 60 | 7 | 7 | 50 | Lofton, Atl | 2 | 1 | 67 | 15 | 9 | 63 |
| Butler B, LA | 15 | 3 | 83 | 6 | 10 | 38 | Martinez D, WSox | 5 | 0 | 100 | 6 | 1 | 86 |
| Castillo F, Col | 10 | 3 | 77 | 0 | 0 | — | Mashore, Oak | 7 | 2 | 78 | 1 | 2 | 33 |
| Clayton, StL | 2 | 1 | 67 | 4 | 6 | 40 | Matheny, Mil | 9 | 2 | 82 | 2 | 2 | 50 |
| Cooke, Pit | 7 | 5 | 58 | 0 | 0 | — | McCracken, Col | 6 | 2 | 75 | 3 | 3 | 50 |
| Cora, Sea | 8 | 1 | 89 | 4 | 7 | 36 | McDonald, Oak | 2 | 1 | 67 | 6 | 9 | 40 |
| Cruz D, Det | 14 | 1 | 93 | 2 | 3 | 40 | McLemore, Tex | 6 | 0 | 100 | 3 | 5 | 38 |
| Damon, KC | 6 | 2 | 75 | 2 | 2 | 50 | McRae, Mets | 4 | 2 | 67 | 3 | 10 | 23 |
| DeShields, StL | 7 | 1 | 88 | 11 | 21 | 34 | Morandini, Phi | 12 | 1 | 92 | 5 | 0 | 100 |
| DiSarcina, Ana | 8 | 0 | 100 | 4 | 1 | 80 | Neagle, Atl | 9 | 7 | 56 | 0 | 0 | — |
| Dunston, Pit | 5 | 0 | 100 | 8 | 7 | 53 | Nixon, LA | 8 | 4 | 67 | 25 | 26 | 49 |
| Durham, WSox | 2 | 0 | 100 | 10 | 10 | 50 | Ordonez R, Mets | 14 | 1 | 93 | 3 | 1 | 75 |
| Estes, SF | 7 | 5 | 58 | 1 | 0 | 100 | Perez N, Col | 5 | 2 | 71 | 6 | 4 | 60 |
| Everett, Mets | 3 | 1 | 75 | 6 | 9 | 40 | Reboulet, Bal | 11 | 0 | 100 | 1 | 1 | 50 |
| Fernandez, Cle | 6 | 1 | 86 | 8 | 4 | 67 | Renteria, Fla | 19 | 1 | 95 | 7 | 4 | 64 |
| Foster, Cubs | 11 | 0 | 100 | 0 | 1 | 0 | Sanchez, Yanks | 9 | 1 | 90 | 1 | 1 | 50 |
| Garcia C, Tor | 10 | 2 | 83 | 0 | 0 | — | Sanders D, Cin | 2 | 3 | 40 | 12 | 14 | 46 |
| Girardi, Yanks | 5 | 4 | 56 | 1 | 2 | 33 | Santangelo, Mon | 12 | 5 | 71 | 1 | 1 | 50 |
| Glanville, Cubs | 9 | 1 | 90 | 4 | 3 | 57 | Schilling, Phi | 12 | 6 | 67 | 1 | 0 | 100 |
| Glavine, Atl | 17 | 2 | 90 | 0 | 0 | — | Stocker, Phi | 2 | 1 | 67 | 7 | 9 | 44 |
| Gonzalez A, Tor | 11 | 2 | 85 | 1 | 1 | 50 | Trachsel, Cubs | 11 | 6 | 65 | 0 | 0 | — |
| Goodwin C, Cin | 6 | 7 | 46 | 7 | 4 | 64 | Tucker, Atl | 4 | 0 | 100 | 6 | 4 | 60 |
| Goodwin T, Tex | 11 | 6 | 65 | 16 | 7 | 70 | Valdes I, LA | 7 | 2 | 78 | 2 | 1 | 67 |
| Guerrero W, LA | 13 | 5 | 72 | 9 | 6 | 60 | Valentin J, Mil | 4 | 1 | 80 | 9 | 1 | 90 |
| Guillen O, WSox | 11 | 2 | 85 | 3 | 2 | 60 | Veras, SD | 9 | 2 | 82 | 3 | 7 | 30 |
| Hamilton, SF | 6 | 0 | 100 | 3 | 8 | 27 | Vina, Mil | 2 | 1 | 67 | 8 | 10 | 44 |
| Hampton, Hou | 10 | 5 | 67 | 0 | 0 | — | Vizcaino, SF | 13 | 2 | 87 | 6 | 3 | 67 |
| Hitchcock, SD | 8 | 7 | 53 | 1 | 0 | 100 | Vizquel, Cle | 16 | 0 | 100 | 7 | 4 | 64 |
| Hollins, Ana | 1 | 1 | 50 | 12 | 7 | 63 | Womack, Pit | 2 | 1 | 67 | 9 | 8 | 53 |
| Holt, Hou | 9 | 5 | 64 | 0 | 0 | — | Young E, LA | 10 | 0 | 100 | 1 | 2 | 33 |
| Hunter B, Det | 8 | 1 | 89 | 4 | 2 | 67 | **MLB Totals** | **1577** | **446** | **78** | **522** | **464** | **53** |

# Which Pitchers Have Misleading Earned Run Averages? (p. 142)

## Predicted ERA versus Actual ERA
### (minimum 100 IP for starters or 50 IP for relievers in 1997)

| Pitcher, Team | ERA Diff | Act ERA | Pred ERA | Pitcher, Team | ERA Diff | Act ERA | Pred ERA |
|---|---|---|---|---|---|---|---|
| Charlton, Sea | -1.42 | 7.27 | 5.85 | Olivares, Sea | -0.24 | 4.97 | 4.73 |
| Bautista, StL | -1.29 | 6.66 | 5.38 | Hitchcock, SD | -0.24 | 5.20 | 4.96 |
| Harris R, Phi | -1.09 | 5.30 | 4.21 | Sager, Det | -0.24 | 4.18 | 3.94 |
| Bochtler, SD | -0.99 | 4.77 | 3.79 | Erickson, Bal | -0.23 | 3.69 | 3.46 |
| Lima, Hou | -0.99 | 5.28 | 4.29 | Rojas, Mets | -0.22 | 4.64 | 4.42 |
| Rogers, Yanks | -0.94 | 5.65 | 4.71 | Sele, Bos | -0.21 | 5.38 | 5.16 |
| Baldwin, WSox | -0.90 | 5.27 | 4.36 | Rincon, Pit | -0.21 | 3.45 | 3.24 |
| Person, Tor | -0.89 | 5.61 | 4.72 | Reyes C, Oak | -0.21 | 5.82 | 5.61 |
| Worrell T, LA | -0.88 | 5.28 | 4.40 | Alvarez, SF | -0.20 | 3.48 | 3.28 |
| Trombley, Min | -0.87 | 4.37 | 3.51 | Sanders, Det | -0.19 | 5.86 | 5.67 |
| Drabek, WSox | -0.83 | 5.74 | 4.91 | Park, LA | -0.19 | 3.38 | 3.18 |
| Ruebel, Pit | -0.78 | 6.32 | 5.54 | Nomo, LA | -0.19 | 4.25 | 4.06 |
| Suppan, Bos | -0.76 | 5.69 | 4.93 | Burba, Cin | -0.18 | 4.73 | 4.54 |
| Bullinger, Mon | -0.76 | 5.56 | 4.80 | Eldred, Mil | -0.17 | 4.99 | 4.82 |
| Leskanic, Col | -0.76 | 5.55 | 4.80 | Patterson B, Cubs | -0.17 | 3.34 | 3.17 |
| Navarro, WSox | -0.72 | 5.79 | 5.07 | Hampton, Hou | -0.16 | 3.83 | 3.67 |
| Gordon, Bos | -0.72 | 3.74 | 3.03 | Powell, Fla | -0.15 | 3.28 | 3.12 |
| Carrasco, KC | -0.66 | 4.40 | 3.73 | Slocumb, Sea | -0.15 | 5.16 | 5.01 |
| Henry D, SF | -0.66 | 4.71 | 4.06 | Jones T, Det | -0.15 | 3.09 | 2.94 |
| Whiteside, Tex | -0.59 | 5.08 | 4.49 | Smiley, Cle | -0.13 | 5.31 | 5.17 |
| Pittsley, KC | -0.58 | 5.46 | 4.88 | Rusch, KC | -0.13 | 5.50 | 5.36 |
| McElroy, WSox | -0.57 | 3.84 | 3.27 | Radke, Min | -0.13 | 3.87 | 3.74 |
| McDonald, Mil | -0.57 | 4.06 | 3.49 | Wengert, Oak | -0.12 | 6.04 | 5.93 |
| Jackson M, Cle | -0.55 | 3.24 | 2.69 | Worrell T, SD | -0.11 | 5.16 | 5.05 |
| DiPoto, Col | -0.50 | 4.70 | 4.21 | Hermanson, Mon | -0.10 | 3.69 | 3.60 |
| Remlinger, Cin | -0.49 | 4.14 | 3.65 | Wells B, Sea | -0.09 | 5.75 | 5.66 |
| Rosado, KC | -0.48 | 4.69 | 4.21 | Castillo T, WSox | -0.07 | 4.91 | 4.83 |
| Springer R, Hou | -0.48 | 4.23 | 3.75 | Leiter A, Fla | -0.07 | 4.34 | 4.27 |
| Stottlemyre, StL | -0.48 | 3.88 | 3.40 | Swindell, Min | -0.07 | 3.58 | 3.51 |
| Heredia F, Fla | -0.46 | 4.29 | 3.83 | Wagner B, Hou | -0.07 | 2.85 | 2.78 |
| Saunders, Fla | -0.46 | 4.61 | 4.15 | Estes, SF | -0.06 | 3.18 | 3.12 |
| Oquist, Oak | -0.45 | 5.02 | 4.57 | Astacio, Col | -0.05 | 4.14 | 4.08 |
| Morgan, Cin | -0.45 | 4.78 | 4.33 | Benes A, StL | -0.05 | 3.10 | 3.05 |
| Ashby, SD | -0.44 | 4.13 | 3.69 | Stanton, Yanks | -0.05 | 2.57 | 2.52 |
| Miceli, Det | -0.43 | 5.01 | 4.58 | Burkett, Tex | -0.03 | 4.56 | 4.53 |
| Guthrie, LA | -0.43 | 5.32 | 4.90 | Dreifort, LA | -0.03 | 2.86 | 2.82 |
| Cunnane, SD | -0.43 | 5.81 | 5.39 | Rhodes, Bal | -0.02 | 3.02 | 3.00 |
| Wohlers, Atl | -0.41 | 3.50 | 3.09 | Bielecki, Atl | -0.02 | 4.08 | 4.06 |
| Robertson, Min | -0.39 | 5.69 | 5.30 | Karsay, Oak | -0.01 | 5.77 | 5.75 |
| Spradlin, Phi | -0.39 | 4.74 | 4.35 | Blair, Det | -0.01 | 4.17 | 4.16 |
| Beck, SF | -0.39 | 3.47 | 3.09 | D'Amico, Mil | -0.01 | 4.71 | 4.70 |
| Lieber, Pit | -0.38 | 4.49 | 4.11 | Juden, Cle | -0.00 | 4.46 | 4.46 |
| Gonzalez, Cubs | -0.36 | 4.25 | 3.89 | Hill, Ana | -0.00 | 4.55 | 4.54 |
| Finley, Ana | -0.35 | 4.23 | 3.87 | Castillo F, Col | -0.00 | 5.42 | 5.42 |
| Ogea, Cle | -0.34 | 4.99 | 4.65 | Belcher, KC | -0.00 | 5.02 | 5.02 |
| Wasdin, Bos | -0.31 | 4.40 | 4.09 | Thomson, Col | 0.00 | 4.71 | 4.71 |
| Leiter M, Phi | -0.31 | 5.67 | 5.35 | Nen, Fla | 0.01 | 3.89 | 3.90 |
| Percival, Ana | -0.31 | 3.46 | 3.15 | Belinda, Cin | 0.01 | 3.71 | 3.73 |
| Myers M, Det | -0.31 | 5.70 | 5.39 | Spoljaric, Sea | 0.02 | 3.69 | 3.71 |
| Rodriguez F, Min | -0.30 | 4.62 | 4.31 | Corsi, Bos | 0.02 | 3.43 | 3.45 |
| Reed S, Col | -0.29 | 4.04 | 3.75 | Vosberg, Fla | 0.04 | 4.42 | 4.46 |
| Eckersley, StL | -0.29 | 3.91 | 3.62 | Glavine, Atl | 0.05 | 2.96 | 3.02 |
| Moyer, Sea | -0.27 | 3.86 | 3.60 | Wells D, Yanks | 0.06 | 4.21 | 4.27 |
| Springer D, Ana | -0.27 | 5.18 | 4.91 | Moehler, Det | 0.06 | 4.67 | 4.73 |
| Urbina, Mon | -0.26 | 3.78 | 3.51 | Jones B, Mets | 0.07 | 3.63 | 3.70 |
| Schmidt, Pit | -0.25 | 4.60 | 4.35 | Taylor, Oak | 0.09 | 3.82 | 3.91 |
| Groom, Oak | -0.25 | 5.15 | 4.90 | Foster, Cubs | 0.09 | 4.61 | 4.70 |
| Bergman, SD | -0.25 | 6.09 | 5.84 | Hoffman, SD | 0.10 | 2.66 | 2.75 |
| Reynolds, Hou | -0.25 | 4.23 | 3.98 | Nelson, Yanks | 0.10 | 2.86 | 2.96 |

| Pitcher, Team | ERA Diff | Act ERA | Pred ERA | Pitcher, Team | ERA Diff | Act ERA | Pred ERA |
|---|---|---|---|---|---|---|---|
| Patterson D, Tex | 0.10 | 3.42 | 3.53 | Rueter, SF | 0.36 | 3.45 | 3.80 |
| Montgomery J, KC | 0.11 | 3.49 | 3.60 | Castillo C, WSox | 0.36 | 4.48 | 4.84 |
| Fassero, Sea | 0.12 | 3.61 | 3.73 | Roa, SF | 0.37 | 5.21 | 5.57 |
| Adams T, Cubs | 0.12 | 4.62 | 4.74 | Holmes, Col | 0.37 | 5.34 | 5.71 |
| James, Ana | 0.12 | 4.31 | 4.43 | Benitez, Bal | 0.38 | 2.45 | 2.83 |
| Tewksbury, Min | 0.12 | 4.22 | 4.34 | Timlin, Sea | 0.38 | 3.22 | 3.60 |
| Perez C, Mon | 0.13 | 3.88 | 4.00 | McMichael, Mets | 0.38 | 2.98 | 3.36 |
| Fernandez A, Fla | 0.13 | 3.59 | 3.72 | Orosco, Bal | 0.39 | 2.32 | 2.71 |
| Neagle, Atl | 0.13 | 2.97 | 3.10 | Ritchie, Min | 0.39 | 4.58 | 4.97 |
| Valdes M, Mon | 0.14 | 3.13 | 3.26 | Bottalico, Phi | 0.39 | 3.65 | 4.04 |
| Beech, Phi | 0.14 | 5.07 | 5.21 | Williams W, Tor | 0.40 | 4.35 | 4.74 |
| Cordova, Pit | 0.14 | 3.63 | 3.76 | Cook, Fla | 0.40 | 3.90 | 4.30 |
| Gooden, Yanks | 0.14 | 4.91 | 5.05 | Witt, Tex | 0.41 | 4.82 | 5.23 |
| Loaiza, Pit | 0.15 | 4.13 | 4.27 | Clemens, Tor | 0.42 | 2.05 | 2.46 |
| Appier, KC | 0.15 | 3.40 | 3.55 | Lidle, Mets | 0.42 | 3.53 | 3.94 |
| Schilling, Phi | 0.15 | 2.97 | 3.12 | Telford, Mon | 0.42 | 3.24 | 3.66 |
| Blazier, Phi | 0.15 | 5.03 | 5.18 | Darwin D, SF | 0.44 | 4.35 | 4.78 |
| Sullivan, Cin | 0.15 | 3.24 | 3.39 | Johnson R, Sea | 0.44 | 2.28 | 2.73 |
| Mercker, Cin | 0.15 | 3.92 | 4.07 | Cooke, Pit | 0.46 | 4.30 | 4.76 |
| Mulholland, SF | 0.15 | 4.24 | 4.40 | DeJean, Col | 0.48 | 3.99 | 4.47 |
| Thompson J, Det | 0.16 | 3.02 | 3.18 | Valdes I, LA | 0.48 | 2.65 | 3.13 |
| Karl, Mil | 0.16 | 4.47 | 4.63 | Martinez R, LA | 0.48 | 3.64 | 4.12 |
| Hamilton, SD | 0.16 | 4.25 | 4.41 | Candiotti, LA | 0.52 | 3.60 | 4.12 |
| Benes A, StL | 0.17 | 2.89 | 3.06 | Garcia, Hou | 0.53 | 3.69 | 4.21 |
| Hentgen, Tor | 0.17 | 3.68 | 3.85 | Ritz, Col | 0.55 | 5.87 | 6.42 |
| Kamieniecki, Bal | 0.18 | 4.01 | 4.19 | Dickson, Ana | 0.56 | 4.29 | 4.84 |
| Petkovsek, StL | 0.18 | 5.06 | 5.24 | Trachsel, Cubs | 0.56 | 4.51 | 5.08 |
| Mussina, Bal | 0.18 | 3.20 | 3.39 | Kile, Hou | 0.57 | 2.57 | 3.14 |
| Watson, Ana | 0.19 | 4.93 | 5.12 | Clark M, Cubs | 0.60 | 3.82 | 4.42 |
| Smoltz, Atl | 0.19 | 3.02 | 3.21 | Hernandez R, SF | 0.61 | 2.45 | 3.07 |
| Wright J, Col | 0.19 | 6.25 | 6.45 | Bottenfield, Cubs | 0.62 | 3.86 | 4.48 |
| Wilkins, Pit | 0.19 | 3.69 | 3.88 | Oliver, Tex | 0.63 | 4.20 | 4.83 |
| Fetters, Mil | 0.20 | 3.45 | 3.65 | Key, Bal | 0.65 | 3.43 | 4.09 |
| Hershiser, Cle | 0.20 | 4.47 | 4.67 | Hawkins, Min | 0.66 | 5.84 | 6.49 |
| Reed R, Mets | 0.20 | 2.89 | 3.10 | Hasegawa, Ana | 0.68 | 3.93 | 4.61 |
| Henry B, Bos | 0.22 | 3.52 | 3.74 | Sodowsky, Pit | 0.69 | 3.63 | 4.33 |
| Wendell, Mets | 0.22 | 4.36 | 4.58 | Osuna, LA | 0.71 | 2.19 | 2.89 |
| Mlicki, Mets | 0.22 | 4.00 | 4.22 | Stephenson, Phi | 0.71 | 3.15 | 3.87 |
| Tomko, Cin | 0.24 | 3.43 | 3.67 | Villone, Mil | 0.73 | 3.42 | 4.14 |
| Jones D, Mil | 0.24 | 2.02 | 2.26 | Kline, Mon | 0.73 | 5.98 | 6.71 |
| Martinez P, Mon | 0.24 | 1.90 | 2.14 | Ayala, Sea | 0.76 | 3.82 | 4.57 |
| Plunk, Cle | 0.24 | 4.66 | 4.90 | Harris P, Ana | 0.77 | 3.62 | 4.39 |
| Rapp, SF | 0.25 | 4.83 | 5.08 | Bailey R, Col | 0.83 | 4.29 | 5.12 |
| Gardner, SF | 0.25 | 4.29 | 4.54 | Prieto, Oak | 0.93 | 5.04 | 5.97 |
| Shaw, Cin | 0.26 | 2.38 | 2.63 | Loiselle, Pit | 0.94 | 3.10 | 4.03 |
| Maddux G, Atl | 0.27 | 2.20 | 2.47 | Frascatore, StL | 0.94 | 2.48 | 3.42 |
| Wakefield, Bos | 0.27 | 4.25 | 4.52 | Rodriguez R, SF | 0.96 | 3.17 | 4.13 |
| Holt, Hou | 0.29 | 3.52 | 3.81 | Karchner, WSox | 1.00 | 2.91 | 3.90 |
| Morris, StL | 0.30 | 3.19 | 3.49 | Brocail, Det | 1.02 | 3.23 | 4.25 |
| Radinsky, LA | 0.30 | 2.89 | 3.19 | Wickman, Mil | 1.02 | 2.73 | 3.75 |
| Brown, Fla | 0.30 | 2.69 | 3.00 | Myers R, Bal | 1.05 | 1.51 | 2.56 |
| Plesac, Tor | 0.31 | 3.58 | 3.88 | Rivera, Yanks | 1.12 | 1.88 | 3.00 |
| Mathews T, Bal | 0.31 | 4.41 | 4.71 | Martin, Hou | 1.16 | 2.09 | 3.25 |
| Pettitte, Yanks | 0.31 | 2.88 | 3.19 | Mathews T, Oak | 1.18 | 3.01 | 4.20 |
| Aguilera, Min | 0.31 | 3.82 | 4.13 | Veres D, Mon | 1.25 | 3.48 | 4.73 |
| Tavarez, SF | 0.31 | 3.87 | 4.18 | Mesa, Cle | 1.26 | 2.40 | 3.67 |
| Wetteland, Tex | 0.31 | 1.94 | 2.25 | Tatis, Cubs | 1.28 | 5.34 | 6.61 |
| Mercedes, Mil | 0.31 | 3.79 | 4.10 | Fossas, StL | 1.28 | 3.83 | 5.11 |
| Small, Oak | 0.31 | 4.28 | 4.60 | Hutton, Col | 1.79 | 4.48 | 6.27 |
| Nagy, Cle | 0.32 | 4.28 | 4.60 | Quantrill, Tor | 2.02 | 1.94 | 3.97 |
| Cone, Yanks | 0.33 | 2.82 | 3.15 | Hall, LA | 2.08 | 2.30 | 4.38 |
| Franco, Mets | 0.34 | 2.55 | 2.89 | | | | |

## Whose Heater Is Hottest? (p. 145)

### Both Leagues — Listed Alphabetically
### (minimum 130 IP or 56 relief games in 1997)

| Pitcher,Team | IP | K | K/9 | Pitcher,Team | IP | K | K/9 |
|---|---|---|---|---|---|---|---|
| Adams T, Cubs | 74.0 | 64 | 7.8 | Glavine, Atl | 240.0 | 152 | 5.7 |
| Aguilera, Min | 68.1 | 68 | 9.0 | Gordon, Bos | 182.2 | 159 | 7.8 |
| Alvarez, SF | 212.0 | 179 | 7.6 | Groom, Oak | 64.2 | 45 | 6.3 |
| Appier, KC | 235.2 | 196 | 7.5 | Guardado, Min | 46.0 | 54 | 10.6 |
| Ashby, SD | 200.2 | 144 | 6.5 | Gunderson, Tex | 49.2 | 31 | 5.6 |
| Assenmacher, Cle | 49.0 | 53 | 9.7 | Guthrie, LA | 69.1 | 42 | 5.5 |
| Astacio, Col | 202.1 | 166 | 7.4 | Hall, LA | 54.2 | 39 | 6.4 |
| Ayala, Sea | 96.2 | 92 | 8.6 | Hamilton, SD | 192.2 | 124 | 5.8 |
| Bailey R, Col | 191.0 | 84 | 4.0 | Hampton, Hou | 223.0 | 139 | 5.6 |
| Baldwin, WSox | 200.0 | 140 | 6.3 | Harris P, Ana | 79.2 | 56 | 6.3 |
| Beck, SF | 70.0 | 53 | 6.8 | Henry D, SF | 70.2 | 69 | 8.8 |
| Belcher, KC | 213.1 | 113 | 4.8 | Hentgen, Tor | 264.0 | 160 | 5.5 |
| Belinda, Cin | 99.1 | 114 | 10.3 | Heredia F, Fla | 56.2 | 54 | 8.6 |
| Benes A, StL | 177.0 | 175 | 8.9 | Hernandez R, SF | 80.2 | 82 | 9.1 |
| Benitez, Bal | 73.1 | 106 | 13.0 | Hershiser, Cle | 195.1 | 107 | 4.9 |
| Blair, Det | 175.0 | 90 | 4.6 | Hill, Ana | 190.0 | 106 | 5.0 |
| Bottalico, Phi | 74.0 | 89 | 10.8 | Hoffman, SD | 81.1 | 111 | 12.3 |
| Bottenfield, Cubs | 84.0 | 74 | 7.9 | Holt, Hou | 209.2 | 95 | 4.1 |
| Brocail, Det | 78.0 | 60 | 6.9 | Holtz, Ana | 43.1 | 40 | 8.3 |
| Brown, Fla | 237.1 | 205 | 7.8 | Jackson M, Cle | 75.0 | 74 | 8.9 |
| Burkett, Tex | 189.1 | 139 | 6.6 | James, Ana | 62.2 | 57 | 8.2 |
| Carrasco, KC | 86.0 | 76 | 8.0 | Johnson R, Sea | 213.0 | 291 | 12.3 |
| Castillo F, Col | 184.1 | 126 | 6.2 | Jones B, Mets | 193.1 | 125 | 5.8 |
| Castillo T, WSox | 62.1 | 42 | 6.1 | Jones D, Mil | 80.1 | 82 | 9.2 |
| Charlton, Sea | 69.1 | 55 | 7.1 | Jones T, Det | 70.0 | 70 | 9.0 |
| Clark M, Cubs | 205.0 | 123 | 5.4 | Kamieniecki, Bal | 179.1 | 109 | 5.5 |
| Clemens, Tor | 264.0 | 292 | 10.0 | Karl, Mil | 193.1 | 119 | 5.5 |
| Cone, Yanks | 195.0 | 222 | 10.2 | Key, Bal | 212.1 | 141 | 6.0 |
| Cook, Fla | 62.1 | 63 | 9.1 | Kile, Hou | 255.2 | 205 | 7.2 |
| Cooke, Pit | 167.1 | 109 | 5.9 | Leiter M, Phi | 182.2 | 148 | 7.3 |
| Cordova, Pit | 178.2 | 121 | 6.1 | Lieber, Pit | 188.1 | 160 | 7.6 |
| Dickson, Ana | 203.2 | 115 | 5.1 | Loaiza, Pit | 196.1 | 122 | 5.6 |
| Dipoto, Col | 95.2 | 74 | 7.0 | Loiselle, Pit | 72.2 | 66 | 8.2 |
| Drabek, WSox | 169.1 | 85 | 4.5 | Maddux G, Atl | 232.2 | 177 | 6.8 |
| Eckersley, StL | 53.0 | 45 | 7.6 | Martinez P, Mon | 241.1 | 305 | 11.4 |
| Eldred, Mil | 202.0 | 122 | 5.4 | Mathews T, Oak | 74.2 | 70 | 8.4 |
| Embree, Atl | 46.0 | 45 | 8.8 | Mathews T, Bal | 63.1 | 39 | 5.5 |
| Erickson, Bal | 221.2 | 131 | 5.3 | McElroy, WSox | 75.0 | 62 | 7.4 |
| Estes, SF | 201.0 | 181 | 8.1 | McMichael, Mets | 87.2 | 81 | 8.3 |
| Fassero, Sea | 234.1 | 189 | 7.3 | Mesa, Cle | 82.1 | 69 | 7.5 |
| Fernandez A, Fla | 220.2 | 183 | 7.5 | Miceli, Det | 82.2 | 79 | 8.6 |
| Finley, Ana | 164.0 | 155 | 8.5 | Mlicki, Mets | 193.2 | 157 | 7.3 |
| Fossas, StL | 51.2 | 41 | 7.1 | Moehler, Det | 175.1 | 97 | 5.0 |
| Franco, Mets | 60.0 | 53 | 8.0 | Morgan, Cin | 162.0 | 103 | 5.7 |
| Frascatore, StL | 80.0 | 58 | 6.5 | Morris, StL | 217.0 | 149 | 6.2 |
| Gardner, SF | 180.1 | 136 | 6.8 | Moyer, Sea | 188.2 | 113 | 5.4 |

| Pitcher,Team | IP | K | K/9 | Pitcher,Team | IP | K | K/9 |
|---|---|---|---|---|---|---|---|
| Mulholland, SF | 186.2 | 99 | 4.8 | Shaw, Cin | 94.2 | 74 | 7.0 |
| Munoz M, Col | 45.2 | 26 | 5.1 | Slocumb, Sea | 75.0 | 64 | 7.7 |
| Mussina, Bal | 224.2 | 218 | 8.7 | Small, Oak | 96.2 | 57 | 5.3 |
| Myers M, Det | 53.2 | 50 | 8.4 | Smoltz, Atl | 256.0 | 241 | 8.5 |
| Myers R, Bal | 59.2 | 56 | 8.4 | Spoljaric, Sea | 70.2 | 70 | 8.9 |
| Nagy, Cle | 227.0 | 149 | 5.9 | Spradlin, Phi | 81.2 | 67 | 7.4 |
| Navarro, WSox | 209.2 | 142 | 6.1 | Springer D, Ana | 194.2 | 75 | 3.5 |
| Neagle, Atl | 233.1 | 172 | 6.6 | Stanton, Yanks | 66.2 | 70 | 9.5 |
| Nelson, Yanks | 78.2 | 81 | 9.3 | Stottlemyre, StL | 181.0 | 160 | 8.0 |
| Nen, Fla | 74.0 | 81 | 9.9 | Sullivan, Cin | 97.1 | 96 | 8.9 |
| Nomo, LA | 207.1 | 233 | 10.1 | Swindell, Min | 115.2 | 75 | 5.8 |
| Olivares, Sea | 177.1 | 103 | 5.2 | Tatis, Cubs | 55.2 | 33 | 5.3 |
| Oliver, Tex | 201.1 | 104 | 4.6 | Tavarez, SF | 88.1 | 38 | 3.9 |
| Orosco, Bal | 50.1 | 46 | 8.2 | Taylor, Oak | 73.0 | 66 | 8.1 |
| Park, LA | 192.0 | 166 | 7.8 | Telford, Mon | 89.0 | 61 | 6.2 |
| Patterson B, Cubs | 59.1 | 58 | 8.8 | Tewksbury, Min | 168.2 | 92 | 4.9 |
| Perez C, Mon | 206.2 | 110 | 4.8 | Thompson J, Det | 223.1 | 151 | 6.1 |
| Pettitte, Yanks | 240.1 | 166 | 6.2 | Thomson, Col | 166.1 | 106 | 5.7 |
| Plesac, Tor | 50.1 | 61 | 10.9 | Timlin, Sea | 72.2 | 45 | 5.6 |
| Poole, SF | 49.1 | 26 | 4.7 | Trachsel, Cubs | 201.1 | 160 | 7.2 |
| Powell, Fla | 79.2 | 65 | 7.3 | Trombley, Min | 82.1 | 74 | 8.1 |
| Quantrill, Tor | 88.0 | 56 | 5.7 | Urbina, Mon | 64.1 | 84 | 11.8 |
| Radinsky, LA | 62.1 | 44 | 6.4 | Valdes I, LA | 196.2 | 140 | 6.4 |
| Radke, Min | 239.2 | 174 | 6.5 | Vosberg, Fla | 53.0 | 37 | 6.3 |
| Reed R, Mets | 208.1 | 113 | 4.9 | Wagner B, Hou | 66.1 | 106 | 14.4 |
| Reed S, Col | 62.1 | 43 | 6.2 | Wakefield, Bos | 201.1 | 151 | 6.8 |
| Remlinger, Cin | 124.0 | 145 | 10.5 | Watson, Ana | 199.0 | 141 | 6.4 |
| Reynolds, Hou | 181.0 | 152 | 7.6 | Wells D, Yanks | 218.0 | 156 | 6.4 |
| Rincon, Pit | 60.0 | 71 | 10.7 | Wendell, Mets | 76.1 | 64 | 7.5 |
| Rivera, Yanks | 71.2 | 68 | 8.5 | Wetteland, Tex | 65.0 | 63 | 8.7 |
| Rodriguez R, SF | 65.1 | 32 | 4.4 | Wickman, Mil | 95.2 | 78 | 7.3 |
| Rojas, Mets | 85.1 | 93 | 9.8 | Wilkins, Pit | 75.2 | 47 | 5.6 |
| Rosado, KC | 203.1 | 129 | 5.7 | Williams W, Tor | 194.2 | 124 | 5.7 |
| Rueter, SF | 190.2 | 115 | 5.4 | Witt, Tex | 209.0 | 121 | 5.2 |
| Rusch, KC | 170.1 | 116 | 6.1 | Wohlers, Atl | 69.1 | 92 | 11.9 |
| Schilling, Phi | 254.1 | 319 | 11.3 | Worrell T, LA | 59.2 | 61 | 9.2 |
| Schmidt, Pit | 187.2 | 136 | 6.5 | **MLB Avg** | | | **6.7** |
| Sele, Bos | 177.1 | 122 | 6.2 | | | | |

# Who Are the Best-Hitting Pitchers? (p. 148)

## 1997 Active Pitchers — Listed Alphabetically
### (minimum 50 PA lifetime)

| Pitcher, Team | AVG | AB | H | HR | RBI | Pitcher, Team | AVG | AB | H | HR | RBI |
|---|---|---|---|---|---|---|---|---|---|---|---|
| Aguilera, Min | .203 | 138 | 28 | 3 | 11 | Green, Phi | .222 | 72 | 16 | 1 | 7 |
| Arocha, SF | .101 | 69 | 7 | 0 | 3 | Greene, Hou | .221 | 213 | 47 | 4 | 19 |
| Ashby, SD | .145 | 262 | 38 | 0 | 11 | Gross, Ana | .161 | 660 | 106 | 6 | 36 |
| Astacio, Col | .115 | 279 | 32 | 0 | 7 | Hamilton, SD | .110 | 227 | 25 | 3 | 14 |
| Avery, Bos | .178 | 409 | 73 | 4 | 31 | Hammond, Bos | .205 | 229 | 47 | 4 | 14 |
| Bailey R, Col | .206 | 97 | 20 | 1 | 8 | Hampton, Hou | .165 | 164 | 27 | 0 | 11 |
| Banks, Yanks | .179 | 67 | 12 | 0 | 1 | Harkey, LA | .183 | 164 | 30 | 0 | 7 |
| Bautista, StL | .100 | 50 | 5 | 0 | 1 | Harnisch, Mil | .116 | 327 | 38 | 0 | 15 |
| Beech, Phi | .136 | 44 | 6 | 0 | 2 | Henry B, Bos | .139 | 151 | 21 | 1 | 12 |
| Belcher, KC | .122 | 378 | 46 | 2 | 25 | Hermanson, Mon | .104 | 48 | 5 | 1 | 1 |
| Benes Al, StL | .151 | 119 | 18 | 0 | 8 | Hershiser, Cle | .213 | 675 | 144 | 0 | 46 |
| Benes An, StL | .139 | 502 | 70 | 4 | 35 | Hill, Ana | .150 | 326 | 49 | 1 | 21 |
| Bielecki, Atl | .078 | 282 | 22 | 0 | 13 | Hitchcock, SD | .100 | 50 | 5 | 0 | 1 |
| Blair, Det | .056 | 90 | 5 | 0 | 5 | Holt, Hou | .088 | 68 | 6 | 0 | 1 |
| Boskie, Bal | .184 | 141 | 26 | 1 | 8 | Honeycutt, StL | .132 | 182 | 24 | 0 | 9 |
| Bottenfield, Cubs | .231 | 65 | 15 | 0 | 3 | Isringhausen, Mets | .212 | 85 | 18 | 2 | 10 |
| Brantley, Cin | .118 | 68 | 8 | 0 | 5 | Jackson D, SD | .126 | 428 | 54 | 0 | 28 |
| Brocail, Det | .164 | 67 | 11 | 0 | 1 | Jarvis, Det | .161 | 62 | 10 | 0 | 2 |
| Brown, Fla | .122 | 148 | 18 | 0 | 7 | Jones B, Mets | .123 | 244 | 30 | 0 | 9 |
| Bullinger, Mon | .188 | 165 | 31 | 4 | 19 | Juden, Cle | .103 | 78 | 8 | 1 | 9 |
| Burba, Cin | .141 | 163 | 23 | 2 | 10 | Kile, Hou | .114 | 368 | 42 | 1 | 24 |
| Burkett, Tex | .090 | 424 | 38 | 0 | 14 | Langston, Ana | .167 | 66 | 11 | 0 | 3 |
| Candiotti, LA | .114 | 298 | 34 | 0 | 12 | Leiter A, Fla | .102 | 118 | 12 | 0 | 2 |
| Castillo F, Col | .110 | 326 | 36 | 0 | 13 | Leiter M, Phi | .112 | 179 | 20 | 0 | 14 |
| Charlton, Sea | .093 | 86 | 8 | 0 | 1 | Lieber, Pit | .123 | 154 | 19 | 0 | 11 |
| Clark M, Cubs | .056 | 178 | 10 | 1 | 6 | Loaiza, Pit | .171 | 129 | 22 | 0 | 8 |
| Cone, Yanks | .153 | 398 | 61 | 0 | 20 | Maddux G, Atl | .173 | 851 | 147 | 2 | 41 |
| Cook, Fla | .276 | 105 | 29 | 2 | 9 | Maddux M, Sea | .068 | 88 | 6 | 0 | 4 |
| Cooke, Pit | .136 | 169 | 23 | 0 | 7 | Martinez D, Sea | .143 | 509 | 73 | 0 | 30 |
| Cordova, Pit | .097 | 72 | 7 | 0 | 2 | Martinez P, Mon | .102 | 246 | 25 | 0 | 11 |
| Cormier, Mon | .185 | 184 | 34 | 0 | 12 | Martinez R, LA | .152 | 552 | 84 | 1 | 32 |
| Darwin D, SF | .135 | 260 | 35 | 2 | 21 | Mercker, Cin | .093 | 162 | 15 | 0 | 10 |
| Davis M, Mil | .156 | 167 | 26 | 1 | 9 | Mimbs, Phi | .129 | 70 | 9 | 0 | 2 |
| Drabek, WSox | .166 | 715 | 119 | 2 | 46 | Mlicki, Mets | .124 | 97 | 12 | 0 | 5 |
| Eckersley, StL | .133 | 181 | 24 | 3 | 12 | Morgan, Cin | .087 | 469 | 41 | 0 | 14 |
| Estes, SF | .141 | 92 | 13 | 1 | 4 | Morris, StL | .205 | 73 | 15 | 0 | 6 |
| Fassero, Sea | .080 | 212 | 17 | 0 | 5 | Moyer, Sea | .143 | 154 | 22 | 0 | 4 |
| Fernandez A, Fla | .152 | 66 | 10 | 0 | 4 | Mulholland, SF | .099 | 505 | 50 | 2 | 13 |
| Fernandez O, SF | .068 | 74 | 5 | 0 | 1 | Munoz B, Phi | .196 | 56 | 11 | 1 | 7 |
| Fernandez S, Hou | .182 | 539 | 98 | 1 | 34 | Myers R, Bal | .186 | 59 | 11 | 0 | 7 |
| Foster, Cubs | .190 | 163 | 31 | 1 | 19 | Navarro, WSox | .154 | 143 | 22 | 0 | 10 |
| Gardner, SF | .124 | 330 | 41 | 0 | 14 | Neagle, Atl | .142 | 282 | 40 | 3 | 26 |
| Glavine, Atl | .201 | 695 | 140 | 1 | 51 | Nomo, LA | .129 | 210 | 27 | 0 | 9 |
| Gonzalez, Cubs | .100 | 40 | 4 | 0 | 1 | Olivares, Sea | .238 | 206 | 49 | 4 | 23 |
| Gooden, Yanks | .196 | 734 | 144 | 7 | 65 | Orosco, Bal | .169 | 59 | 10 | 0 | 4 |

| Pitcher, Team | AVG | AB | H | HR | RBI | Pitcher, Team | AVG | AB | H | HR | RBI |
|---|---|---|---|---|---|---|---|---|---|---|---|
| Osborne, StL | .181 | 221 | 40 | 1 | 19 | Smith L, Mon | .047 | 64 | 3 | 1 | 2 |
| Painter, StL | .161 | 56 | 9 | 0 | 5 | Smith P, SD | .122 | 263 | 32 | 0 | 14 |
| Park, LA | .141 | 71 | 10 | 0 | 4 | Smoltz, Atl | .163 | 614 | 100 | 4 | 39 |
| Patterson B, Cubs | .125 | 56 | 7 | 0 | 4 | Stottlemyre, StL | .230 | 122 | 28 | 0 | 6 |
| Perez C, Mon | .156 | 109 | 17 | 2 | 7 | Swift, Bal | .214 | 224 | 48 | 1 | 15 |
| Petkovsek, StL | .109 | 64 | 7 | 0 | 2 | Swindell, Min | .192 | 240 | 46 | 0 | 13 |
| Portugal, Phi | .191 | 397 | 76 | 2 | 32 | Tapani, Cubs | .146 | 41 | 6 | 0 | 2 |
| Pugh, Det | .202 | 109 | 22 | 0 | 4 | Tewksbury, Min | .132 | 379 | 50 | 0 | 19 |
| Quantrill, Tor | .098 | 61 | 6 | 0 | 0 | Thompson M, Col | .174 | 86 | 15 | 1 | 3 |
| Rapp, SF | .123 | 235 | 29 | 1 | 13 | Thomson, Col | .213 | 47 | 10 | 0 | 5 |
| Reed R, Mets | .168 | 95 | 16 | 1 | 8 | Torres, Mon | .152 | 46 | 7 | 0 | 0 |
| Rekar, Col | .133 | 45 | 6 | 0 | 0 | Trachsel, Cubs | .161 | 224 | 36 | 1 | 15 |
| Remlinger, Cin | .058 | 52 | 3 | 0 | 7 | Valdes I, LA | .110 | 191 | 21 | 0 | 4 |
| Reynolds, Hou | .147 | 231 | 34 | 2 | 8 | Valenzuela, StL | .200 | 936 | 187 | 10 | 84 |
| Reynoso, Mets | .155 | 200 | 31 | 3 | 9 | VanLandingham, SF | .122 | 164 | 20 | 1 | 6 |
| Ritz, Col | .155 | 168 | 26 | 1 | 7 | Wagner P, Mil | .167 | 150 | 25 | 0 | 9 |
| Rojas, Mets | .119 | 59 | 7 | 0 | 3 | Wakefield, Bos | .125 | 72 | 9 | 1 | 3 |
| Rueter, SF | .110 | 173 | 19 | 0 | 13 | Wall, Cin | .169 | 59 | 10 | 0 | 1 |
| Ruffin, Col | .081 | 295 | 24 | 0 | 7 | Watson, Ana | .255 | 165 | 42 | 0 | 19 |
| Saberhagen, Bos | .127 | 181 | 23 | 0 | 1 | Weathers, Cle | .111 | 99 | 11 | 1 | 3 |
| Sanders, Det | .180 | 111 | 20 | 0 | 7 | Wetteland, Tex | .167 | 42 | 7 | 1 | 8 |
| Schilling, Phi | .161 | 354 | 57 | 0 | 15 | Williams B, Bal | .163 | 80 | 13 | 0 | 7 |
| Schmidt, Pit | .087 | 92 | 8 | 0 | 5 | Williams M, KC | .168 | 101 | 17 | 0 | 7 |
| Schourek, Cin | .172 | 221 | 38 | 2 | 17 | Worrell T, SD | .116 | 69 | 8 | 0 | 4 |
| Smiley, Cle | .145 | 504 | 73 | 2 | 35 | Wright J, Col | .108 | 74 | 8 | 0 | 3 |

# Which Starters Combine Quality With Quantity? (p. 150)

The table below shows the percentage (**%**) of Quality Starts (**QS**) among each pitcher's Games Started (**GS**).

### Both Leagues — Listed Alphabetically
### (minimum 15 GS in 1997)

| Player,Team | GS | QS | % | Player,Team | GS | QS | % | Player,Team | GS | QS | % |
|---|---|---|---|---|---|---|---|---|---|---|---|
| Aldred, Min | 15 | 3 | 20.0 | Hentgen, Tor | 35 | 20 | 57.1 | Pettitte, Yanks | 35 | 24 | 68.6 |
| Alvarez, SF | 33 | 21 | 63.6 | Hermanson, Mon | 28 | 13 | 46.4 | Pittsley, KC | 21 | 5 | 23.8 |
| Appier, KC | 34 | 19 | 55.9 | Hernandez L, Fla | 17 | 8 | 47.1 | Prieto, Oak | 22 | 9 | 40.9 |
| Ashby, SD | 30 | 17 | 56.7 | Hershiser, Cle | 32 | 16 | 50.0 | Radke, Min | 35 | 20 | 57.1 |
| Astacio, Col | 31 | 19 | 61.3 | Hill, Ana | 31 | 16 | 51.6 | Rapp, SF | 25 | 8 | 32.0 |
| Avery, Bos | 18 | 6 | 33.3 | Hitchcock, SD | 28 | 12 | 42.9 | Reed R, Mets | 31 | 22 | 71.0 |
| Bailey R, Col | 29 | 12 | 41.4 | Holt, Hou | 32 | 22 | 68.8 | Reynolds, Hou | 30 | 15 | 50.0 |
| Baldwin, WSox | 32 | 14 | 43.8 | Johnson M, Mon | 16 | 3 | 18.8 | Reynoso, Mets | 16 | 9 | 56.3 |
| Beech, Phi | 24 | 11 | 45.8 | Johnson R, Sea | 29 | 23 | 79.3 | Ritz, Col | 18 | 6 | 33.3 |
| Belcher, KC | 32 | 18 | 56.3 | Jones B, Mets | 30 | 20 | 66.7 | Robertson, Min | 26 | 8 | 30.8 |
| Benes Al, StL | 23 | 16 | 69.6 | Juden, Cle | 27 | 13 | 48.1 | Rodriguez F, Min | 15 | 6 | 40.0 |
| Benes An, StL | 26 | 20 | 76.9 | Kamieniecki, Bal | 30 | 17 | 56.7 | Rogers, Yanks | 22 | 4 | 18.2 |
| Blair, Det | 27 | 12 | 44.4 | Karl, Mil | 32 | 19 | 59.4 | Rosado, KC | 33 | 15 | 45.5 |
| Brown, Fla | 33 | 27 | 81.8 | Karsay, Oak | 24 | 10 | 41.7 | Rueter, SF | 32 | 21 | 65.6 |
| Bullinger, Mon | 25 | 12 | 48.0 | Key, Bal | 34 | 19 | 55.9 | Rusch, KC | 27 | 11 | 40.7 |
| Burba, Cin | 27 | 13 | 48.1 | Kile, Hou | 34 | 26 | 76.5 | Sanders, Det | 20 | 4 | 20.0 |
| Burkett, Tex | 30 | 12 | 40.0 | Leiter A, Fla | 27 | 13 | 48.1 | Saunders, Fla | 21 | 12 | 57.1 |
| Candiotti, LA | 18 | 9 | 50.0 | Leiter M, Phi | 31 | 13 | 41.9 | Schilling, Phi | 35 | 26 | 74.3 |
| Castillo F, Col | 33 | 12 | 36.4 | Lieber, Pit | 32 | 18 | 56.3 | Schmidt, Pit | 32 | 16 | 50.0 |
| Clark M, Cubs | 31 | 20 | 64.5 | Lira, Sea | 18 | 7 | 38.9 | Schourek, Cin | 17 | 3 | 17.6 |
| Clemens, Tor | 34 | 26 | 76.5 | Loaiza, Pit | 32 | 21 | 65.6 | Sele, Bos | 33 | 17 | 51.5 |
| Colon, Cle | 17 | 5 | 29.4 | Maddux G, Atl | 33 | 27 | 81.8 | Smiley, Cle | 26 | 13 | 50.0 |
| Cone, Yanks | 29 | 21 | 72.4 | Martinez P, Mon | 31 | 25 | 80.6 | Smith P, SD | 15 | 7 | 46.7 |
| Cooke, Pit | 32 | 16 | 50.0 | Martinez R, LA | 22 | 12 | 54.5 | Smoltz, Atl | 35 | 25 | 71.4 |
| Cordova, Pit | 29 | 17 | 58.6 | McDonald, Mil | 21 | 12 | 57.1 | Springer D, Ana | 28 | 11 | 39.3 |
| D'Amico, Mil | 23 | 9 | 39.1 | Mendoza, Yanks | 15 | 7 | 46.7 | Stephenson, Phi | 18 | 12 | 66.7 |
| Darwin D, SF | 24 | 14 | 58.3 | Mercedes, Mil | 23 | 9 | 39.1 | Stottlemyre, StL | 28 | 17 | 60.7 |
| Dickson, Ana | 32 | 20 | 62.5 | Mercker, Cin | 25 | 13 | 52.0 | Suppan, Bos | 22 | 9 | 40.9 |
| Drabek, WSox | 31 | 12 | 38.7 | Mlicki, Mets | 32 | 20 | 62.5 | Telgheder, Oak | 19 | 5 | 26.3 |
| Eldred, Mil | 34 | 15 | 44.1 | Moehler, Det | 31 | 12 | 38.7 | Tewksbury, Min | 26 | 15 | 57.7 |
| Erickson, Bal | 33 | 22 | 66.7 | Morgan, Cin | 30 | 12 | 40.0 | Thompson J, Det | 32 | 25 | 78.1 |
| Estes, SF | 32 | 20 | 62.5 | Morris, StL | 33 | 22 | 66.7 | Thomson, Col | 27 | 15 | 55.6 |
| Fassero, Sea | 35 | 22 | 62.9 | Moyer, Sea | 30 | 19 | 63.3 | Tomko, Cin | 19 | 14 | 73.7 |
| Fernandez A, Fla | 32 | 22 | 68.8 | Mulholland, SF | 27 | 14 | 51.9 | Trachsel, Cubs | 34 | 16 | 47.1 |
| Finley, Ana | 25 | 13 | 52.0 | Mussina, Bal | 33 | 25 | 75.8 | Valdes I, LA | 30 | 20 | 66.7 |
| Foster, Cubs | 25 | 17 | 68.0 | Nagy, Cle | 34 | 18 | 52.9 | Valenzuela, StL | 18 | 4 | 22.2 |
| Garcia, Hou | 20 | 11 | 55.0 | Navarro, WSox | 33 | 16 | 48.5 | VanLanding., SF | 17 | 7 | 41.2 |
| Gardner, SF | 30 | 16 | 53.3 | Neagle, Atl | 34 | 27 | 79.4 | Wakefield, Bos | 29 | 15 | 51.7 |
| Glavine, Atl | 33 | 26 | 78.8 | Nomo, LA | 33 | 18 | 54.5 | Watson, Ana | 34 | 18 | 52.9 |
| Gonzalez, Cubs | 23 | 9 | 39.1 | Ogea, Cle | 21 | 11 | 52.4 | Wells D, Yanks | 32 | 17 | 53.1 |
| Gooden, Yanks | 19 | 8 | 42.1 | Olivares, Sea | 31 | 12 | 38.7 | Williams W, Tor | 31 | 18 | 58.1 |
| Gordon, Bos | 25 | 14 | 56.0 | Oliver, Tex | 32 | 15 | 46.9 | Witt, Tex | 32 | 16 | 50.0 |
| Hamilton, SD | 29 | 16 | 55.2 | Oquist, Oak | 17 | 5 | 29.4 | Wolcott, Sea | 18 | 6 | 33.3 |
| Hampton, Hou | 34 | 20 | 58.8 | Park, LA | 29 | 21 | 72.4 | Wright J, Col | 26 | 10 | 38.5 |
| Hawkins, Min | 20 | 6 | 30.0 | Perez C, Mon | 32 | 15 | 46.9 | Wright J, Cle | 16 | 9 | 56.3 |
| Helling, Tex | 16 | 6 | 37.5 | Person, Tor | 22 | 8 | 36.4 | **MLB Avg** | | | **49.4** |

# How Costly Is a Blown Save? (p. 152)

## W-L in Games with Blown Saves—1997

| Team | 6th Inning W-L | Pct | 7th Inning W-L | Pct | 8th Inning W-L | Pct | 9th Inning W-L | Pct | 10th+ Inning W-L | Pct |
|------|------|------|------|------|------|------|------|------|------|------|
| Anaheim | 0-3 | .000 | 6-5 | .545 | 3-5 | .375 | 0-5 | .000 | 0-0 | — |
| Baltimore | 1-1 | .500 | 2-1 | .667 | 1-3 | .250 | 0-1 | .000 | 0-0 | — |
| Boston | 1-3 | .250 | 4-4 | .500 | 3-4 | .429 | 2-4 | .333 | 0-1 | .000 |
| Chicago | 0-0 | — | 2-2 | .500 | 4-5 | .444 | 3-1 | .750 | 1-0 | 1.000 |
| Cleveland | 1-1 | .500 | 1-3 | .250 | 2-2 | .500 | 1-3 | .250 | 0-1 | .000 |
| Detroit | 0-2 | .000 | 2-4 | .333 | 2-8 | .200 | 1-3 | .250 | 0-0 | — |
| Kansas City | 1-2 | .333 | 1-6 | .143 | 1-6 | .143 | 2-2 | .500 | 0-0 | — |
| Milwaukee | 1-2 | .333 | 3-2 | .600 | 1-3 | .250 | 0-3 | .000 | 0-0 | — |
| Minnesota | 0-4 | .000 | 1-3 | .250 | 1-3 | .250 | 3-3 | .500 | 1-0 | 1.000 |
| New York | 2-1 | .667 | 2-3 | .400 | 1-7 | .125 | 3-6 | .333 | 0-0 | — |
| Oakland | 3-2 | .600 | 3-2 | .600 | 2-2 | .500 | 5-3 | .625 | 0-1 | .000 |
| Seattle | 0-0 | — | 1-8 | .111 | 1-5 | .167 | 4-8 | .333 | 0-0 | — |
| Texas | 4-0 | 1.000 | 3-6 | .333 | 2-5 | .286 | 2-2 | .500 | 0-0 | — |
| Toronto | 0-3 | .000 | 0-3 | .000 | 1-6 | .143 | 3-4 | .429 | 0-1 | .000 |
| **American League** | **14-24** | **.368** | **31-52** | **.373** | **25-64** | **.281** | **29-48** | **.377** | **2-4** | **.333** |
| | | | | | | | | | | |
| Atlanta | 0-1 | .000 | 2-1 | .667 | 3-5 | .375 | 1-3 | .250 | 0-0 | — |
| Chicago | 0-0 | — | 0-3 | .000 | 3-3 | .500 | 0-9 | .000 | 0-0 | — |
| Cincinnati | 0-2 | .000 | 1-0 | 1.000 | 2-2 | .500 | 4-2 | .667 | 0-1 | .000 |
| Colorado | 1-0 | 1.000 | 3-2 | .600 | 2-5 | .286 | 3-5 | .375 | 0-1 | .000 |
| Florida | 0-1 | .000 | 1-4 | .200 | 2-4 | .333 | 4-4 | .500 | 0-0 | — |
| Houston | 0-1 | .000 | 4-3 | .571 | 2-8 | .200 | 1-2 | .333 | 1-0 | 1.000 |
| Los Angeles | 1-1 | .500 | 3-0 | 1.000 | 4-1 | .800 | 4-5 | .444 | 0-1 | .000 |
| Montreal | 1-0 | 1.000 | 4-4 | .500 | 2-3 | .400 | 0-4 | .000 | 0-0 | — |
| New York | 0-4 | .000 | 2-8 | .200 | 4-6 | .400 | 3-2 | .600 | 0-0 | — |
| Philadelphia | 0-2 | .000 | 2-2 | .500 | 0-5 | .000 | 2-2 | .500 | 0-0 | — |
| Pittsburgh | 0-3 | .000 | 1-3 | .250 | 3-3 | .500 | 2-2 | .500 | 0-1 | .000 |
| San Diego | 2-4 | .333 | 1-2 | .333 | 2-5 | .286 | 2-1 | .667 | 0-1 | .000 |
| San Francisco | 2-3 | .400 | 3-2 | .600 | 3-5 | .375 | 3-3 | .500 | 0-0 | — |
| St. Louis | 0-0 | — | 1-2 | .333 | 3-6 | .333 | 0-6 | .000 | 1-0 | 1.000 |
| **National League** | **7-22** | **.241** | **28-36** | **.438** | **35-61** | **.365** | **29-50** | **.367** | **2-5** | **.286** |
| **MLB Totals** | **21-46** | **.313** | **59-88** | **.401** | **60-125** | **.324** | **58-98** | **.372** | **4-9** | **.308** |

# Who Gets the "Red Barrett Trophy"? (p. 154)

### Most Pitches In a Game By Starting Pitchers in 1997

| Date | Opp | Score | Pitcher | W/L | IP | H | R | ER | BB | SO | #Pit | Time |
|------|-----|-------|---------|-----|-----|----|----|----|----|----|------|------|
| 6/5 | @Mil | 2-1 | Wakefield, Bos | W | 8.2 | 7 | 1 | 0 | 7 | 10 | 168 | 2:47 |
| 7/18 | KC | 5-4 | Johnson R, Sea | W | 9.0 | 9 | 4 | 4 | 3 | 16 | 154 | 2:50 |
| 5/23 | @Tor | 12-2 | Springer D, Ana | W | 9.0 | 7 | 2 | 2 | 4 | 3 | 149 | 3:13 |
| 8/8 | WSox | 5-0 | Johnson R, Sea | W | 9.0 | 5 | 0 | 0 | 3 | 19 | 149 | 2:27 |
| 6/29 | @Sea | 2-3 | Springer D, Ana | ND | 8.0 | 4 | 2 | 2 | 4 | 5 | 145 | 2:54 |
| 6/5 | Tex | 3-6 | Appier, KC | ND | 9.0 | 4 | 3 | 3 | 5 | 11 | 143 | 3:37 |
| 6/24 | Oak | 1-4 | Johnson R, Sea | L | 9.0 | 11 | 4 | 4 | 0 | 19 | 143 | 2:21 |
| 9/23 | Ana | 4-3 | Johnson R, Sea | W | 8.0 | 8 | 3 | 3 | 1 | 11 | 143 | 3:01 |
| 9/28 | Bos | 3-2 | Clemens, Tor | ND | 8.1 | 7 | 2 | 2 | 2 | 8 | 143 | 2:55 |
| 5/26 | Oak | 1-2 | Appier, KC | ND | 9.0 | 5 | 1 | 0 | 1 | 10 | 141 | 3:29 |
| 6/20 | Fla | 1-2 | Martinez P, Mon | L | 9.0 | 5 | 2 | 2 | 4 | 12 | 140 | 2:18 |
| 7/23 | @Cin | 8-1 | Fernandez A, Fla | W | 8.0 | 6 | 1 | 1 | 3 | 5 | 140 | 2:46 |

### Fewest Pitches In a Nine-Inning Complete Game By Starting Pitchers in 1997

| Date | Opp | Score | Pitcher | W/L | IP | H | R | ER | BB | SO | #Pit | Time |
|------|-----|-------|---------|-----|-----|----|----|----|----|----|------|------|
| 7/22 | @Cubs | 4-1 | Maddux G, Atl | W | 9.0 | 5 | 1 | 1 | 0 | 6 | 78 | 2:07 |
| 8/1 | @Mon | 8-2 | Hamilton, SD | W | 9.0 | 4 | 2 | 2 | 1 | 2 | 82 | 2:24 |
| 9/2 | Yanks | 5-0 | Grace, Phi | W | 9.0 | 3 | 0 | 0 | 0 | 1 | 84 | 2:22 |
| 7/2 | @Yanks | 2-0 | Maddux G, Atl | W | 9.0 | 3 | 0 | 0 | 0 | 8 | 86 | 2:09 |
| 8/19 | Bal | 9-2 | Bones, KC | W | 9.0 | 7 | 2 | 2 | 0 | 1 | 88 | 2:26 |
| 6/27 | Phi | 7-1 | Maddux G, Atl | W | 9.0 | 6 | 1 | 1 | 0 | 8 | 90 | 2:08 |
| 8/15 | Cubs | 5-1 | Hitchcock, SD | W | 9.0 | 4 | 1 | 1 | 0 | 4 | 90 | 2:23 |
| 6/18 | @Bal | 1-0 | Perez C, Mon | W | 9.0 | 8 | 0 | 0 | 0 | 2 | 92 | 2:29 |
| 6/23 | Cin | 5-0 | Bullinger, Mon | W | 9.0 | 4 | 0 | 0 | 1 | 0 | 93 | 2:16 |
| 9/3 | Bos | 1-0 | Perez C, Mon | W | 9.0 | 2 | 0 | 0 | 0 | 8 | 94 | 1:54 |
| 4/25 | Mets | 4-1 | Perez C, Mon | W | 9.0 | 6 | 1 | 1 | 1 | 5 | 95 | 2:13 |
| 9/16 | Cin | 5-0 | Tapani, Cubs | W | 9.0 | 1 | 0 | 0 | 2 | 5 | 96 | 1:57 |
| 7/15 | @Atl | 8-1 | Stephenson, Phi | W | 9.0 | 4 | 1 | 1 | 2 | 3 | 97 | 2:08 |
| 7/20 | @Mon | 9-0 | Kile, Hou | W | 9.0 | 4 | 0 | 0 | 1 | 6 | 97 | 2:14 |
| 9/19 | @Tex | 7-1 | Hill, Ana | W | 9.0 | 2 | 1 | 1 | 1 | 0 | 97 | 2:36 |
| 9/26 | @Mon | 7-1 | Morgan, Cin | W | 9.0 | 3 | 1 | 1 | 1 | 7 | 97 | 2:00 |
| 8/27 | Det | 2-0 | Tewksbury, Min | W | 9.0 | 5 | 0 | 0 | 1 | 5 | 98 | 2:13 |
| 7/29 | @WSox | 3-1 | Blair, Det | W | 9.0 | 3 | 1 | 1 | 1 | 3 | 98 | 2:18 |
| 9/2 | Det | 5-0 | Neagle, Atl | W | 9.0 | 4 | 0 | 0 | 0 | 7 | 98 | 2:18 |
| 9/25 | Cubs | 9-1 | Hampton, Hou | W | 9.0 | 4 | 1 | 1 | 1 | 6 | 98 | 2:42 |
| 4/11 | @Cin | 10-0 | Rapp, SF | W | 9.0 | 5 | 0 | 0 | 2 | 1 | 99 | 2:16 |
| 5/28 | @Mon | 7-0 | Jones B, Mets | W | 9.0 | 4 | 0 | 0 | 2 | 7 | 99 | 2:15 |
| 6/10 | @SF | 9-0 | Brown, Fla | W | 9.0 | 0 | 0 | 0 | 0 | 7 | 99 | 2:21 |
| 6/30 | Mon | 1-2 | Hentgen, Tor | L | 9.0 | 6 | 2 | 2 | 1 | 3 | 99 | 2:03 |
| 7/19 | @Mil | 8-0 | Wells D, Yanks | W | 9.0 | 3 | 0 | 0 | 0 | 4 | 99 | 2:44 |
| 5/6 | Min | 7-2 | Wells D, Yanks | W | 9.0 | 8 | 2 | 2 | 1 | 3 | 100 | 2:40 |
| 6/23 | @Hou | 6-0 | Cordova, Pit | W | 9.0 | 2 | 0 | 0 | 2 | 5 | 100 | 2:24 |
| 6/5 | Fla | 6-0 | Reynoso, Mets | W | 9.0 | 5 | 0 | 0 | 1 | 4 | 100 | 2:09 |
| 7/2 | Cle | 6-2 | Hampton, Hou | W | 9.0 | 10 | 2 | 2 | 1 | 3 | 100 | 2:33 |
| 7/16 | Mon | 6-0 | Schilling, Phi | W | 9.0 | 4 | 0 | 0 | 0 | 7 | 100 | 2:31 |

# Which Pitchers Heat Up in the Cold? (p. 156)

## Best ERA, Temperature Unber 50 Degrees—1993-97
### (minimum 5 GS)

| Pitcher | GS | W-L | ERA |
|---|---|---|---|
| Alex Fernandez | 8 | 6-1 | 1.70 |
| Danny Darwin | 5 | 1-1 | 2.31 |
| Tom Gordon | 5 | 3-0 | 2.36 |
| Dave Burba | 6 | 2-2 | 2.67 |
| Wilson Alvarez | 9 | 4-2 | 2.83 |
| Andy Benes | 5 | 1-1 | 3.06 |
| Dennis Martinez | 10 | 5-2 | 3.11 |
| Andy Pettitte | 5 | 3-1 | 3.13 |
| Ben McDonald | 7 | 4-0 | 3.30 |
| Alan Benes | 5 | 2-1 | 3.41 |
| David Cone | 5 | 3-1 | 3.44 |
| Doug Drabek | 8 | 4-3 | 3.47 |
| Jose Rijo | 5 | 1-2 | 3.58 |
| Frank Castillo | 9 | 2-6 | 3.90 |
| Steve Trachsel | 5 | 1-3 | 4.20 |
| Jack McDowell | 9 | 3-4 | 4.34 |
| Charles Nagy | 5 | 3-2 | 4.41 |
| Kevin Appier | 5 | 2-3 | 4.45 |
| John Smiley | 5 | 1-3 | 4.85 |
| Jaime Navarro | 8 | 1-2 | 5.15 |
| Kevin Tapani | 5 | 1-3 | 5.58 |
| Ricky Bones | 8 | 3-4 | 5.84 |
| Kevin Ritz | 5 | 1-2 | 6.17 |
| Bobby Jones | 5 | 2-1 | 7.11 |
| Cal Eldred | 6 | 2-3 | 7.84 |

## Who Knows How to Handle Their Inheritance? (p. 158)

The table below shows the percentage (**%**) of Inherited Runners (**IR**) each relief pitcher allowed to score (**SC**)

### Both Leagues — Listed Alphabetically
### (minimum 23 IR in 1997)

| Pitcher, Team | IR | SC | % | Pitcher, Team | IR | SC | % | Pitcher, Team | IR | SC | % |
|---|---|---|---|---|---|---|---|---|---|---|---|
| Adams T, Cubs | 43 | 7 | 16.3 | Jackson M, Cle | 29 | 5 | 17.2 | Rincon, Pit | 35 | 9 | 25.7 |
| Assenmacher, Cle | 74 | 17 | 23.0 | James, Ana | 36 | 12 | 33.3 | Ritchie, Min | 24 | 7 | 29.2 |
| Ayala, Sea | 55 | 14 | 25.5 | Johnson D, Oak | 35 | 19 | 54.3 | Roa, SF | 23 | 6 | 26.1 |
| Belinda, Cin | 49 | 18 | 36.7 | Jones T, Det | 35 | 10 | 28.6 | Rodriguez F, Min | 28 | 10 | 35.7 |
| Benitez, Bal | 57 | 12 | 21.1 | Karchner, WSox | 37 | 10 | 27.0 | Rodriguez R, SF | 64 | 19 | 29.7 |
| Blazier, Phi | 27 | 8 | 29.6 | Kline, Mon | 29 | 14 | 48.3 | Rojas, Mets | 24 | 11 | 45.8 |
| Bochtler, SD | 38 | 11 | 28.9 | Lacy, Bos | 23 | 11 | 47.8 | Ruebel, Pit | 36 | 12 | 33.3 |
| Boehringer, Yanks | 30 | 8 | 26.7 | Leskanic, Col | 25 | 11 | 44.0 | Sager, Det | 41 | 12 | 29.3 |
| Bottenfield, Cubs | 53 | 19 | 35.8 | Lidle, Mets | 29 | 11 | 37.9 | Shaw, Cin | 25 | 7 | 28.0 |
| Brandenburg, Bos | 28 | 10 | 35.7 | Lima, Hou | 36 | 15 | 41.7 | Simas, WSox | 30 | 11 | 36.7 |
| Brocail, Det | 30 | 13 | 43.3 | Lloyd, Yanks | 39 | 10 | 25.6 | Slocumb, Sea | 27 | 12 | 44.4 |
| Bruske, LA | 31 | 9 | 29.0 | Loiselle, Pit | 26 | 16 | 61.5 | Small, Oak | 52 | 15 | 28.8 |
| Carrasco, KC | 36 | 13 | 36.1 | Magnante, Hou | 39 | 9 | 23.1 | Sodowsky, Pit | 23 | 8 | 34.8 |
| Casian, KC | 34 | 14 | 41.2 | Martin, Hou | 39 | 19 | 48.7 | Spoljaric, Sea | 46 | 12 | 26.1 |
| Castillo C, WSox | 31 | 10 | 32.3 | Mathews T, Oak | 25 | 8 | 32.0 | Spradlin, Phi | 40 | 13 | 32.5 |
| Castillo T, WSox | 48 | 15 | 31.3 | Mathews T, Bal | 42 | 12 | 28.6 | Springer R, Hou | 37 | 12 | 32.4 |
| Charlton, Sea | 54 | 19 | 35.2 | McCarthy, Sea | 24 | 4 | 16.7 | Stanton, Yanks | 49 | 13 | 26.5 |
| Clontz, Atl | 32 | 15 | 46.9 | McElroy, WSox | 42 | 10 | 23.8 | Sullivan, Cin | 39 | 16 | 41.0 |
| Cook, Fla | 24 | 5 | 20.8 | McMichael, Mets | 52 | 15 | 28.8 | Swindell, Min | 60 | 19 | 31.7 |
| Corsi, Bos | 41 | 14 | 34.1 | Mecir, Yanks | 35 | 9 | 25.7 | Tatis, Cubs | 49 | 15 | 30.6 |
| Cunnane, SD | 30 | 10 | 33.3 | Mesa, Cle | 36 | 8 | 22.2 | Tavarez, SF | 80 | 32 | 40.0 |
| Daal, Tor | 41 | 13 | 31.7 | Miceli, Det | 62 | 29 | 46.8 | Taylor, Oak | 48 | 15 | 31.3 |
| DeJean, Col | 27 | 11 | 40.7 | Mohler, Oak | 55 | 17 | 30.9 | Telford, Mon | 53 | 10 | 18.9 |
| DeLucia, Ana | 26 | 6 | 23.1 | Montgomery J, KC | 24 | 10 | 41.7 | Timlin, Sea | 30 | 8 | 26.7 |
| Dipoto, Col | 46 | 15 | 32.6 | Morman, Cle | 26 | 3 | 11.5 | Trombley, Min | 51 | 17 | 33.3 |
| Dreifort, LA | 28 | 6 | 21.4 | Munoz M, Col | 52 | 11 | 21.2 | Urbina, Mon | 36 | 9 | 25.0 |
| Embree, Atl | 43 | 6 | 14.0 | Myers M, Det | 81 | 27 | 33.3 | Valdes M, Mon | 33 | 10 | 30.3 |
| Florie, Mil | 32 | 14 | 43.8 | Naulty, Min | 30 | 7 | 23.3 | Veres D, Mon | 33 | 15 | 45.5 |
| Fossas, StL | 60 | 6 | 10.0 | Nelson, Yanks | 53 | 11 | 20.8 | Veres R, KC | 28 | 13 | 46.4 |
| Frascatore, StL | 38 | 15 | 39.5 | Olson, KC | 30 | 12 | 40.0 | Villone, Mil | 37 | 8 | 21.6 |
| Groom, Oak | 72 | 15 | 20.8 | Orosco, Bal | 68 | 16 | 23.5 | Vosberg, Fla | 45 | 13 | 28.9 |
| Guardado, Min | 57 | 17 | 29.8 | Osuna, LA | 24 | 3 | 12.5 | Wagner B, Hou | 34 | 13 | 38.2 |
| Gunderson, Tex | 54 | 14 | 25.9 | Patterson B, Cubs | 68 | 17 | 25.0 | Wainhouse, Pit | 25 | 8 | 32.0 |
| Guthrie, LA | 32 | 9 | 28.1 | Patterson D, Tex | 50 | 19 | 38.0 | Walker, KC | 46 | 17 | 37.0 |
| Hall, LA | 46 | 12 | 26.1 | Percival, Ana | 27 | 5 | 18.5 | Wasdin, Bos | 28 | 12 | 42.9 |
| Harris P, Ana | 54 | 13 | 24.1 | Peters, Pit | 25 | 8 | 32.0 | Wengert, Oak | 36 | 14 | 38.9 |
| Harris R, Phi | 34 | 11 | 32.4 | Pichardo, KC | 24 | 5 | 20.8 | Whisenant, KC | 23 | 7 | 30.4 |
| Hasegawa, Ana | 37 | 9 | 24.3 | Plesac, Tor | 52 | 14 | 26.9 | Whiteside, Tex | 38 | 16 | 42.1 |
| Henry D, SF | 39 | 11 | 28.2 | Plunk, Cle | 46 | 14 | 30.4 | Wickman, Mil | 48 | 15 | 31.3 |
| Heredia F, Fla | 37 | 13 | 35.1 | Poole, SF | 53 | 24 | 45.3 | Wilkins, Pit | 31 | 5 | 16.1 |
| Hernandez R, SF | 46 | 14 | 30.4 | Powell, Fla | 30 | 8 | 26.7 | Worrell T, SD | 28 | 11 | 39.3 |
| Hernandez X, Tex | 37 | 13 | 35.1 | Quantrill, Tor | 55 | 16 | 29.1 | **MLB Avg** | | | **32.2** |
| Hoffman, SD | 44 | 14 | 31.8 | Radinsky, LA | 56 | 11 | 19.6 | | | | |
| Holtz, Ana | 56 | 12 | 21.4 | Reed S, Col | 34 | 11 | 32.4 | | | | |
| Hudson, Bos | 24 | 8 | 33.3 | Remlinger, Cin | 50 | 8 | 16.0 | | | | |
| Hutton, Col | 24 | 9 | 37.5 | Rhodes, Bal | 38 | 11 | 28.9 | | | | |

# If You Hold the Fort, Will You Soon Be Closing the Gate? (p. 160)

A Hold (**Hld**) is a Save Opportunity passed on to the next pitcher. If a pitcher comes into the game in a Save Situation and leaves the game having gotten at least one out and without having blown the lead, this is a "passed on" Save Opportunity and the pitcher is credited with a Hold.

## Both Leagues — Listed By Most Holds
### (minimum 3 Holds in 1997)

| Pitcher, Team | Hld | Pitcher, Team | Hld | Pitcher, Team | Hld | Pitcher, Team | Hld |
|---|---|---|---|---|---|---|---|
| Belinda, Cin | 28 | Groom, Oak | 12 | DeLucia, Ana | 8 | Cunnane, SD | 4 |
| Wickman, Mil | 28 | Gunderson, Tex | 12 | Mathews T, Bal | 8 | Hammond, Bos | 4 |
| Plesac, Tor | 27 | James, Ana | 12 | McCarthy, Sea | 8 | Henry B, Bos | 4 |
| Radinsky, LA | 26 | Karchner, WSox | 12 | Naulty, Min | 8 | Hutton, Col | 4 |
| Stanton, Yanks | 26 | Mathews T, Oak | 12 | Ruebel, Pit | 8 | Lopez, Cle | 4 |
| Tavarez, SF | 26 | Swindell, Min | 12 | Small, Oak | 8 | McCurry, Col | 4 |
| Powell, Fla | 24 | Adams T, Cubs | 11 | Tatis, Cubs | 8 | Mendoza, Yanks | 4 |
| Nelson, Yanks | 22 | Corsi, Bos | 11 | Villone, Mil | 8 | Pichardo, KC | 4 |
| Patterson B, Cubs | 22 | Fetters, Mil | 11 | Vosberg, Fla | 8 | Rodriguez F, Min | 4 |
| Henry D, SF | 21 | Miceli, Det | 11 | Fox, Atl | 7 | Sanders, Det | 4 |
| Orosco, Bal | 21 | Mohler, Oak | 11 | Heredia F, Fla | 7 | Shuey, Cle | 4 |
| Assenmacher, Cle | 20 | Telford, Mon | 11 | Martin, Hou | 7 | Stanifer, Fla | 4 |
| Benitez, Bal | 20 | Trombley, Min | 11 | Mills, Bal | 7 | Veres R, KC | 4 |
| McMichael, Mets | 19 | Wasdin, Bos | 11 | Rojas, Mets | 7 | Acevedo, Mets | 3 |
| Munoz M, Col | 19 | Dipoto, Col | 10 | Taylor, Oak | 7 | Brandenburg, Bos | 3 |
| Myers M, Det | 18 | Harris P, Ana | 10 | Cruz, WSox | 6 | Castillo C, WSox | 3 |
| Rincon, Pit | 18 | King, StL | 10 | Helling, Tex | 6 | Daal, Tor | 3 |
| Spradlin, Phi | 18 | Osuna, LA | 10 | Leskanic, Col | 6 | Davis M, Mil | 3 |
| Brocail, Det | 16 | Pisciotta, Cubs | 10 | Boehringer, Yanks | 5 | Frascatore, StL | 3 |
| Embree, Atl | 16 | Plunk, Cle | 10 | Brewer, Phi | 5 | Gomes, Phi | 3 |
| Fossas, StL | 16 | Reed S, Col | 10 | Bruske, LA | 5 | Hasegawa, Ana | 3 |
| Quantrill, Tor | 16 | Sager, Det | 10 | Casian, KC | 5 | Kashiwada, Mets | 3 |
| Worrell T, SD | 16 | Spoljaric, Sea | 10 | Foulke, WSox | 5 | Levine, WSox | 3 |
| Ayala, Sea | 15 | Veres D, Mon | 10 | Holmes, Col | 5 | Lima, Hou | 3 |
| Castillo T, WSox | 15 | Bochtler, SD | 9 | Jones T, Det | 5 | Magnante, Hou | 3 |
| Hall, LA | 15 | Charlton, Sea | 9 | Karp, Phi | 5 | Martinez P, Cin | 3 |
| McElroy, WSox | 15 | Dreifort, LA | 9 | Kline, Mon | 5 | Montgomery J, KC | 3 |
| Wilkins, Pit | 15 | Hernandez R, SF | 9 | Lacy, Bos | 5 | Painter, StL | 3 |
| Holtz, Ana | 14 | Lidle, Mets | 9 | Loiselle, Pit | 5 | Plantenberg, Phi | 3 |
| Jackson M, Cle | 14 | Mesa, Cle | 9 | Mahay, Bos | 5 | Ritchie, Min | 3 |
| Remlinger, Cin | 14 | Patterson D, Tex | 9 | Morman, Cle | 5 | Service, KC | 3 |
| Rodriguez R, SF | 14 | Poole, SF | 9 | Olson, KC | 5 | Simas, WSox | 3 |
| Cook, Fla | 13 | Rhodes, Bal | 9 | Petkovsek, StL | 5 | Slocumb, Sea | 3 |
| DeJean, Col | 13 | Springer R, Hou | 9 | Shaw, Cin | 5 | Walker, KC | 3 |
| Guardado, Min | 13 | Timlin, Sea | 9 | Sodowsky, Pit | 5 | Wallace, Pit | 3 |
| Guthrie, LA | 13 | Bottenfield, Cubs | 8 | Wells B, Sea | 5 | White, Cin | 3 |
| Hernandez X, Tex | 13 | Carrasco, KC | 8 | Whisenant, KC | 5 | | |
| Sullivan, Cin | 13 | Christiansen, Pit | 8 | Cather, Atl | 4 | | |
| Bielecki, Atl | 12 | Crabtree, Tor | 8 | Cummings, Det | 4 | | |

# Which Relievers Can Be Counted on to Convert? (p. 162)

The table below lists a reliever's Holds (**Hld**), Saves (**Sv**), Blown Saves (**BS**), and Hold + Save Percentage (**%**), which is Holds plus Saves divided by Holds plus Saves plus Blown Saves.

### Both Leagues — Listed Alphabetically
### (minimum 5 Holds+Saves+Blown Saves in 1997)

| Pitcher | Hld | Sv | BS | % |
|---|---|---|---|---|
| Acevedo, Mets | 3 | 0 | 4 | 43 |
| Adams T, Cubs | 11 | 18 | 4 | 88 |
| Aguilera, Min | 0 | 26 | 7 | 79 |
| Assenmacher, Cle | 20 | 4 | 1 | 96 |
| Ayala, Sea | 15 | 8 | 4 | 85 |
| Beck, SF | 1 | 37 | 8 | 83 |
| Belinda, Cin | 28 | 1 | 4 | 88 |
| Benitez, Bal | 20 | 9 | 1 | 97 |
| Bevil, KC | 1 | 1 | 4 | 33 |
| Bielecki, Atl | 12 | 2 | 4 | 78 |
| Bochtler, SD | 9 | 2 | 1 | 92 |
| Boehringer, Yanks | 5 | 0 | 3 | 63 |
| Bottalico, Phi | 0 | 34 | 7 | 83 |
| Bottenfield, Cubs | 8 | 2 | 2 | 83 |
| Brewer, Phi | 5 | 0 | 2 | 71 |
| Brocail, Det | 16 | 2 | 7 | 72 |
| Bruske, LA | 5 | 0 | 1 | 83 |
| Carrasco, KC | 8 | 0 | 2 | 80 |
| Casian, KC | 5 | 0 | 2 | 71 |
| Castillo T, WSox | 15 | 4 | 5 | 79 |
| Cather, Atl | 4 | 0 | 3 | 57 |
| Charlton, Sea | 9 | 14 | 11 | 68 |
| Christiansen, Pit | 8 | 0 | 2 | 80 |
| Cook, Fla | 13 | 0 | 2 | 87 |
| Corsi, Bos | 11 | 2 | 7 | 65 |
| Crabtree, Tor | 8 | 2 | 3 | 77 |
| Cruz, WSox | 6 | 0 | 0 | 100 |
| Cunnane, SD | 4 | 0 | 2 | 67 |
| Daal, Tor | 3 | 1 | 2 | 67 |
| DeJean, Col | 13 | 2 | 2 | 88 |
| DeLucia, Ana | 8 | 3 | 4 | 73 |
| Dipoto, Col | 10 | 16 | 5 | 84 |
| Dreifort, LA | 9 | 4 | 3 | 81 |
| Eckersley, StL | 0 | 36 | 7 | 84 |
| Embree, Atl | 16 | 0 | 0 | 100 |
| Ericks, Pit | 0 | 6 | 1 | 86 |
| Escobar, Tor | 1 | 14 | 3 | 83 |
| Fetters, Mil | 11 | 6 | 5 | 77 |
| Fossas, StL | 16 | 0 | 1 | 94 |
| Foulke, WSox | 5 | 3 | 3 | 73 |
| Fox, Atl | 7 | 0 | 1 | 88 |
| Franco, Mets | 0 | 36 | 6 | 86 |
| Frascatore, StL | 3 | 0 | 4 | 43 |
| Gordon, Bos | 0 | 11 | 2 | 85 |
| Groom, Oak | 12 | 3 | 2 | 88 |
| Guardado, Min | 13 | 1 | 0 | 100 |
| Gunderson, Tex | 12 | 1 | 3 | 81 |
| Guthrie, LA | 13 | 1 | 3 | 82 |
| Hall, LA | 15 | 2 | 3 | 85 |
| Hammond, Bos | 4 | 1 | 1 | 83 |
| Harris P, Ana | 10 | 0 | 3 | 77 |
| Helling, Tex | 6 | 0 | 1 | 86 |
| Henry B, Bos | 4 | 6 | 2 | 83 |
| Henry D, SF | 21 | 3 | 3 | 89 |
| Heredia F, Fla | 7 | 0 | 1 | 88 |
| Hernandez R, SF | 9 | 31 | 8 | 83 |
| Hernandez X, Tex | 13 | 0 | 1 | 93 |
| Hoffman, SD | 0 | 37 | 7 | 84 |
| Holmes, Col | 5 | 3 | 1 | 89 |
| Holtz, Ana | 14 | 2 | 6 | 73 |
| Hudek, Hou | 2 | 4 | 4 | 60 |
| Hutton, Col | 4 | 0 | 3 | 57 |
| Jackson M, Cle | 14 | 15 | 2 | 94 |
| James, Ana | 12 | 7 | 6 | 76 |
| Johnson D, Oak | 2 | 2 | 2 | 67 |
| Jones D, Mil | 0 | 36 | 2 | 95 |
| Jones T, Det | 5 | 31 | 5 | 88 |
| Karchner, WSox | 12 | 15 | 1 | 96 |
| Karp, Phi | 5 | 0 | 1 | 83 |
| Kashiwada, Mets | 3 | 0 | 2 | 60 |
| King, StL | 10 | 0 | 3 | 77 |
| Kline, Mon | 5 | 0 | 3 | 63 |
| Lacy, Bos | 5 | 3 | 0 | 100 |
| Leskanic, Col | 6 | 2 | 2 | 80 |
| Lidle, Mets | 9 | 2 | 1 | 92 |
| Lima, Hou | 3 | 2 | 0 | 100 |
| Loiselle, Pit | 5 | 29 | 5 | 87 |
| Lopez, Cle | 4 | 0 | 1 | 80 |
| Magnante, Hou | 3 | 1 | 4 | 50 |
| Mahay, Bos | 5 | 0 | 1 | 83 |
| Martin, Hou | 7 | 2 | 1 | 90 |
| Mathews T, Oak | 12 | 3 | 6 | 71 |
| Mathews T, Bal | 8 | 1 | 1 | 90 |
| McCarthy, Sea | 8 | 0 | 0 | 100 |
| McCurry, Col | 4 | 0 | 2 | 67 |
| McElroy, WSox | 15 | 1 | 5 | 76 |
| McMichael, Mets | 19 | 7 | 11 | 70 |
| Mendoza, Yanks | 4 | 2 | 2 | 75 |
| Mesa, Cle | 9 | 16 | 5 | 83 |
| Miceli, Det | 11 | 3 | 5 | 74 |
| Mills, Bal | 7 | 0 | 0 | 100 |
| Minor, Hou | 2 | 1 | 2 | 60 |
| Mohler, Oak | 11 | 1 | 3 | 80 |
| Montgomery J, KC | 3 | 14 | 3 | 85 |
| Morman, Cle | 5 | 2 | 0 | 100 |
| Munoz M, Col | 19 | 2 | 0 | 100 |
| Myers M, Det | 18 | 2 | 3 | 87 |
| Myers R, Bal | 2 | 45 | 1 | 98 |
| Naulty, Min | 8 | 1 | 2 | 82 |
| Nelson, Yanks | 22 | 2 | 6 | 80 |
| Nen, Fla | 0 | 35 | 7 | 83 |
| Olson, KC | 5 | 1 | 3 | 67 |
| Orosco, Bal | 21 | 0 | 4 | 84 |
| Osuna, LA | 10 | 0 | 0 | 100 |
| Patterson B, Cubs | 22 | 0 | 3 | 88 |
| Patterson D, Tex | 9 | 1 | 7 | 59 |
| Percival, Ana | 0 | 27 | 4 | 87 |
| Petkovsek, StL | 5 | 2 | 0 | 100 |
| Pichardo, KC | 4 | 11 | 2 | 88 |
| Pisciotta, Cubs | 10 | 0 | 1 | 91 |
| Plesac, Tor | 27 | 1 | 4 | 88 |
| Plunk, Cle | 10 | 0 | 2 | 83 |
| Poole, SF | 9 | 0 | 0 | 100 |
| Powell, Fla | 24 | 2 | 2 | 93 |
| Quantrill, Tor | 16 | 5 | 5 | 81 |
| Radinsky, LA | 26 | 3 | 2 | 94 |
| Reed S, Col | 10 | 6 | 7 | 70 |
| Remlinger, Cin | 14 | 2 | 0 | 100 |
| Rhodes, Bal | 9 | 1 | 1 | 91 |
| Rincon, Pit | 18 | 4 | 2 | 92 |
| Ritchie, Min | 3 | 0 | 2 | 60 |
| Rivera, Yanks | 0 | 43 | 9 | 83 |
| Rodriguez F, Min | 4 | 0 | 2 | 67 |
| Rodriguez R, SF | 14 | 1 | 4 | 79 |
| Rojas, Mets | 7 | 15 | 7 | 76 |
| Ruebel, Pit | 8 | 0 | 1 | 89 |
| Ruffin, Col | 2 | 7 | 2 | 82 |
| Sager, Det | 10 | 3 | 1 | 93 |
| Sanders, Det | 4 | 2 | 2 | 75 |
| Shaw, Cin | 5 | 42 | 7 | 87 |
| Shuey, Cle | 4 | 2 | 1 | 86 |
| Simas, WSox | 3 | 1 | 1 | 80 |
| Slocumb, Sea | 3 | 27 | 6 | 83 |
| Small, Oak | 8 | 4 | 2 | 86 |
| Smith L, Mon | 2 | 5 | 1 | 88 |
| Sodowsky, Pit | 5 | 0 | 2 | 71 |
| Spoljaric, Sea | 10 | 3 | 2 | 87 |
| Springer R, Hou | 9 | 3 | 4 | 75 |
| Stanifer, Fla | 4 | 1 | 1 | 83 |
| Stanton, Yanks | 26 | 3 | 2 | 94 |
| Sullivan, Cin | 13 | 1 | 1 | 93 |
| Swindell, Min | 12 | 1 | 6 | 68 |
| Tatis, Cubs | 8 | 0 | 1 | 89 |
| Tavarez, SF | 26 | 0 | 3 | 90 |
| Taylor, Oak | 7 | 23 | 7 | 81 |
| Telford, Mon | 11 | 1 | 4 | 75 |
| Timlin, Sea | 9 | 10 | 8 | 70 |
| Trombley, Min | 11 | 1 | 0 | 100 |
| Urbina, Mon | 1 | 27 | 5 | 85 |
| Veres D, Mon | 10 | 1 | 3 | 79 |
| Veres R, KC | 4 | 1 | 2 | 71 |
| Villone, Mil | 8 | 0 | 2 | 80 |
| Vosberg, Fla | 8 | 1 | 2 | 82 |
| Wagner B, Hou | 1 | 23 | 6 | 80 |
| Wasdin, Bos | 11 | 0 | 2 | 85 |
| Wells B, Sea | 5 | 2 | 2 | 78 |
| Wendell, Mets | 2 | 5 | 2 | 78 |
| Wetteland, Tex | 0 | 31 | 6 | 84 |
| Whisenant, KC | 5 | 0 | 0 | 100 |
| Whiteside, Tex | 2 | 0 | 4 | 33 |
| Wickman, Mil | 28 | 1 | 4 | 88 |
| Wilkins, Pit | 15 | 2 | 2 | 89 |
| Wohlers, Atl | 1 | 33 | 7 | 83 |
| Worrell T, SD | 16 | 3 | 4 | 83 |
| Worrell T, LA | 0 | 35 | 9 | 80 |
| **MLB Avg** | | | | **83** |

# Who Gets the Easy Saves—And Who Toughs It Out? (p. 164)

## Both Leagues—Listed Alphabetically
### (minimum 5 Save Opportunities in 1997)

| Reliever | Easy | Regular | Tough | Reliever | Easy | Regular | Tough |
|---|---|---|---|---|---|---|---|
| Adams T, Cubs | 10/12 | 6/7 | 2/3 | Mesa, Cle | 10/12 | 4/6 | 2/3 |
| Aguilera, Min | 16/16 | 8/15 | 2/2 | Miceli, Det | 1/2 | 2/4 | 0/2 |
| Assenmacher, Cle | 2/2 | 1/1 | 1/2 | Montgomery J, KC | 9/9 | 5/8 | 0/0 |
| Ayala, Sea | 1/1 | 5/5 | 2/6 | Myers M, Det | 1/1 | 0/1 | 1/3 |
| Beck, SF | 24/26 | 13/17 | 0/2 | Myers R, Bal | 26/26 | 18/19 | 1/1 |
| Belinda, Cin | 1/1 | 0/1 | 0/3 | Nelson, Yanks | 0/0 | 1/5 | 1/3 |
| Benitez, Bal | 0/1 | 6/6 | 3/3 | Nen, Fla | 26/30 | 8/11 | 1/1 |
| Bevil, KC | 1/2 | 0/2 | 0/1 | Patterson D, Tex | 0/0 | 1/3 | 0/5 |
| Bielecki, Atl | 0/0 | 1/5 | 1/1 | Percival, Ana | 21/23 | 4/4 | 2/4 |
| Bottalico, Phi | 17/17 | 14/18 | 3/6 | Pichardo, KC | 3/3 | 6/8 | 2/2 |
| Brocail, Det | 1/2 | 0/2 | 1/5 | Plesac, Tor | 0/0 | 1/2 | 0/3 |
| Castillo T, WSox | 1/1 | 3/6 | 0/2 | Quantrill, Tor | 2/3 | 2/2 | 1/5 |
| Charlton, Sea | 5/6 | 7/13 | 2/6 | Radinsky, LA | 0/0 | 2/3 | 1/2 |
| Corsi, Bos | 0/1 | 2/5 | 0/3 | Reed S, Col | 2/2 | 4/9 | 0/2 |
| Crabtree, Tor | 0/0 | 1/2 | 1/3 | Rincon, Pit | 1/1 | 3/4 | 0/1 |
| DeLucia, Ana | 0/0 | 1/3 | 2/4 | Rivera, Yanks | 28/28 | 13/21 | 2/3 |
| Dipoto, Col | 9/10 | 6/8 | 1/3 | Rodriguez R, SF | 1/2 | 0/0 | 0/3 |
| Dreifort, LA | 0/0 | 4/6 | 0/1 | Rojas, Mets | 2/3 | 12/17 | 1/2 |
| Eckersley, StL | 25/26 | 11/14 | 0/3 | Ruffin, Col | 1/1 | 5/5 | 1/3 |
| Ericks, Pit | 6/6 | 0/1 | 0/0 | Shaw, Cin | 23/23 | 16/21 | 3/5 |
| Escobar, Tor | 8/8 | 5/8 | 1/1 | Slocumb, Sea | 14/14 | 10/12 | 3/7 |
| Fetters, Mil | 4/4 | 1/3 | 1/4 | Small, Oak | 0/1 | 4/5 | 0/0 |
| Foulke, WSox | 0/1 | 2/4 | 1/1 | Smith L, Mon | 2/2 | 3/3 | 0/1 |
| Franco, Mets | 24/26 | 9/12 | 3/4 | Spoljaric, Sea | 0/0 | 1/1 | 2/4 |
| Gordon, Bos | 4/4 | 5/5 | 2/4 | Spradlin, Phi | 1/2 | 0/1 | 0/2 |
| Groom, Oak | 0/0 | 2/2 | 1/3 | Springer R, Hou | 2/2 | 1/1 | 0/4 |
| Hall, LA | 1/1 | 0/0 | 1/4 | Stanton, Yanks | 2/2 | 1/1 | 0/2 |
| Henry B, Bos | 0/0 | 3/3 | 3/5 | Swindell, Min | 0/0 | 1/2 | 0/5 |
| Henry D, SF | 1/1 | 1/4 | 1/1 | Taylor, Oak | 8/11 | 12/14 | 3/5 |
| Hernandez R, SF | 15/16 | 11/14 | 5/9 | Telford, Mon | 0/0 | 1/4 | 0/1 |
| Hoffman, SD | 23/24 | 7/10 | 7/10 | Timlin, Sea | 3/3 | 4/9 | 3/6 |
| Holtz, Ana | 0/1 | 1/2 | 1/5 | Urbina, Mon | 7/8 | 12/13 | 8/11 |
| Hudek, Hou | 4/5 | 0/2 | 0/1 | Wagner B, Hou | 8/8 | 12/13 | 3/8 |
| Jackson M, Cle | 5/5 | 8/9 | 2/3 | Wendell, Mets | 1/1 | 2/3 | 2/3 |
| James, Ana | 0/1 | 4/7 | 3/5 | Wetteland, Tex | 23/25 | 7/8 | 1/4 |
| Jones D, Mil | 25/26 | 9/9 | 2/3 | Wickman, Mil | 0/1 | 1/2 | 0/2 |
| Jones T, Det | 16/16 | 11/13 | 4/7 | Wohlers, Atl | 19/20 | 10/13 | 4/7 |
| Karchner, WSox | 4/4 | 8/9 | 3/3 | Worrell T, SD | 1/2 | 2/4 | 0/1 |
| Loiselle, Pit | 18/19 | 9/11 | 2/4 | Worrell T, LA | 25/26 | 10/18 | 0/0 |
| Magnante, Hou | 0/0 | 1/3 | 0/2 | **AL Totals** | **268/297** | **223/356** | **77/208** |
| Mathews T, Oak | 2/2 | 1/4 | 0/3 | **NL Totals** | **296/329** | **222/349** | **53/168** |
| McElroy, WSox | 1/2 | 0/1 | 0/3 | **MLB Totals** | **564/626** | **445/705** | **130/376** |
| McMichael, Mets | 3/3 | 3/7 | 1/8 | | | | |

# Which Reliever Is Best at Preventing Runs? (p. 167)

## Runs Prevented Point Totals—1997 (minimum 70 IP)

| Reliever, Team | Pts | Reliever, Team | Pts | Reliever, Team | Pts |
|---|---|---|---|---|---|
| Quantrill, Tor | 21.8 | Beck, SF | 1.8 | Wasdin, Bos | -1.6 |
| Shaw, Cin | 20.5 | Astacio, Col | 1.8 | Adams T, Cubs | -1.6 |
| Rivera, Yanks | 19.8 | Mercker, Cin | 1.4 | Juden, Cle | -1.6 |
| Jones D, Mil | 19.5 | Mohler, Oak | 1.4 | Tomko, Cin | -2.0 |
| Mesa, Cle | 18.2 | Loaiza, Pit | 1.4 | Foster, Cubs | -2.1 |
| Hernandez R, SF | 16.8 | Telgheder, Oak | 1.4 | Loiselle, Pit | -2.2 |
| Rhodes, Bal | 16.1 | VanLandingham, SF | 1.4 | Clark M, Cubs | -2.4 |
| McMichael, Mets | 15.6 | Hamilton, SD | 1.3 | Suppan, Bos | -2.5 |
| Powell, Fla | 14.5 | Henry B, Bos | 1.3 | Bottalico, Phi | -2.7 |
| Hoffman, SD | 14.0 | Park, LA | 1.3 | Rusch, KC | -2.7 |
| Benitez, Bal | 13.9 | Burba, Cin | 1.2 | Castillo F, Col | -2.8 |
| Hasegawa, Ana | 12.5 | Stephenson, Phi | 1.1 | Florie, Mil | -2.9 |
| Wickman, Mil | 12.4 | Johnson R, Sea | 0.9 | Whiteside, Tex | -2.9 |
| Swindell, Min | 11.9 | Lieber, Pit | 0.9 | Bones, KC | -3.0 |
| Valdes M, Mon | 11.1 | Erickson, Bal | 0.9 | Reyes C, Oak | -3.1 |
| Telford, Mon | 10.8 | Sager, Det | 0.8 | Oquist, Oak | -3.2 |
| Frascatore, StL | 9.9 | Robertson, Min | 0.8 | Nen, Fla | -3.4 |
| Helling, Tex | 8.9 | Witt, Tex | 0.7 | Avery, Bos | -3.4 |
| Jackson M, Cle | 8.7 | Wolcott, Sea | 0.7 | Ritchie, Min | -3.5 |
| Sullivan, Cin | 8.5 | Holt, Hou | 0.5 | Mulholland, SF | -4.0 |
| Jones T, Det | 7.9 | Saunders, Fla | 0.5 | Worrell T, SD | -4.1 |
| Mathews T, Oak | 7.0 | Spradlin, Phi | 0.4 | Springer D, Ana | -4.1 |
| Belinda, Cin | 6.7 | Maduro, Phi | 0.4 | Dipoto, Col | -4.3 |
| Nelson, Yanks | 6.7 | Colon, Cle | 0.3 | Watson, Ana | -4.4 |
| Rodriguez F, Min | 6.6 | Aldred, Min | 0.3 | Bohanon, Mets | -4.8 |
| Wilkins, Pit | 5.9 | Blair, Det | 0.2 | Garcia, Hou | -4.9 |
| Harris P, Ana | 5.4 | Hermanson, Mon | 0.2 | Boskie, Bal | -4.9 |
| Mendoza, Yanks | 5.4 | Spoljaric, Sea | 0.1 | Santana, Tex | -5.1 |
| Fetters, Mil | 5.0 | Hitchcock, SD | 0.0 | Cunnane, SD | -5.1 |
| Lidle, Mets | 5.0 | Gooden, Yanks | -0.4 | Henry D, SF | -5.3 |
| Ayala, Sea | 4.7 | Perez C, Mon | -0.5 | Sanders, Det | -5.6 |
| Patterson D, Tex | 4.6 | Olivares, Sea | -0.6 | Wendell, Mets | -5.7 |
| Bottenfield, Cubs | 4.3 | Taylor, Oak | -0.6 | Carrasco, KC | -5.8 |
| Remlinger, Cin | 4.0 | Foulke, WSox | -0.8 | Lira, Sea | -5.8 |
| Rogers, Yanks | 4.0 | Adamson, Mil | -0.8 | Wengert, Oak | -7.0 |
| Timlin, Sea | 3.7 | Bullinger, Mon | -0.9 | Lima, Hou | -7.0 |
| Johnson M, Mon | 3.3 | Mercedes, Mil | -0.9 | Holmes, Col | -7.9 |
| Trombley, Min | 3.0 | Schourek, Cin | -1.0 | Rojas, Mets | -10.3 |
| Brocail, Det | 2.9 | Gordon, Bos | -1.1 | Smith P, SD | -10.6 |
| Candiotti, LA | 2.8 | Morgan, Cin | -1.1 | Miceli, Det | -11.9 |
| McElroy, WSox | 2.8 | Darwin D, SF | -1.1 | Petkovsek, StL | -12.6 |
| Small, Oak | 2.3 | Carpenter, Tor | -1.3 | Bergman, SD | -12.6 |
| Reed R, Mets | 2.3 | Person, Tor | -1.3 | Slocumb, Sea | -14.3 |
| Dickson, Ana | 2.2 | Wakefield, Bos | -1.4 | Lopez, Cle | -20.1 |
| Tavarez, SF | 2.1 | Rapp, SF | -1.4 | | |

# Which Pitchers "Scored" the Highest in 1997? (p. 171)

## Best Game Scores—1997

| Player, Team | Date | Opp | W/L | IP | H | R | ER | BB | K | Score |
|---|---|---|---|---|---|---|---|---|---|---|
| R Clemens, Tor | 09/07 | Tex | W | 9.0 | 2 | 0 | 0 | 0 | 14 | 97 |
| M Mussina, Bal | 05/30 | Cle | W | 9.0 | 1 | 0 | 0 | 0 | 10 | 95 |
| F Cordova, Pit | 07/12 | Hou | ND | 9.0 | 0 | 0 | 0 | 2 | 10 | 95 |
| K Brown, Fla | 06/10 | SF | W | 9.0 | 0 | 0 | 0 | 0 | 7 | 94 |
| D Wells, Yanks | 07/30 | Oak | W | 9.0 | 3 | 0 | 0 | 3 | 16 | 94 |
| A Fernandez, Fla | 04/10 | Cubs | W | 9.0 | 1 | 0 | 0 | 0 | 8 | 93 |
| A Benes, StL | 05/16 | Atl | ND | 9.0 | 1 | 0 | 0 | 3 | 11 | 93 |
| P Martinez, Mon | 06/14 | Det | W | 9.0 | 3 | 0 | 0 | 2 | 14 | 93 |
| P Martinez, Mon | 07/13 | Cin | W | 9.0 | 1 | 0 | 0 | 1 | 9 | 93 |
| R Johnson, Sea | 08/08 | WSox | W | 9.0 | 5 | 0 | 0 | 3 | 19 | 93 |
| R Johnson, Sea | 06/08 | Det | W | 8.0 | 1 | 0 | 0 | 3 | 15 | 92 |
| S Sanders, Det | 09/09 | Tex | W | 9.0 | 1 | 0 | 0 | 1 | 8 | 92 |
| S Estes, SF | 04/26 | Hou | W | 9.0 | 2 | 0 | 0 | 1 | 9 | 91 |
| S Estes, SF | 07/04 | Col | W | 8.2 | 1 | 0 | 0 | 2 | 11 | 91 |
| S Woodard, Mil | 07/28 | Tor | W | 8.0 | 1 | 0 | 0 | 1 | 12 | 91 |
| C Perez, Mon | 09/03 | Bos | W | 9.0 | 2 | 0 | 0 | 0 | 8 | 91 |
| K Brown, Fla | 07/16 | LA | W | 9.0 | 1 | 1 | 0 | 1 | 8 | 90 |
| R Johnson, Sea | 06/02 | Tor | W | 9.0 | 2 | 0 | 0 | 3 | 9 | 89 |
| G Maddux, Atl | 07/02 | Yanks | W | 9.0 | 3 | 0 | 0 | 0 | 8 | 89 |
| C Finley, Ana | 07/06 | Sea | W | 9.0 | 4 | 0 | 0 | 3 | 13 | 89 |
| P Martinez, Mon | 07/29 | Col | W | 9.0 | 5 | 0 | 0 | 1 | 13 | 89 |
| M Gardner, SF | 08/08 | Mon | W | 9.0 | 2 | 0 | 0 | 1 | 7 | 89 |
| M Gardner, SF | 04/30 | Pit | W | 9.0 | 3 | 1 | 1 | 0 | 11 | 88 |
| P Martinez, Mon | 05/01 | Hou | W | 9.0 | 3 | 0 | 0 | 2 | 9 | 88 |
| P Hentgen, Tor | 05/04 | Min | W | 9.0 | 4 | 0 | 0 | 1 | 10 | 88 |
| F Lira, Det | 05/13 | Tor | W | 9.0 | 4 | 0 | 0 | 1 | 10 | 88 |
| C Ogea, Cle | 05/23 | Bal | W | 9.0 | 2 | 1 | 0 | 2 | 9 | 88 |
| R Johnson, Sea | 05/28 | Tex | W | 8.0 | 4 | 0 | 0 | 1 | 15 | 88 |
| C Eldred, Mil | 05/30 | WSox | W | 9.0 | 3 | 0 | 0 | 1 | 8 | 88 |
| M Mussina, Bal | 06/25 | Mil | W | 9.0 | 3 | 1 | 1 | 1 | 12 | 88 |
| R Clemens, Tor | 07/06 | Yanks | W | 9.0 | 4 | 0 | 0 | 1 | 10 | 88 |
| C Schilling, Phi | 08/10 | StL | W | 9.0 | 3 | 0 | 0 | 1 | 8 | 88 |
| S Erickson, Bal | 08/12 | Oak | W | 9.0 | 3 | 0 | 0 | 1 | 8 | 88 |
| K Tapani, Cubs | 09/16 | Cin | W | 9.0 | 1 | 0 | 0 | 2 | 5 | 88 |
| B Moehler, Det | 04/26 | Ana | W | 9.0 | 2 | 0 | 0 | 0 | 4 | 87 |
| C Schilling, Phi | 05/11 | Col | W | 9.0 | 4 | 1 | 1 | 0 | 12 | 87 |
| J Juden, Mon | 07/01 | Tor | W | 8.1 | 2 | 1 | 1 | 2 | 14 | 87 |
| B Radke, Min | 07/20 | Oak | W | 9.0 | 5 | 0 | 0 | 0 | 10 | 87 |
| D Neagle, Atl | 07/28 | Cubs | W | 9.0 | 3 | 0 | 0 | 0 | 6 | 87 |
| M Mussina, Bal | 09/13 | Yanks | W | 9.0 | 3 | 1 | 0 | 1 | 9 | 87 |
| C Schilling, Phi | 04/01 | LA | W | 8.0 | 2 | 0 | 0 | 3 | 11 | 86 |
| F Cordova, Pit | 06/23 | Hou | W | 9.0 | 2 | 0 | 0 | 2 | 5 | 86 |
| P Martinez, Mon | 06/30 | Tor | W | 9.0 | 3 | 1 | 1 | 1 | 10 | 86 |
| R Clemens, Tor | 07/12 | Bos | W | 8.0 | 4 | 1 | 1 | 0 | 16 | 86 |
| D Hermanson, Mon | 07/15 | Fla | W | 9.0 | 5 | 0 | 0 | 0 | 9 | 86 |
| C Schilling, Phi | 07/16 | Mon | W | 9.0 | 4 | 0 | 0 | 0 | 7 | 86 |
| S Erickson, Bal | 07/27 | Min | W | 9.0 | 5 | 0 | 0 | 0 | 9 | 86 |
| J Smoltz, Atl | 08/04 | Pit | W | 9.0 | 4 | 0 | 0 | 2 | 9 | 86 |
| D Neagle, Atl | 09/02 | Det | W | 9.0 | 4 | 0 | 0 | 0 | 7 | 86 |
| T Glavine, Atl | 09/10 | LA | W | 9.0 | 4 | 0 | 0 | 0 | 7 | 86 |

## How Bad Was Navarro? (p. 174)

### Worst ERAs (minimum 200 IP)

| Year | Pitcher | ERA |
|---|---|---|
| 1894 | Harry Staley, Bos | 6.81 |
| 1894 | Mike Sullivan, Was-Cle | 6.48 |
| 1895 | Bert Inks, Lou | 6.40 |
| 1894 | Dad Clarkson, StL | 6.36 |
| 1894 | Dan Daub, Bro | 6.32 |
| 1897 | Bill Hart, StL | 6.26 |
| 1931 | Pat Caraway, WSox | 6.22 |
| 1930 | Guy Bush, Cubs | 6.20 |
| 1897 | Red Donahue, StL | 6.13 |
| 1894 | Bill Hutchison, Cubs | 6.06 |
| 1894 | Ad Gumbert, Pit | 6.02 |
| 1895 | Red Ehret, StL | 6.02 |
| 1895 | Mike McDermott, Lou | 5.99 |
| 1894 | Al Maul, Was | 5.98 |
| 1887 | Ed Cushman, Giants | 5.97 |
| 1883 | Jack Neagle, Phils-Bal-Pit | 5.94 |
| 1895 | Varney Anderson, Was | 5.89 |
| 1894 | Duke Esper, Was-Bal | 5.86 |
| 1894 | Willie McGill, Cubs | 5.84 |
| 1894 | Bill Hawke, Bal | 5.84 |
| 1936 | Buck Ross, A's | 5.83 |
| 1939 | Jack Kramer, Browns | 5.83 |
| 1894 | Gus Weyhing, Phi | 5.81 |
| 1895 | Gus Weyhing, Phi-Pit-Lou | 5.81 |
| 1939 | Vern Kennedy, Det-Browns | 5.80 |
| 1896 | Red Donahue, StL | 5.80 |
| 1997 | Jaime Navarro, WSox | 5.79 |
| 1899 | Charlie Knepper, Cle | 5.78 |
| 1890 | George Haddock, Buf | 5.76 |
| 1936 | Gordon Rhodes, A's | 5.74 |
| 1982 | Matt Keough, Oak | 5.72 |
| 1930 | Ray Benge, Phils | 5.70 |
| 1950 | Herm Wehmeier, Cin | 5.67 |
| 1895 | Con Lucid, Bro-Phi | 5.66 |
| 1890 | Bert Cunningham, Buf-A's | 5.63 |
| 1894 | Tom Parrott, Cin | 5.60 |
| 1996 | Tom Gordon, Bos | 5.59 |
| 1940 | Vern Kennedy, Browns | 5.59 |
| 1936 | Chief Hogsett, Det-Browns | 5.58 |
| 1889 | Kid Gleason, Phils | 5.58 |
| 1894 | Kid Carsey, Phi | 5.56 |
| 1975 | Joe Coleman, Det | 5.55 |
| 1953 | Harry Byrd, A's | 5.51 |
| 1897 | Jack Fifield, Phi | 5.51 |
| 1930 | Larry Benton, Giants-Cin | 5.50 |
| 1941 | Eldon Auker, Browns | 5.50 |
| 1894 | Phil Knell, Pit-Lou | 5.49 |
| 1983 | Frank Viola, Min | 5.49 |
| 1950 | Alex Kellner, A's | 5.47 |

### Worst Relative ERAs (minimum 200 IP)

| Year | Pitcher | ERA | Lg ERA | ERA/Lg ERA |
|---|---|---|---|---|
| 1883 | Jack Neagle, Phils-Bal-Pit | 5.94 | 3.25 | 1.825 |
| 1876 | George Zettlein, Phi | 3.88 | 2.31 | 1.684 |
| 1917 | Elmer Myers, A's | 4.42 | 2.66 | 1.660 |
| 1885 | Pete Conway, Buf | 4.67 | 2.82 | 1.658 |
| 1880 | Curry Foley, Bos | 3.89 | 2.37 | 1.641 |
| 1888 | Lev Shreve, Ind | 4.63 | 2.83 | 1.634 |
| 1876 | Dory Dean, Cin | 3.73 | 2.31 | 1.619 |
| 1907 | Irv Young, Braves | 3.96 | 2.46 | 1.607 |
| 1913 | Dan Griner, Cards | 5.08 | 3.20 | 1.589 |
| 1904 | Tom Fisher, Braves | 4.25 | 2.73 | 1.558 |
| 1883 | John Coleman, Phils | 4.87 | 3.14 | 1.551 |
| 1906 | George Winter, RSox | 4.12 | 2.69 | 1.531 |
| 1905 | Kaiser Wilhelm, Braves | 4.53 | 2.99 | 1.515 |
| 1908 | Gus Dorner, Braves | 3.54 | 2.35 | 1.508 |
| 1886 | Pete Conway, KC-Det | 4.95 | 3.29 | 1.506 |
| 1899 | Charlie Knepper, Cle | 5.78 | 3.85 | 1.500 |
| 1898 | Chick Fraser, Lou-Cle | 5.36 | 3.60 | 1.489 |
| 1892 | George Cobb, Bal | 4.86 | 3.28 | 1.480 |
| 1910 | Bob Harmon, Cards | 4.46 | 3.03 | 1.475 |
| 1907 | Vive Lindaman, Braves | 3.63 | 2.46 | 1.475 |
| 1903 | Al Orth, Was | 4.34 | 2.95 | 1.471 |
| 1966 | Sammy Ellis, Cin | 5.29 | 3.61 | 1.468 |
| 1975 | Joe Coleman, Det | 5.55 | 3.79 | 1.465 |
| 1885 | Billy Serad, Buf | 4.10 | 2.82 | 1.456 |
| 1897 | Bill Hart, StL | 6.26 | 4.30 | 1.456 |
| 1909 | Dolly Gray, Was | 3.59 | 2.47 | 1.453 |
| 1904 | Willie Sudhoff, Browns | 3.76 | 2.60 | 1.450 |
| 1909 | George Ferguson, Braves | 3.73 | 2.59 | 1.441 |
| 1980 | Dennis Lamp, Cubs | 5.20 | 3.61 | 1.440 |
| 1905 | Mal Eason, Bro | 4.30 | 2.99 | 1.439 |
| 1902 | Snake Wiltse, A's-Bal | 5.13 | 3.57 | 1.436 |
| 1884 | Billy Serad, Buf | 4.27 | 2.98 | 1.433 |
| 1892 | Ted Breitenstein, StL | 4.69 | 3.28 | 1.427 |
| 1897 | Red Donahue, StL | 6.13 | 4.30 | 1.425 |
| 1891 | Pat Luby, Cubs | 4.76 | 3.34 | 1.424 |
| 1931 | Pat Caraway, WSox | 6.22 | 4.38 | 1.420 |
| 1957 | Chuck Stobbs, Was | 5.36 | 3.79 | 1.414 |
| 1905 | Bill Dinneen, RSox | 3.73 | 2.65 | 1.409 |
| 1915 | Bill Bailey, Bal-Whales | 4.27 | 3.03 | 1.407 |
| 1899 | Jim Hughey, Cle | 5.41 | 3.85 | 1.404 |
| 1907 | Casey Patten, Was | 3.56 | 2.54 | 1.404 |
| 1909 | Harry McIntire, Bro | 3.63 | 2.59 | 1.402 |
| 1982 | Matt Keough, Oak | 5.72 | 4.08 | 1.401 |
| 1902 | Ham Iburg, Phils | 3.89 | 2.78 | 1.400 |
| 1884 | Jersey Bakely, A's-Wil-KC | 4.29 | 3.07 | 1.398 |
| 1884 | Ed Begley, Giants | 4.16 | 2.98 | 1.398 |
| 1901 | Bill Phillips, Cin | 4.64 | 3.32 | 1.397 |
| 1885 | Charlie Sweeney, Cards | 3.93 | 2.82 | 1.394 |
| 1887 | Ed Cushman, Giants | 5.97 | 4.29 | 1.393 |

# Who's Best in the Infield Zone? (p. 178)

## Zone Ratings — Infielders
### (minimum 550 defensive innings in 1997)

| FIRST BASE | 1997 | | | | 1995-97 | | |
|---|---|---|---|---|---|---|---|
| | | In | | Zone | In | | Zone |
| Player, Team | Innings | Zone | Outs | Rating | Zone | Outs | Rating |
| King, KC | 1291.0 | 309 | 298 | .964 | 517 | 501 | .969 |
| Young D, StL | 590.2 | 114 | 108 | .947 | 123 | 116 | .943 |
| Young K, Pit | 576.0 | 149 | 141 | .946 | 205 | 185 | .902 |
| Clark T, Det | 1383.2 | 261 | 243 | .931 | 458 | 413 | .902 |
| Conine, Fla | 991.2 | 219 | 203 | .927 | 326 | 300 | .920 |
| Palmeiro R, Bal | 1356.0 | 252 | 227 | .901 | 788 | 710 | .901 |
| Stahoviak, Min | 629.0 | 131 | 118 | .901 | 451 | 411 | .911 |
| Joyner, SD | 1045.2 | 192 | 172 | .896 | 625 | 567 | .907 |
| Grace, Cubs | 1291.0 | 278 | 249 | .896 | 817 | 715 | .875 |
| Olerud, Mets | 1236.1 | 271 | 242 | .893 | 681 | 618 | .907 |
| Bagwell, Hou | 1391.0 | 285 | 252 | .884 | 807 | 724 | .897 |
| Karros, LA | 1447.2 | 292 | 258 | .884 | 832 | 749 | .900 |
| Delgado C, Tor | 1035.2 | 212 | 184 | .868 | 262 | 226 | .863 |
| Brogna, Phi | 1200.0 | 234 | 202 | .863 | 553 | 470 | .850 |
| Martinez T, Yanks | 1309.1 | 260 | 224 | .862 | 734 | 646 | .880 |
| Galarraga, Col | 1325.2 | 334 | 287 | .859 | 950 | 836 | .880 |
| Thome, Cle | 1224.2 | 268 | 230 | .858 | 268 | 230 | .858 |
| Nilsson, Mil | 589.2 | 125 | 107 | .856 | 164 | 141 | .860 |
| Sorrento, Sea | 1057.2 | 176 | 150 | .852 | 558 | 467 | .837 |
| Clark W, Tex | 848.1 | 177 | 150 | .847 | 603 | 513 | .851 |
| Snow, SF | 1333.1 | 252 | 212 | .841 | 674 | 562 | .834 |
| Segui, Mon | 1071.2 | 202 | 168 | .832 | 536 | 463 | .864 |
| Thomas, WSox | 822.2 | 168 | 139 | .827 | 526 | 430 | .817 |
| Erstad, Ana | 1083.0 | 195 | 161 | .826 | 195 | 161 | .826 |
| McGriff, Atl | 1263.2 | 234 | 193 | .825 | 678 | 570 | .841 |
| Morris, Cin | 749.0 | 130 | 107 | .823 | 507 | 445 | .878 |
| McGwire, StL | 1287.1 | 273 | 223 | .817 | 639 | 539 | .844 |
| Vaughn M, Bos | 1137.0 | 232 | 175 | .754 | 725 | 595 | .821 |
| MLB Avg | | | | .869 | | | .875 |

| SECOND BASE | 1997 | | | | 1995-97 | | |
|---|---|---|---|---|---|---|---|
| | | In | | Zone | In | | Zone |
| Player, Team | Innings | Zone | Outs | Rating | Zone | Outs | Rating |
| Sandberg, Cubs | 991.1 | 319 | 306 | .959 | 785 | 736 | .938 |
| Lansing, Mon | 1234.0 | 425 | 402 | .946 | 1286 | 1170 | .910 |
| Castillo L, Fla | 575.1 | 195 | 184 | .944 | 315 | 303 | .962 |
| Young E, LA | 1327.1 | 555 | 521 | .939 | 1286 | 1185 | .921 |
| Offerman, KC | 870.0 | 274 | 256 | .934 | 363 | 340 | .937 |
| Kent, SF | 1227.1 | 450 | 420 | .933 | 866 | 799 | .923 |
| Biggio, Hou | 1384.1 | 517 | 481 | .930 | 1484 | 1316 | .887 |
| McLemore, Tex | 742.1 | 263 | 244 | .928 | 966 | 912 | .944 |
| Lemke, Atl | 849.2 | 342 | 315 | .921 | 1142 | 1047 | .917 |
| Morandini, Phi | 1220.2 | 364 | 335 | .920 | 1113 | 1025 | .921 |
| Spiezio, Oak | 1256.0 | 461 | 424 | .920 | 461 | 424 | .920 |
| Knoblauch, Min | 1316.2 | 462 | 422 | .913 | 1307 | 1190 | .910 |
| DeShields, StL | 1226.0 | 424 | 387 | .913 | 1226 | 1133 | .924 |
| Boone B, Cin | 1115.1 | 374 | 341 | .912 | 1175 | 1076 | .916 |
| Veras, SD | 1192.1 | 461 | 420 | .911 | 1017 | 927 | .912 |
| Alicea, Ana | 890.0 | 290 | 262 | .903 | 1053 | 962 | .914 |
| Fernandez, Cle | 840.1 | 327 | 295 | .902 | 338 | 305 | .902 |
| Frye, Bos | 703.0 | 253 | 228 | .901 | 886 | 798 | .901 |
| Guerrero W, LA | 739.2 | 256 | 229 | .895 | 256 | 229 | .895 |
| Vina, Mil | 657.1 | 246 | 219 | .890 | 921 | 842 | .914 |
| Alomar R, Bal | 896.2 | 345 | 306 | .887 | 1250 | 1139 | .911 |
| Baerga, Mets | 1048.2 | 415 | 361 | .870 | 1275 | 1133 | .889 |
| Duncan, Tor | 638.1 | 232 | 200 | .862 | 580 | 507 | .874 |
| Valentin J, Bos | 707.1 | 287 | 247 | .861 | 287 | 247 | .861 |
| Garcia C, Tor | 821.2 | 308 | 263 | .854 | 820 | 695 | .848 |
| Womack, Pit | 1292.2 | 485 | 413 | .852 | 496 | 421 | .849 |
| Durham, WSox | 1339.2 | 472 | 401 | .850 | 1280 | 1123 | .877 |

| Player, Team | Innings | In Zone | Outs | Zone Rating | In Zone | Outs | Zone Rating |
|---|---|---|---|---|---|---|---|
| Cora, Sea | 1192.2 | 365 | 299 | .819 | 1034 | 884 | .855 |
| Easley, Det | 1161.2 | 460 | 369 | .802 | 717 | 603 | .841 |
| **MLB Avg** | | | | **.899** | | | **.904** |

## THIRD BASE

| | | 1997 | | | 1995-97 | | |
|---|---|---|---|---|---|---|---|
| Player, Team | Innings | In Zone | Outs | Zone Rating | In Zone | Outs | Zone Rating |
| Cirillo, Mil | 1294.1 | 416 | 369 | .887 | 964 | 831 | .862 |
| Brosius, Oak | 825.2 | 276 | 243 | .880 | 736 | 633 | .860 |
| Alfonzo, Mets | 1117.0 | 364 | 319 | .876 | 582 | 500 | .859 |
| Gaetti, StL | 1075.1 | 321 | 276 | .860 | 933 | 780 | .836 |
| Fryman, Det | 1331.2 | 412 | 348 | .845 | 1257 | 1052 | .837 |
| Rolen, Phi | 1337.0 | 406 | 342 | .842 | 484 | 407 | .841 |
| Williams M, Cle | 1284.2 | 405 | 337 | .832 | 889 | 739 | .831 |
| Orie, Cubs | 901.0 | 301 | 248 | .824 | 301 | 248 | .824 |
| Mueller, SF | 916.0 | 306 | 252 | .824 | 420 | 350 | .833 |
| Jones C, Atl | 1300.2 | 326 | 268 | .822 | 940 | 765 | .814 |
| Boggs, Yanks | 611.0 | 201 | 165 | .821 | 741 | 611 | .825 |
| Valentin J, Bos | 552.2 | 178 | 146 | .820 | 197 | 158 | .802 |
| Hayes, Yanks | 806.0 | 250 | 205 | .820 | 1053 | 854 | .811 |
| Coomer, Min | 1008.2 | 301 | 244 | .811 | 332 | 270 | .813 |
| Strange, Mon | 803.1 | 243 | 196 | .807 | 394 | 310 | .787 |
| Castilla, Col | 1372.0 | 465 | 373 | .802 | 1366 | 1103 | .807 |
| Ripken C, Bal | 1401.0 | 444 | 356 | .802 | 462 | 373 | .807 |
| Caminiti, SD | 1117.0 | 410 | 326 | .795 | 1260 | 1006 | .798 |
| Randa, Pit | 970.1 | 353 | 280 | .793 | 599 | 462 | .771 |
| Zeile, LA | 1431.1 | 360 | 285 | .792 | 878 | 693 | .789 |
| Naehring, Bos | 602.1 | 156 | 122 | .782 | 806 | 652 | .809 |
| Davis R, Sea | 992.0 | 318 | 248 | .780 | 494 | 376 | .761 |
| Paquette, KC | 585.2 | 206 | 158 | .767 | 429 | 327 | .762 |
| Sprague, Tor | 1120.1 | 299 | 229 | .766 | 963 | 771 | .801 |
| Berry, Hou | 629.1 | 199 | 152 | .764 | 764 | 574 | .751 |
| Palmer, KC | 1227.0 | 362 | 276 | .762 | 789 | 611 | .774 |
| Snopek, WSox | 692.0 | 182 | 138 | .758 | 257 | 190 | .739 |
| Bonilla, Fla | 1268.2 | 343 | 255 | .743 | 521 | 398 | .764 |
| Hollins, Ana | 1148.1 | 374 | 277 | .741 | 744 | 592 | .796 |
| Greene W, Cin | 848.0 | 259 | 188 | .726 | 486 | 367 | .755 |
| **MLB Avg** | | | | **.800** | | | **.802** |

## SHORTSTOP

| | | 1997 | | | 1995-97 | | |
|---|---|---|---|---|---|---|---|
| Player, Team | Innings | In Zone | Outs | Zone Rating | In Zone | Outs | Zone Rating |
| Reese, Cin | 853.1 | 288 | 285 | .990 | 288 | 285 | .990 |
| DiSarcina, Ana | 1330.1 | 445 | 440 | .989 | 1252 | 1217 | .972 |
| Clayton, StL | 1287.1 | 495 | 489 | .988 | 1344 | 1308 | .973 |
| Bogar, Hou | 586.1 | 223 | 219 | .982 | 300 | 287 | .957 |
| Vizquel, Cle | 1307.1 | 474 | 465 | .981 | 1379 | 1327 | .962 |
| Ordonez R, Mets | 956.1 | 366 | 358 | .978 | 867 | 826 | .953 |
| Renteria, Fla | 1328.2 | 450 | 437 | .971 | 820 | 796 | .971 |
| Cruz D, Det | 1184.0 | 461 | 445 | .965 | 461 | 445 | .965 |
| Gil, Tex | 860.2 | 374 | 359 | .960 | 807 | 777 | .963 |
| Gonzalez A, Tor | 1102.1 | 366 | 351 | .959 | 1102 | 1058 | .960 |
| Bordick, Bal | 1335.1 | 462 | 443 | .959 | 1357 | 1317 | .971 |
| Rodriguez A, Sea | 1233.2 | 456 | 432 | .947 | 1044 | 975 | .934 |
| Garciaparra, Bos | 1344.1 | 520 | 491 | .944 | 586 | 549 | .937 |
| Weiss, Col | 971.2 | 401 | 377 | .940 | 1361 | 1276 | .938 |
| Bell J, KC | 1271.0 | 476 | 447 | .939 | 1469 | 1380 | .939 |
| Vizcaino, SF | 1221.0 | 474 | 443 | .935 | 937 | 868 | .926 |
| Valentin J, Mil | 1150.1 | 435 | 406 | .933 | 1282 | 1242 | .969 |
| Grudzielanek, Mon | 1368.1 | 512 | 474 | .926 | 1160 | 1045 | .901 |
| Polcovich, Pit | 635.0 | 303 | 280 | .924 | 303 | 280 | .924 |
| Stocker, Phi | 1262.1 | 422 | 389 | .922 | 1225 | 1160 | .947 |
| Meares, Min | 1131.1 | 463 | 426 | .920 | 1227 | 1126 | .918 |
| Guillen O, WSox | 1191.1 | 422 | 386 | .915 | 1165 | 1079 | .926 |
| Gomez, SD | 1279.2 | 480 | 439 | .915 | 1226 | 1133 | .924 |
| Jeter, Yanks | 1417.0 | 525 | 480 | .914 | 1097 | 992 | .904 |
| Blauser, Atl | 1235.0 | 431 | 394 | .914 | 1067 | 986 | .924 |
| Gagne, LA | 1223.0 | 383 | 346 | .903 | 1237 | 1177 | .951 |
| Dunston, Pit | 979.2 | 333 | 287 | .862 | 1002 | 887 | .885 |
| **MLB Avg** | | | | **.940** | | | **.938** |

# Who Can Turn the Pivot? (p. 181)

## Both Leagues — Listed Alphabetically
### 1997 Active Players with 15 or more DP Opp (1992-97)

| Player, Team | DP Opp | DP | Pct | Player, Team | DP Opp | DP | Pct |
|---|---|---|---|---|---|---|---|
| Abbott K, Fla | 37 | 16 | .432 | Hudler, Phi | 88 | 60 | .682 |
| Alexander, Mets-Cubs | 60 | 40 | .667 | Huson, Mil | 54 | 34 | .630 |
| Alfonzo, Mets | 45 | 24 | .533 | Ingram, LA | 20 | 12 | .600 |
| Alicea, Ana | 356 | 220 | .618 | Jefferies, Phi | 121 | 47 | .388 |
| Alomar R, Bal | 673 | 392 | .582 | Kelly P, Yanks | 301 | 183 | .608 |
| Amaral, Sea | 85 | 49 | .576 | Kent, SF | 281 | 183 | .651 |
| Arias A, Fla | 24 | 13 | .542 | King, KC | 76 | 40 | .526 |
| Baerga, Mets | 573 | 358 | .625 | Knoblauch, Min | 596 | 363 | .609 |
| Bates, Col | 64 | 43 | .672 | Lansing, Mon | 297 | 178 | .599 |
| Batista, Oak | 28 | 18 | .643 | Lemke, Atl | 452 | 263 | .582 |
| Bell D, StL | 38 | 22 | .579 | Lewis M, SF | 137 | 76 | .555 |
| Bellhorn, Oak | 15 | 9 | .600 | Liriano, LA | 232 | 120 | .517 |
| Belliard, Atl | 50 | 31 | .620 | Listach, Hou | 43 | 26 | .605 |
| Benjamin, Bos | 26 | 16 | .615 | Lockhart, Atl | 85 | 56 | .659 |
| Biggio, Hou | 501 | 265 | .529 | Lopez L, Mets | 30 | 14 | .467 |
| Boone B, Cin | 335 | 223 | .666 | Loretta, Mil | 53 | 35 | .660 |
| Bordick, Bal | 64 | 42 | .656 | Martin N, WSox | 35 | 18 | .514 |
| Bournigal, Oak | 42 | 29 | .690 | McLemore, Tex | 336 | 210 | .625 |
| Branson, Cin-Cle | 79 | 49 | .620 | Mejia, StL | 55 | 26 | .473 |
| Brito, Tor-Oak | 19 | 15 | .789 | Milliard, Fla | 16 | 10 | .625 |
| Candaele, Cle | 91 | 58 | .637 | Morandini, Phi | 440 | 251 | .570 |
| Castillo L, Fla | 63 | 40 | .635 | Naehring, Bos | 57 | 28 | .491 |
| Cedeno D, Tex | 90 | 55 | .611 | Offerman, KC | 90 | 49 | .544 |
| Cirillo, Mil | 17 | 12 | .706 | Perez N, Col | 41 | 29 | .707 |
| Cora, Sea | 420 | 255 | .607 | Perez T, Tor | 54 | 37 | .685 |
| Cordero, Bos | 28 | 13 | .464 | Phillips T, WSox-Ana | 219 | 130 | .594 |
| Counsell, Col-Fla | 30 | 19 | .633 | Randa, Pit | 20 | 7 | .350 |
| DeShields, StL | 529 | 297 | .561 | Reboulet, Bal | 44 | 25 | .568 |
| Duncan, Yanks-Tor | 277 | 155 | .560 | Reed J, Det | 593 | 377 | .636 |
| Durham, WSox | 246 | 140 | .569 | Ripken B, Tex | 325 | 213 | .655 |
| Easley, Det | 195 | 128 | .656 | Rivera L, Hou | 17 | 9 | .529 |
| Espinoza, Sea | 33 | 22 | .667 | Roberts, KC-Cle | 205 | 104 | .507 |
| Fernandez, Cle | 75 | 37 | .493 | Samuel, Tor | 229 | 100 | .437 |
| Fonville, LA-WSox | 30 | 15 | .500 | Sanchez, Cubs-Yanks | 110 | 64 | .582 |
| Fox, Yanks | 26 | 14 | .538 | Sandberg, Cubs | 526 | 291 | .553 |
| Franco J, Cle-Mil | 256 | 132 | .516 | Scarsone, StL | 84 | 55 | .655 |
| Frye, Bos | 258 | 143 | .554 | Shipley, SD | 35 | 19 | .543 |
| Gallego, StL | 218 | 134 | .615 | Shumpert, SD | 131 | 76 | .580 |
| Garcia C, Tor | 327 | 202 | .618 | Sojo, Yanks | 240 | 146 | .608 |
| Gates, Sea | 217 | 131 | .604 | Spiers, Hou | 62 | 36 | .581 |
| Gomez, SD | 38 | 24 | .632 | Spiezio, Oak | 80 | 50 | .625 |
| Gonzales, Col | 81 | 53 | .654 | Stankiewicz, Mon | 32 | 20 | .625 |
| Graffanino, Atl | 25 | 16 | .640 | Strange, Mon | 123 | 75 | .610 |
| Grebeck, Ana | 64 | 41 | .641 | Valentin J, Bos | 65 | 40 | .615 |
| Guerrero W, LA | 35 | 14 | .400 | Velarde, Ana | 122 | 70 | .574 |
| Hale, LA | 22 | 15 | .682 | Veras, SD | 186 | 104 | .559 |
| Hansen J, KC | 17 | 10 | .588 | Vina, Mil | 196 | 149 | .760 |
| Hardtke, Mets | 16 | 7 | .438 | Vizcaino, SF | 102 | 70 | .686 |
| Harris, Cin | 127 | 61 | .480 | Womack, Pit | 112 | 52 | .464 |
| Hernandez J, Cubs | 23 | 11 | .478 | Young E, Col-LA | 287 | 168 | .585 |
| Howard D, KC | 59 | 32 | .542 | MLB Avg | | | .591 |

## Which Catchers Catch Thieves? (p. 184)

The chart below lists the Stolen Bases (**SB**) while this catcher was behind the plate, the runners he caught stealing (**CCS**), that percentage (**CS%**), the runners he picked off (**CPk**), the SB allowed per 9 innings (**SB/9**), the runners caught stealing (**PCS**) and picked off (**PPk**) by his pitchers.

### Both Leagues — Listed Alphabetically
### (minimum 500 Innings Caught in 1997)

| Catcher, Team | SB | CCS | CS% | CPk | SB/9 | PCS | PPk |
|---|---|---|---|---|---|---|---|
| Alomar S, Cle | 84 | 33 | 28.2 | 0 | 0.75 | 6 | 3 |
| Ausmus, Hou | 47 | 38 | 44.7 | 1 | 0.41 | 8 | 5 |
| Casanova, Det | 72 | 20 | 21.7 | 0 | 0.89 | 8 | 1 |
| Difelice, StL | 62 | 30 | 32.6 | 1 | 0.81 | 4 | 1 |
| Fabregas, WSox | 63 | 29 | 31.5 | 0 | 0.68 | 6 | 4 |
| Flaherty, SD | 125 | 42 | 25.1 | 0 | 1.09 | 8 | 1 |
| Fletcher, Mon | 71 | 12 | 14.5 | 0 | 0.93 | 4 | 3 |
| Girardi, Yanks | 71 | 20 | 22.0 | 0 | 0.65 | 17 | 14 |
| Haselman, Bos | 63 | 20 | 24.1 | 0 | 1.07 | 2 | 3 |
| Hatteberg, Bos | 95 | 22 | 18.8 | 1 | 1.02 | 6 | 3 |
| Hoiles, Bal | 74 | 13 | 14.9 | 0 | 0.91 | 7 | 6 |
| Hundley, Mets | 79 | 21 | 21.0 | 0 | 0.71 | 4 | 5 |
| Johnson B, SF | 61 | 20 | 24.7 | 0 | 0.71 | 6 | 2 |
| Johnson C, Fla | 62 | 50 | 44.6 | 2 | 0.52 | 6 | 1 |
| Kendall, Pit | 95 | 51 | 34.9 | 3 | 0.70 | 5 | 4 |
| Kreuter, Ana | 36 | 15 | 29.4 | 2 | 0.51 | 11 | 1 |
| Lampkin, StL | 55 | 18 | 24.7 | 4 | 0.90 | 4 | 1 |
| Leyritz, Tex | 48 | 30 | 38.5 | 0 | 0.75 | 7 | 1 |
| Lieberthal, Phi | 75 | 35 | 31.8 | 1 | 0.64 | 5 | 8 |
| Lopez J, Atl | 72 | 29 | 28.7 | 2 | 0.68 | 4 | 0 |
| Macfarlane, KC | 26 | 10 | 27.8 | 0 | 0.35 | 1 | 0 |
| Manwaring, Col | 83 | 25 | 23.1 | 0 | 0.90 | 3 | 2 |
| Matheny, Mil | 69 | 34 | 33.0 | 5 | 0.67 | 3 | 1 |
| Mayne, Oak | 57 | 14 | 19.7 | 1 | 0.80 | 9 | 2 |
| O'Brien, Tor | 25 | 27 | 51.9 | 3 | 0.38 | 4 | 3 |
| Oliver, Cin | 65 | 25 | 27.8 | 3 | 0.70 | 6 | 0 |
| Piazza, LA | 112 | 34 | 23.3 | 0 | 0.84 | 9 | 4 |
| Reed J, Col | 47 | 23 | 32.9 | 0 | 0.70 | 3 | 10 |
| Rodriguez I, Tex | 37 | 40 | 51.9 | 9 | 0.28 | 7 | 0 |
| Santiago, Tor | 48 | 26 | 35.1 | 2 | 0.53 | 5 | 4 |
| Servais, Cubs | 92 | 42 | 31.3 | 2 | 0.86 | 4 | 10 |
| Steinbach, Min | 59 | 21 | 26.3 | 0 | 0.54 | 8 | 3 |
| Sweeney M, KC | 32 | 20 | 38.5 | 0 | 0.50 | 3 | 2 |
| Webster, Bal | 68 | 23 | 25.3 | 1 | 0.90 | 6 | 6 |
| Widger, Mon | 116 | 18 | 13.4 | 0 | 1.50 | 5 | 5 |
| Wilson D, Sea | 74 | 46 | 38.3 | 0 | 0.55 | 10 | 1 |
| **MLB Avg** | | | 27.6 | | 0.74 | | |

# Who's Best in the Outfield Zone? (p. 186)

## Zone Ratings — Outfielders
### (minimum 550 defensive innings in 1997)

| Player, Team | Innings | 1997 In Zone | Outs | Zone Rating | 1995-97 In Zone | Outs | Zone Rating |
|---|---|---|---|---|---|---|---|
| **LEFT FIELD** | | | | | | | |
| Giles, Cle | 647.1 | 162 | 144 | .889 | 179 | 160 | .894 |
| Gant, StL | 1084.1 | 284 | 240 | .845 | 769 | 629 | .818 |
| Surhoff, Bal | 1135.0 | 277 | 231 | .834 | 451 | 375 | .831 |
| Rodriguez H, Mon | 1010.2 | 232 | 191 | .823 | 354 | 295 | .833 |
| Cordova, Min | 863.2 | 245 | 201 | .820 | 990 | 832 | .840 |
| Higginson, Det | 809.2 | 231 | 189 | .818 | 520 | 425 | .817 |
| Roberts, Cle | 682.2 | 188 | 152 | .809 | 288 | 241 | .837 |
| Glanville, Cubs | 803.0 | 211 | 170 | .806 | 235 | 193 | .821 |
| Bonds, SF | 1372.1 | 334 | 267 | .799 | 984 | 784 | .797 |
| Belle, WSox | 1333.0 | 428 | 342 | .799 | 1135 | 930 | .819 |
| Anderson G, Ana | 1084.2 | 310 | 246 | .794 | 906 | 747 | .825 |
| Greer, Tex | 1219.1 | 341 | 270 | .792 | 758 | 630 | .831 |
| Vaughn G, SD | 758.1 | 182 | 144 | .791 | 516 | 403 | .781 |
| Gonzalez L, Hou | 1257.2 | 317 | 248 | .782 | 886 | 718 | .810 |
| Gilkey, Mets | 1179.2 | 312 | 241 | .772 | 920 | 743 | .808 |
| Justice, Cle | 622.1 | 147 | 112 | .762 | 147 | 112 | .762 |
| Cruz Jr, Tor | 858.2 | 224 | 170 | .759 | 224 | 170 | .759 |
| Klesko, Atl | 992.1 | 238 | 180 | .756 | 617 | 477 | .773 |
| Cordero, Bos | 1199.1 | 318 | 235 | .739 | 370 | 275 | .743 |
| Jefferies, Phi | 1021.2 | 279 | 206 | .738 | 507 | 392 | .773 |
| Alou, Fla | 716.0 | 159 | 117 | .736 | 326 | 253 | .776 |
| Bichette, Col | 1000.1 | 270 | 198 | .733 | 533 | 386 | .724 |
| Martin A, Pit | 929.2 | 177 | 127 | .718 | 585 | 426 | .728 |
| **MLB Avg** | | | | **.798** | | | **.807** |
| **CENTER FIELD** | | | | | | | |
| Cameron, WSox | 836.2 | 331 | 293 | .885 | 344 | 304 | .884 |
| Johnson L, Cubs | 836.1 | 266 | 229 | .861 | 1117 | 940 | .842 |
| Hunter B, Det | 1422.2 | 474 | 403 | .850 | 1016 | 855 | .842 |
| White D, Fla | 586.2 | 175 | 147 | .840 | 839 | 686 | .818 |
| Buford, Tex | 909.2 | 318 | 267 | .840 | 425 | 364 | .856 |
| Lofton, Atl | 1047.1 | 337 | 282 | .837 | 1062 | 890 | .838 |
| McRae, Mets | 1222.0 | 358 | 299 | .835 | 1156 | 966 | .836 |
| Finley, SD | 1179.0 | 395 | 329 | .833 | 1163 | 991 | .852 |
| Nixon, LA | 1263.2 | 410 | 341 | .832 | 1268 | 1026 | .809 |
| Grissom, Cle | 1250.2 | 409 | 340 | .831 | 1178 | 957 | .812 |
| Edmonds, Ana | 967.0 | 362 | 298 | .823 | 1131 | 957 | .846 |
| White R, Mon | 1339.0 | 448 | 363 | .810 | 964 | 787 | .816 |
| Goodwin T, Tex | 1228.0 | 435 | 351 | .807 | 892 | 723 | .811 |
| Griffey Jr, Sea | 1330.2 | 468 | 377 | .806 | 1154 | 935 | .810 |
| Sanders D, Cin | 654.2 | 194 | 156 | .804 | 434 | 358 | .825 |
| Williams G, Mil | 1071.2 | 358 | 286 | .799 | 482 | 393 | .815 |
| Williams B, Yanks | 1122.2 | 332 | 264 | .795 | 1225 | 1013 | .827 |
| Bragg, Bos | 945.0 | 345 | 274 | .794 | 470 | 382 | .813 |
| Allensworth, Pit | 837.2 | 232 | 184 | .793 | 393 | 318 | .809 |
| Lankford, StL | 1141.1 | 356 | 281 | .789 | 1152 | 910 | .790 |
| Mashore, Oak | 557.0 | 213 | 167 | .784 | 237 | 181 | .764 |
| Hamilton, SF | 961.2 | 297 | 232 | .781 | 1091 | 867 | .795 |
| Becker, Min | 932.0 | 360 | 280 | .778 | 1082 | 867 | .801 |
| Anderson B, Bal | 1096.0 | 347 | 267 | .769 | 855 | 677 | .792 |
| Burks, Col | 650.0 | 202 | 152 | .752 | 462 | 341 | .738 |
| McCracken, Col | 756.0 | 271 | 192 | .708 | 453 | 313 | .691 |
| **MLB Avg** | | | | **.814** | | | **.814** |

| Player, Team | Innings | 1997 In Zone | Outs | Zone Rating | 1995-97 In Zone | Outs | Zone Rating |
|---|---|---|---|---|---|---|---|
| **RIGHT FIELD** | | | | | | | |
| Javier, SF | 580.0 | 169 | 148 | .876 | 208 | 176 | .846 |
| Guerrero V, Mon | 721.0 | 164 | 141 | .860 | 172 | 148 | .860 |
| Dye, KC | 600.0 | 184 | 158 | .859 | 324 | 277 | .855 |
| Sanders R, Cin | 753.0 | 206 | 176 | .854 | 633 | 549 | .867 |
| Sosa, Cubs | 1416.2 | 364 | 310 | .852 | 994 | 858 | .863 |
| Merced, Tor | 827.0 | 220 | 187 | .850 | 729 | 607 | .833 |
| Salmon, Ana | 1372.2 | 396 | 336 | .848 | 1136 | 946 | .833 |
| Jones A, Atl | 553.2 | 166 | 140 | .843 | 216 | 184 | .852 |
| Burnitz, Mil | 989.1 | 242 | 204 | .843 | 301 | 251 | .834 |
| Ramirez, Cle | 1253.2 | 292 | 246 | .842 | 868 | 720 | .829 |
| Mondesi, LA | 1390.0 | 387 | 323 | .835 | 1066 | 870 | .816 |
| O'Leary, Bos | 967.2 | 252 | 210 | .833 | 625 | 503 | .805 |
| Nieves, Det | 752.1 | 227 | 188 | .828 | 428 | 355 | .829 |
| Buhner, Sea | 1326.0 | 349 | 287 | .822 | 872 | 694 | .796 |
| Tucker, Atl | 828.0 | 207 | 169 | .816 | 380 | 304 | .800 |
| O'Neill, Yanks | 1263.0 | 343 | 279 | .813 | 919 | 754 | .820 |
| Gwynn, SD | 1203.1 | 253 | 203 | .802 | 739 | 619 | .838 |
| Daulton, Fla | 556.2 | 167 | 133 | .796 | 167 | 133 | .796 |
| Bell D, Hou | 767.2 | 200 | 157 | .785 | 728 | 569 | .782 |
| Sheffield, Fla | 1115.1 | 284 | 222 | .782 | 697 | 553 | .793 |
| Hill, SF | 744.2 | 198 | 150 | .758 | 674 | 520 | .772 |
| Gonzalez J, Tex | 555.2 | 161 | 121 | .752 | 367 | 277 | .755 |
| Berroa, Bal | 661.1 | 180 | 135 | .750 | 406 | 312 | .768 |
| Guillen J, Pit | 1108.2 | 293 | 216 | .737 | 293 | 216 | .737 |
| Walker L, Col | 1235.1 | 303 | 220 | .726 | 641 | 476 | .743 |
| **MLB Avg** | | | | **.814** | | | **.814** |

# Which Outfielders Know How to Hold 'Em? (p. 188)

## Both Leagues—1997—Listed by Advance Percentage
### (minimum 30 baserunner opportunities to advance)

### Left Field

| Player, Team | Opp | XB | Pct |
|---|---|---|---|
| Whiten, Yanks | 33 | 4 | 12.1 |
| Curtis, Yanks | 33 | 7 | 21.2 |
| Green S, Tor | 40 | 9 | 22.5 |
| Kelly R, Sea | 30 | 7 | 23.3 |
| Lesher, Oak | 45 | 11 | 24.4 |
| Alou, Fla | 89 | 22 | 24.7 |
| Cruz Jr, Tor | 113 | 28 | 24.8 |
| Voigt, Mil | 32 | 8 | 25.0 |
| Stynes, Cin | 30 | 8 | 26.7 |
| Cordero, Bos | 143 | 39 | 27.3 |
| Greer, Tex | 121 | 34 | 28.1 |
| Gilkey, Mets | 119 | 34 | 28.6 |
| Gonzalez L, Hou | 138 | 41 | 29.7 |
| Bonds, SF | 137 | 41 | 29.9 |
| Vaughn G, SD | 96 | 29 | 30.2 |
| Hollandsworth, LA | 36 | 11 | 30.6 |
| Belle, WSox | 137 | 42 | 30.7 |
| Stairs, Oak | 35 | 11 | 31.4 |
| Surhoff, Bal | 76 | 24 | 31.6 |
| Higginson, Det | 90 | 29 | 32.2 |
| Anderson G, Ana | 124 | 40 | 32.3 |
| Giambi, Oak | 76 | 25 | 32.9 |
| Martin A, Pit | 97 | 32 | 33.0 |
| Justice, Cle | 69 | 23 | 33.3 |
| Glanville, Cubs | 92 | 31 | 33.7 |
| Klesko, Atl | 64 | 22 | 34.4 |
| Giles, Cle | 60 | 21 | 35.0 |
| Burks, Col | 31 | 11 | 35.5 |
| Bichette, Col | 111 | 40 | 36.0 |
| Cordova, Min | 111 | 40 | 36.0 |
| Amaral, Sea | 30 | 11 | 36.7 |
| Damon, KC | 38 | 14 | 36.8 |
| Jefferies, Phi | 97 | 36 | 37.1 |
| Raines, Yanks | 61 | 23 | 37.7 |
| Rodriguez H, Mon | 89 | 34 | 38.2 |
| Roberts, Cle | 91 | 35 | 38.5 |
| Ashley, LA | 31 | 12 | 38.7 |
| Henderson, Ana | 54 | 21 | 38.9 |
| Benitez, KC | 31 | 13 | 41.9 |
| Lawton, Min | 52 | 22 | 42.3 |
| Gant, StL | 99 | 45 | 45.5 |
| **MLB Avg** | | | **32.0** |

| Player, Team | Opp | XB | Pct |
|---|---|---|---|
| Martinez D, WSox | 37 | 17 | 45.9 |
| Mouton J, Hou | 40 | 19 | 47.5 |
| White D, Fla | 69 | 33 | 47.8 |
| Stewart S, Tor | 48 | 23 | 47.9 |
| Allensworth, Pit | 121 | 58 | 47.9 |
| Hunter B, Det | 174 | 84 | 48.3 |
| Johnson L, Cubs | 88 | 43 | 48.9 |
| Jackson D, Mil | 46 | 23 | 50.0 |
| Young E, Oak | 58 | 29 | 50.0 |
| Goodwin C, Cin | 34 | 17 | 50.0 |
| Buford, Tex | 137 | 70 | 51.1 |
| Jones A, Atl | 45 | 23 | 51.1 |
| Williams B, Yanks | 157 | 81 | 51.6 |
| Curtis, Yanks | 53 | 28 | 52.8 |
| Giles, Cle | 34 | 18 | 52.9 |
| Cameron, WSox | 134 | 71 | 53.0 |
| Mashore, Oak | 84 | 45 | 53.6 |
| Magee, Phi | 37 | 20 | 54.1 |
| White R, Mon | 159 | 86 | 54.1 |
| Hamilton, SF | 146 | 81 | 55.5 |
| Damon, KC | 61 | 34 | 55.7 |
| Anderson B, Bal | 126 | 71 | 56.3 |
| Lankford, StL | 108 | 61 | 56.5 |
| Williams G, Mil | 168 | 95 | 56.5 |
| Becker, Min | 125 | 71 | 56.8 |
| Bragg, Bos | 146 | 83 | 56.8 |
| Finley, SD | 183 | 105 | 57.4 |
| Alou, Fla | 54 | 31 | 57.4 |
| McDonald, Oak | 85 | 49 | 57.6 |
| Grissom, Cle | 163 | 94 | 57.7 |
| Ward, Pit | 38 | 22 | 57.9 |
| Bell D, Hou | 31 | 18 | 58.1 |
| Mack, Bos | 53 | 31 | 58.5 |
| Nunnally, Cin | 37 | 22 | 59.5 |
| Butler B, LA | 50 | 30 | 60.0 |
| Goodwin T, Tex | 181 | 110 | 60.8 |
| Cummings, Phi | 49 | 30 | 61.2 |
| Sanders D, Cin | 78 | 48 | 61.5 |
| Brown A, Pit | 34 | 21 | 61.8 |
| Cedeno R, LA | 42 | 26 | 61.9 |
| Everett, Mets | 54 | 34 | 63.0 |
| Nixon, LA | 131 | 84 | 64.1 |
| Burks, Col | 104 | 68 | 65.4 |
| Otero, Phi | 47 | 31 | 66.0 |
| McCracken, Col | 125 | 83 | 66.4 |
| McRae, Mets | 115 | 77 | 67.0 |
| **MLB Avg** | | | **54.6** |

| Player, Team | Opp | XB | Pct |
|---|---|---|---|
| Nieves, Det | 84 | 32 | 38.1 |
| Newson, Tex | 34 | 13 | 38.2 |
| Phillips T, Ana | 39 | 15 | 38.5 |
| Tarasco, Bal | 36 | 14 | 38.9 |
| Merced, Tor | 86 | 34 | 39.5 |
| Mieske, Mil | 48 | 19 | 39.6 |
| O'Neill, Yanks | 131 | 52 | 39.7 |
| Salmon, Ana | 141 | 56 | 39.7 |
| Walker L, Col | 151 | 60 | 39.7 |
| Bragg, Bos | 40 | 16 | 40.0 |
| Martinez D, WSox | 47 | 19 | 40.4 |
| Kelly R, Sea | 44 | 18 | 40.9 |
| Sosa, Cubs | 129 | 53 | 41.1 |
| Green S, Tor | 41 | 17 | 41.5 |
| Barron, Phi | 35 | 15 | 42.9 |
| Sanders R, Cin | 57 | 25 | 43.9 |
| Higginson, Det | 54 | 24 | 44.4 |
| Mondesi, LA | 109 | 49 | 45.0 |
| Javier, SF | 50 | 23 | 46.0 |
| Bell D, Hou | 65 | 30 | 46.2 |
| Jones A, Atl | 56 | 26 | 46.4 |
| Ramirez, Cle | 153 | 72 | 47.1 |
| Buhner, Sea | 127 | 60 | 47.2 |
| Guerrero V, Mon | 59 | 28 | 47.5 |
| Mabry, StL | 54 | 26 | 48.1 |
| Dye, KC | 72 | 35 | 48.6 |
| Huskey, Mets | 47 | 23 | 48.9 |
| Gwynn, SD | 120 | 59 | 49.2 |
| Mouton L, WSox | 46 | 23 | 50.0 |
| Stairs, Oak | 61 | 31 | 50.8 |
| Sheffield, Fla | 106 | 54 | 50.9 |
| Lawton, Min | 43 | 22 | 51.2 |
| Guillen J, Pit | 99 | 51 | 51.5 |
| Hill, SF | 77 | 40 | 51.9 |
| Burnitz, Mil | 74 | 39 | 52.7 |
| Berroa, Bal | 71 | 39 | 54.9 |
| Greene W, Cin | 30 | 17 | 56.7 |
| Hammonds, Bal | 35 | 20 | 57.1 |
| Tucker, Atl | 73 | 42 | 57.5 |
| Grieve, Oak | 34 | 20 | 58.8 |
| Gonzalez J, Tex | 68 | 41 | 60.3 |
| Daulton, Fla | 56 | 35 | 62.5 |
| Everett, Mets | 38 | 24 | 63.2 |
| Canseco, Oak | 36 | 23 | 63.9 |
| O'Leary, Bos | 125 | 83 | 66.4 |
| Davis E, Bal | 30 | 21 | 70.0 |
| McGee, StL | 31 | 22 | 71.0 |
| Damon, KC | 38 | 28 | 73.7 |
| **MLB Avg** | | | **48.1** |

### Center Field

| Player, Team | Opp | XB | Pct |
|---|---|---|---|
| Edmonds, Ana | 158 | 65 | 41.1 |
| Carr, Hou | 64 | 27 | 42.2 |
| Lofton, Atl | 105 | 45 | 42.9 |
| Griffey Jr, Sea | 170 | 76 | 44.7 |
| Lewis D, LA | 33 | 15 | 45.5 |

### Right Field

| Player, Team | Opp | XB | Pct |
|---|---|---|---|
| Abreu, Hou | 37 | 11 | 29.7 |
| Ochoa, Mets | 47 | 16 | 34.0 |

## Which Fielders Have the Best "Defensive Batting Average"? (p. 191)

Each chart summarizes, by position, the STATS Defensive Batting Average: a player's zone rating (**ZR**), his fielding percentage (**FP**), his pivot rating (**PR**) if he was a second baseman, and, if he was an outfielder, his outfield arm rating (**OA**). A weighting system (see article on page 224) was used to determine a player's all-around fielding rating (**DBA**). The ML average in each category is .275.

### Both Leagues — Sorted by Defensive Batting Average
### (minimum 550 defensive innings in 1997)

| First Base | ZR | FP | PR | OA | DBA |
|---|---|---|---|---|---|
| King, KC | .334 | .308 | — | — | .328 |
| Young K, Pit | .323 | .314 | — | — | .321 |
| Clark T, Det | .313 | .283 | — | — | .306 |
| Conine, Fla | .310 | .271 | — | — | .301 |
| Joyner, SD | .291 | .309 | — | — | .295 |
| Young D, StL | .323 | .207 | — | — | .294 |
| Grace, Cubs | .291 | .301 | — | — | .293 |
| Olerud, Mets | .289 | .297 | — | — | .291 |
| Palmeiro R, Bal | .294 | .279 | — | — | .290 |
| Stahoviak, Min | .294 | .249 | — | — | .283 |
| Bagwell, Hou | .283 | .278 | — | — | .282 |
| Karros, LA | .283 | .274 | — | — | .281 |
| Brogna, Phi | .270 | .288 | — | — | .274 |
| Martinez T, Yanks | .269 | .291 | — | — | .274 |
| Sorrento, Sea | .263 | .306 | — | — | .274 |
| Clark W, Tex | .260 | .303 | — | — | .271 |
| Thome, Cle | .267 | .275 | — | — | .269 |
| Snow, SF | .256 | .297 | — | — | .266 |
| Galarraga, Col | .267 | .258 | — | — | .265 |
| Delgado C, Tor | .273 | .239 | — | — | .264 |
| Nilsson, Mil | .265 | .260 | — | — | .264 |
| Segui, Mon | .250 | .294 | — | — | .261 |
| McGwire, StL | .240 | .297 | — | — | .255 |
| Morris, Cin | .244 | .256 | — | — | .247 |
| McGriff, Atl | .245 | .253 | — | — | .247 |
| Erstad, Ana | .246 | .251 | — | — | .247 |
| Thomas, WSox | .247 | .220 | — | — | .240 |
| Vaughn M, Bos | .200 | .236 | — | — | .209 |
| **Second Base** | **ZR** | **FP** | **PR** | **OA** | **DBA** |
| Lansing, Mon | .310 | .300 | .284 | — | .302 |
| Boone B, Cin | .284 | .346 | .316 | — | .301 |
| Sandberg, Cubs | .320 | .287 | .235 | — | .294 |
| Spiezio, Oak | .290 | .315 | .290 | — | .294 |
| Castillo L, Fla | .308 | .226 | .297 | — | .293 |
| Kent, SF | .300 | .263 | .289 | — | .292 |
| Morandini, Phi | .290 | .316 | .278 | — | .291 |
| Lemke, Atl | .291 | .269 | .298 | — | .289 |
| McLemore, Tex | .296 | .270 | .281 | — | .288 |
| Vina, Mil | .268 | .275 | .343 | — | .288 |
| Young E, LA | .304 | .259 | .264 | — | .287 |
| Biggio, Hou | .298 | .263 | .264 | — | .284 |
| Knoblauch, Min | .285 | .289 | .278 | — | .284 |

| Second Base | ZR | FP | PR | OA | DBA |
|---|---|---|---|---|---|
| Frye, Bos | .276 | .318 | .281 | — | .283 |
| Offerman, KC | .301 | .270 | .248 | — | .283 |
| DeShields, StL | .285 | .231 | .293 | — | .279 |
| Fernandez, Cle | .277 | .270 | .250 | — | .269 |
| Veras, SD | .283 | .287 | .223 | — | .269 |
| Alicea, Ana | .278 | .257 | .253 | — | .268 |
| Alomar R, Bal | .265 | .306 | .248 | — | .267 |
| Baerga, Mets | .252 | .257 | .299 | — | .264 |
| Guerrero W, LA | .271 | .310 | .209 | — | .261 |
| Duncan, Tor | .246 | .269 | .286 | — | .259 |
| Valentin J, Bos | .245 | .246 | .286 | — | .256 |
| Garcia C, Tor | .240 | .273 | .263 | — | .251 |
| Durham, WSox | .237 | .237 | .281 | — | .248 |
| Easley, Det | .201 | .272 | .317 | — | .240 |
| Womack, Pit | .238 | .241 | .235 | — | .238 |
| Cora, Sea | .214 | .234 | .260 | — | .228 |
| **Third Base** | **ZR** | **FP** | **PR** | **OA** | **DBA** |
| Brosius, Oak | .328 | .317 | — | — | .324 |
| Cirillo, Mil | .333 | .294 | — | — | .317 |
| Gaetti, StL | .314 | .319 | — | — | .316 |
| Alfonzo, Mets | .325 | .300 | — | — | .315 |
| Fryman, Det | .304 | .318 | — | — | .309 |
| Boggs, Yanks | .287 | .319 | — | — | .300 |
| Williams M, Cle | .295 | .305 | — | — | .299 |
| Orie, Cubs | .289 | .307 | — | — | .296 |
| Rolen, Phi | .302 | .269 | — | — | .289 |
| Coomer, Min | .280 | .299 | — | — | .287 |
| Mueller, SF | .289 | .282 | — | — | .286 |
| Jones C, Atl | .288 | .281 | — | — | .285 |
| Naehring, Bos | .260 | .322 | — | — | .285 |
| Hayes, Yanks | .286 | .269 | — | — | .279 |
| Valentin J, Bos | .287 | .262 | — | — | .277 |
| Castilla, Col | .274 | .279 | — | — | .276 |
| Strange, Mon | .277 | .269 | — | — | .274 |
| Ripken C, Bal | .274 | .272 | — | — | .273 |
| Caminiti, SD | .269 | .258 | — | — | .265 |
| Randa, Pit | .268 | .253 | — | — | .262 |
| Zeile, LA | .267 | .243 | — | — | .257 |
| Davis R, Sea | .259 | .254 | — | — | .257 |
| Palmer, KC | .247 | .270 | — | — | .256 |
| Sprague, Tor | .249 | .265 | — | — | .255 |
| Paquette, KC | .250 | .249 | — | — | .250 |

| Third Base | ZR | FP | PR | OA | DBA |
|---|---|---|---|---|---|
| Bonilla, Fla | .234 | .253 | — | — | .241 |
| Berry, Hou | .248 | .226 | — | — | .239 |
| Snopek, WSox | .244 | .218 | — | — | .233 |
| Greene W, Cin | .221 | .247 | — | — | .232 |
| Hollins, Ana | .232 | .228 | — | — | .230 |
| **Shortstop** | ZR | FP | PR | OA | DBA |
| Vizquel, Cle | .305 | .314 | — | — | .307 |
| Bogar, Hou | .306 | .310 | — | — | .307 |
| DiSarcina, Ana | .312 | .284 | — | — | .306 |
| Ordonez R, Mets | .303 | .306 | — | — | .303 |
| Clayton, StL | .311 | .267 | — | — | .302 |
| Reese, Cin | .312 | .243 | — | — | .299 |
| Gonzalez A, Tor | .287 | .315 | — | — | .293 |
| Renteria, Fla | .297 | .275 | — | — | .293 |
| Cruz D, Det | .292 | .291 | — | — | .292 |
| Bordick, Bal | .287 | .295 | — | — | .289 |
| Bell J, KC | .271 | .313 | — | — | .279 |
| Weiss, Col | .272 | .303 | — | — | .278 |
| Gil, Tex | .288 | .229 | — | — | .276 |
| Garciaparra, Bos | .275 | .260 | — | — | .272 |
| Vizcaino, SF | .267 | .279 | — | — | .269 |
| Rodriguez A, Sea | .278 | .226 | — | — | .267 |
| Stocker, Phi | .257 | .297 | — | — | .265 |
| Valentin J, Mil | .266 | .247 | — | — | .262 |
| Gomez, SD | .251 | .285 | — | — | .258 |
| Polcovich, Pit | .258 | .250 | — | — | .257 |
| Jeter, Yanks | .250 | .275 | — | — | .255 |
| Meares, Min | .255 | .253 | — | — | .255 |
| Guillen O, WSox | .251 | .270 | — | — | .255 |
| Blauser, Atl | .250 | .268 | — | — | .254 |
| Grudzielan., Mon | .260 | .202 | — | — | .248 |
| Gagne, LA | .241 | .260 | — | — | .245 |
| Dunston, Pit | .207 | .254 | — | — | .217 |
| **Left Field** | ZR | FP | PR | OA | DBA |
| Giles, Cle | .346 | .275 | — | .260 | .318 |
| Surhoff, Bal | .307 | .309 | — | .292 | .304 |
| Cordova, Min | .297 | .306 | — | .250 | .289 |
| Rodriguez H, Mon | .299 | .288 | — | .243 | .287 |
| Higginson, Det | .296 | .250 | — | .281 | .286 |
| Vaughn G, SD | .277 | .314 | — | .288 | .285 |
| Bonds, SF | .283 | .283 | — | .292 | .285 |
| Gant, StL | .315 | .263 | — | .199 | .284 |
| Glanville, Cubs | .287 | .287 | — | .266 | .283 |
| Anderson G, Ana | .279 | .300 | — | .272 | .280 |
| Belle, WSox | .282 | .249 | — | .290 | .279 |
| Roberts, Cle | .289 | .277 | — | .239 | .277 |
| Gonzalez L, Hou | .271 | .278 | — | .291 | .276 |
| Greer, Tex | .277 | .222 | — | .306 | .275 |
| Gilkey, Mets | .264 | .299 | — | .291 | .275 |
| Cruz Jr, Tor | .254 | .251 | — | .325 | .268 |
| Cordero, Bos | .240 | .309 | — | .311 | .265 |
| Justice, Cle | .256 | .282 | — | .273 | .264 |
| Alou, Fla | .238 | .262 | — | .328 | .260 |
| Klesko, Atl | .252 | .238 | — | .269 | .254 |
| Bichette, Col | .236 | .304 | — | .257 | .251 |

| Left Field | ZR | FP | PR | OA | DBA |
|---|---|---|---|---|---|
| Jefferies, Phi | .240 | .291 | — | .246 | .249 |
| Martin A, Pit | .225 | .203 | — | .274 | .232 |
| **Center Field** | ZR | FP | PR | OA | DBA |
| Cameron, WSox | .334 | .266 | — | .275 | .306 |
| Hunter B, Det | .307 | .295 | — | .298 | .302 |
| Lofton, Atl | .296 | .264 | — | .321 | .299 |
| White D, Fla | .298 | .281 | — | .299 | .296 |
| Buford, Tex | .298 | .292 | — | .288 | .294 |
| Johnson L, Cubs | .315 | .211 | — | .296 | .294 |
| Edmonds, Ana | .285 | .270 | — | .319 | .293 |
| Griffey Jr, Sea | .271 | .272 | — | .312 | .284 |
| Grissom, Cle | .291 | .301 | — | .259 | .283 |
| Finley, SD | .293 | .287 | — | .257 | .281 |
| White R, Mon | .275 | .303 | — | .278 | .280 |
| Nixon, LA | .292 | .312 | — | .238 | .279 |
| Williams B, Yanks | .263 | .305 | — | .288 | .277 |
| Williams G, Mil | .266 | .295 | — | .270 | .271 |
| McRae, Mets | .295 | .282 | — | .222 | .271 |
| Allensworth, Pit | .261 | .249 | — | .299 | .271 |
| Goodwin T, Tex | .272 | .302 | — | .250 | .270 |
| Bragg, Bos | .262 | .308 | — | .265 | .270 |
| Mashore, Oak | .254 | .290 | — | .274 | .265 |
| Sanders D, Cin | .270 | .262 | — | .247 | .262 |
| Anderson B, Bal | .242 | .290 | — | .266 | .256 |
| Hamilton, SF | .251 | .250 | — | .268 | .256 |
| Becker, Min | .249 | .263 | — | .266 | .256 |
| Lankford, StL | .258 | .209 | — | .268 | .254 |
| Burks, Col | .229 | .282 | — | .237 | .239 |
| McCracken, Col | .194 | .251 | — | .221 | .210 |
| **Right Field** | ZR | FP | PR | OA | DBA |
| Merced, Tor | .300 | .293 | — | .303 | .300 |
| Javier, SF | .319 | .284 | — | .276 | .299 |
| Salmon, Ana | .299 | .263 | — | .309 | .297 |
| Sanders R, Cin | .303 | .270 | — | .297 | .296 |
| Sosa, Cubs | .301 | .276 | — | .294 | .295 |
| Nieves, Det | .284 | .281 | — | .314 | .294 |
| Mondesi, LA | .289 | .300 | — | .289 | .291 |
| O'Neill, Yanks | .274 | .289 | — | .312 | .289 |
| Dye, KC | .307 | .253 | — | .279 | .289 |
| Ramirez, Cle | .295 | .271 | — | .279 | .285 |
| Buhner, Sea | .280 | .316 | — | .278 | .285 |
| Jones A, Atl | .295 | .259 | — | .276 | .283 |
| Guerrero V, Mon | .307 | .176 | — | .276 | .277 |
| Burnitz, Mil | .295 | .258 | — | .251 | .274 |
| Gwynn, SD | .266 | .287 | — | .267 | .269 |
| Tucker, Atl | .276 | .279 | — | .241 | .264 |
| Bell D, Hou | .253 | .250 | — | .276 | .261 |
| O'Leary, Bos | .288 | .288 | — | .204 | .259 |
| Sheffield, Fla | .250 | .282 | — | .256 | .257 |
| Walker L, Col | .210 | .306 | — | .303 | .257 |
| Daulton, Fla | .261 | .279 | — | .217 | .248 |
| Berroa, Bal | .227 | .267 | — | .251 | .242 |
| Hill, SF | .233 | .214 | — | .252 | .237 |
| Gonzalez J, Tex | .228 | .263 | — | .236 | .236 |
| Guillen J, Pit | .218 | .247 | — | .253 | .234 |

# Which First Basemen Are the Best at Starting Double Plays? (p. 196)

## Double Plays Started by First Basemen—1995-97
## (minimum 8 opportunities)

| Player | DP | Opp | Pct | Player | DP | Opp | Pct |
|---|---|---|---|---|---|---|---|
| Jeff Bagwell | 13 | 45 | .289 | Tino Martinez | 24 | 54 | .444 |
| Rico Brogna | 11 | 31 | .355 | Don Mattingly | 8 | 13 | .615 |
| Mark Carreon | 1 | 14 | .071 | Fred McGriff | 6 | 24 | .250 |
| Archi Cianfrocco | 2 | 9 | .222 | Mark McGwire | 9 | 32 | .281 |
| Tony Clark | 12 | 33 | .364 | Hal Morris | 11 | 36 | .306 |
| Will Clark | 6 | 35 | .171 | Dave Nilsson | 2 | 11 | .182 |
| Greg Colbrunn | 14 | 36 | .389 | Jose Offerman | 5 | 9 | .556 |
| Jeff Conine | 11 | 20 | .550 | John Olerud | 19 | 54 | .352 |
| Carlos Delgado | 9 | 15 | .600 | Rafael Palmeiro | 17 | 47 | .362 |
| Darin Erstad | 3 | 14 | .214 | Roberto Petagine | 2 | 8 | .250 |
| Cecil Fielder | 2 | 16 | .125 | J.R. Phillips | 5 | 8 | .625 |
| Julio Franco | 6 | 17 | .353 | David Segui | 14 | 19 | .737 |
| Andres Galarraga | 30 | 60 | .500 | Kevin Seitzer | 4 | 13 | .308 |
| Jason Giambi | 5 | 13 | .385 | J.T. Snow | 18 | 51 | .353 |
| Mark Grace | 8 | 51 | .157 | Paul Sorrento | 10 | 37 | .270 |
| Bob Hamelin | 3 | 8 | .375 | Scott Stahoviak | 7 | 26 | .269 |
| Butch Huskey | 5 | 12 | .417 | Lee Stevens | 5 | 12 | .417 |
| John Jaha | 12 | 25 | .480 | Frank Thomas | 3 | 9 | .333 |
| Gregg Jefferies | 5 | 10 | .500 | Jim Thome | 9 | 13 | .692 |
| Mark Johnson | 5 | 17 | .294 | Mo Vaughn | 21 | 42 | .500 |
| Wally Joyner | 22 | 42 | .524 | Eddie Williams | 6 | 8 | .750 |
| Eric Karros | 19 | 53 | .358 | Dmitri Young | 5 | 10 | .500 |
| Jeff King | 23 | 43 | .535 | Kevin Young | 3 | 13 | .231 |
| John Mabry | 4 | 29 | .138 | **MLB Totals** | **519** | **1431** | **.363** |
| Dave Martinez | 1 | 8 | .125 | | | | |

# Glossary

### Batting Average

Hits divided by At-Bats.

### Bequeathed Runners

Any runner on base when a pitcher leaves a game is considered "bequeathed" by the departing hurler; the opposite of "inherited" (see below).

### Brock2/Brock6

A complex set of several hundred interlocking formulas devised by Bill James, designed to project a player's final career totals on the basis of his age and past performance. The method was first introduced as Brock2; the most recent version is called Brock6.

### Defensive Batting Average

A composite statistic incorporating various defensive statistics to arrive at a number akin to batting average. Zone rating and fielding percentage are the primary determinants.

### Earned Run Average

Earned Runs times nine, divided by Innings Pitched.

### Expected Winning Percentage

The offensive winning percentage (see below) compiled by the batters facing a particular pitcher. This estimates what the pitcher's actual winning percentage should be, given average run support.

### Favorite Toy

The Favorite Toy is a method that is used to estimate a player's chance of achieving a specific goal—in the following example, we'll say 3,000 hits.

Four things are considered:

1) Need Hits—the number of hits needed to reach the goal. (This, of course, could also be "Need Home Runs" or "Need Doubles"—Whatever.)

2) Years Remaining. The number of years remaining to meet the goal is estimated by the formula (42-age)/2. This formula assigns a 20-year-old player 11.0 remaining seasons, a 25-year-old player 8.5 remaining seasons, a 30-year-old player 6.0 remaining seasons, and a 35-year-old player 3.5 remaining seasons. Any player who is still playing regularly is assumed to have at least 1.5 seasons remaining, regardless of his age.

3) Established Hit Level. For 1998, the established hit level would be found by adding 1995 hits, two times 1996 hits, and three times 1997 hits, and dividing by six. However, a player cannot have an established performance level that is less than three-fourths of his most recent performance—that is, a player who had 200 hits in 1997 cannot have an established hit level below 150.

4) Projected Remaining Hits. This is found by multiplying the second number (years remaining) by the third (established hit level).

Once you get the projected remaining hits, the chance of getting to the goal is figured by (projected remaining hits) divided by (need hits), minus .5. By this method, if your "need hits" and your "projected remaining hits" are the same, your chance of reaching the goal is 50 percent. If your projected remaining hits are 20 percent more than your need hits, the chance of reaching the goal is 70 percent.

Three special rules, and a note:

1) A player's chance of continuing to progress toward a goal cannot exceed .97 per year. (This rule prevents a player from figuring to have a 148 percent chance of reaching a goal.)

2) If a player's offensive winning percentage is below .500, his chance of continuing to progress toward the goal cannot exceed .75 per season. (That is, if a below-average hitter is two years away from reaching a goal, his chance of reaching that goal cannot be shown as better than nine-sixteenths, or three-fourths times three-fourths, regardless of his age.)

3) If a player's offensive winning percentage is greater than .500 and he's within four seasons of a goal, his chance of continuing to progress toward the goal cannot be less than .70 per season.

4) For 1995, we used projected stats based on a full season of play.

## Fielding Percentage

(Putouts plus Assists) divided by (Putouts plus Assists plus Errors).

## Game Score

A tool designed by Bill James to quantify how well a starting pitcher performed in a single game. To calculate, start with 50. Add one point for each out recorded, two points for each inning completed after the fourth and one point for each strikeout. Subtract one point for each walk, two points for each hit, four points for each run and two points for each unearned run. A score of 50 is about average; anything above 90 is outstanding.

## Go-Ahead RBI

Any time a player drives in a run which gives his team the lead, he is credited with a go-ahead RBI.

## Go-Ahead RBI Opportunities

The total of a player's Go-Ahead RBI and the number of times he made an out with the go-ahead run in scoring position.

## Ground/Fly Ratio (Grd/Fly)

A hitter's ground balls divided by his fly balls. All batted balls except line drives and bunts are included.

## Hold

A Hold is credited any time a relief pitcher enters a game in a Save Situation (see definition below), records at least one out and leaves the game never having relinquished the lead. Note: a pitcher cannot finish the game and receive credit for a hold, nor can he earn a hold and a save in the same game.

## Inherited Runner

Any runner on base when a relief pitcher enters a game is considered "inherited" by that pitcher.

## Isolated Power

Slugging Percentage minus Batting Average.

## K/BB Ratio

Strikeouts divided by Walks.

## No Decision (ND)

The result when a starter is credited with neither a win nor a loss.

## Offensive Winning Percentage (OWP)

Jeff Bagwell's offensive winning percentage equals the percentage of games a team would win with nine Jeff Bagwells in the lineup (given average pitching and defense). The formula: (Runs Created per 27 outs) divided by the League average of runs scored per game. Square the result and divide it by (1+itself).

## On-Base Percentage

(Hits plus Walks plus Hit by Pitcher) divided by (At-Bats plus Walks plus Hit by Pitcher plus Sacrifice Flies).

## OPS

On-Base Percentage plus Slugging Percentage.

## Outfield Advance Percentage

A statistic used to evaluate outfielders' throwing arms. "Advance Percentage" is computed by dividing extra bases taken by baserunners by the number of opportunities. For example, if a single is lined to center field with men on first and second, and one man scores while the other stops at second, that is one extra base taken on two opportunities, a 50.0 advance percentage.

## Park Index

A method of measuring the extent to which a given ballpark influences a given statistic, such as home runs. A park index for home runs is derived by dividing the team's home runs per game plus home runs allowed per home game by the team's (home runs plus home runs allowed per road game and multiplying by 100. An index of 100 means the park is completely neutral. A park index of 118 for home runs means that games played in the park feature 18 percent more home runs than the average park.

## Pivot Percentage

The number of double plays turned by a second baseman as the pivot man, divided by the number of opportunities. An "opportunity" is any situation where the double play is in order, the ball is hit to an infielder and the second baseman takes the throw.

## Plate Appearances

At-Bats plus Walks plus Hit By Pitcher plus Sacrifice Hits plus Sacrifice Flies plus Times Reached on Defensive Interference.

## Pickoffs (Pk)

The number of times a runner was picked off base by a pitcher.

## Predicted ERA

Opponent on-base percentage multiplied by opponent slugging average multiplied by 31.

## Quality Start

Any start in which a pitcher works six or more innings while allowing three or fewer earned runs.

## Quick Hooks and Slow Hooks

A Quick Hook is the removal of a pitcher who has pitched less than six innings and given up three or fewer runs. A Slow Hook goes to a pitcher who pitches more than nine innings, or allows seven or more runs, or whose combined innings and runs total 13 or more.

## RBI Opportunities

The number of RBI a hitter would have accumulated if he had hit a home run every time up, given the total number of men that were on base when he batted. No RBI opportunities are charged if the batter reaches base via a base on balls, hit by pitch or catcher's interference.

## Relative Batting Average

Batting average divided by league batting average.

## Relative OPS

OPS divided by league OPS.

## Relief Conversion Percentage

(Saves plus Holds) divided by (Saves plus Blown Saves plus Holds).

## Run Support Per 9 IP

The number of runs scored by a pitcher's team while he was still in the game times nine divided by his Innings Pitched.

## Runs Created

A way to combine a batter's total offensive contributions into one number. The formula: (H + BB + HBP - CS - GIDP) times (TB + .26(TBB - IBB + HBP) + .52(SH + SF + SB)) divided by (AB + TBB + HBP + SH + SF).

## Runs Prevented

A linear-weights system that attempts to measure how many runs a reliever prevents, given the opposition's scoring potential both when the reliever enters and exits the game. The scoring potential depends on the number of outs, the number of men on base and the bases they occupy, if any.

## Save Percentage

Saves divided by Save Opportunities.

## Save Situation

A Relief Pitcher is in a Save Situation when:

upon entering the game with his club leading, he's not the pitcher of record and meets any one of the three following conditions:

(1) he has a lead of no more than three runs and has the opportunity to pitch for at least one inning; or

(2) he enters the game, regardless of the count, with the potential tying run either on base, at bat, or on deck; or

(3) he pitches three or more innings regardless of the lead and the official scorer credits him with a save.

## SBA

Stolen-base attempts against a catcher.

## Secondary Average

A way to look at a player's extra bases gained, independent of Batting Average. The formula: (TB - H + TBB + SB - CS) divided by AB.

## Similarity Score

A method of measuring the degree of similarity of two statistical lines (the stats may be team stats or player stats). Two identical stat lines would generate a score of 1,000.

## Slugging Percentage

Total Bases divided by At-Bats.

## Zone Rating

The percentage of balls fielded by a player in his typical defensive "zone," as measured by STATS reporters, along with outs recorded on balls hit outside the zone. Players receive additional credit (outs) for starting a double play.

# About STATS, Inc.

STATS, Inc. is the nation's leading independent sports information and statistical analysis company, providing detailed sports services for a wide array of commercial clients.

As one of the fastest-growing sports companies—in 1994, we ranked 144th on the "Inc. 500" list of fastest-growing privately held firms—STATS provides the most up-to-the-minute sports information to professional teams, print and broadcast media, software developers and interactive service providers around the country. Some of our major clients are ESPN, the Associated Press, Fox Sports, Electronic Arts, MSNBC, SONY and Topps. Much of the information we provide is available to the public via STATS On-Line. With a computer and a modem, you can follow action in the four major professional sports, as well as NCAA football and basketball. . . as it happens!

STATS Publishing, a division of STATS, Inc., produces 12 annual books, including the *Major League Handbook*, *The Scouting Notebook*, the *Pro Football Handbook*, the *Pro Basketball Handbook* and the *Hockey Handbook* as well as the *STATS Fantasy Insider* magazine. These publications deliver STATS' expertise to fans, scouts, general managers and media around the country.

In addition, STATS offers the most innovative—and fun—fantasy sports games and support products around, from *Bill James Fantasy Baseball* and *Bill James Classic Baseball* to *STATS Fantasy Football* and *STATS Fantasy Hoops*. Check out the latest STATS and Bill James fantasy game, *Stock Market Baseball* and our immensely popular Fantasy Portfolios.

Information technology has grown by leaps and bounds in the last decade, and STATS will continue to be at the forefront as a supplier of the most up-to-date, in-depth sports information available. For those of you on the information superhighway, you can always catch STATS in our area on America Online or at our Internet site.

For more information on our products, or on joining our reporter network, contact us on:

**America On-Line** — (Keyword: STATS)

**Internet** — www.stats.com

**Toll Free in the USA** at 1-800-63-STATS (1-800-637-8287)

**Outside the USA** at 1-847-676-3383

**Or write** to:

**STATS, Inc.**
**8131 Monticello Ave.**
**Skokie, IL 60076-3300**

# Index

# Track YOUR Fantasy Team

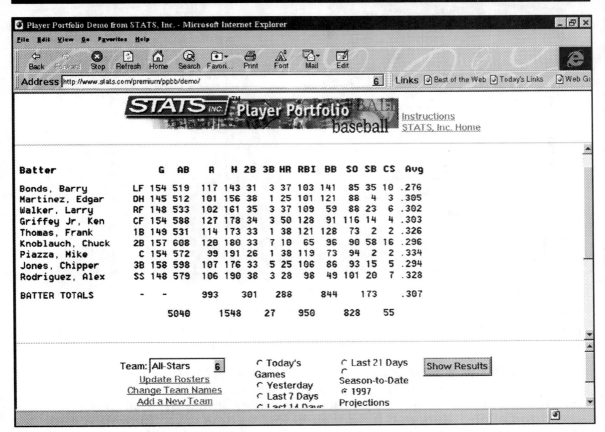

**Player Portfolio Demo from STATS, Inc. - Microsoft Internet Explorer**

File  Edit  View  Go  Favorites  Help

Back  Forward  Stop  Refresh  Home  Search  Favori...  Print  Font  Mail  Edit

Address http://www.stats.com/premium/ppbb/demo/

Links  Best of the Web  Today's Links  Web G

**STATS INC. Player Portfolio baseball**

Instructions
STATS, Inc. Home

| Batter | | G | AB | R | H | 2B | 3B | HR | RBI | BB | SO | SB | CS | Avg |
|--------|----|-----|-----|-----|-----|----|----|----|-----|-----|-----|----|----|------|
| Bonds, Barry | LF | 154 | 519 | 117 | 143 | 31 | 3 | 37 | 103 | 141 | 85 | 35 | 10 | .276 |
| Martinez, Edgar | DH | 145 | 512 | 101 | 156 | 38 | 1 | 25 | 101 | 121 | 88 | 4 | 3 | .305 |
| Walker, Larry | RF | 148 | 533 | 102 | 161 | 35 | 3 | 37 | 109 | 59 | 88 | 23 | 6 | .302 |
| Griffey Jr, Ken | CF | 154 | 588 | 127 | 178 | 34 | 3 | 50 | 128 | 91 | 116 | 14 | 4 | .303 |
| Thomas, Frank | 1B | 149 | 531 | 114 | 173 | 33 | 1 | 38 | 121 | 128 | 73 | 2 | 2 | .326 |
| Knoblauch, Chuck | 2B | 157 | 608 | 120 | 180 | 33 | 7 | 10 | 65 | 96 | 90 | 58 | 16 | .296 |
| Piazza, Mike | C | 154 | 572 | 99 | 191 | 26 | 1 | 38 | 119 | 73 | 94 | 2 | 2 | .334 |
| Jones, Chipper | 3B | 158 | 598 | 107 | 176 | 33 | 5 | 25 | 106 | 86 | 93 | 15 | 5 | .294 |
| Rodriguez, Alex | SS | 148 | 579 | 106 | 190 | 38 | 3 | 28 | 98 | 49 | 101 | 20 | 7 | .328 |
| BATTER TOTALS | - | - | | 993 | | 301 | | 288 | | 844 | | 173 | | .307 |
| | | | 5040 | | 1548 | | 27 | | 950 | | 828 | | 55 | |

Team: All-Stars
Update Rosters
Change Team Names
Add a New Team

○ Today's Games
○ Yesterday
○ Last 7 Days
○ Last 14 Days

○ Last 21 Days
○
Season-to-Date
◉ 1997
Projections

[Show Results]

# Every Play. Every Game. Every Day.

Manage your fantasy player's statistics with **STATS Player Portfolio for Baseball**

- Interactive & fully customizable fantasy roster-tracking software

- Player & team stats — search today, yesterday, this week, last week, season-to-date...

- Real-time results. Log-in to in-progress games...*see how your ace pitcher is doing after 5 innings*

- In-depth info keeps you totally informed! (Upcoming schedules, injury reports, player projections and more)

**STATS makes your fantasy life easy. Track all your players with no fuss.**

# at **www.stats.com**

**STATS INC.**

# 10th ANNIVERSARY EDITION!

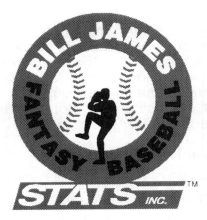

Bill James Fantasy Baseball enters its 10th season of offering baseball fans the most unique, realistic and exciting game that fantasy sports has to offer.

As team owner and GM, you draft a 26-player roster and can expand to as many as 28. Players aren't ranked like in rotisserie leagues— you'll get credit for everything a player does, like hitting homers, driving in runs, turning double plays, pitching quality outings and much more!

The team which scores the most points among all leagues, and wins the World Series, will receive the John McGraw Award, which includes a one-week trip to the Grapefruit League in spring training, a day at the ballpark with Bill James and a new fantasy league named in his/her honor!

## *Unique Features Include:*

Playable on the web @ www.stats.com

- **Live fantasy experts** — available seven days a week

- **The best weekly reports in the business** — detailing who is in the lead, win-loss records, MVPs, and team strengths and weaknesses

- **On-Line computer system** — a world of information, including daily updates of fantasy standings and stats

- **Over twice as many statistics as rotisserie**

- **Transactions that are effective the very next day!**

"My goal was to develop a fantasy league based on the simplest yet most realistic principles possible. A league in which the values are as nearly as possible what they ought to be, without being distorted by artificial category values or rankings...."

*- Bill James*

## Order from STATS INC. Today!

*Use Order Form in This Book, or Call 1-800-63-STATS or 847-676-3383 or visit www.stats.com*

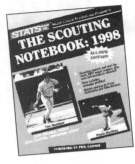

# ROUNDING OUT THE STARTING LINEUP...

## STATS Pro Football Handbook 1998

- A complete season-by-season register for every active NFL player
- Numerous statistical breakdowns for hundreds of NFL players
- Leader boards in a number of innovative and traditional categories
- Exclusive evaluations of offensive linemen
- Foreword by Mike Ditka
- **Item #FH98, $19.95, Available NOW!** *Comb-bound Available.*

## STATS Pro Football Revealed 1998
### The 100-Yard War

- Profiles each team, complete with essays, charts and play diagrams
- Detailed statistical breakdowns on players, teams and coaches
- Essays about NFL trends and happenings by leading experts
- Same data as seen on ESPN's *Sunday Night Football* broadcasts
- **Item #PF98, $19.95, Available 7/1/98**

## STATS Pro Basketball Handbook 1997-98

- Career stats for every player who logged minutes during 1996-97
- Team game logs with points, rebounds, assists and much more
- Leader boards from points per game to triple doubles
- Essays cover the hottest topics facing the NBA. Foreword by Bill Walton
- **Item #BH98, $19.95, Available Now!** *BH99 Available 9/1/98.*

## STATS Hockey Handbook 1997-98

- Complete career register for every 1996-97 NHL player and goalie
- Exclusive breakdowns identify player strengths and weaknesses
- Specific coverage for each team, plus league profiles
- Standard and exclusive leader boards
- **Item #HH98, $19.95, Available Now!** *HH99 Available 8/15/98.*

# Order from STATS INC.™ Today!

*Use Order Form in This Book, or Call 1-800-63-STATS or 847-676-3383 or visit www.stats.com*

# Get Into STATS Fantasy Hoops!

Soar into next season with STATS Fantasy Hoops! SFH lets YOU make the calls. Don't just sit back and watch Grant Hill, Shawn Kemp and Michael Jordan—get in the game and coach your team to the top!

## How to Play SFH:
1. Sign up to coach a team
2. You'll receive a full set of rules and a draft form with SFH point values for all eligible players—anyone who played in the NBA last year, plus all NBA draft picks
3. Complete the draft form and return it to STATS
4. You will take part in the draft with nine other owners, and we will send you league rosters
5. You make unlimited weekly transactions including trades, free-agent signings, activations and benchings
6. Six of the 10 teams in your league advance to postseason play, with two teams ultimately advancing to the Finals

SFH point values are based on actual NBA results, mirroring the real thing. Weekly reports will tell you everything you need to know to lead your team to the SFH Championship!

# *PLAY STATS Fantasy Football!*

STATS Fantasy Football puts YOU in charge! You draft, trade, cut, bench, activate players and even sign free agents each week. SFF pits you head-to-head against 11 other owners.

STATS' scoring system applies realistic values, tested against actual NFL results. Each week, you'll receive a superb in-depth report telling you all about both team and league performances.

## How to Play SFF:
1. Sign up today!
2. STATS sends you a draft form listing all eligible NFL players
3. Fill out the draft form and return it to STATS, and you will take part in the draft along with 11 other team owners
4. Go head-to-head against the other owners in your league. You'll make week-by-week roster moves and transactions through STATS' Fantasy Football experts, via phone, fax or on-line!

## *STATS Fantasy Football on the Web? Check it out! www.stats.com*

# Order from STATS INC. Today!

*Use Order Form in This Book, or Call 1-800-63-STATS or 847-676-3383 or visit www.stats.com*

# STATS, Inc. Order Form

Name_____

Address_____

City_____ State_____ Zip_____

Phone_____Fax_____E-mail Address_____

## Method of Payment (U.S. Funds Only):

❑ Check    ❑ Money Order    ❑ Visa    ❑ MasterCard

## Credit Card Information:

Cardholder Name_____

Credit Card Number_____ Exp. Date_____

Signature_____

## PUBLICATIONS (STATS books include FREE first class shipping; magazines — add $2)

| Qty. | Product Name | Item # | Price | Total |
|------|--------------|--------|-------|-------|
| | STATS All-Time Major League Handbook | ATHA | $79.95 | |
| | STATS All-Time Baseball Sourcebook | ATSA | $79.95 | |
| | STATS All-Time Major League COMBO (BOTH books!) | ATCA | `$149.95 | |
| | STATS Major League Handbook 1998 | HB98 | $19.95 | |
| | STATS Major League Handbook 1998 (Comb-bound) | HC98 | $21.95 | |
| | STATS Projections Update 1998 (MAGAZINE) | PJUP | $9.95 | |
| | The Scouting Notebook 1998 | SN98 | $19.95 | |
| | The Scouting Notebook 1998 (Comb-bound) | SC98 | $21.95 | |
| | STATS Minor League Scouting Notebook 1998 | MN98 | $19.95 | |
| | STATS Minor League Handbook 1998 | MH98 | $19.95 | |
| | STATS Minor League Handbook 1998 (Comb-bound) | MC98 | $21.95 | |
| | STATS Player Profiles 1998 | PP98 | $19.95 | |
| | STATS Player Profiles 1998 (Comb-bound) | PC98 | $21.95 | |
| | STATS 1998 BVSP Match-Ups! | BP98 | $19.95 | |
| | STATS Baseball Scoreboard 1998 | SB98 | $19.95 | |
| | STATS Diamond Chronicles 1998 | CH98 | $19.95 | |
| | Pro Football Revealed: The 100-Yard War (1998 Edition) | PF98 | $19.95 | |
| | STATS Pro Football Handbook 1998 | FH98 | $19.95 | |
| | STATS Pro Football Handbook 1998 (Comb-bound) | FC98 | $21.95 | |
| | STATS Basketball Handbook 1997-98 | BH98 | $19.95 | |
| | STATS Hockey Handbook 1997-98 | HH98 | $19.95 | |
| | STATS Diamond Diagrams 1998 | DD98 | $19.95 | |
| | STATS Fantasy Insider: 1998 Baseball Edition (MAGAZINE) | IB98 | $5.95 | |
| | STATS Fantasy Insider: 1998 Pro Football Edition (MAGAZINE) | IF98 | $5.95 | |
| | **Prior Editions** (Please circle appropriate year) | | | |
| | STATS Major League Handbook  '90 '91 '92 '93 '94 '95 '96 '97 | | $9.95 | |
| | The Scouting Report/Notebook  '94 '95 '96 '97 | | $9.95 | |
| | STATS Player Profiles  '93 '94 '95 '96 '97 | | $9.95 | |
| | STATS Minor League Handbook  '92 '93 '94 '95 '96 '97 | | $9.95 | |
| | STATS BVSP Match-Ups!  '94 '95 '96 '97 | | $5.95 | |
| | STATS Baseball Scoreboard  '92 '93 '94 '95 '96 '97 | | $9.95 | |
| | STATS Basketball Scoreboard/Handbook  '93-'94 '94-'95 '95-'96 '96-'97 | | $9.95 | |
| | Pro Football Revealed: The 100-Yard War  '94 '95 '96 '97 | | $9.95 | |
| | STATS Pro Football Handbook  '95 '96 '97 | | $9.95 | |
| | STATS Minor League Scouting Notebook  '95 '96 '97 | | $9.95 | |
| | STATS Hockey Handbook  '96-'97 | | $9.95 | |

## FANTASY GAMES

| Qty. | Product Name | Item Number | Price | Total |
|------|--------------|-------------|-------|-------|
|  | Bill James Classic Baseball | BJCB | $129.00 |  |
|  | STATS Fantasy Hoops | SFH | $79.00 |  |
|  | STATS Fantasy Football | SFF | $69.00 |  |
|  | Bill James Fantasy Baseball | BJFB | $89.00 |  |

1st Fantasy Team Name (ex. Colt 45's):_____ _____

   What Fantasy Game is this team for?_____

2nd Fantasy Team Name (ex. Colt 45's):_____ _____

   What Fantasy Game is this team for?_____

        **NOTE: $1.00/player is charged for all roster moves and transactions.**

**For Bill James Fantasy Baseball:**

Would you like to play in a league drafted by Bill James?    ❏ Yes    ❏ No

## MULTIMEDIA PRODUCTS (Prices include shipping & handling charges)

| Qty. | Product Name | Item Number | Price | Total |
|------|--------------|-------------|-------|-------|
|  | Bill James Encyclopedia CD-Rom | BJCD | $49.95 |  |

| TOTALS | Price | Total |
|--------|-------|-------|
| **Product Total (excl. Fantasy Games)** |  |  |
| Canada—all orders—add: | $2.50/book |  |
| Magazines—shipping—add: | $2.00/each |  |
| Order 2 or more books—subtract: | $1.00/book |  |
| (**NOT** to be combined with other specials) |  |  |
| **Subtotal** |  |  |
| **Fantasy Games Total** |  |  |
| IL residents add 8.5% sales tax |  |  |
| **GRAND TOTAL** |  |  |

**NOTE:** Orders for shipments outside the USA or Canada are Credit Card only.
    Actual shipping charges will be added to your order.